JOHN GEORGE PHILLIMORE

AF824169

INTRODUCTION

TO THE

STUDY AND HISTORY

OF

THE ROMAN LAW

Elibron Classics
www.elibron.com

Elibron Classics series.

ISBN 0-543-97093-0 (paperback)
ISBN 0-543-97092-2 (hardcover)

This Elibron Classics book contains the complete text of the edition published in 1848 by William Benning & Co., London.

"Il faut éclairer l'histoire par les lois, et les lois par l'histoire."

Montesquieu, *Esprit des Lois,* liv. xxxi. c.2.

"Das moralische Gesetz in uns, und der gestirnte Himmel über uns."

Kant.

(The moral law within, and the starry heaven above us.)

PREFACE

THAT striking passage in the Gorgias of Plato[1] where Socrates points out the difference between science and empiricism, as it on other accounts well deserves attentive perusal, so for those engaged in the study and practice of the law in this age and country, it has a peculiar value and importance. The reasons given by Socrates why any particular study or pursuit cannot be dignified with the name of science, an occupation fit for liberal and enlarged intellects, but must be transferred to the inferior category that includes the trivial and ignoble employments in which mechanical dexterity and irrational routine are the chief ingredients, are exactly and in terms applicable to the English law. For, while the treasures of ancient wisdom and modern science lie untouched before us, while our neighbours on both sides of the Rhine elicit truth by the collision of their opinions, and vie with each other in endeavouring to raise the grand and harmonious fabric of jurisprudence on an imperishable basis, we live in our mud hovel, content with acorns when bread is within our reach, and with a state of things which, ruinous as it is to some, and dangerous to all, few have more reason (if they know what is really, and for its own sake, desirable, or if they covet future

[1] Gor.§56.: Ἡ μέν τοντου οὗ θεραπένει καὶ τήν φύσιν εσκεπται, τήν αιτίαν ϖν πράττει, καὶ λόγον έχει τούτων έκστον δούναι..... ή δέ έτέρα.... ἄλογός τε παντάπασιν, ώς έπος ειπεῖν,ούέν διαριθμησαμένη τριζή καὶέμπειρια,μνήμην μόνονσωζομενη τοῦ ειωθοτος γιγνεσθαι.

fame,) to regret, than those who have acquired high rank and large fortunes by its operation.

Demosthenes told the Athenians that their military expeditions against Philip reminded him of nothing so much as the boxing of a barbarian: for, said he, "if the clown is struck here, he moves his hands here; if there, he moves his hands there: his arms follow the blow; but he has no system, no foresight, by which to guard against and to anticipate it."

It is just so with us in civil matters. A particular case is decided, and the law is then for the first time ascertained. Meanwhile, it is deposited, not in a code, but in the breast of the judge. There is no general and authentic collection of principles from which the theory of law can be deduced. The circumstance that, in the opinion of one judge, prevents a given case from being a precedent for another, does not so qualify its effect in the opinion of his colleague. In short, our judges *legislate* without the responsibility of legislation, or the control of any constituency; and that not only in a few cases which, perhaps, would be, in any state of things, an inevitable evil, but in by far the majority of those that are brought under their consideration. The power given to them by our detestable system of pleading, as the art of making the plainest matter unintelligible is facetiously called, alone (I speak of the common law) is as prodigious and as little known by the public at large, as it is misplaced and impolitic. Hume said, that, in the actual state of society, the wars of European sovereigns made him always, think of a match of cudgel-playing in a china shop, and this happy illustration has, over and over again, occurred to me in the Court of Exchequer; when I have seen the welfare or absolute ruin of whole families depending on the construction that the judge might choose to put on an uncouth and unintelligible jargon invented in the dark ages, and with which the real merit of the cause had no sort of connexion; when I have seen the most precious rights, the means of education for youth, of comfort for age, and, in this most money-worshipping[2] of countries, of respectability itself perhaps, the sport of conflicting gibberish, hanging on some wretched quibble, and dancing on the tremulous balance of irrational caprice; when I have watched the distempered strength of a contracted and disproportioned intellect, like the Homeric courser bounding without bit or bridle in the fresh pastures, disporting itself in the mere wanton exuberance of pernicious subtilty, and have known, not only that it was a perfect chance which way the wind of chicane might happen to blow, but that by all his sophistry and crotchets, all his shadowy speculations, false refinements, mock-difficulties, provoking pedantry, and unnecessary doubts, that by every quotation from the writers of an age to which every principle of Jurisprudence was as much unknown as the law of gravitation, the judge was, unconsciously no doubt, aggravating the distress of the actual suitor, as well as scattering broadcast the seeds of future misery and litigation.

I have been most anxious, in the following pages, to refer the reader to the authorities which I have consulted, to put him in the track I myself have followed. If, however, it should happen that any particular obligation is not acknowledged, I must appeal to the candour of the reader, and ask him to ascribe the omission to accident or negligence, not to the wish to dissemble the origin of my remark.

In the meantime, I acknowledge fully and unequivocally my obligations, which, indeed, can hardly be exaggerated, to the various writers whom I have cited, especially to Savigny, Hugo, Marezoll, Schilling, Zimmern, and Walther, among the German; and Domat, Toullier, Beaufort, Laboulaye, Giraud, and Warnkönig among the French authorities.

What I have said will, I hope, account for what might otherwise seem an ostentatious and pedantic display of French

---

[2] Worship is too feeble a word, even adoration does not fully convey the idea of the intense and absorbing veneration that wealth (even when quite useless to the votary, and surrounded by all that is most revolting to our nature) commands in England. It is loved, as literature should be, for its own sake.
"Chaste matrons court it, and grave bishops bless."

and German quotations. But I am driven to ask how otherwise, in the present state of our literature, can a writer guard himself?

Why is my lot to be different from that of others? Why is not some anonymous writer in the Quarterly Review[3], especially as this book is not published in Albemarle Street, whose wish to give pain to man or woman is only equalled by his ignorance of the subject he presumes to discuss, and only surpassed by his effrontery, animated by the noble desire of blackening the character and of marring the prospects of one whose political opinions are different from his own, to impute to me, as he has done to others, equally without foundation, the crime of plagiarism?

I must touch on one topic more before I consign this book to the indulgence of my readers. Many, on whose judgment and friendship I place the most entire reliance, wish that I had omitted some passages in the notes to the following pages that may give offence, not only to the numerous class, worshipping Diana of the Ephesians, who, thinking only of the preferments held out by the law to its votaries, are content to pace in the beaten road which has led so many to their attainment, and consider him with aversion who would alter the track to which they are accustomed; but to the powerful class who, having obtained those preferments, look in many cases

---

[3] The Quarterly Review, in spite of some very able articles in the earlier numbers, answers generally to the Index Expurgatorius of Rome. If a book was put in the latter, it was a sign it was worth reading; if a book is abused in the former, it is a proof that the views of its author are wide, his language vigorous, and that his philanthropy is not guided exclusively by Debrett and Burke in its sympathies. So it praises Sir Egerton Brydges, and abuses with the utmost virulence Sydney Smith, Hallam's Constitutional History, Romilly's Memoirs, and Napier's Peninsula War. It is melancholy to think that the majority of the English landed gentry and of those to whom their education is entrusted have no other ideas on political subjects, but what are infused into them by this journal, in which the most grotesque prejudices, every where else exploded, are stated as axioms, and embodied in a style which, when it does not deviate into mere scurrilous ribaldry, is heavy, barbarous, insipid, and pedantic. Can the degraded state of all that ought to be great and elevating in this country be wondered at, when nobody dares question any one established authority in literature, fashion, law, church or state?

"Et si quis suaves mergos edixerit assos,
Parebit pravi docilis Romana juventus."

The abuse of periodical criticism in the Quarterly Review is well pointed out in Stirling's Essays.

with the blindness and jealous affection of a parent on some of the worst and most mischievous of the absurdities of which I complain. I concur in the apprehensions of my friends, but I have not followed their advice. Had my motive been popularity as a writer, I should undoubtedly have struck out the remarks to which it points; but I would not purchase the "*euge et belle*" of a single reader by the sacrifice of that frankness which is the first privilege of a writer, the right to which has not been taken away from us on all subjects, and without which, indeed, to write and to deceive would be synonymous. How soon an act of parliament may be passed to make the censure of special pleading felony, I cannot tell. It is true, I have seen strange things. I have seen, in a free country, the classes usually called educated hasten to tender their abject and trivial homage to the scourge of Poland; the tyrant who respected, in his career of wickedness, the honour of women no more than the rights of men; and from whom mere instinct would have made the French peasant recoil, as our Elizabeth did from a less atrocious criminal,[4] But although the time foretold by Goldsmith, when this country

"A heap of level avarice shall lie,"

seems to have arrived; though we live in an age when, in a mere effusion and ecstasy of spontaneous baseness (for which, as the records of Carthage are destroyed, no parallel can be found), a subscription has been raised to reward a broker in railway shares for making his own fortune; though the triumph of the love of gain and of the mediocrity which is its inseparable companion is visible wherever we cast our eyes; though, in short, the remark of an acute English writer, that we are "naturally tradesmen," was never more verified by high and low, noble and plebeian, than at the present moment; notwithstanding, I say, all these reasons for disbelieving that any measure pointed exclusively at the public good is likely to be insisted upon, it is, I verily think, impossible that the law can

---

[4] From Bonner "she turned aside, as from a man polluted with blood, who was a just object of horror to every heart susceptible of humanity." — *Hume, Eliz.* p. 3. "Il faut appeler les choses par leur nom, si on veut arrêter les tyrans."

continue much longer without reform, and that the abuses which prevail in it, from the double summons of jurors to the nefarious proceedings before parliamentary committees, from the court of quarter sessions to the highest court of appeal (in both of which a body of men, who may never have opened a law book in their lives, have a right to vote),[5] can be tolerated much longer even among us. An inquiry into the Roman law furnished a just and natural opportunity for occasionally pointing out (and I have done no more) a contrast so humiliating and so complete. There are many abuses in support of which a host of amiable and generous feelings often are enlisted. The English church abounds with sinecures and abuses, with pomps and vanities, and marks of worldliness that are inconsistent with its true dignity, and in most insolent contrast with its doctrines. The Irish church is, and has been since the first minute of its existence, a great standing outrage on reason, justice, and humanity. Good and honourable men, however, will be found, as well as profligate time-servers, among the indiscriminating champions of both. But the advocate of chicane must be swayed by motives which it is difficult to think of even with patience. He must oppose reform either from the love of gain, as the country proctors successfully resisted all attempts to reform the local ecclesiastical courts; or from the love of power, which induced all the judges to oppose the reforms brought forward by Sir Samuel Romilly; or from the *esprit de corps,* which prevents men from perceiving that, if a profession sets itself against a nation, the nation, sooner or later, will set itself against a profession. There is nothing in any of these motives to conciliate the sympathies of the present time, or to mitigate the indignation of posterity. He alone is a good citizen who pursues, under all obloquy and discouragement, the interest of his country, whose success is her prosperity, and whose failure is her degradation, who adheres with a resolution that neither the fear of personal danger, nor what is more hard for a

[5]"Il y avait une cour de boyards qui décidait en dernier ressort des affaires contentieuses: le rang et la naissance y donnaient séance. Il fallait que la science la donnât; cette cour fut cassée."— *Histoire de Pierre le Grand.*

generous and active nature to endure, the chilling gloom of undeserved obscurity, can overcome, to the grand principle enshrined in the most glorious language that ever was uttered by the lips of man: τὰς τιμὰς δυναστείας, τὰς εὐδοξίας, τὰς της πατρίδος θεραπεύειν — ταύτας αὔξειν — μετα τούτων είναι.

INTRODUCTION

CHAPTER I

To consider the moral and intellectual progress of mankind daring so many ages, as that of an individual acquiring wisdom by experience, and schooled by suffering into virtue, is the method which has distinguished those who have studied the history of our species with most success, and who have explained the lessons it contains with most sagacity. Whether, indeed, the view which these writers have taken is not one more favourable to man than a due consideration of his past fate and his present condition will altogether justify— whether, in this country for instance, the same crimes, the same follies, the same prejudices, which others in their day have been called upon to encounter, are entirely without effect upon ourselves— whether comparative inferiority, not to say utter insignificance, in some pursuits, is not the price we pay for our success in others— nay, whether even in those material advantages which we systematically sacrifice so much that is great and elevated to obtain, other nations are not and have not been our masters, are questions which it is beyond my present purpose to discuss. That Vico[6] and Montesquieu were right in considering the acquisitions of one age as the inheritance of another is unquestionable; and though their doctrine may have been expressed too generally and was not guarded by sufficient

---

[6] This is the doctrine of Hegel, Philosophie der Geschichte; and Lessing, Erziehung des Men-schen Geschlechts; and Gans, the pupil of Hegel, Erbrecht, Scholien zum Gaius; Obligationenrecht.

See also Warnkœnig und Stein, Französische Staats- und Rechtsgeschichte, vol. iii. p. 25., Kampf der Systeme.

Nobody has seized upon the true character of the early Roman law more sagaciously than Vico. Niebuhr owes much to him, far more than is usually supposed.

qualifications, it is one which ought ever to be kept in view by him who would take a wide and philosophical view of human affairs. Were there in our nature no principle of improvement, history might indeed still, as now, amuse the specious idleness of antiquarians—it might still, as now, be inculcated by thoughtless tutors, and studied by insignificant meditation, as if it were an account of birds in the air or of wild beasts in the forest —but it never could be turned to a more salutary and a nobler purpose. "Ad illa," said the greatest and most eloquent of historians, "ad illa mihi pro se quisque acriter intendat animum, quæ vita, qui mores, fuerint, per quos viros, quibusque artibus, domi, militiæque, et partum et auctum imperium sit."

It is the contemplation of man in all his different characters that gives to historical studies their real dignity and importance—him it is that history enables us to behold in disaster and prosperity, in war and peace, in life and death, as the denizen of the wilderness, as the inhabitant of the town, as crushed by oppression or exalted by liberty, as ruler and subject, as slave and tyrant, as persecutor or as martyr, as refined by philosophy or made sordid by the love of gain, as checked by bigotry and prejudice, or exerting the whole strength of his capacity without contradiction or restraint, as struggling with barbarity or disguised under the various forms of arbitrary refinement and long-established policy.

By observing the various passions, qualities, and energies, developed by man amid the various situations in which his lot is cast, as woven into the canvass that history is ever unrolling for our instruction, the spot we inhabit is enlarged, and the span of oar existence is prolonged, we are transported beyond the present hour, and the dead become the companions and the teachers of the living. It is to the collision of parties and opinions that society always owes activity in its origin, and sometimes regeneration in its decay. In those states and during those periods where one principle has exclusively predominated, either because its supremacy never was disputed, or because it was disputed ineffectually, the reader will find nothing but servility and corruption. The most ancient histories of the East present to us much the same spectacle as at present, identity of every thing with a ruling power and the consequent loss of all individual energy.

In Greece we find, on the contrary, the qualities of the individual developed to the highest degree of excellence that man was ever destined to attain—every character of the intellect placed in the clearest light, every element of genius awakened into complete activity—we see civilised man acting, thinking, speaking, writing, as if the condition of the universe depended on his own individual efforts, animated by resistance, triumphing over obstacles, achieving prodigies. The defeat of Xerxes, the humiliation of Persia, the triumphs of Alexander, prove the infinite difference between that state of things, where the will of every individual is exercised, and that in which impulse is unknown, volition extinguished, and thought, feeling, reason, are merged in obedience to a blind and irresistible authority. The myriads of Darius and Xerxes wanted the great element of human superiority—they wanted will; they were defeated by a handful of troops, but in every individual of which that body consisted, individual will, that great distinguishing attribute of our species, had been wrought up to the highest point of resolution and intensity.

In Rome we meet, for the first time in the same nation, with both principles[7]—the principle of the state and that of individual will, the element of Asiatic uniformity and of Grecian variety, engaged in a long and uncertain contest. That contest terminated when the contending principles had weakened and corrupted each other by the triumph of a third which absorbed and annihilated both. After many furious and destructive efforts, the popular and aristocratic elements were alike enervated and paralysed. The people accustomed to the indulgence of licentious caprice, but stripped of solid power,

---

[7] Hier in Rom finden wir nunmehr diese freie Allgemeinheit, diese abstrakte Freiheit, welche einer seits den abstrakten Staat die Politik, und die Gewalt uber die concrete Individualitat setzt, und diese durchaus unterordnet, anderer seits dieser Allgemeinheit gegenüber die Personlichkeit erschafft.

Diese beiden Momente welche Rom bilden die politische Allgemeinheit fur sich, und die abstrakte Freiheit des Individualismus in sich selbst, sind zunachst in der Form der Innerlichkeit selbst befasst. — *Philosophie der Genschichte. Hegel, theil* 3. *Die Romische Welt.*

lost all idea of permanent freedom, of the institutions in which it is embodied, and of the virtues by which alone it can be guaranteed.[8] (b)While the nobles, who supposed themselves to be trafficking only with the rights of others, found that they had made a shameful barter of their own and that they were the fellow-slaves of those whom they had employed all the resources of wealth, and all the instruments of violence, to intimidate and corrupt. After the victories of the legions, the patrician and plebeian, the bribing senator and the hireling voter, were slaves alike. The tumults and factions of the Roman state were succeeded by the lethargy of despotism, and the history of the Roman emperors is the history of continual decrepitude and of chronical decay. Even the vigorous and successful reigns of some virtuous or able rulers, furnish the strongest and most invincible proofs of this assertion. The extremities were sacrificed to preserve the centre. Momentary vigour was restored by sudden and violent retrenchment. It was like the convulsive effort of a dying man, not a token of recovery, but a forerunner of dissolution. When by Augustus, that most consummate of pagan hypocrites, the liberties of Rome were finally destroyed, it was his first object to close up all the avenues to political distinction, and as far as was consistent with the safety of the empire, even those to military renown. Many of those men, who in happier days would have been the statesmen, captains, and orators of the commonwealth, driven out of the sphere in which their ancestors had shone, endeavoured by the study of jurisprudence to keep alive some traditions of the republic, and to entitle themselves to the gratitude of their countrymen,[9] The Labeos, the Ulpians, and

---

[8] As he said, who ennobled his country, not only by his sublime genius, but by his deep and passionate love of freedom: —

"*Licence* they mean, when they cry liberty,
For who loves that, must first be wise and good."

[9] §357. Hegel, Philosophie des Rechts.

Die Auflösung des Ganzen endigt sich in das allgemeine Unglück, und den Tod des sittlichen Lebens, worin die Völker Individualitäten in der Einheit eines Pantheons ersterben, alle einzelne zu Privatpersonen und zu gleichen mit formellem Rechte herabsinken, welche hiermit nur eine Abstrakte ins ungeheure sich treibende Willkür zusammenhält. — *Gans, Erbrecht,* vol. i. p. 9.

the Papinians took the place of the Marcellus's, the Gracchi, and the Catos.

To this cause for the astonishing progress of jurisprudence during the decline of every other generous and elevating pursuit, must be added another less honourable to those among whom it operated. We behold in the Roman state, during the time of the emperors, a ruler exempt from the control of law, and almost of opinion, a gigantic and boundless caprice, wielding at will, during the short period of its precarious power, the destinies of the most civilised portion of the universe; and a society disfigured by the most hideous vices, where the name of citizen was synonymous with that of slave; the repose of servitude can hardly be said to have been interrupted by the wretched conspiracies of courtiers, parasites, and menials, or by the sordid ferocity of the legions. As if to inculcate the great lesson that to live by one man's will is the cause of all men's misery, Rome, like modern Russia, exhibited for centuries, in all its disgusting lineaments, the appalling spectacle of material power uninformed by a single ray of probity or genius,[10] An utter indifference to public affairs became of course almost universal. The desire of power, which had distinguished the

---

[10] Illustrating Aristotle's remark: —"Ωσπερ γὰρ καὶ τελεωθέν βέλτιστον τῶν ζών ανθρωπός έστιν, οὕτω καὶ χωρισθέν νόμον καὶ δίκης χεὶριστον πὰντων χαλεπωτὰτη γὰρ ἄδικὶα έχουσα ὃπλα.—πολ. i. C. 1.§12.

The following description by a Russian of that frightful despotism called in Russia by the name of government, is the best commentary on Aristotle's text: — " Nous sommes un peuple esclave; chez nous point de liberté, point de respect pour la dignité humaine: c'est le despotisme hideux, sans frein dans ses caprices, sans bornes dans son action; nuls droits, mille justice... nous n'avons rien de ce qui constitue la dignité et l'orgueil des nations; il est impossible d'imaginer une position plus malheureuse... à l'extérieur notre position n'est pas moins déplorable. Exécuteurs passifs d'une pensée qui nous est étrangère, d'une volonté qui est aussi contraire à nos intérêts qu'à notre honneur, on nous regarde partout comme les ennemis de la civilisation et de l'humanité. Sans parler de la Pologne, nous nous déshonorons chaque jour par des violences atroces, par des infamies sans nom; nous ne sommes que les rouages inanimés de cette monst.rueuse machine d'oppression et de conquête qu'on appelle l'empire russe. Les affaires intérieures du pays vont horriblement mal: c'est une compléte anarchie avec tous les semblants de l'ordre; une organisation, étudiée et savante, de l'iniquité, de la barbarie, du pillage, car tous les serviteurs du czar jusqu'aux plus petits employés de village ruinent, volent le pays, commettent les injustices les plus criantes, les plus détestables violences sans honte, sans crainte, avec une insolence et une brutalité sans exemple.—*Discours par M. Bakounine,* Paris, 1847.

citizens of Borne, was exchanged for a love of wealth and a craving for sensual enjoyment, which no profusion could satisfy and no indulgence could appease.

The natural consequence of this state of things, was the intense and assiduous study of the rules by which property was acquired, transmitted, and secured; and thus, as we often find throughout history occasion to observe, good was elicited from evil, and the vices and enormities of the very period when man was apparently steeped in degradation the most hopeless, and depravity the most appalling, laid a foundation for the permanent improvement and welfare of the species. To examine further, how, from the violent reaction produced by the doctrines of Christianity and the constant migrations of barbarous tribes, mankind were raised from the lethargy which for so many ages had benumbed their faculties, would be beyond the scope of this investigation.

Turning from these wider views to the Roman law, we may observe, that, from the expulsion of the first monarchs to the days of Sylla, the conflict between liberality and form — between the active will, the eagerness for improvement, the susceptibility of the people, and the iron rule of an inflexible aristocracy, clinging with tenacious resolution to its privileges at home, and pursuing with a sternness of purpose, like the Greek destiny, its course to foreign empire— is perpetually apparent. Who can refuse his admiration to the wonderful exhibition of moral energy so repeatedly developed during this memorable period?—not Pyrrhus, not Hannibal thundering at their gates—not the loss of armies— not internal faction, not even the revolt of confederated Italy, ever caused that matchless aristocracy to swerve for a single moment from its grand and glorious object. They drew some advantage from every turn of fortune, and, victorious or vanquished, persisted in one uniform comprehensive plan of breaking to pieces every thing which obstructed their greatness, or endangered their security. The same spirit pervades every period of their history. The senate congratulates Varro after the defeat of Cannæ, and Sylla turns aside at the most critical period of a civil war, to annihilate the enemies of the commonwealth. When mention is made, however, of a patrician and plebeian principle in the Roman law, the expression is not meant to convey the notion of particular laws affecting each of these classes separately. At a very early period of Roman history, the distinction as to private law between the patrician and plebeian was substantially at an end.

After the laws of the Twelve Tables, the law of Canuleius, above all, the law of Hortensius, the distinction between the two classes is effaced in one legal system; but, though the law was nominally one, it contained a double element. The "*strictum jus*" represents the influence of the aristocracy, the "*bonum et œquum,*" by which its rigour was mitigated, the working of the popular principle;, on the one side was the letter of the law, the rigour of its doctrine deduced with inflexible severity—ancient tradition, and obstinate forms; on the other, a more liberal construction, a system pliant and adapting itself to various exigencies — indulgent, and showing a disregard of forms when they oppose the claims of justice and the essential interest of society. Thus we may trace throughout, in the history of the Roman law, the rule and its mitigation, the evil and its remedy. Slowly and gradually the evil disappears and the remedy remains; that which was first the rule gives way to the exception. Marriage at first is the complete and absolute dominion of the husband, the wife is a chattel; this is the *conventio in manum;* the reaction against this doctrine produces a different kind of marriage, governed by a laxer principle and free from this degrading bondage. Again, at first, there is the property of the Roman alone recognised by the state—the *dominium ex jure Quiritium;* the reaction against this doctrine creates the property *in bonis,* which was recognised by the prætor; the *patria potestas* at first appears in its harshest and most terrible form; the son is a slave, whom the father may sell, kill, or mutilate at his pleasure; these evils elicited the doctrine of *emancipatio,* by which the son became independent,[11]

[11] So we meet this dualism in the first clause of Gaius, " Populus itaque Romanus partim suọ ptoprio, partim communi omnium hominum jure utitur quæ singula, qualia sint, suis locis propo-nemua." *Comm.* 1.1.

To the same powerful principle may be traced the division of property into the *res mancipi* and *non mancipi.* It was, lone, however, before the liberal element could force its way. Step by step its progress was resisted, barrier after barrier was raised to oppose its triumph. The secession to Mount Aventine, the tribuneship, the admission of plebeians to public offices, the publication of the forms which the patricians endeavoured to conceal under a veil of religious mystery, the introduction of the formulæ, the prætorian system, are among the most decisive and important proofs of the triumph of sound reason over the selfish ambition and narrow interest of one class, and the traditional superstition and dependent habits of another. The efforts of the Jurists were continually directed, in republican Rome, to give the same stability to their more liberal and extensive system, which had belonged to that of their predecessors. In the time of the emperors, their countless rescripts and edicts were added to the laws, commentaries, and edicts which had emanated from other sources, and thus a mass of jurisprudence was accumulated, which no human judgment could digest, and no human memory retain, resembling in the multiplicity of its details the English law of the present day, though as superior to it, in the wisdom and precision of each separate part, as the results of reflection and knowledge are to those of chance, ignorance, and pedantic barbarity. The evils

---

So Topica Cicero, C.3.: — "Genus enim est uxor, ejus duæ formæ; una matrumfamilias, earum, quæ in manum convenerunt, altera earum, quæ tantummbdo uxores habentur."

At last the opposite principle prevailed so far, that the husband might bring an action against his wife. Dig. ix. 2.§§29, 30. Ad. Leg. Ag.

"Si cum maritus uxori, margaritas extricatas dedisset in usu, eaque invito vel inscio viro perfo-rasset, ut pertusis in linea uteretur, teneri eam Lege Aquilia, sive divertit, sive nupta est adhuc." Dig. i. 56, eodem. " Mulier, si in rem viri damnum dederit, pro tenore legis Aquiliæ convenitur." Aulus Gel-lius, 18. 6. Ulpian, Frag. 4. 2. — Compare with the German Marriage, Eichhorn, Dents. St. und R. G. vol. ii. pp.371. 523.

With regard to the son: — " Patria potestas debet in pietate non in atrocitate consistere" was the expression of the modern law. Dig. 48. 9. 5. Ulp. Frag. 20. 1. 10.

Mancipi aut nec Mancipi. Ulp. Frag. 19. 1., omnes res sunt mancipi aut nec mancipi.

So again, " Sequitur ut admoneamus, apud peregrinos quidem *unum* esse dominium, ita ut do-minus quisque sit aut dominus non intelligatur. Quo jure etiam populus Romanus olim utebatur; aut enim ex jure Quiritium unusquisque dominus erat, aut non intelligebatur dominus: sed postea *divisionem accepit dominium,* ut alius possit esse *ex jure Quiritium* dominus, alius *in bonis* habere." — *Gaius,* ii.§40.

thus produced made a code necessary, and the attempts at its compilation were the last memorable efforts of the Roman intellect. For, while by the doctrines of Christianity some rulers hoped to accomplish the regeneration of the empire, an attempt was made to graft the wisdom of past ages on its corrupted jurisprudence. Christianity, however, could not renovate the stagnant mass of Roman corruption, or infuse fresh vigour into its tainted stamina, but was forced to seek in the rude energies and yet unpolluted nature of the barbarous tribes, fitter instruments to work withal—and the Roman code, when the spirit of Rome and Romans had passed away, was like a tree forced into the earth without roots, goodly to the eye for a moment, but without any power of continuance, or any principle of vitality.

The soil into which its roots had once struck themselves so deeply was now taken away. That in the Eastern empire it never was understood there is abundant proof; and in the West, soon after jurisprudence had attained its height in the third century of the Christian æra, all its life and energy disappeared. The task of applying the law of another age to actual practice became every day more difficult, as all activity of thought and all independent energy became less and less discernible among the degraded inhabitants of the empire.

So[12] complete, indeed, was the consciousness of intellectual decrepitude, that, in conformity with many edicts of his predecessors, Justinian actually forbade the attempt to create a new legal literature. The Greek translation of the Latin text, and an abridgment of the chapters as a means of mechanical instruction, were alone tolerated, and a separate treatise or commentary on the law exposed the writer to the punishment of forgery. Besides the sources of Roman law in the time of the

---

[12] Cod. de Vet. Jure enucleando, lib.i. 17.1.§12.; ii.§,21.; iii.§21. It is a curious proof of the superficial knowledge of Justinian a workmen, that in the 78th Novel., Caracalla is confounded with M. Antoninus. The similarity of name led to the mistake. (Ulpian, 1. 17. de Statu Hominum.) Prerhaps an ukas of the present emperor of Russia, may be ascribed to some virtuous successor.

Pilati gives another instance, Traité des Loix civiles, 1 Partie. c.5 c. 8. p. 35., "Les insensés compilateurs des Pandectes," &c. "Justinian qui ne fit guères que de mauvaises loix," c. 5. 201. " Ce législateur stupide," ib. c. 8. p. 35. Procop. Ann.

republic, the empire had, as has been observed, opened others of its own. The edicts and rescripts of its rulers—these were for the most part declarations of the law, in answer to the questions of the magistrates and of private persons. As with the progress of Christianity, the opinions and habits of the countries subject to the Roman government were changed or abolished altogether, these edicts became more frequent and comprehensive,[13] In this state, the inheritance of Roman wisdom was transmitted to the fierce barbarians of the West; and as they wrought the materials of the temple and amphitheatre into their own rude fortresses and dwellings, so did they occasionally incorporate the precious fragments of Roman law with their own unformed and scanty jurisprudence.

This, however, they did sometimes unconsciously, and almost always against their will. But[14] when society improved, men looked on the Roman law with increasing veneration, as the surest basis of civil order.[15]

---

[13] The epoch of barbarian legislation in France reaches from the fifth to the tenth century. This period includes the laws of the Salian and Ripuarian Franks, of the Burgundians, the Visigoths, the Bavarians, the Lombards, the Thuringians, the Saxons, and the Anglo-Saxons.

[14] There are two maxims of the civil law in their proper terms in the Code of Canute: —
"Negatio potiorest affirmatione."
"Possessio proprior est habenti quam deinceps repetenti." *Cited by Burke,* Ab. English Hist. vol. x. c. 9. p.563.
Marina, Ensayo, vol. i. p. 40.

[15] (a) Eichhorn, vol. i.§41. p. 277.Deutsche Staat und Rechts geschichte.
Von alien diesen Gesetzen.unterscheidet sich Theoderícts Edict vom Jahre 500 weniger in dem Gegenstanden, als dadurch dass es bloss aus dem römischen Rechte geschöpft ist; das bisherige gothische Gewohneitsrecht wurde durch dieses Edict nicht aufgehoben, aber manche in dem Edicte enthaltene Verordnungen standen seiner Anwendung in Wege, 42.
Den Römern war in den neuen germanischen Staaten verstattet worden nach ihrem bisherigen Rechte zu leben; die germanischen Gesetzo sorgten für eine Entscheidungsquelle für Rechtigkeiten zwischen ihnen und Germaniern. Ensayo sobre la Legislacion, por Martinez Marina, p. 45., where the reader will find the sentiments of a Spanish patriot, and the language of an accomplished writer. He certainly shows that Robertson was very superficially acquainted with the history of Spanish law, " Es un sueno la description che hace," &c. Canciani Leges Bar. In Leg. Wisigoth. Monitum — Codex ita comparatus est, ut jus nec mere Barbarum regnet, neque mere Romanum.
Cujacius says the laws of the Visigoths were written in emulation, Codicis Justiniani. " Pero esta opinion," says Marina, " tampoco es cierta puesto que muchas Leyes Goticas se hallen en contradicion con las Romanas.
Canciani Leg. Barb. Prefatio, p. 13.

It would have been as easy for barbarians who allowed any form of government so perfectly detestable as those founded on the feudal and Gothic systems to grow up among them, to vie with the Grecian philosophy, or poetry, or eloquence, as out of the materials strictly their own to construct a system of social obligation. It is the true character of barbarians to consider themselves and their institutions alone, and to despise the inhabitants of other countries. In no country has this spirit prevailed so much, or lasted so long, or produced effects so pernicious, as in our own. And, in spite of all its wealth and all its physical science, England furnishes every day, as new meshes are added to the snares of chicanery by the ingenuity of the judge, and new absurdities are crowded into the statute book by the blundering ignorance of the legislator, fresh examples of its unhappy consequences,[16]

Guizot, Hist. de la Civilization en France, vol. i. p. 301. A work of which France may well be proud.

"Praise deserved no enemy can grudge.

* * * * *

"Oh had he been content to serve the crown
With virtues only proper to the grown!"

[16]"Nusquam pejores laquei quam laquei legum." See Meeson and Welsby's Reports, 15 vols. *passim,* a magazine of cobwebs, in most of which the reader (fremant omnes licet, dicam quod sentio) will look in vain for the ghost of a principle, except in about three judgments of my Lord Abinger's; two of which were overruled immediately by his colleagues. One of the last, Gibson v. Carruthers, is as masterly a specimen of judicial reasoning as our reports contain; and in that, as well as in the purity and vigour of its language, forms a marked contrast to those of his brethren; who " nusquam putant esse subtilitatem nisi ubi nihil est præter subtilitatem." We are shocked by a series of scholastic and arbitrary distinctions, invented by fraud in the dark ages for the support of violence, odious to the common sense, and inconsistent with the common necessities of mankind. If the judges of the Exchequer had been ordinary men, the mischief which the law has compelled them to do, would be less surprising and not nearly so vexatious. But as most of them, during the time that all this wretched μικρολογια has been going on under their auspices, have been, and are, men, if not of enlarged minds, of acuteness, sagacity, and thorough masters of their art, the frightful growth of chicane and its demoralizing effect on all concerned in the administration of justice, as it is infinitely more provoking, forms the strongest proof of the inveterate and detestable evils of the system which some of these very judges might have destroyed, and thought it expedient to perpetuate.

As the English law is based on a system completed in the dark ages, it not only consists of a series of absurdities, but it has produced among its expounders an equally connected system of maxims and arguments to justify them; literally, " ratione ut insaniant."

To resume the subject of this Chapter. In the history of Rome and her institutions, we observe for the first time the struggle of two conflicting elements, one of which had never before played so conspicuous a part in the great drama of the universe. In the East, it is the ruler alone who fills the scene; this is despotism. In Greece all is animated and inspired by the efforts of individual will — we see nothing but the people enlisted indeed in hostile factions, but acknowledging one common principle of government[17]; this is democracy. In Rome we find an aristocracy never without a rival, but brought into contact at first with the Eastern, and afterwards with the Grecian element, triumphant over and exterminating the first, and carrying on with the latter a long, perilous, and doubtful struggle. The history of the world exhibits no grander or more instructive spectacle. For against that aristocracy, great in arts, and great in arms — with monarchs for its vassals and kingdoms for its patrimony, powerful from prescriptive right, powerful from hereditary virtue, powerful from religious association, and surrounded by a blaze of accumulated glories, there arose a principle, the progress of which was slow, and for a time almost imperceptible, still mightier and far more generous — deriving from its parent earth, when baffled and overthrown, a fresh supply of vigour, which for a few short and glorious years was lord of the ascendant. Thus was produced the balanced government of Rome. That constitution was no exception to the works which are wrought by man, and which bear the marks of human frailty. It fell. The struggle of the patrician and plebeian ended in joint corruption and common

---

The merely empirical knowledge of law which has always been the favourite character of our judges, from Sir Edward Coke to Lord Eldon, and still continues to be their chosen attribute, is, in the words of perhaps the greatest of modern philosophers, like the wooden head in Phædrus, which appears beautiful, but within which are no brains.—*Kant, Rechfslehre Einleitung,* p. 30. Ed. Leipzig, 1838.

Perhaps after all, considering the known opinions of the selected reformers, we ought to be thankful that the opportunity was not seized upon of reviving trial by battle, by which the likeness of our present system to that of the Plantagenets would have been even more complete than it is. Setting English judges to reform law is, in most cases, like setting the makers of graven images to reform idolatry.

[17] Das Princip. der Aristocratie und das der Demokratie. Dieser Dualismus ist es der eigentlich Roms innerstes Wesen bedeutet. — *Hegel, Philosophie der Geschichte, theil* 3. *Die Römische Welt.*

servitude. But while that struggle lasted, it mingled in every class of life, and pervaded every relation of society. It may be traced in the election of magistrates, in the prevalence of particular customs, in dissensions at home, and in the administration of affairs abroad, but in nothing more clearly and emphatically than in the progress of Roman jurisprudence. In that jurisprudence there is no doctrine so obscure, no law so private, scarcely any analogy so refined, that does not bear stamped upon it the marks of this incessant contest. The Licinian rogations, the Agrarian law, the law of Canuleius, all that concerns the relation of debtor and creditor, the law of contracts, the law of marriage, the very forms of civil process[18], above all, the law of inheritance, speak the same language and carry with them the same testimony. I shall now endeavour to lay before the reader a more detailed account of some of these institutions.

CHAPTER II

As a particular and distinct examination of every branch of the Roman law would far exceed the limits of the present undertaking, I shall confine myself to those parts of it, the study of which appears to me most adapted to enlarge the views, and fortify the judgment, of the jurist; and to create that fine tact and sense of jurisprudence, and that quick perception of legal fitness, method, and analogy, which the French possess in such a remarkable degree from nature — which the Germans acquire by diligence and meditation — and in which, owing to the absence of both these causes, almost all intrusted with the making and administration of law in this country, are so unfortunately and notoriously deficient.

---

[18]"Sed istæ omnes legis actiones paulatim in odium venerunt: *namque ex nimiâ subtilitate veterum qui tunc* jura *condiderunt,* eo res perducta est, ut vel qui minimum errasset, litem perderet. Itaque per Legem Æbutiam et duas Julias sublatæ sunt istæ legis actiones, effectumque est ut per concepta verba, id est, per formulas, litigaremus."

With this view, omitting the law of marriage, the law of families, the law of guardianship, and the criminal law — topics most interesting in themselves, and well deserving deep and attentive consideration, but less immediately bearing on the business of the day than those which I am about to enumerate— I propose to investigate, first, the law of civil process; a subject which, when its contrast to the shocking and oppressive state of our law on that head is considered, may, I cannot help believing it, awaken even official apathy to the amendment of the latter, romantic as experience shows such hope to be, when neither title nor income, nor any thing but the gratitude of all the enlightened part of the community, is to be the reward of such exertions. After this will come an account of the edict of the prætor, and its effect on Roman jurisprudence. Then I propose to consider the law of possession, the law of property, the law of contracts, and the law of inheritance.

I also propose to give an account of the tribunal before which state criminals were impeached in the latter days of the republic. I shall conclude by an outline of what, since the days of Leibnitz, most writers on the subject have agreed to call the external history of the Roman law.

PART I

LAW OF CIVIL PROCESS —

It is hardly possible to conceive a stronger proof of that ignorance of the most ordinary topics connected with general jurisprudence, which has so long been the characteristic of the most eminent lawyers in this country, than the notion, so vehemently maintained and so popularly received, that the jury is of a peculiarly English origin. The absurdity of obliging twelve men to say upon their oaths that they agree when in fact they differ, is indeed, emphatically our own; but the principle and essence of a jury, which involves the selection of judges, unknown beforehand to the executive magistrate, from a particular body, and which gives to those judges the power of deciding, with certain restrictions and under the direction of certain rules, on the question in dispute, is to be found in the institutions of many other countries; possibly throughout the institutions of the West, though from accident or design it has, on the Continent, been suffered to fall into oblivion and disuse,[19]

---

[19] Was nun das erstere, das eigne *Gemeindegericht in Strafsachen* betrifft, so sind die ursprüng-lichsten und einfachsten Grundsatze darüber wohl folgende gewesen: dass jedes Verbrechen eines Communemitgliedes sowohl gegen den anderen Juratus als gegen das Nichtmitglied innerhalb des Communegebiets und zweitens sogar ausserhalb desselben, nur von dem Major und den Scabinis zu richten seien. Das Privil. von Corbie, von Ludw. VI., drückt diess vielleicht in seiner anfänglichsten Form aus.

Allerdings gilt der Grundsatz allenthalben, class die Verbrechenmder Communeglieder nur von Major und Juratis gerichtet werden sollen. — *Warnkœnig und Stein, französische Staats- und Bechtsgeschichte,* band 3. p. 278. Rogge, Salitschgesetz.

So Tacitus (De M. G. c. 11.), after telling us " de minoribus," &c. adds "licet etiam apud concilium (mallum) accusare quoque et discrimen capitis intendere."

So I b.§12. "Eliguntur in eisdem conciliis principes qui jura per pagos vicosque reddunt—centeni singulis ex plebe comites consilium simul et auctoritas adsunt."

The trial of a citizen by other citizens, and a judicial authority in causes civil as well as criminal, inherent in every free member of the community, was the corner stone of the Athenian constitution[20]; it was thence transferred to Borne, and it is attested by Cicero[21] in words which, if it were not for the purity of the Latin, one might suppose were to be met with in Lord Coke's Reports: — "Neminem voluerunt majores nostri, non modo de existimatione cujusquam, sed ne pecuniariâ quidem de re minimâ esse judicem, nisi qui inter adversarios convenisset." Accordingly, the distinction between the

---

Pardessus has given this passage its true meaning. Loi Salique, p. 575: " Le préteur ne jugeait pas, il donnait des juges dont il déterminait la mission, et faisait exécuter leur décision, ce qui s'appelait *judicare, jus reddere*. Précisément, à la seule exception que le *princeps* germain ne donnait pas des juges, mais avait seulement la présidence des hommes libres, ce *princeps* ressemblait, sous le rapport judiciaire, au préteur romain. Tel est donc le sens dans lequel Tacite a pu dire: jura reddunt. Les mots *centeni singulis ex plebe comites* expriment trés bien la réunion des hommes libres auprés du chef de justice." See De Rachinburgiis, Lex Salica, tit. 60: "Si quidem rachinburgii in mallo resedentes, cum causa discussa fuerit inter duos causatores, ammoniti ab eo qui causam requiret, ut legem salicam dicant, et si legem dicere noluerint, tunc ab eo qui causam requiret sint iterum ammoniti usque tertia vice."

Capitul. C. Magni, a. D. 706: "De incendio convenit quod nullus infra patriam præsumat facere propter iram aut iniroicitiam.... Si talis fuerit rebellis... ut in præsentia nostra justitiam reddat, venire despexerit, condicto commune placito simul ipsi pagenses veniant;.et si unanimiter consenserint pro districtione illius casa incendatur... de ipso placito commune consilio facto fiat peractum."

Capit. Lud. Pii, A.D. 815: "Ipsi... pro majoribus causis sicut sunt homicidia, raptus, incendia, deprædationes, membrorum amputationes, furta, latrocinia, alienarum rerum invasiones, et undecumque a vicino suo... fuerit accusatus, et ad placitum venire jussus, ad comitis sui mallum omnimodis venire non recusent."

[20] Πολιτης δ απλϖς ουδενι τϖν αλλων οριζεται μαλλον η τϖ ετεχεν κρισεως και αρχης. — Aristot. Πολιτ. 3. 1.

And Aristoph. —

Ξνλλεγέντες γαρ καθ έσμούς, ώσπερεί τάνθρήνια,
Οί μέν ήμών ούπερ άρχων, οί δέ παρά τούς ένδεκα,
Οί δ έν ώδε?ώ δικάξονσ, οί δέ πρός τοίς τείχίοις
Ξνμξεξνσμένοι. Σφήκες, 1107., ed. Dindorf.

Plato, not in his Republic, but in his Laws, which were intended for actual use, insists upon the jury as the test of freedom, not only in political but civil causes. Πâsa δέ δή πον πόλις ãπολις ãν γιγνοιτο έν η δικαστηρια μη καθεστϖτα ειη κατα τροπν.... περι δέ τϖν δημοσιων έγκληματων αναγκαιον πρϖτον μέντϖ πλήθει μεταδιδοναι της κρισεως... δει δέ δη και των ιδιων δικων κοιωνειν ϖν έξουσιας του συνδικαζειν, ηγειται τοπαραπαν της πολεως ου μετοχος δια ταυτ ουν δή και κατα φιλας αναγκαιον στας έκ τον παραχρημα αδιαφθορους ταις δεησεσι δικαζειν. — Νόμ??, b. 6. P. 280. Bipont. Ed.

[21] Pro Cluentio, 43.

magistratus, the person under whose jurisdiction a particular cause arose and particular individuals contended, and a judge or judges to whom the investigation of the facts in dispute was referred, is to be traced throughout the changes of Roman jurisprudence. The administration of justice was not, among the Romans, the exclusive duty of any single magistrate; the persons to whom this function was assigned held in the state offices of high political importance, varying from those which conferred upon their possessor power almost absolute, to those of limited but still considerable authority. To have entrusted these functionaries with judicial duties must have led to the most obvious and flagrant abuses. The method by which this evil was avoided was as simple as it was judicious: the duty of the magistrate in matters of contentious jurisdiction was generally (for we shall see that some cases formed an exception to the rule) to conduct the preliminary proceedings, to ascertain the points really in dispute between the parties, to instruct the judges, and to sanction their appointment; in this division of the judicial functions between the *magistratus* and the *judex* consisted the "*ordo judiciorum priva-torum,*" which probably derived its origin from Servius Tullus, and it was afterwards improved by the introduction of a simple mode of proceeding and the establishment of a standing body of judges, and continued till the time of the Christian emperors. This proceeding may be divided into two parts: first, the proceeding "*in jure*" before the magistrate, in which the process received its shape, and the points in dispute between the parties were elicited; secondly, the proceeding "*in judicio*" before the judge, which is terminated by the "*sententia judicis.*" Together with this method of judicial proceeding there existed, also, for particular cases a mode of proceeding, "*extra ordinem,*" the "*eastraordinaria cognitio*"and *persecutio;* in this proceeding the whole conduct of the cause was entrusted to the magistrate, and the assistance of the *judex* was not called in. All the *extra-ordinaria judicia* we know of were "*in personam,*" none "*in rem.*" They were employed only in proceedings growing out of the "*jus civile,*" and not in proceedings before the prætor. It has been disputed whether the numerous interdicts were classed with the *ordinaria* or *extraordinaria judicia;* but Savigny has proved *(Recht des Besitzes,* § 34.), that they are to be numbered among the former. During the nourishing period of Roman jurisprudence, this mode of proceeding by the "*cognitio extraordinaria*" was comparatively rare, till, under the later emperors, as all ideas of freedom and justice were obliterated, it became universal. Justinian speaks of it in his time as the only known proceeding[22] The *ordo judiciorum privatorum* had then entirely disappeared. In the usual mode of proceeding, where the *magistratus* was separate from the judge, if the parties agreed upon the judge, he was, of course, if eligible, assigned to them by the magistrate. In order to produce this agreement, when the parties met before the magistrate, the plaintiff had the right first to propose the judge, *judicem nominare;* and he was appointed, unless the opposite party objected to his nomination — "*Ejero, iniquus mihi est:"* the objecting party was not called upon, in the first instance, to assign any special reason for his negative; but a perverse and wanton rejection exposed the defendant to the consequences of contumacy: this proceeding was designated by the expression "*sumere judicem."* There was also another proceeding, called "*rejicere judicem:*" the prætor named a certain quantity of "*recuperatores*" or "*judices,"* of whom each party was entitled to reject an equal number, and the prætor selected the judges from the rest. Under the emperors the republican principle of the selection of the judges by the parties themselves, was gradually lost sight of; and though the parties retained the power of rejecting the judges, they were nominated in a regular series, by the prætor at Rome, to their duties; as were the "*decuriones,"* by another list, to the discharge of their municipal functions. That the parties no longer named their own judges is proved by a rescript of Hadrian (Callistratus, libro I. Quæstionum) — "Ob-servandum est, ne is judex detur, quern altera pars nominatim petat, id enim iniqui exempli esse Divus Hadrianus rescripsit, nisi hoc specialiter a principe ad verecundiam petiti judicis respiciente permittetur."[23] The task of the magistrate and the judge, at a

---

[22] Quoties extra ordinem jus dicitur qualia sunt hodie omnia judicia. — *Inslit. i.* §8. de Interdictis.

[23] Dig. viii. 1—47.

very early period of Roman history, was not to inquire and determine only. Strange as it will appear to English readers[24], it appeared to the Romans, as their views expanded and their notions of society became more accurate, that it was part of the duty of the state to take care, not only that a tribunal should exist, but that it should be accessible, and that, in consequence, the suitor should be guided by the law itself amid the pitfalls and snares into which, if left to himself without the assistance of the judge, he might chance to fall. In a word, those great jurists conceived it right to insure the decision of a cause upon its merites — a result which, up to the present time, it has been the great object of the English system to prevent, and of its admirers to explode; and which, at the time I am writing, is, in more than one half the cases upon which our judges decide with perfect equanimity, and, with all the solemnity and pomp which many people seem to suppose the chief object of their institution, unattained and unattainable. By means of the *"formulæ"* an intelligible state of facts was presented to the judge or judges. As, however, this system was unknown in the early ages of the republic, it is requisite to mention a state of law, less intolerable indeed, but in oppressive pedantry not entirely dissimilar to our own. After the expulsion of the Tarquins, the government of Rome was an aristocracy. As the Romans were a people extremely governed by religious notions, the patricians secured to themselves the highest functions of the priesthood; as they were a people extremely tenacious of established custom, by instituting certain forms known only to themselves, and making any, even the slightest, deviation from those forms fatal to the suitor, the same caste became the exclusive depositaries of the law. By the use of these artifices the patricians protracted, to a very late period, the struggle between themselves and the patriot party. The manner in which they made religion subservient to their selfish purpose it is not necessary to expatiate upon, but some account of the

---

[24] I cannot forbear quoting a passage from Minucius Felix, which exactly applies to those who from bigotry or necessity employ learning and study to make the absurdities of our ignorant ancestors plausible. " Fabulas et errores ab imperitis parentibus discimus, et quod est gravius *ipsis studiis et di- sciplinis eloboramus."* — P. 203.

way in which they perverted law for the same object is essential to our inquiry. The mode of proceeding which they invented, was that by the *"legis actiones,"* which Gaius has described[25]:—The authors of the Digest tell us: "Deinde ex his legibus eodem tempore fere actiones compositæ sunt, quibus inter se homines disceptarent; quas actiones, ne populus, prout vellet, institueret, certas sollennesque esse voluerunt; et appellatur hæc pars juris legis actiones, id est, legitimæ actiones omnium tamen harum et interpretandi scientia, et actiones, apud collegium Ponficum erant, ex quibus constituebatur quis quoquo anno præssset privatis; et fere populus annis prope centum hac consuetudine usus est." These were the *legis actiones.*[26]

They consisted in symbolical[27] forms and actions and particular words. As they were almost entirely abolished by the

[25] Actiones quas in usu veteres habuerunt, legis actiones appellabantur, vel ideo quod legibus proditæ erant, quia tune edicta prætoris quibus complures actiones introductæ sunt, nondum in usu habebantur; vel ideo quia ipsarum legum verbis adcommodatas erant, et ideo immutabiles proinde atque leges observabantur. Unde eum *qui* de *vitibus succisis* ita egisset, ut in actione *vites nominaret,* responsum [eum] *rem perdidisse* est, quia debuisset *arbores nominare, eo* quod lex XII. Tabularum, ex qua de vitibus succisis actio competeret, generaliter de arboribus succisis loqueretur. — *Gaius,* 2.§11. It is hardly possible to believe that this is not a translation from Meeson & Wellsby.

[26] Lege autem agebatur modis quinque: Sacramento, per judicis postulationem, per condictionem, per manus injectionem, per pignoris capionem.

[27] The laws of a rude people almost always endeavour to supply the want of written documents, and perpetuate the memory of particular facts, by an appeal to the senses; and the phrases that they employ, both in their etymology and in the form, often metrical, into which they are cast, bear the traces of this intention. Livy, i. 10. Lex horrendi carminis. Id. 13. Verba carminis, rogationis carmen. Cicero (Pro Rab.) has " Cruciatus carmen" " Qua; verba jampridem tenebris vetustatis et luce libertatia oppressa sunt." — 3. 32. Pactum pangere. The Roman lex comes from legere (eligere), to choose, custom. So the old German law was called Kür. (Willkühr, Grimm, Zeitsch. für Gesch. W., vol. ii. p. 33.) The same motive dictated the tautology so incessant in all early and some modern laws. Vocamus addicimusque, jus fasque, juste pieque. So from this res dare, facere, solvere, censeo, consentio, conscisco, of Livy (1. 13.) to the voluimus, jussimus, et mandavimus of the Middle Ages. So in our Liturgy, " acknowledge and confess," " sins and wickedness," " dissemble nor cloak," " assemble and meet together," " requisite and necessary," " pray and beseech," " erred and strayed," " devices and desires; " here it will be found. generally that one word is of a Saxon, and the other of a Latin stock. So the Homeric ούτ είρομαι οὔτε μεταλλώ ήγήτορες ήδε μέδοντες μένος καί ζνμός μίνύνθα οὔτι μάλα δήν. Alliteration, of course, is common: Quod felix faustumque sit: fidem et f?dera serva; puro pioque duello; vis victoriaque

operation of the *lex Æbutia* and the *Leges Juliæ,* a very slight notice of them will be sufficient for our present purpose. The

---

(Liv. viii. 8.); potest polletque (Liv. i. 9. ii. 20. viii. 6.); lance et licio furtum concipere; aqua et igni interdicere; ferro flammaque vastare; templa tesquaque; sane sarteque (exactly the German ganz und gar). So out of the Sachsen Spiegel: eigen und erbe, gut und gelt; haut und haar, hand und hahn: in more modern times, "Bausch und Bogen." There was a very curious symbol among the northern nations: the children born before marriage sat on the mother's knees during her marriage, and so became legitimate. So " kniesetzen " is " adoptare." So we find in the Greek γόννγένος (genu-genus). The Twelve Tables forbid the laceration and shrieks of women at funerals; ἀμφιδρυφῆς ἂλοχο. " Mulier faciem ne carpito; mulieres genas ne radunto, neve lessum funeris ergo habento." Grimm remarks, as a curious trait of national character (Von der Poesie und Recht. Savigny, Zeitschrift fur ges. Rechtswissenschaft, vol. ii. p. 36.) that all the poetry of the laws of Friesland is completely lost in the Anglo-Saxon law, which is a close and almost literal imitation of it. There never was a more prosaic race than the Anglo-Saxon before the Conquest, Among other symbols, the vellicare, touching the ear of the witness, *Ωτων ΕπιΨαυσεις* should not be forgotten. So, in the Middle Ages we find the plural " testes per aurem tacti." Grimm, *ubi supra.* Greek and Roman formsof oath. Livy, i. 9. II. iii. 268. The house searching, requisitio rei furtivæ secundum veterem observantiam, Inst. part i.§4., borrowed from the Greek, see Aristoph. Νεφ 497. The search of a suspected house was called *φωράν* (fur). The searcher entered naked, except as will be stated, lest he should carry any thing under his garments with him, to inculpate the owner; he was cinctus with the licio, and held the lancem before his eyes. Festus vv.Lance et Licio. Furtum per lancem et licium concipere, was long a technical phrase in Roman law. Aulus Gell. Noctes Att. 21:—φωρᾶν δέ,?ν ἐθέλῃ τις τι παρ' ότφοῦν γυμνὸς, ἤ χιτωνίσκον ἔχων?ζωστος..... οὔτω φωρᾶν. Platonis Νομ. 12. P.202. 16. 10. ed. Bipont. Another conclusive proof of the derivation of Roman from Greek laws. But of all ancient symbols, probably the one of which Livy has given so striking an account (i. 32.) reaches back to the most remote antiquity. "Fieri solitum, ut fecialis h*astam ferratam* aut *sanguineam præustam,* ad fines eorum ferret, et non minus tribus puberibus præsentibus, diceret: 'Quod populi priscorum Latinorum, hominesque prisci Latini adversus, populum Romanum Quiritium fecerunt, deliquerunt, quod populus Romanus Quiritium bellum cum priscis Latinis jussit esse, senatusque populi Romani Quiritium censuit, consensit, conscivit, ut bellum cum priscis Latinis fieret; ob eam rem ego, populusque Romanus, populis priscorum Latinorum, homini- busque priscis Latinis, bellum indico facioque.' Id ubi dixisset, h*astam in fines eorum emittebat."* This is the Gaelic crauntair. " When one Highland chieftain received any provocation or slight from another, or when he had reason to apprehend an invasion of his territories, he straightway formed a cross of light wood, *seared* its extremities *in the fire,* and extinguished it *in the blood* of some animal (commonly a goat) slain for the purpose, and thus from place to place was this instrument conveyed through extensive districts, with a celerity that can scarcely be credited. Degradation or death fell upon all who refused the summons of this mute messenger of bloodshed. In 1745 the crauntair or croistair traversed the wide district of Breadalbane upwards of thirty miles in three hours." So the angebrannter stock among the northern nations, Grimm, Rechtsalterthümer, p. 165.; and Gans, Vermischte Schriften, vol. i. p. 124.

leqis actio sacramento[28] took its name and formal character from the money forfeited by the defeated party to the "*œrarium.*" This, when the value of the object in dispute was equal to or above 3000 *asses,* was fixed by the Twelve Tables at 500 *asses;* for less valuable objects the sum was fixed at 50 *asses.* This sum was deposited by both parties *"in sacro."* The successful party received his stake back. In later times the money was not paid, but sureties were taken for its payment. The money lost was called "*sacramentum,"* and the proceeding, "*sacramento contendere."* This was so expressed, "*D. œris sacramento, te vrovoco." "Et ego te."* In particular cases where a dispute arose concerning the property to an individual thing, the preliminary proceedings "*in jure"* were called *vindicatio,* or "*in jure manum*[29] *conserere."* The plaintiff touched the object with a stick which he held *(festucâ,* or *vindictâ),* to represent the spear —— the emblem of conquest and of dominion, "Omnium enim," says Gaius, in words which show the origin of the

---

[28] The sacramentum is the παρακαταζολή of the Athenians (not to be confounded with the παράστασις). Dem.: Πρὸς μακάρτατον ούκόλμησε παρακαταζαλεῖν ἀλλ' αύτς ἑαυτψέδίκασεν, κ. τ. λ.Isæus.?.τού φιλ. κλήρου. Budæus, Comment, fol. ed. p. 11. " Pecuniam deponebant... ut tam: actor quam reus apud acta decimam partem æstimationis litis depone rent mulctam, scilicet, futuram temere litigantis;" and yet we are told that the idea of the Romans having borrowed the groundwork of their institutions from the Athenians is a myth! A myth, believed by Livy, Cicero, Tacitus, Varro, the authors of the Digest, which grave writers of legal treatises take for granted, as much as Lord Coke and Blackstone do the existence of Magna Charta and the Norman conquest, is entitled to some consideration.

Though it may appear out of place, I cannot here forbear quoting a fact that may interest legal antiquarians, and indeed all etymologists, as it is a very curious instance of the transmission of a word from one age and country to another. " Essoign-day was the word used to describe the last day on which excuses were received. And thereon the court sits to take essoigns or excuses for such as do not appear according to the summons of the writ."—*Blackstone,* iii. 277. This was borrowed imme- diately from the Norman French, but it came originally from the Greek word ἐξομνύναι — ἐξομνυμᾶι τήν πρεσζείαν—in Law French, "exoniare," of which Budæus, Comm. Ling. G. p. 10. gives the following derivation: " Lingua nostra vernacula ut alia multa, a Græcis habet: *exoniare* enim appellant jure- jurando excusare ejus absentiæ causam qui vadimonio obstrictus est: q. q. " ἐξομνύσθαι" et *exoniatos* vulgus appellat, vulnere aut mutilatione causarios, qui detrectare jure militiam possunt."

[29] So Ennius,

"Non ex jure manu consertum sed mage ferro
Rem repetunt."

Festus v.Vindex, Au. Gell. 16. 10. " Assiduo vindex assiduus esto." "Assiduo," says Hugo (vol. i. p. 204.), ab asses et dare, celui dont on peut tirer beaucoup d'argent"

Roman state, "maxime sua esse credebant quæ ex hostibus cepissent;" saying "Hunc ego hominem (as the case might be) ex jure Quiritium meum esse aio, secundum suam causam, sicut dixi, ecce tibi vindictam imposui." The defendant did the same. Then the prætor said, "Mittite ambo hominem." When land was in dispute, the prætor in the earliest times went with the litigants to the ground. In later days a clod of earth was substituted, which the parties brought with them before the prætor. The plaintiff then said, asserting his right as a challenge to his adversary, "Fundum qui est in agro qui Sabinus vocatur, ego ex jure Quiritium meum esse aio, inde ibi ego te ex jure consertum voco." The defendant, answering to the challenge, replies, "Unde tu me ex jure manum consertam vocâsti[30] inde ibi ego te revoco." Then the prætor said, as a symbol of his interference and to declare his cognisance of the matter, "Suis utrisque superstitibus præsentibus vindicias sumite— inite viam," and as the clod was produced "Redite viam." After the vindication and the prætor's order, followed the "*sacramento contendere.*" The plaintiff said, "Postulo anne dicas quâ ex causâ vindicaveris?" To which the other answered, "Jus peregi, sicut vindictam imposui." The prætor pronounced on the *vindiciæ,* that is, he decided who should remain in possession of the thing claimed while the suit was going on, and ordered him to give security "prædes litis et vindiciarum," to the other, "secundum alterum eorum vindicias dicebat," The object of the former part of these proceedings was, as Keller acutely observes, to settle on which of the parties the *onus probandi* should rest. Different from this "*vindicias sumere,*" was another proceeding called "*deductio;*" Cicero twice calls it "*Deductio quæ moribus fit.*"[31] One party formally turned the other out of

---

[30] See the famous passage, Cic. Pro Murena, c. 12. Festus, " Superstites...vindiciæ ex jure manu consertum vocari."

Cicero, De Off. 3. 10. Prædarum a magistratibus morem *rogandi judicis,* &c. Dig. 40. 7.§21. De Statu Lib.

[31] Keller, Ueber die " Deductio quas moribus fit." Zeitschrift für geschichtliche Rechtswissen-schaft, vol. ix. art. 9. p. 287. Deductio quæ moribus fit. This Gellius calls "vis civilis " "festucaria." It was a form used in Cicero's days, I would suggest, for the purpose of giving the prætor jurisdiction; as the clause of trespass was in writs for civil actions, to give the Queen's Bench jurisdiction. It is, however, remarkable that it is borrowed from Athens, and corresponds exactly with the

possession, became the plaintiff, and gave the *vadimonium* (Cæcina ad eum fundum profectus ex quo, *ex conventu vim fieri* oportebat).[32]

The second "*legis actio*" was *judicis (arbitrive) postulatio,* Gaius's account of which is unfortunately lost. Both of these, the two oldest "*legis actiones,*" were applicable also to every kind of complaint. But the third, the "*legis actio per condictionem,*" was more limited. It was introduced by the Silian and Calpurnian laws, "Lege quidem Siliâ certæ pecuniæ, Lege vero Calpurniâ de omni certa." Why it was introduced, as all it gave was already accomplished, Graius tells us was matter of much speculation. It deserves notice, however, as a kind of link between the old law and the system of *formulæ;* and this Savigny thinks the right answer to Gaius's inquiry,[33] The *condictio* is the fixing of a certain day with the opposite party. "*Legis actio per manus injectionem*" applied to cases where the *in jus vocatio* had no effect; 1*st.* to a debtor, *indefensus vel confessus; 2d.* to *a fur manifestus;* and to a slave, "Virgini, venienti in forum,.... minister decemviri libidinis *manum injecit;* servâ suâ natam esse servamque appellans: sequique se jubebat."[34] According to this process, the plaintiff seized upon the defendant at once and carried him before the prætor.

The "*pignoris capio*" is like the last proceeding, one in which the plaintiff asserts his own right without the assistance of the state. It bears some resemblance to our action of replevin. It consisted in carrying off a particular thing, after uttering

---

έξγωγή. Budæus, Comment. Linguæ Græcæ, p. 329. fol. ed. Isæus, p. 28. Πλήν δυοίν οίκιδίοιν έξω τείχους ούδέν κεκομίσμεθα.... ήμεῖς ούκ έξαγομεν δεδίαμεν, γὰρ μή οφλωμεν ικας. The claimant allowed himself to be turned out of possession by the actual possessor, έξαγεσθαι. Dem. K. *Ζην.* 887; *κατὰ Λεωχ.* 1090. Zeitschrift, Savigny, vol. iii. p. 426. Cicero, Pro Cæcina, cap. 7. " Placuit Cæcinæ, de amicorum sententia cunstituere, quo die in rem præsentem veniretur, et de fundo Cæcina moribus deduceretur. Colloquuntur. Dies ex utriusque. commodo sumitur. Cæcina cum amicis ad diem venit," etc. Ib. cap. 8. "Ad eum fundum profectus, ex quo ex conventu vim fieri oportebat." Cicero, Pro Tullio, cap. 16. "Appellat Fabius, ut aut ipse Tullium deduceret, aut ab eo deduceretur. Dicit deducturum se Tullius, vadimonium Fabio Romam promissurum."

[32] Pro Tullio, 20. Pro Cæcina, 7, 8. Gaius, iv. 19.

[33] System des heut. R. R. vol. v. p. 59.

[34] Livy, iii. 44.

certain formal words in which the reason of the proceeding was declared. If the article was not redeemed by the original owner, it might be sold. The Twelve Tables gave the *"pignoris capio"* against the purchaser of an animal for sacrifice, who did not pay the price. It was also given to the *publicanus* against the state debtor; and it was given to the soldier for his pay, which was not in early times paid by the treasury, but by certain appointed persons. Livy, i. 43.: "Quibus equos alerent, viduas attributæ, quæ bina millia æris in annos singulos penderent." Gaius, iv. 27.: "Propter stipendium licebat militi ab eo qui æs tribuebat, nisi daret, pignus capere." I may remark, in passing, on behalf of a favourite writer, that both the account of the *manus injeclio* by Gaius, and Livy's account of the proceeding towards Virginia, and this last case, where the passage (i. 43.) as to the support of the equites is so fully, though indirectly, corroborated and explained by Gaius, are strongly in favour of the fidelity and truth for which, in his own age, and long after, Livy was as much celebrated as for his almost inspired and never ceasing eloquence.

TRIBUNAL

The first judges at Rome, in all cases, were the *pontifices,* and the king at their head, as *pontifex maximus.* There was no distinction between private and public law. Every transaction between its members interested the state alike. Of this state of things we may see the most obvious traces in the law of wills, and the ceremonies requisite for their validity. So Scævola says, "Nullum bonum pontificem esse, nisi qui jus civile cognôsset" (which, by the way, we may compare with the saying of William of Malmesbury[35], "Nullus clericus, nisi causidicus"). However, it is certain that the *pontifices* were the primitive guardians of Roman law. "Omnium tamen harum (legum) et interpretandi scientia et actiones apud collegium pontificum

---

[35] 4. 7. col. 1.

erant, ex quibus constituebatur, quis quoquo anno præesset privatis."[36] Servius Tullus established the *decemviri*

for the trial of private causes,[37] The Lex Horatia, which was passed A. U. C. 305, "lit, qui tribunis plebis, ædilibus[38], judicibus, *decemviris*[39] nocuisset, ejus caput Jovi sacrum esset."

THE CENTUMVIRI

The first accurate knowledge which we acquire of this tribunal[40] is taken from the times of the emperors. Niebuhr thinks, and, as it appears to me, on sufficient grounds, that it was instituted by Servius Tullus, and there can be no doubt that it goes back to very remote antiquity; it consisted, when there were thirty-five tribes, of one hundred and five members, three from each tribe, who were in all probability chosen by the

---

[36] Dig. i. 2.§6.

[37] Dion. Hal. iv. 25.

[38] The interpolation of the words populus Romanus (Gaius, iv. 15.) after ante earn legem is, as Puchta says, an obvious error. Zimmern, G. 3 Band. Puchta, 1. Tigerström, Innere Gesch. p. 134. Noodt, De Juris 1—12. Cicero in Rull. ii. 17. "Auctio decemviralig, hasta decemviralis." In Rull. i.§§2, 3.

[39] Livy, iii. 55. This again corroborates Livy. Was the existence of those decemvirs and their office a myth, to borrow that affected language? and if the records were all destroyed, how happens his account to coincide in such minute details with that of Gaius?

[40] See Pliny, Ep. vi. 33. in which he is coxcomb enough to tell us that all the judges rose up from the effect of his eloquence. Val. Max. vii. 7.: "Omnibus non solum consiliis sed sententiis;" with which compare Cic. de Nat. Deor. i. 38. Quintil. xii.§5. "Quatuor judicia ut moris est cogerentur, circa inofficiosi quædam plerumque evenire solet ut in unâ atque eâdem causâ diversæ sententiæ proferantur." Suetonius, Aug. c. 36. "Auctor et aliarum rerum fuit.... ut centumviralem hastam, quam quæsturâ functi consueverant cogere, decemviri cogerent." Dialogus de Orat. 38. Gellius, 14. 2. De Orat. 38.

"Nec jam tibi turba reorum
Vestibulo querulive rogant exire clientes.
Cessat centeni moderatrix judicis hasta,
Qua tibi sublimi jam nunc celeberrima fama
Eminet."

STATIUS, *Sylv. iv.* 4. 41. Ad Vict. Marcellum Ep.

" Res quoque privatas statui sine crimine judex,
Deque mea fassa est, pars quoque victa fide."

ovid. *Trist.* ii. 96.

prætor.[41] Cicero has enumerated the causes brought before it, which seem to be those growing out of the peculiar technicalities and primitive character of the Roman law. Accordingly, the old forms and "*legis actiones*" were preserved before this tribunal, when elsewhere they were obsolete. "Sed enim cum proletarii.... omnisque illa Duodecim Tabularum antiquitas, nisi in legis actionibus centumviralium causarum, Lege Æbutiâ latâ, consopita sit."[42] "Ideo cum ad centumviros itur, ante lege agitur sacramento apud prætorem urbanum vel peregrinum."[43] Its sittings were denoted by a spear, the ancient emblem of property, and therefore Gaius says, "In centumviralibus judiciis hasta præponitur;" the number of its members was increased by Augustus to 180; they were divided into four consilia, which made so many separate tribunals, and sat in the Basilica Julia. The prætor was the president of the whole, but a quæstor presided judicially over the management of each separate cause, till Augustus transferred that office to decemviri, *"stlitibus ordinandis."* Some cases were, however, brought before two of these *consilia;* and for the consideration of some all the four were collected. To decide upon questions of disputed inheritance was the peculiar, if not exclusive, duty of this tribunal; in later times it adjudicated upon the "*Querela inofficiosi testamenti."* It appears to me that the duties of the *decemviri* appointed by Augustus, corresponded to those of the *judex quœstionis* in other cases: so Pomponius, "Deinde quum esset necessarius magistratus qui hastæ præesset, decemviri in litibus judicandis sunt constituti."[44]

---

[41] Pliny tells us the causes before this tribunal were "parvæ et exiles." Ep. ii. 14. " Nam vo-litare in foro jactare se in caussis centumviralibus, in quibus usucapionum, tutelarum, gentilitatum, agnationum, alluvionum, circumluvionum, nexorum, mancipiorum, parietum, luminum, stillicidiorum, testamentorum ruptorum [aut ratorum] ceterarumque rerum innumerabilium jura versentur, quum omnino, quid suum, quid alienum, quare denique civis aut peregrinus, servus aut liber ignoret, insignis eat impudentiæ." Cic. de Orat. 1. 73. Puchta, Institutiones, vol. ii. p. 37. Zimmern, Gesch.des Röm. Privat-Rechts, 3 Band. p. 94. Tigerström, Innere Geschichte des Röm. Rechts, p. 130. Quintilian, xii. 5, 6. Seneca, de Ben. iii. 9.

[42] Aul. Gell. N. Att. xvi. 10.

[43] Gaius, iv. 31.

[44] Dig. i. 22. 29.

RECUPERATORES

As there was intercourse without community of law between the Roman *civis* and the *peregrinus,* particular magistrates were required to adjust litigation that arose between them, and these were the *recuperatores.* It was usual for the Romans in their treaties, to stipulate expressly that a tribunal should be constituted, to determine the differences of individuals belonging to the foreign nation and to their own. These judges, therefore, were not to proceed according to the strict rules of Roman law, but according to substantial equity. The *recuperatores* were at first not included in the list of judges between Roman citizens *(decuriæ judicium).* They were called *judices:* the word was confined to those we have mentioned, and to the judges in the provinces, who were called *peregrini recuperatores,* in the same sense as one of the prætors was called *peregrinus*[45] The proceeding before *recuperatores* afterwards was extended to the disputes of Roman citizens.[46] The matter was thus brought to a more speedy conclusion. "*Protinus.*"[47] To this tribunal, for this reason, were assigned "*injuriarum actio*"[48], or "*bon. rapt. actio*", "*interdict, unde vi hominis armat.*" Questions of status.

---

[45] Gaius, iv. 105. "Imperia vero continentur recuperatoria, et quæ sub uno judice accipiuntur interveniente peregrini persona judicis aut litigatoris," where the recuperatores are opposed to a single judge.

[46] Festus v. Recuperatio: Cum inter populum et reges nationesque, et civitates peregrinas, lex convenit quomodo per recuperatores reddantur res reciperenturque, resque privatas inter se persequantur.

[47] Gaius, iv. 145,

[48] Aul. Gell. xx. 1.

PART II

LAW OF CIVIL PROCESS

FORMULÆ

It is to the discovery of the work of Gaius that we owe the means of explaining some of the greatest difficulties that have hitherto embarrassed the interpreters of the Roman law. This precious treatise, far superior in my opinion not only in the purity of its style and the lucid precision of its statements, but in its scientific method, to the Institutes of Justinian, the feeble work of a degenerate age from which the spirit of jurisprudence had departed, contains a detailed and minute account of the Roman formula, that great instrument which in the most flourishing period of Roman jurisprudence was employed not to impede, but to insure the triumph of substantial justice. A close and strict attention to this formula is therefore of the utmost importance, not to the jurist only, but to the general scholar, as it explains much that up to the time that Gaius was discovered was unintelligible. As in Justinian's time the use of the formula was abolished, all explanation of it was of course omitted in his compilations, and the allusions to it, which occur sometimes[49], are cursory and accidental.

---

[49] Inst. 8. de Interdictis. So Dig. 47. 2.§42: " Si servus navem exerceat non voluntate domini, de eo quod ibi periit, vulgaris formula in dominum danda est." The *intentio* of the formula is mentioned in a remarkable passage which probably escaped the vigilance of the compilers. Dig. 44. 1.§12: " Generaliter in præjudiciis is actoris partes sustinet qui habet *intentionem* secundum id quod *in-tendit"* So Dig. 5. 3.§47: "Non ideo repelli ab *intentione* non jure facti testamenti." So Dig. 44. 1§9: " Non utique existimatur confiteri de *intentione* adversarius quocum agitur, quia exceptione utitur." Dig. 5. 2.§14; 21. 2.§17; 15. 1.§32.

The formula probably came into use soon after the sixth century, A. U. C. It became, except before the centumviri, and for cases where the *extraordinaria cognitio* was used, universal in the time of Augustus, and lasted from his days to those of Alexander Severus. Under Diocletian the provincial rulers decided themselves all questions but those of "*status* "[50] without appeal, except to the emperor.

The *legis actiones* consisted, as we have seen, in the utterance of certain words and the performance of certain actions by the contending parties, in the presence of the prætor.[51] A mistake in this form was fatal to the suit; but as the jurisdiction of the Roman magistrate increased, and he was called upon more frequently to decide in disputes to which a foreigner was a party, a more rational system was adopted on such occasions. The *legis actiones,* however, remained the only means of obtaining a civil remedy in disputes which arose among Romans, until the period of the "*Lex Æbutia,*"[52] about 520 A. U. C., more fully developed and established finally by the two *Leges Juliœ,* in the time of Julius Cæsar and Augustus, which in all probability borrowing the system in use when foreigners were litigant parties, applied it with the happiest effect to the controversies of Roman citizens. According to this method, the proceedings began by a written instrument, *i. e. a formula*[53], in which the magistrate stated the point in dispute

---

[50] Cod. iii.§§2, 3. de ped. Jud. Cod. vii.§§11. 16. de lib. causâ.

[51] Théorie de la procédure civile par M. Boncenne, page 56. *Introd.* The study of isolated decisions arréte les progrés de l'étude, 54. ib. " Leur loi commune (ours) est une masse indigeste de coutûmes dont les recueils de jugemens sont l'unique depôt. Leur jurisprudence n'est pas la science du droit, elle n'est que la mémoire des précédens. Ils ne s'attachent point dans la discussion d'une affaire à examiner la loi, et à en développer les principes, mais seulement, à en rechercher ces précédens... ainsi la plus grande partie des lois qui régissent les personnes et les propriétés en Angleterre n'a été éditée que par la bouche *d'un jvge* statuant sur un cas particulier." How disgraceful, and how true.

[52] Not to be confounded with that mentioned by Cicero, de Lege Agr. ii. 8. 24. This Æbutia " lata est ab Æbutio incertum quo et quo tempore." Onomas. Tull. p. 126.

[53] There is a passage in Cicero's letters to Trebatius, which shows that in his time the formulæ were common; he laughs at his correspondent's economy for writing on a Palimpsest, and says he could have obliterated nothing to make place for his letter, that was not worth more than what he had written, except a formula. Ad Fam. vii. 18:" Nam quod in Palimpsesto—laudo equidem parcimoniam, sed miror quid in

between the parties "*per concepta verba;*" this contained the appointment of the judge or judges before whom the trial was to take place, "*Octavius Judex esto,*" or "*Recuperatores sunto;*" and the direction to the magistrate, which, after stating first the point in dispute between the parties, ended with instructing the judge to decide under one state of facts, for the plaintiff; under another state of facts, for the defendant.[54] Thus, from an almost passive spectator during the most important part of the cause (as English judges now are), the *Lex Æbutia* and the *Leges Juliœ,* converted the magistrate into an instrument for obtaining justice. Both plaintiff and defendant assisted in the preparation of the *formula,* which, when most expanded, contained four parts.[55] The *demonstratio,* the *intentio,* the *adjudicatio,* the *condemnatio;* the *adjudicatio* we may at once set aside, as it was used only in three actions, "Si inter coheredes, familiæ erciscundæ, agatur; aut inter socios communi dividundo; aut inter vicinos finium regundorum: nam illic ita est; quantum adjudicari oportet, judex Silio adjudicato."[56]

DEMONSTRATIO

The *demonstratio,* Gaius tells us, stated the fact in dispute, it was the narrative and introductory part of the *formula, e. g.* "Quod Aulus Agerius, Numerio Negidio hominem vendidit."

"Item hæc quod Aulus Agerius (apud) Numerium Negidium hominem deposuit,"

"Quod A. Agerius de N. Negidio incertum stipulatus est," were respectively the demonstrations, for the *actio venditi,*

---

illa chartula fuerit, quod delere malueris quam hæc exscribero, nisi forte tuas formulas."

[54]"Mes amis," disoit Henri IV. " *la barbarie* et la confusion de la jurisprudence voilà l'ennemi." Worse than the furies of the Ligue-Jesuits, Guises, and Philip II., we have the same enemy still.

[55] Savigny, System des heutigen Römischen Rechts, vol.v. Zimmern, Geschichte des Römis-chen Rechts, vol. i. p. 116. Puchta, Institutiones, vol. ii.

[56] Gaius, iv. These were the "judicia divisoria," and corresponded with the δικη εις δατητῶν α'Lρεσιν of the Athenians. Harpocration, v. " δατεισθαι."

depositi, ex stipulatu. The *demonstratio* was only used in in personal actions, and those personal actions which were *in jus conceptœ,* and even in these last only where the *intentio* was *incerta.* In the *demonstratio,* an error in asking too much or too little was immaterial, it was at once rectified by the *"judex quœstionis;"* and hence the maxim "F*alsa demonstratio non nocet."* It often happened that the "*intentio,"* contained every thing that the *demonstratio* was used to introduce. Gaius tells us, that in certain cases the action was specially limited by a form, sometimes prefixed to the *"demonstratio"* itself; sometimes substituted for it; and sometimes incorporated with it, which was called *"prœscriptio."*[57] The use of the *prœscriptio* was this:—Proof of the same fact may entitle the party adducing it, not only to what he actually demands, but to some claim hereafter to be made. The same instrument, for instance, may prove, that on a particular day money is due from A to B, and that it will continue to be due at certain intervals hereafter. *The formula* then being *"Quicquid ob earn rem dare facere oportet,"* it is necessary to limit it to that particular part of the object which the plaintiff is now entitled to demand, and this is done in the case of money to be paid by instalments, some of which only had become due, by adding to the *"demonstratio"* the words *"Ea res agatur, cujus rei dies fuit;"* without this the plaintiff would have recovered the instalment due, but would have been excluded from enforcing his subsequent demand. These *prœscriptiones* supposed an *actio incerfa;* in one case it might, however, be necessary where the *actio* was *certa,* and that is where a contract had been entered into by a slave for his master. Here, as the *certa actio* had no *demonstratio* — but begins *"Si paret A. A, N. N. decem dare oportere,"* it was necessary that the *"prœscriptio"* should state *"loco demonstrationis,"* that the person with whom the contract really was made, was not the master, but his slave; and this is the meaning of the passage in Gaius, iv.§ 134.: "Inpræscriptione de

[57] The instance of the præscriptio is where it was used for the benefit of the plaintiff, but it might be used for the defendant. This last class, in the time of Gaius, was comprised under the head of exceptiones. Gaius, iv.§133.

pacto quæritur quod secundum naturalem significationem verum ease debet."

INTENTIO[58]

We now proceed to the *intentio;* this is the part of the *formula* which is most nearly connected with the rights it is intended to enforce, and which, therefore, had the most material influence on the matter in litigation; it is here, therefore, that the different kinds of action, as they depend on the different nature of the plaintiff's right, are most prominent and conspicuous; it is that part of the *formula* in which the object of the plaintiff is expressed, "*qua actor desiderium suum concludit,"* e. g.

"*Quicquid paret ob eam rem. N. N. A. A. dare facere, oportere.* Or, *Si paret N. N. A. A. sestertium X millia dare oportere."* In these cases the *intentio* is directly aimed at an individual; it is called "*intentio in personam,"* and the *actio* was "*in personum actio."* Or it might run

"*Si paret fundum Tusculanum A. A. dare oportere."* In this case the *intentio* was *in rem,* and the *actio* was *in rem actio;* this *intentio in rem* corresponds in the process of the *formula* with the *vindicatio,* under the old *legis actiones,* and was therefore called *vindicatio,* or at a still latter period "*fictitia formula petitoria,"* and the *"in rem actiones"* are called sometimes "*vindicationes,"* sometimes "*petitioner".* Gaius has described the two forms of action with his usual perspicuity: — "In personam actio est, quoties cum aliquo agimus qui nobis vel ex contractu vel ex delicto obligatus est; id est, cum intendimus dare, facere, præstare oportere. In rem actio est, cum aut corporalem rem intendimus nostram *ease,* aut jus aliquod nobis competere, velut utendi aut fruendi, eundi, agendi,

---

[58] The object of this was when in jus, what the object of all pleading ought to be, " diriger la justice dans le choix des analogies." Boncenne, Intr. p. 31. "Il ne faut pas donner à l'une des parties le bien de l'autre sans examen, *ni les ruiner toutes deux* à *force d'examiner"* Esprit des Loix. 29. c. 1. We reject the latter maxim altogether, and make the former useless. More injustice is done under colour of law in this country in a week than in all France in a year.

aquamve.ducendi, vel altius tollendi vel prospiciendi."[59] Although in this last case the person asserting the opposite right must be named. All these *intentiones* are *"in jus concepts"*

The best key to the *intentiones* is to consider the *obligationes* which were framed with reference to them.[60] The *obligationes* were three: — *Ad dandum, — faciendum, — prœstandum.* The *obligationes ad dandum* corresponded with the *intentio "dare oportere;"* — the *obligationes ad dandum faciendum,* with the *intentio "dare facere;"* — and the *obligationes ad prœstandum* were met neither by the *intentio "dare,"* nor *"dare facere,"* but by an *intentio* framed in the words *"dam-nurn decidere:"*—this *"damnum decidere"* relates entirely to the class of *obligationes "ex delicto"*

INTENTIONES IN JUS CONCEPTŒ: CERTA FORMULA, INTENTIO "DARE" "CONDICTIO CERTI"

The *"certa formula"* supposes a specific object, *"res corporalis,"* or a specific right, such as an easement or beneficial interest, *"res incorporalis," "usus," "jus eundi," "usus fructus;"* and it must demand that the object should be placed within the plaintiff's power, as the owner by the civil law; *e. g.* that if a thing, it should be given to him as his property, *"ex jure Quiritium;"* if a servitude, it should be allowed as his *"jure civili;"* hence an object really belonging to the plaintiff could not be claimed through the *"intentio dare oportere,"* as nobody can give another what actually is his own; the *"intentio oportere dare"* was employed to demand a certain sum of money, *"si paret N. N. A. A. sestertium X millia dare oportere."*

---

[59] Gaius, iv.§§2, 3. 39, 40.

[60] Actions:
Vindicationes — Condictiones.
Real. Personal.
Intentiones:
In jus — in factum.
Utiles — directæ.

INTENTIO INCERTA., "DARE FACERE" "CONDICTIO INCERTI"

We now come to the "*intentio incerta,*" "*dare facere oportere.*" This was used in all cases where the object sought to be recovered, had not the fixed definite character that has already been described, and which was expressed by the word "*dare.*" For the "*incerta*" the word "*facere*" was introduced, "*quicquid N. N. A. A. dare facere oportere.*" Where the "*certa formula*" was used, the task of the judge was only to determine, as in the case of "*certa pecunia,*" whether the sum required was due. But as the object of the "*incerta intentio*" is not any thing fixed and specific, the judge may include in his decision the "*fructus,*—as Papinian expressly says[61] —*postea capti.*"[62]

INTENTIONES IN JUS CONCEPTŒ

Both these *formulœ,* in which the *intentio* was "*dare,*" or "*dare facere,*" were called *condictiones.*[63] "Appellantur autem in rem quidem actiones vindicationes; in personam vero actiones quibus dare fierive oportere intendimus, condictiones."[64] Thus there was a "*certi,*" *or* an "*incerti condictio.*"[65] There was, moreover, a third species of "*condictio,*" in which the "*condictio*" was conceived, not for a specific sum of money, "*pecunia numerata,*" but for "*alia certa res.*" This the Roman lawyers called "*condictio triticaria*" "*triticarius,*" "*triticiarius*" a "*tritico nomen trahens.*" Thus we have three *condictiones,* corresponding to the two "*intentiones,*" "*dare*" and "*dare facere.*"

1. *Condictio certi. Si paret S. S. N. N. x millia dare oportere.*

---

[61] Dig.xxii.§§1.4.
[62] Ibid. xxxii.§§1.7. 38.
[63] V. supra, p.22.
[64] Gaius, iv.§4.
[65] Dig.xii.§§1.24.

2. *Condictio triticaria. Si paret, A. A. N. N. Vini Campani amphoras L dare oportere.*

3. *Condictio incerti, quicquid dare facere oportere.*

INTENTIO EX FIDE BONA

In a great number of actions in which the "*intentio dare facere oportere*" was used, considerable latitude was given to the powers of the judge by the addition of the words "*ex fide bona.*" This principle of equity, which existed in the time of the "*legis actiones,*" "*judicis, arbitrive*[66], *postulatio,* "was transferred to the system of *formulas;* hence these actions were called "*bonæ fidei judicia,*" and the obligations out of which they arose, "*bonæ fidei obligationes.*" Gains (iv.§ 62.) enumerates "Ex empto, vehdito, locato, conducto, negotiorum gestorum, mandati, depositi fiduciæ, pro socio, tutelæ, rei uxoriæ, commodati."[67] Thus the actions from contracts were divided into *condictiones,* or *stricti juris actiones,* and *bonæ fidei actiones.* The *intentio ex fide bona* could not belong to a *formula "in factum concepta,"* or to a *formula in rem.*

INTENTIO UTILIS

Another very important variety of the *intentio* may be next considered[68]: that is, the fiction by means of which a legal remedy was extended to cases for which it was not intended originally to provide; e. *g.* if the person who succeeded, by the prætor's interposition, and not by strict law, to the estate of a

[66] Cic. Pro Roscio,§4, where the distinction is made between the judge and the arbiter. V. infra, p. 44. This was borrowed from the Athenian system.

[67] Inst. de Act. (46) 28.

[68] Savigny, Sys. heut. R.R. p. 72. vol. V. lib. 2. c. 4.; Gaius, ii.§253. The words "*fictitia actio*" do not occur in the Justinian compilation;" *utiles actiones* " is the expression everywhere; " Quoties deficit actio vel exceptio, utilis actio vel exceptio danda est." Dig xix.§§5. 21. Gaius. iv.§§34—38. " Ficto se hærede agit." " Fingitur rem usucepisse." " Civitas ei Romana fingitur." "Fingimus adversarium nostrum capite diminutum non esse."

relation, claimed on that account a particular farm, he could not directly say that what belonged to the deceased was his by the Roman law, *ex jure Quiritium;* and therefore the *formula* directed the judge to give him the farm, if, setting aside the technical objection, he would have had a right to it. So, if a purchaser lost his slave before the time when his right by "*usucapio*" would have accrued, he could not claim it, "*ex jure Quiritium,"* as his own; and therefore the *intentio* directed the judge to give him the slave, if, supposing the slave to have been in his possession a year, he would have been the property of the purchaser; in other words, not to allow the plaintiff to be defeated by a mere wrong-doer, on the objection that he had not acquired a prescriptive title to his property, but to decide on the hypothesis that the prescriptive title had been acquired. Actions in which the *formulœ* were thus framed, were called *"fictitiœ,"* or afterwards "*utiles actiones,"* and were opposed to the "*actiones directœ,"* those, for instance, in which the heir or proprietor, in the cases above cited, would have had a legal title. The "*intentiones*" we have hitherto examined were "*in jus conceptœ;"* but there are numerous cases when the judge was called upon to say, not whether such a sum was Iegally due to the plaintiff, or if such a piece of ground legally belonged to him, but to ascertain whether a particular fact was true or false, and, according to the result of that inquiry, to pronounce for or against the plaintiff; these were called *"formulœ in factum conceptœ."* and in these the "*de-monstratio*" was lost in the *intentio,* the fact usually stated in the former, being transferred[69] to the latter.

These *formulœ in factum* were many of them set forth in the edict, some as concurrent, others as exclusive remedies; but there were also a vast number of such *formulœ* not set forth in the edict, but the mere result of advancing necessity and experience, the children, if I may use the expression, of that analogy which was the fruitful parent of so many blessings in the Roman law. The *formulœ in factum conceptœ* not mentioned in the edict, led to the *actiones in factum.* Such of

---

[69] Savigny, v. Sys. des heut. R. Rechts. 21. *a.* Bonjean, Traité des Actions, vol. i.

these *formulæ* as were of common use, found their way into the edict and became the foundation of the *actiones honorariæ.* But neither in the structure nor the effect of the *formulæ* did its omission from, or incorporation with, the edict make the slightest difference. The *actiones in factum* were therefore one and the same with *the formulæ in factum concepts,* which the invaluable work of Gaius has explained to us[70]; and if some *actiones* of this sort were, like *"Serviana"* or the *"actio doli quod metus causâ,"* called by particular names, this was only for the sake of convenience, and they were not the less *actiones in factum or formulæ in factum conceptæ.*

"Cæteras formulas in factum conceptas vocamus, id est, in quibus nulla talis intentionis conceptio est, sed initio formulæ nominato eo quod factum est adjiciuntur ea verba per quæ judici damnandi absolvendive potestas datur."[71] From the *"fictitia intentio,"* it is but a very short step to the *"formula in factum concepfa,"* where the *"intentio"* framed in the previous cases was omitted altogether, and a fact stated, on the decided truth or falsehood of which the success of the litigant parties was to depend. These actions, in which the *"formula in factum concepta,"* was used, arose where, to use the *"intentio juris civilis,"* would be impossible, that is, —where the right which it is intended to assert was one which the civil law did not recognise, and, therefore, where, if the judge had been obliged to decide whether the claimant was entitled according to the rules of the civil law, *"si paret secundum jus civile,"* his decision, whatever might in fact be the justice of the claimant's demand, must have been against him; this evil was in some measure guarded against by the *"fictitia formula;"* but there were cases where the application of this remedy would be inconvenient or impracticable, hence came the *"in factum actiones"* which Pomponius has accounted for: "Quia actionum non plenus numerus esset ideo plerumque actiones in factum desiderantur. Sed et eas actiones quas legibus proditæ sunt, si lex justa ac necessaria sit, supplet prætor in eo, quod legi deest, quod facit in Lege Aquilia reddendo actiones in factum

---

[70] Corn. iv. 106, *107.*

[71] Gaius, iv. 45.

accommodatas Legi Aquiliæ: idque utilitas ejus legis exigit."[72] As an illustration of this, let us consider the case where the son, not emancipated, has lent or deposited any article.[73] He cannot have recourse to *the formula "in jus concepta,"* as the property is in reality not his; but he must have recourse to a *formula in factum concepta,* in which he states the facts that give him an equitable right, and obliges his antagonist to dispute them, or abandon his defence. Another difference between the *formula in jus concepta* and that *in factum* was this. When the action was at the same time a personal action, a *"legitimum judicium,"* and *"in jus conceptum,"* the complaint, when once brought forward, was *"ipso jure"* extinguished. But in all other cases it was necessary if that defence was relied on, to (plead it, as we should say,) enforce it by an *"exceptio rel judicatæ".*

Care must be taken to distinguish the *"actio in factum"* and the *"formula in factum concepta,"* of which mention has been made, from the *"actio præscriptis verbis,"* and the "*actio in factum civilis."* These last-mentioned actions which are synonymous expressions, were those by which the "*con-tractus innominati"* were enforced. In these the *formula* began with a *demonstratio,* which did not, as in other cases, state concisely and generally the nature of the complaint, but set it out in full detail; hence the expression "*præscriptis verbis,"* which here, as in the "*præscriptiones,"* came before the *intentio.* The name *in factum* is derived from the long enumeration of facts; then came the "*intentio in jus concepta."* "Quidquid eum ob eam rem dare facere oportet," and as this was quite indefinite, the action is often called "*incerti actio,"* and often *actio civilis,* and sometimes both, as *"civili intentione incerti[74],"* *"civilis incerti."*[75] Now it will be obvious to any one who has read the preceding pages, that an "*incerti actio"* must be quite

---

[72] Dig. xix.§§5. 11.

[73] Dig. v. 1.§18. Ulpian says that this, where the matter was ex maleficio, had been established before. " Unde ego probavi, si res non ex maleficio veniat sed ex contractu, debeat filius agere utili ju-dicio forte depositum repetens, vel mandati agens, vel pecuniam quam credidit, petens. Si forte pater in provinciâ, ipse autem Romæ studiorum causâ,... agat ne," &c.

[74] Dig. xix.§§5, 6.

[75] Dig. ii.§§2. 14.

inconsistent with a *"formula in factum concepta"* in the sense first assigned to it, as nothing could be more certain or less arbitrary than the object, of such an action. The *"in factum actio"* in this last-mentioned sense, and the *civilis incerti actio,* are opposed to each other in a passage of the Digest, which effectually points out the difference between the two.[76]

CONDEMNATIO

"Judex Numerium Negidium Aulo Agerio sestertium x millia condemna: si non paret, absolve. — Quidquid ob eam rem N. N. A. A.—dare facere oportet ex fide bona ejus, id judex N. N. A. A. condemnafo; si non paret, absolvito. _ Quanti ea res erit, tantam pecuniam Judex N. N. A. A. con-demnato; si non paret, absolvito."

The *condemnatio* was employed almost in *every formula,* except in the *"actiones prœjudiciales,"* that is, the actions by which the mere existence of a fact or of a legal relation was established, in order that the plaintiff might avail himself of it in another suit. It was that part of *the formula* by which the judge was commanded to condemn or to acquit if it referred to a sum of money; this might be certain or indefinite; in the first case the judge was obliged to acquit if the precise sum demanded by the plaintiff was not due. Cic. Pro Roscio iv.: "Pecunia tibi debebatur certa, quæ nunc petitur per judicem; in qua legitimæ partis sponsio facta est. Hic tu si amplius H.S. nummo petisti, quam tibi debitum est, causam perdidisti: propterea quod aliud est judicium, aliud arbitrium. Judicium est pecuniæ certæ; arbitrium, incertæ. Ad judicium hoc modo venimus, ut totam aut obtineamus aut amittamus; ad arbitrium hoc animo adimus, ut neque nihil neque tantum quantum postula(vi)mus consequamur."

---

[76] Dig. ii.§14. viii§2.

In the other, a sum was sometimes mentioned as a limit to the discretion of the judge, "*duntaxat decem millia.*"[77] The condemnation was, Gaius expressly says, always pecuniary.[78]

So, where the defendant might only be liable for a certain portion, or the heir for so much as he had inherited; "*de eo duntaxat quod ad heredem pervenit,*" or the father for so much of the son's *peculium* as was added to his inheritance.

Some of the *condemnationes* belonged to the class of "*formulæ arbitrariæ,*" and have been already touched upon.

There is a passage in the Institutes of Justinian,[79] which, as it explains the nature of the *arbitrariæ actiones,* I shall set out and comment upon: —

"Præterea quasdam actiones arbitrarias, id est, ex arbitrio judicis, pendentes appellamus, in quibus, nisi arbitrio judicis is, cum quo agitur, actori satisfaciat, veluti rem restituat, vel exhibeat, vel solvat, vel ex noxali causa servum dedat, condemnari debeat. Bed istæ actiones tam in rem, quam in personam inveniuntur. In rem veluti Publiciana, Serviana de rebus coloni, quasi Serviana, quæ etiam hypothecaria vocatur. In personam, veluti quibus de eo agitur, quod aut metus causa, aut dolo malo factum est; item quum id, quod certo loco promissum est, petitur. Ad exhibendum quoque actio ex arbitrio judicis pendet. In his enim actionibus et ceteris similibus permittitur judici ex bono et æquo secundum cujusque rei, de qua actum est, naturam æstimare, quemadmodum actori satisfieri oporteat."[80]

Now, it is important to distinguish the "*arbitrariæ actiones*" here mentioned from those "*bonæ fidei*" before described. In the *arbitrariæ actiones* we are now considering, which are a subdivision of the "*bonæ fidei actiones,*" it was the duty of the *arbiter* to call upon the defendant, in cases where

---

[77] Gains, iv.§43.

[78] Omnium autem formularum quæ condemnationem habent ad pecuniariam æstimationem condemnatio concepta est, itaque, &c. Gaius, iv.§48.

[79] Savigny, Sys. des heut. R. Rechts, v. 100.

[80] Inst. iv.§§6. 27.

the plaintiff established his demand, to satisfy the latter by giving such compensation as the *arbiter* should appoint. If this compensation was made, the defendant was acquitted; if it was not, he was condemned: the importance of this process appears from the peculiarity of the ancient proceeding, according to which the judge could only condemn the defendant to the payment of a sum of money; hence an obstinate or perverse litigant might compel his antagonist to receive money as a substitute for any thing that he had taken possession of. It was to avert this consequence, that the "*arbiter*" in the "*arbitrariœ actiones*" had the power to insist, before pronouncing sentence, on a restitution of the thing demanded. The method of compulsion was efficacious, though indirect; if the defendant refused to make the satisfaction required by the *arbiter,* the plaintiff might state on his oath the amount due to him as compensation; this, of course, where the thing itself was sought, would far exceed its intrinsic value. In some cases the consequences were still more serious. In the *"actio quod metus causa,"* fourfold the value of the object was required; and in the "*actio doli,"* the defendant became infamous. The peculiar nature of these *actiones arbitrariœ* was expressed by the addition of the words "*nisi exhibeatur," "nisi restituatur*" to *the formula.*

In the *actiones prœjudiciales* no *condemnatio* was used. In these cases the Prætor sent the parties before a judge simply to decide a fact:

"Si paret Stichum esse libertum Titii."[81]

[81] See post, p. 58.

EXCEPTIONES[82]

After the form by which the plaintiff may enforce redress has been considered, the question arises how the person assailed may protect himself against an unjust demand; since, from the opposite situation in which the parties stand to each other, opposite rights arise, which it requires no ordinary skill and experience to reconcile and adjust. Generally speaking, there are two parties, one who complains, and another who denies the justice of the complaint; but even this state of things is not universal, for there is a small number of excepted cases, in which both parties fill, in some degree and in a certain sense, the situation of plaintiff and defendant. These were called by the Romans "*duplices actiones,*" "*duplicia judicia,*" and those among them which were interdicts, "*duplicia interdicta*;" they were also called "*mixtce actiones,*" "*mixtœ actiones in quibus uterque actor est.*" Such were the "*communi dividundo,*" "*familiœ erciscundœ,*" "*retinendœ possessionis;*" among the interdicts, the "*uti possidetis*" and the "*utendi fruendi.*" In all these cases either party may be condemned, whereas in most the loss of the suit is the punishment of the unsuccessful plaintiff. The great difficulty in such cases is to find out on

---

[82] *παραγραφή* opposed to the *εὐθυδικία εισιεναι* of the Athenian Law. Dem. *Πρὸς Φορ.* 908. 7. *περί στεφ.* 1103. 2. Demosthenes, *πρὸς Φορ.* says it is " *Κατηγορειν τού διώκοντος.*." Seven speeches of Dem. turn on παραγραφαι. They might relate either to the plaintiff's action, *e.g.* πρὸς' Απ. where the law forbidding the loan of bottomry money on any ship that did not bring corn to Athens is relied on, or to some fact adduced by the defendant as the exceptio rei judicatæ. In civil cases the Athenians, like the Romans, held the doctrine, " res judicata tantummodo inter partes jus tacit." The seven speeches of Demosthenes are against Apollodorus, Zenothemis, Lacritus, Phormio (who seems to have been a sort of Athenian Baring, as Pasio was a sort of Rothschild), Pantænetus, Nausimachus, Xenopeithes.

"Neque est quod illam exceptionem in interdicto pertimescas." — *Cic. Ad Trebat. Fam. Epist.* vii. 13.

"Exceptiones opponuntur, aut quia factum sit quod fieri oportet, aut quia factum sit quod fieri non oportuit, aut quia factum non sit quod fieri debuerat."

"Quia factum est quod fieri oportuit, datur exceptio rei venditæ et traditæ, et rei judicatæ;. Quia factum est quod fieri non oportuit, datur exceptio doli mali. Quia non factum est quod fieri debuit, ut bonorum possessionis non datæ."— *Paul. Lib. Singul. de Conceptione Formularum,* lib. xx. Zimmern, vol. iii. p. 283.; Savigny, Sys. des heut. R. Rechts, vol. v. p. 160.; Puchta, Institutiones, vol. ii.; Dig. xliv.§1.; Cod. viii.§36.; Inst. iv.§13, 14.

whom the "*onus probandi*" ought to be cast; and it was held that the party first complaining should be considered the plaintiff on such occasions; or if both complained at the same time, that the question should be settled by lot: "In tribus duplicibus judiciis; familiæ erciscundæ, communi dividundo, finium regundorum, quæritur, quis actor intelligatur, quia par causa omnium videtur."[83] Again, "Sed magis placuit, eum videri actorem, qui ad judicium provocasset."[84] "Sed quum ambo ad judicium provocant, sorte res discerni solet."[85]

Let us now turn to the consideration of the ordinary case: the defendant may either deny the right asserted by his antagonist, or he may oppose to it a right of his own, by which the right of the plaintiff is controlled and paralysed. Again, he may, if he deny the right of his antagonist, deny it absolutely; or admitting its former and partial existence, deny its actual validity. The question on whom the burden of proof shall be cast, is determined by the course adopted by the defendant,[86] It

---

[83] Dig. x.§§1, 2, 3.

[84] Ibid. 5. 1.§13.

[85] Ibid.§54.

[86] e. g. 1847. Doe d. Bather v. Braine; a case on a disputed will. A dispute arose which side should begin; it was decided one way, the Court above decided another. The consequence is a new trial. All the witnesses must be summoned over again; all the expense, &c., of the former trial is flung away; and this for a point which could be a question at the present time in no country governed by law founded on principle. As specimens of judicial legislation, take the following contradictions:—

"The new rule of practice made by the judges, as to the right to begin, does not extend to actions of contract." — *Lewis* v. *Wells, 7* C.& P. 221.

"If in an action for false imprisonment the defendant plead, as a justification, that the plaintiff stole feathers, and that he was therefore imprisoned, arid the *plaintiff reply de injuriâ,* the *plaintiff* is *entitled to begin,* although the *affirmative is on the defendant,* and there be no general issue."—*Atkinson* v. *Warne,* 6 C. & P. 687

"The plaintiff is entitled to begin where damages of an unascertained amount are the object of the action, though the affirmative of the issues on the record be with the defendant." —Carter v. Jones, 1 M. & R. 281.

"In an action on a bill of exchange defendant pleaded payment. Held, that the admission of all the facts, the proof of which was on the plaintiff; did *not* entitle the defendant to begin."—*Pontifex* v. *Jolly,* 9 C. & P. 202.

"If, in an action for non-repair, &c., the defendant plead *affirmative pleas,* which are denied by the replication, the *defendant is entitled to begin."—Lewis* v. *Wells,* 7 C. & P. 221.

"In covenant, where the affirmative of the issues is *on the defendant, he is entitled to begin, though* the damages are *unascertained."* — *Wooton* v. *Barton,* 1 M. & R. 518.

is a question of great importance, which the English law, so punctilious, where minuteness is almost certain to work injustice, and so loose and slovenly where accuracy is important, has, up to the present hour (incredible as the fact may appear), left open, amid confused, conflicting, and isolated *dicta,* to every possible doubt and misconception. Now, there may be enumerated these three modes of defence:—1. absolute denial; 2. partial denial; 3. the existence of a right in the adverse party, involving absolute denial.

1. The defendant in an action of debt denies the contract altogether, or, in the "*rei vindicatio*" he denies the "*traditio,*" the *"onus probandi"* is on the plaintiff; this is absolute denial.

2. Partial denial. In the "*rei vindicatio,*" defendant admits that the plaintiff has been the proprietor of what he claims, but affirms that he has parted with it. Or, in an action of debt, he admits the debt, and affirms that it has been paid. The "*onus probandi*" is on the defendant.

3. Assertion of an opposite right. Defendant has, in any case, recourse to the *exceptio rei judicatœ;* in the *vindicatio rei* he appeals to the "*exceptio juris in re*;" in the "*Actio Publiciana,*" to the "*exceptio dominii.*" The burden of proof in all these cases is cast upon him.

"In assumpsit, the plea was as to 20*l.* payment; and as to the residue, a set-off. The *defendant must* begin."— *Coxhead* v. *Huish,* 7 C. & P. 63.

"The defendant pleaded a general plea of payment to the whole declaration. Held, that, under these circumstances, the *defendant* must begin."—*Birt* v. *Leigh,* 1 Carr. & K.611.

"In all cases at Nisi Prius, in which the *plaintiff* claims damages, the amount of which is unascertained, *he* has a right to begin, although the affirmative of the issue on the record rests with the defendant."—*Mercer* v. *Whall,* Derby Summer Assizes, 1841.

"A motion being made on the above ruling, Lord Denman observed, ' I had to decide this point *against the authority of a case* entitled to great consideration *(Stanton* v. *Paton,* 1 Carr. & K. 148.), which was an action for breach of promise of marriage, and the only plea, a plea of release. Lord Abin-ger, who tried that cause, held, after argument, and after consulting my brother Patteson, that the *defendant* was entitled to begin.' " Reported in Q.B. Rep.—14 Law, J., Q. B.,267. *Warner* v. *Haines,* C. & P. 69.; *Soward* v. *Leggatt,* 7 C. & P. 613.; *Fanes* v. *Salter,* 1 M. & R. 501.; *Crowley* v. *Page,* 7 C. & P. 789.; *Smart* v. *Rayner,* 6 C. & P. 721.; *Colstone* v. *Hiscolbs,* 1 M. & R. 301.

And then we are told the objection to a code is its uncertainty!

Quis tulerit Gracchos! &c.

With regard to the absolute denial, it should be recollected that the denial may sometimes be in the shape of an affirmative; still the "*onus probandi*" is on the plaintiff. In the "*condictio indebiti,*" the plaintiff denied that any debt was due to the defendant; the assertion that a debt *was* due amounted to a direct denial of the statement. But it was incumbent on the plaintiff to establish his assertion. Another form which the inquiry may take also deserves consideration. Certain ingredients are essential to every claim. If the defendant denied the existence of any of those ingredients, he was in the same position as if under a relative denial (No. 2.) he maintained a right neutralising that of his adversary, and the burden of proof falls upon him. So, if in an action of contract the minority or insanity of the contracting party is insisted upon, or that an admitted promise was modified by certain limitations as to time and place, or that it was in the alternative, the relative denial may be considered as either negative or affirmative. Negative, inasmuch as it denies the right of the adversary; affirmative[87], as it states a fact not before put forward; viewed in one light, it falls under the first class; viewed in another, under the third. To take it as belonging to the first class is most in conformity with the analogies of Roman law.[88] The third class may be substantially distinguished from the naked denial, in some cases; though, in others, the distinction appears to rest merely on positive law. The "*exceptio*" from the minority or want of reason in the defendant, belongs to the second class of denial; that from error or violence, to the third. If the defendant asserted that the debt was extinguished by the "*acceptilatio,*" or the easement by nonuser, these were relative denials; but the great feature of the third class is, that two distinct and

---

[87]"De Bibuli edicto nihil movi, præter illam exceptionem, de qua tu ad me scripseras, *nimis gravi prcejudicio in ordinem nostrum.* Ego tamen habeo, sed tectiorem, ex Q. Mucii P. filii edicto Asiatico, Extra quam si ita negotium gestum est, ut eo stari non oporteat; ex fide bona: multaque sum secutus Scævolæ: in iis illud, in quo sibi libertatem consent Græci datam, ut Græci inter se disceptent suis legibus."—*Cic. Ad. Att.* 6. 1. This is a remarkable passage. Cicero is speaking of his edict in the province. He does not transfer Bibulus's, edict in words, for the reason given in italics, because it was too direct an obstacle to the extortions of the aristocracy; but he tranfers it in effect, by giving an exceptio from another edict.

[88] This is admirably explained in Toullier, Droit civil Francois, vol.viii. p. 18.

independent rights are to be considered, each of which may exist and be destroyed by circumstances peculiar to itself, so *that jus in re,* on which, as we have seen, an *exceptio* might be grounded, may be itself destroyed. The *"exceptio rei judicatœ"* may be destroyed by subsequent compact. So in the usufruct[89]: — "Pactus, ne peteret, postea convenit ut peteret, prius pactum per posterius elidetur non quidem ipso jure, sicut tollitur stipulatio per stipulationem si hoc actum est; quia in stipulationibus jus continetur, in pactis factum versatur; et ideo replicatione exceptio elidetur." Now, if this class of defences be compared with those resting on a denial, it will be found that if, in a vindication, the loss of property, or, in an action of contract, payment, is set up against the plaintiff's right, it is impossible that the effect of these circumstances can be invalidated by any subsequent transaction. "Non enim ex novo pacto prior obligatio resuscitatur sed proficiet pactum ad novum contractual." Of these circumstances, if they are proved, neither can be invalidated by any subsequent transaction. The *"formula in jus concepta"* affords a very strong illustration of this doctrine. The *intentio "fundum Sempronii esse,"* or *"Caio cerium dare,"* was sufficient to let in the defence of a direct absolute, or of a relative denial.[90] To have added *"nisi soluta pecunia"* would have been useless repetition; if the money had been paid, the debt was not due. But if the defendant appealed to a *res judicata,* that is, to another right, the insertion of this in *the formula "si ea res judicata non sit,"* was necessary. It was not asserted by, or comprised in, the original statement.

With this wonderful accuracy and refinement did the *Roman formulœ,* while they rendered technical error almost impossible, announce, provide for, and distinguish, by their construction, every method of defence. "Sunt jura sunt formulæ de omnibus rebus constitutæ *ne quis* aut in genere injuriæ aut ratione actionis *errare possit,* expressæ sunt enim ex unius cujusque damno, dolore, incommode, calamitate, injuriâ, publicæ a prætore formulæ, ad quas privata lis accomodatur."

---

[89] Dig. ii. 14—27§2.

[90] "Intentione per exceptionem elisa," says the Digest in a passage which, before the discovery of Gaius, must have been unintelligible.

How different from the system which, invented in the dark ages, is obstinately continued in our own, where technicality exists merely for the sake of technicality, multiplying the chances in favour of dishonesty and injustice! Though the forms insisted upon with so much rigour, convey no information, even to the judges in many cases, or to the jury in any, as to the real nature and character of the question in dispute, still, however, we make the prejudices of mankind, while ignorant and without experience, the guide and test of judicial proceedings in the present age, and appeal to the crude notions of our rude ancestors, as if they were the infallible dictates of mature reflection and advanced civility.

The *exceptiones* will now be considered more in detail. The *exceptio* was always negative: "Si in ea re nihil dolo malo Auli Agerii factum sit, neque fiat;" or, "si inter Aulum Agerium et Numerium Negidium non convenit ne ea pecunia peteretur."

It was that part of the *formula* which was inserted for the benefit of the defendant, he might insist upon a defence without an exception. If the defendant's defence consisted only in a mere denial, the direction to the judge at the end of the *formula* "Si paret, condemnato — si non paret, absolvito," in that case would be sufficient for the purpose of the defendant.

But where the *exceptio* was inserted, the right of the plaintiff was neutralised by an opposite right which belonged to the defendant. It was the expression by which the Roman lawyer designated that species of defence which required, on the part of the defendant, the proof of some particular right inherent in him; it excluded the case of the defendant from the operation of the "*intentio*" or the "*condemnatio,*" accordingly it was for the defendant to establish it, "*reus in exceptione actor est,*"[91] unless it was met by a "*replicatio,*" which was the *exceptio* of the plaintiff. It made the "*condemnatio*" conditional, "id est, ne aliter judex eum cum quo agitur, condemnet, quam si nihil in ea re de qua agitur, dolo actoris factum sit." Under the

[91] "Agere etiam is videtur qui excipit."—*Dig.xxii. 3. 19;* xliv. I.

old *legis actiones* the *exceptiones* were unknown[92], as they asserted an independent and substantive right of the defendant, and therefore must have been enforced in a separate action,[93] They were the growth of the prætorian law; every right on which an action could be grounded might be the matter of an exception. Some, like the causes of action, were set forth in the edict of the prætor, some were adapted to the particular exigences of the case, *"alias in edicto prœtor habet propositas, alias causa cognita adcommodat."*[94] Some arose from the civil law, *"lex aut quod legis vicem obtinet;* some from the prætorian law; some extended by parity of reason from the cases to which they were originally applied, to others involving the same principle were called (or the actions were under the same circumstances entitled) *utiles.*[95] *"Quoties deficit actio vel exceptio, utilis actio vel exceptio est;"*[96] *"cui damns actionem, eidem et exceptionem competere multo magis quis dixerit."* Some *exceptlones* were only valid for a particular time, or with reference to a particular state of facts, e. g. *exceptio facti in diem,* when payment was required before it was due, or the *"fori exceptio,"* otherwise *"prœjudicialis,"* when the complaint was brought before the wrong tribunal, these were called *dilatoriœ* or *temporales;* the others which were general, were *peremptoriœ* and *perpetuœ.* Again, there were *"personœ"* and "*rei exceptiones;*" these first were very uncommon, and, as in the case "*quod metus causa factum est*" might be employed against these persons, not against the heir or purchaser only. But the most important of all charges of exception was that which arose from the conflict between equity and the civil law. Where equity was admitted, the prætor insured its triumph, sometimes by the "*in factum actiones,*" sometimes by the *exceptio,* in the former case directing the *condemnatio.*

---

[92] "Alia causa fuit legis actionum... nec omnino ita ut nunc usus erat illis temporibus exceptio-num."—*Gaius,* iv.§108.

[93] And are so cited in the Digest, " Quod jure civili debebat, jure prætorio non debebat, i. c. per exceptionem."—*Dig.* xiii. 5. 3.§1.

[94] Gaius, iv. 118.

[95] Dig. xix.§§5. 21.

[96] Ib. xliii.§§18. 1.4.

It is obvious that the plaintiff ought to be able to attack[97] the defence in as many ways as the defendant has questioned his (the plaintiff's) right; he may deny it altogether, or he may deny it relatively, or he may assert a right inconsistent with it. If he adopted the last course, the defence was termed *replicatio,* and was defined "*exceptionis exceptio,*" which, like most of the definitions in the civil law, is explanatory, literal, and concise. As the prætor, after directing the judge, if the *intentio* was proved, to condemn, limited the instruction by saying that, if the *exceptio* was proved, he was nevertheless to acquit; so again he limited this last instruction by saying that he was to acquit only if the fact asserted in the *replicatio* was false: this was expressed in *the formula* thus, "Si paret fundum de quo agitur Numerii esse, judex Negidium condemna; si ab Agerio is fundus, locatus Negidio non sit — aut, si dolo Negidii factum sit quo minus locaretur." He was to condemn in two cases: first, if the defendant did not prove his right; or, secondly, though if he did establish his right, that right became inoperative from his own fraud or another right established by the plaintiff. The *replicatio* was met by a *duplicatio;* the *duplicatio,* by a *triplicatio;* and so forth. If the proceedings were carried beyond these limits, the words *adjectiones* or *exceptiones* were employed to describe them — no especial and appropriate terminology,[98]

---

[97] This, however, he is not allowed to do by the English law. If the defendant advance two falsehoods, in answer to a fact alleged by plaintiff, plaintiff is compelled to admit one of those falsehoods to be true. " The effect," says a most learned writer, " of this state of law is *somewhat remarkable;* for example, it empowers a defendant to plead to a declaration in assumpsit for goods sold and delivered—1. Non assumpsit; 2. That the cause of action did not accrue within six years; 3. That he was an infant at the time of the contract."..."Yet, though the defendant had the advantage of his three pleas cumulatively, the plaintiff is obliged to make his election between these several answers, and can reply but one of them to each plea."—*Stephen on Pleading,* p. 311. Thus a cause is terminated by compelling one of the parties to hold his tongue. " Quand les sauvages de la Louisiane veulent avoir du fruit, ils coupent l'arbre au pied, et cuillent le fruit. Voilà le gouvernment despotique." — *Montesquieu, Esprit des Loix,* v. 13. Law in England is what " Julian" Johnson called transubstantiation, — " not the name of one single absurdity, but it signifies many thousands in one." — *Impossibility of Transubstantiation.*— p.1.

[98] Theoph. iv. 14.§3. uses the word καδρουπλικατιόν.—So Cod. viii. 36.2.§3. The replication was in the form of a condition, which, if it existed, invalidated

LITIS CONTESTATIO[99]

The object of judicial proceeding, i.*e*. the restoration of a violated right, is liable to be prevented by events which happen after the suit is begun and before the sentence of the judge is pronounced[100], If it were possible for a suit to be ended as soon

---

defendant's condition—" Exceptio actorem excludit; replicatio, reum." Gaius, iv.§116.: '• Comparatæ sunt autem exceptiones defendendorum reorum gratia cum quibus agitur: sæpe enim accidit ut quis jure civili teneatur, sed iniquum sit eum judicio condemnari, velut stipulatus sim a te pecuniam tamquam credendi causa numeraturus, nec numeraverim; nam eam pecuniam a te peti posse certum est, dare enim te oporteret cum ex stipulatu tenearis; sed quia iniquum est te eo nomine condemnari, placet per exceptionem doli mali te defendi debere. Item si pactus fuero tecum ne id quod mihi debeas a te petam, nihilominus id ipsum a te petere possum dare mihi oportere, quia obligatio pacto convento non tollitur: sed placet debere me petentem per exceptionem pacti conventi repelli."§117.: "In his quoque actionibus quæ *(non) in* personam sunt, exceptiones locum habent; velut si metu me coegeris aut dolo induxeris, ut tibi rem aliquam mancipio dem *(jure Quiritium; nam)* si *(nunc)* eam rem a me petas, datur mihi exceptio per quam, si metus causa te fecesse vel dolo malo arguero, repelieris. Item, si fundum litigiosum sciens a non possidente emeris, eumque a possidente petas, opponitur tibi exceptio per quam omnimodo summoveris."§118.:" Exceptiones autem alias in edicto prætor habet propositas, alias causa cognita adcommodat; quæ; omnes vel ex legibus, vel ex his quæ legis vicem obtinent, substantiam capiunt, vel ex jurisdictione prætoris proditæ; sunt."§119: " Omnes autem esceptiones in contrarium concipiuntur, quam adfirmat is cum quo agitur; nam si verbi gratia reus dolo malo aliquid actorem facere dicat, qui forte pecuniam petit quam non numeravit, sic exceptio concipitur; si in ea re nihil dolo malo Auli Agerii factum sit, neque fiat.

"Et denique in ceteris causis similiter solet; ideo scilicet, qua omnis exceptio objicitur quidem a reo, sed ita formulæ inseritur ut conditionalem faciat condemnationem, id est, ne aliter judex cum cum quo agitur, dolo actoris factum sit; item, ne aliter judex eum condemnet, quam si nullum pactum conventum de non pentenda pecunia factum erit."§120: " Dicuntur autem exceptiones aut per-emptoriæ aut dilatoriæ."

[99] Dig.xlvii. 1. Cod. de Litis Contest, iii. 9. Dig. xliv. 2. De Sent. vii. 45. De Re Judicatâ, viii. 52. This Litis. Cont. was the ἀνάκρισις; of the Athenian Law. The magistrate made preliminary enquiries, in order to instruct the cause, and take care that it did not fail for want of what might be supplied. This was exactly the office of the Roman prætor; in England it is not considered any part of the duty of the state. Budæus, Sing. Græ. Comment, fol. edit. 1529. p. 132. At the same the *πρυτανεϊα* were deposited by both parties. Pollux, viii. 38. Budæus, p. 15. After the ἀνάκρισις the documents on both sides were put into the *ἐχινος*.. Before the διαιτηταὶ, the *ἐχινος* was open to both parties till the judgment. I cannot agree, by the way, that they were a kind of jury. Liddell and Scott, v. *διαιτητής*. I have no doubt that the Roman arbiter was taken from them.

[100] Savigny, System des heut. R. Rechts, vol. vi. pt. 2.§256. Schilling, R. R. vol. ii. p. 401. Tigerström, I. G. p. 181. Zimmern, Th. ii. B. 3..§121. Mackeldey, Systema Juris. R. curâ et Int. Heindenburg,§200. Gaius, Comment, iii. 180.: " Tollitur adhuc obligatio litis contestatione, si modo legitimo judicio fuerit actum, nam tunc

as it begins — for the decision to follow immediately upon the complaint, this evil would be avoided altogether; and in proportion to the narrowness of the compass within which the delay, in some cases inevitable, in all mischievous, can be contracted, it may be diminished or removed. It is to the utter neglect of this important principle of jurisprudence, if it ought not rather to be called the wilful endeavour, for sordid purposes, to prevent its operation, that many of the frightful evils which abound in the English law, are to be attributed,[101] The problem to be solved with regard to this point is. How can the parties to a suit be placed in the situation in which they would have been, if the same sentence which is finally given had been immediately pronounced? The time when a suit really begins is an important element of this inquiry, and this in the Roman law has been fixed by the "*litis contestatio*" although the "*litis contestatio*" survived the "*formulœ,*" and was to the last an important element of judicial inquiry; it is to the time of the "*formulœ,*" to the time when the *ordo judiciorum privatorum* prevailed, that we must appeal, in order to gain an accurate knowledge of the subject. Whether the "*litis contestatio*" was the last act before the prætor, or the first

---

obligatio quidem principalis dissolvitur, incipit autem te neri reus litis contestatione; sed si condemnatus sit, sublata litis contestatione, incipit ex causa judicati teneri, et hoc (est) quod apud veteres scriptum est, ante litem contestatam dare debitorem oportere, post litem contestatam condemnari oportere, post condemnationem judicatum facere oportere."

[101] Many of the actual evils of the English law may be traced to the desire of finding an excuse for giving fees to the officers of justice. The unmeaning form in the confirmation of bishops, which, to the disgrace of English legislation, engrossed so much time that ought to have been rationally employed, was probably continued for some such object. In Chancery, a suitor, in order to obtain without delay the payment of money decided to be his, was obliged to pay 300*l*. for copies of which he had no need, and which, in all probability, were never taken at all. *(Evidence before Committee on Fees, House of Commons,* 1847.) Even now persons acquitted of a misdemeanour are obliged to pay fees to the officer of the court. A system more oppressive to the poor than the English law, as it existed some few years back, probably never prevailed in any civilised country. Even now, in the hands of the rich, it is a scourge of scorpions for the weak and needy, however undeniable the justice of their cause; and is entitled to as eminent a place among the causes of human misery as Shakspeare assigned to it. It is a great pity that its improvement cannot, like free trade or toleration, be made a party question; in other words, that nobody supposes he has any thing to gain by promoting it. But if, as Homer says, the day that makes man a slave takes away half his value, the day that gives him office takes away all his zeal as a reformer.

before the judge, is matter of dispute,[102] The proceedings before the prætor *were "jus;"* those before the judge, *judicium.* I confess, notwithstanding the great authority of Savigny and some very plausible reasons that he has alleged, I entertain great doubts whether the "*litis contestatio*" does not belong to the *"judicium,"* instead of belonging, as he supposes, to *"jus."* It is extremely difficult to reconcile a passage so clear and peremptory as the following with any other construction: — "Res in judicium deducta non videtur si tantum postulatio simplex celebrata sit, vel actionis species ante judicium reo cognita. Inter litem enim contestatam et editam actionem permultum interest. Lis enim tunc contestata videtur quum judex per narrationem negotii causam audire cœperit."[103] On the other hand, the ceremony from which the "*litis contestatio"* takes its name, namely, the calling of witnesses by each party, not for the purpose of proving their case, but as a sort of living record of the proceeding, and which probably was first adopted under the "*legis actiones,"* when the proceedings were oral, and before the use of the *formulæ,* is much in favour of Savigny's opinion. The "li*s contestata,"* however, was undoubtedly intended to mark a precise and important period in the process between the parties, that is, the time when property became "*res litigiosa,"* and therefore could not be disposed of by the party from whom it was claimed, when in some cases bail was given, in others, possession was taken by the Court of the property in dispute.[104] It consisted in the ceremony of calling witnesses by both parties; and when it took place, "li*s in judicium deducitur."*

---

[102] Dig. ii. 2.§19: " Quum quædam puella apud competentem judicem litem susceperat, deinde condemnata erat, posteaque ad viri matrimonium alii jurisdictioni subjecti pervenerat, quærebatur, an prioris judicis sententia exsequi possit? Dixi posse, quia ante fuerat sententia dicta. Sed *et si post susceptam cognitionem ante sententiam hoc eveniet, idem putarem,* sententiaque a priore judice recte fertur."

Dig. v. 1.§34: Javolenus, libro xv. ex Cassio. — " Si is, qui Romæ; judicium acceperat, deces-sit, heres ejus, quamvis domicilium trans mare habet, Romætamen defendi debet, quia succedit in ejus locum, a quo heres relictus est." — *Cass.* vii. 5. 34.

[103] Cod. de Litis Contestatione, 319, A.D. 209, lib. 3. tit. 9. I Impp. Severus et Antonius, A. A. Valenti.

[104] The Twelve Tables, as we learn from the Digest, forbade the dedication of a res litigiosa to the gods, under the penalty of forfeiting twice its value. Dig. xliv. 6.§3. Gaius, lib. vi. 3. Ad Legem XII. Tabularum: " Reni, de qua controversia est, prohibemur in sacrum dedicare, alioquin dupli pœnam patimur; nec immerito, neliceat eo modo duriorem adversarii conditionem facere."

Besides the consequences already stated, it marked the time also when prescription was interrupted; it changed the relations of the plaintiff and the defendant to each other, "*tollitur obligatio litis contestatione.*" Paulus[105] says, "Non potest videri in judicium venisse id quod post judicium acceptum accidisset, ideoque aliâ interpellatione opus est." Again, after the "*litis contestatio*" the plaintiff was entitled to "*omnis causa rei,*" of the thing he sought. "Ut et *causa rei* restituatur, id est, ut omne habeat petitor, quod habiturus foret, si eo tempore quo judicium accipiebatur, restitutus illi homo fuisset."[106] It compelled both parties to abide the sentence of the judge before whom it took place, even if either of them changed his *forum.* "Ubi acceptum semel est judicium, ibi et finem accipere debet."[107] It made the heir in most cases liable; and lastly, it was for the plaintiff the "*consumtio*" of his right of action which he could not again bring forward: were he to attempt it in an action "*in personam,*" with an "*intentio juris civilis,*" the "*condemnatio,*" was "*ipso jure,*"[108] Were he to attempt it in any other action, he might be met by an "*exceptio rei judicatœ.*"[109]

---

[105] De Jud. v.§1. 23.

[106] Dig. vi. 1. 20.

[107] Dig. v. 1.§30.

[108] Gaius, iii. 180, 181.

[109] Id. iv. 98. 106, 107. Id. iv.§89.: " Si verbi gratia in rem tecum agam, satis mihi dare debes; æquum enim visum est, *te* de eo quod interea tibi rem qua; an ad te pertineat dubium est, possidere conceditur, cum satisdatione mihi cavere ut, si victus sis rem nec ipsam restituas, nec litis æstimationem sufferas, sit mihi potestas aut tecum agendi aut cum sponsoribus tuis." Dig. v. 325.§7.: " Si ante litem contestatam, inquit, fecerint, hoc ideo adictum, quoniam post litem contestatam omnes incipiunt malæ fidei possessores esse, quinimo, post controversiam motam. Quamquam enim litis contestatæ mentio fiat in Senatusconsulto, tamen et post motam controversiam omnes possessores pares fiunt et quasi prædones tenentur. Et hoc jure hodie utimur; cœpit enim scire rem ad se non pertinentem possidere se is qui interpellatur qui vero prædo est, et ante litem contestatam doli nomine.tenebitur, hic est enim dolus præteritus." So the bonâ fide possessor was responsible for neglect after the " lis contestata." Dig. v. 3. 31.§3.: " Et ipse prædo est." The question of " *Mora"* often turned upon the " *litis contestatio. "* An appeal sine dolo made to a legal tribunal was not held to be a " mora " (Dig. 1. 17.§63.); but " mora" was incurred by him who " litigare maluit quam resistere." Dig. xlv. 1. 82.§22.

Festus, Contestari. Auct. Linguæ; Latinæ, p. 271. ed. 1595: " Contestari est, cum uterque reus dicit, Testes estote. Contestari litem dicuntur duo, aut plures adversarii, quod ordinato indicio utraque pars dicere solet, Testes estote."

LAW OF ACTIONS[110]

The examination of *the formulæ* necessarily leads us to the mention of the different kinds of actions known to the Roman law. The word "*actio,*" as the reader has already had occasion to observe, was used originally to denote the particular form in which certain legal proceedings were carried on; from this it was transferred to signify the legal remedy by which every person might enforce his right, "*jus persequendi injudicio quod sibi debetur.*" It had, moreover, as the authors of the Digest tell us, a special and a general signification. In the latter it included proceedings "*in personam*" as well as "*in rem;* " in the former it was confined to proceedings in *personam* only; the distinguishing word for proceedings *in rem* being "*petilio,*" or "*vindicatio,*" besides which the word "*persecutio*" was used to denote extraordinary proceedings. In every action, using that word in the comprehensive sense, three ingredients were requisite: 1. The plaintiff, *"actor," "qui agit," "agens," "petitor"* 2. The defendant, *"reus," "is unde petitur," "cum quo agitur,"* in a corrupted idiom "*fugiens.*"[111] 3. A cause of action vested in the plaintiff and against the defendant. With reference to the authority from which they emanated, actions were divided into *civiles* and *honorariæ,* the former springing from positive law, the latter from the edict of the magistrate. The civil actions are denominated from the law[112] which granted them, *e.g. "Legis Aquiliæ actio;"* or from the particular transaction, as "*commodali,*" "*depositi,*" "*ex stipulatu;*" or from the occasion, "*damni,*" "*injuriæ actio;*" or the parties, "*pro socio actio*" Again, with reference to the *formulæ,* they were called "*vulgares,*"[113] *actiones (Judicia prodita),* or "*in factum*" *actiones;* the "*vulgares*" included those "*in jus conceptæ,*"

---

[110] Schilling, R. R. vol. ii. Savigny, vol. v. Zimmern Th. 2. 1. 3. Bethman, Hollweg. Civ. Process. Mackeldey, Heindenburgii, p. 192. Inst. de Actionibus, iv. 6. Dig. de Obl. et Act. xliv. 7. Cod. iv. 16. Gaius, Comment, iv. Hugo Histoire du Droit Romain, vol. i. 179.

[111] From the Greek φεύγων, but it is not used by any writer of a classical period in this sense.

[112] Hostilianæ Actiones. Cic. de Or.i. 57.

[113] Dig. de Verb. Sign. xvi. 178.§2.

which rested on a ground of action recognised by the civil law; and those "*in factum conceptæ,*" in which no such ground of action was expressed, but the *factum* on which the action turned was placed at the head of the *formula.* "Sed eas quidem formulas in quibus de jure quæritur, in jus conceptas vocamus: quales sunt quibus intendimus nostrum esse aliquid ex jure Quiritium aut nobis dare oportere, aut pro jure damnum (decidere oportere); in quibua juris civilis intentio est."[114] "Ceteras vero in factum conceptas vocamus, id est, in quibus nulla talis intentionis conceptio est; sed initio formulæ nominato eo quod factum est, adjiciuntur ea verba per quæ judici damnandi absolvendive potestasdatur."[115] This last-mentioned subdivision must be carefully distinguished from the "*in factum actiones,*" which form a class by themselves, consisting of several subdivisions, and which are thus described and carefully exemplified by the authors of the Digest, "De Præscriptis Verbis et in Factum Actionibus." "Non-nunquam evenit, ut cessantibus judiciis proditis et vulgaribus actionibus, quum proprium nomen invenire non possumus, facile descendamus ad eas quæ in factum appellantur. Sed ne res exemplis egeat, paucis agam. Domino mercium in magistrum navis, si sit incertum, utrum navem conduxerit, an merces vehendas locaverit, civilem actionem in factum esse dandam, Labeo scribit."[116] To this last class belong —

1. The *prætoriæ in factum actiones,* which the prætor gave in cases where there was no legal remedy. The Digest[117] illustrates this kind of action: "Et ideo puto recte Julianum a Mauriciano reprehensum in hoc dedi tibi Stichum, ut Pamphilum manumittas; manumisisti, evictus est Stichus. Julia-nus scribit in factum actionem a prætore dandam, ille ait, civilem incerti actionem id est, prsescriptis verbis, sufficere, esse enim contractum, quod Aristo..... dicit, unde hæc nascitur actio."

2. The "*præscriptis verbis actiones,*" these were "*in factum actio,*" "*judicium,*" "*civilis actio in factum,*" "*præscriptis*

---

[114] Gaius, iv.§46.
[115] Id.§46.
[116] Dig. xix. 5.§1.
[117] ii. 14. 7.§2.

verbis in factum actio," "præscriptis verbis incerta civilis actio," "civilis incerti actio," "incerta civilis actio," "incertum indicium." These actions rested, indeed, on a ground of obligation recognised by the civil law; but, on account of some peculiarity, could not be brought under the head of any definite contract, or within the words of any of the established *formulæ,* and therefore the peculiar nature of the case, or its accidental modification, was expressed at the beginning of the *formulæ "præscriptis verbis."* "Præscriptiones autem appellatas esse ab eo quod ante formulas præscribuntur, plus quam manifestum est."[118].... "Utilis actio, quæ præscriptis verbis rem gestam demonstrat...."[119] And again, "Nam cum deficiant vulgaria atquæ usitata actionum nomina præscriptia verbis agendum est, in quam necesse est confugere, quoties contractus existunt quorum appellationes nullæ jure civili proditæ sunt; natura enim rerum conditum est, ut plura sint negotia quam vocabula."[120]

3. The *utiles actiones* which we shall have presently occasion to consider in contradistinction to the *directæ.*

Again, actions were divided with reference to the cause from which they arose, and the object at which they were pointed, into those "*in rem,*" and those "*in personam.*" 1. "In rem actiones cum aut corporalem rem intendimus nostram esse, aut jus aliquod nobis competere." The "*in rem actio*" relates to a specific object, whether that object be physical, or the assertion of an incorporal right. "Veluti si rem corporalem possideat quis, quam Titius suam esse affirmet, et possessor dominum se esse dicat; nam si Titius suam esse intendat, in rem actio est. Æque si agat jus sibi esse de fundo forte vel asdibus utendi, fruendi, vel per fundum vicini eundi, agendi, vel ex fundo vicini aquam ducendi, in rem actio est. Ejusdem generis est actio de jure prædiorum urbanorum."[121].... These actions are called

[118] Gaius, iv.§132.

[119] L. C. de Transact, iv. 4.

[120] Dig. hoc tit. 24.

[121] *De Condictione triticaria,* 1 Ulpianus, lib. xxvii. ad Edictum: " Qui certam pecuniam nume-ratam petit, ilia actione utitur, si certam petetur; qui autem alias res, per triticiariam condictionem petet. Et generaliter dicendum *est,* eas res per hanc

"*vindicationes,*" or "*petitiones*"; sometimes, also, when the "*status*" of a person is in question, "*prœjudiciales.*" 2. Personal actions are those which grow out of an obligation contracted by one individual or more persons, as the case may be, towards another. "In personam actio est, qua cum eo agimus, qui obligatus est nobis ad faciendum aliquid, vel dandum, et semper adversus eundem locum habet; " or in the words of Gaius, iv. 2.: "Quoties cum aliquo agimus, qui nobis vel ex contractu, vel ex delicto obligatus est, id est, cum intendimus dare, facere, præstare oportere." The common name for personal actions was *condictio,* which, as has been stated, was of three kinds:—

" Condictio certi."

" Condictio incerti"

" Condictio triticaria," (ff)

Many of the condictiones were distinguished by particular names: —

"Condictio sine causa."

"Condictio causâ datâ, causâ non secutâ."

"Condictio ob turpem causam."

"Condictio indebiti."

If a personal action rested on a law which did not give it a specific name, it was called "condictio ex lege."

The "prœjudicia," or "prœjudiciales formulœ," were so called, because they were intended to procure a preliminary decision on a collateral point, by which a subsequent question

---

actionem peti, si quæ sint præter pecuniam numeratam sive in pondere, sive in mensura constent, sive mobiles sint, sive soli. Quare fundum quoque per hanc actionem petimus, etsi vectigalis sit, sive jus stipulatus quis sit, veluti usumfructum, vel servitutem utrorumque prædiorum."

Dig. xii. 1. 2.§i.: " *Certi condictio competit ex omni causa, ex omni obligations, ex qua certum petitur,* sive ex certo contractu petatur, sive ex incerto; licot enim nobis ex omni contractu certum condicere, dummodo præsens sit obligatio.... Competit hæc actio etiam ex legati causa et ex Lege Aquilia; sed et ex causa furtiva per hanc actionem condicitur, sed et si ex Senatusconsulto agetur, competit hæc actio."... Dig. L. 1. 24 eod: " Si quis certum stipulatus fuerit... ilia *condicticia actione* id persequi debet, *per quam certum petitur,"*

was, or might be, affected. Their object was, not to condemn a particular defendant, but to ascertain a specific fact, as Gaius[122] tells us: "In præjudicialibus formulis; qualisest qua quæritur, aliquis libertus sit, vel quanta dos sit, et aliæ complures." See a very remarkable instance[123]: "Rei majoris pecuniæ præjudicium fieri videtur, quum ea quæstio in judicium deducitur, quæ vel tota, vel ex aliqua parte, communis est quaestioni de re majori." But questions of "Status, an aliquis liber vel libertus sit, vel de partu agnoscendo," were the most remarkable of those included under this head.[124]

Actions were divided, according to the number of the objects they embraced, into those "de universitate proposiœ,"[125] those, for instance, which demanded the assemblage of objects constituting an estate; or special, those which sought particular things, "in omnibus rebus mobilibus, tam animalibus quam his quæ animâ carent."

Actions are also divided into actiones directœ and actiones utiles. Actiones directœ are those which were originally created for the redress of the specific injury to which they immediately apply. Utiles (jfictitiœ) are actions framed by analogy to the "directœ," for cases which the latter did not include. This analogy to the "directœ actiones" is often expressed in the name of the former, by the addition of the word "quasi," or "exemplo," or "ad exemplum," to the "directa actio," so the "quasi Serviana" actio in "quasi Publiciana," "exempio Aquiliœ," "ad exemplum institoriœ," "quasi ex Lege Aquilia." The object of the actiones utiles was to fill up the omissions and to correct the errors of the civil law, so.... "Quia iniquum erat... non posse stipulatorem ad suum pervenire, ideo

---

[122] Supra, page 44.
[123] Dig. xliv 1.§§16.18. 21.
[124] Quintilian, v. 2. Inst. 1 Orat.
[125] Dig. viii. 5. 4. 7. "Competit autem de servitute actio domino ædificii, neganti servitutem se vicino debere, cujus ædes non in totum liberæ sunt, sed ei cum quo agitur, servitutem non debent, verbi gratia. Habeo ædes, quibus sunt vicinæ Sejanæ et Sempronianæ, Sempronianis servitutem debeo, adversus dominum Sejanarum volo experiri altius me tollere prohibentem, in rem actione experiar; licet enim serviant ædes meæ, ei tamen, cum quo agitur, non serviunt. Hoc igitur intendo, habere me jus altius tollendi invito eo cum quo ago; quantum enim ad eum pertinet, liberas ædes habeo."

visum est, utilem actionem in eam rem comparare."[126] Some of the utiles actiones were introduced by the emperors, they differed only in name from the actiones directœ. "Nec refert, directa quis, an utili actione agat vel conveniatur;... cum utraque actio ejusdem potestatis est, eundemque habet effectum."[127]

With reference to the relation in which the contending parties stood to each other, actions were divided into "simplicia," or "duplicia judicia," or into actiones directœ and contrariœ. Actiones directœ were those which grew immediately out of a contract. Actiones contrariœ were those which were subsidiary and collateral to it, and in which the defendant of an actio directa might enforce the rights with which the contract that the plaintiff had insisted upon, had invested him, and the liabilities he had incurred for the plaintiff (and for which no "actio directa" would lie), might be compensated. Again, actiones were "privatœ" or " populares:" the former were those which any private citizen might bring; the latter those "qua jus suum populus tuetur." With reference to their object, again, actions were divided into those—1. "Rei persequendœ gratia," or "pœnœ prosequendœ gratia comparatœ," or both, and "mixtœ." The first class includes all real actions and those personal actions which arise from contracts or quasi contracts, which relate merely to the surrender of the thing sought, or to recover compensation even where the conduct of the defendant would fall under the cognisance of criminal justice, condictio furtiva.[128] 2."Pœnales" are those which are instituted for the sake of a penalty. 3.The "mixtœ" are those which aim at a penalty as well as simple compensation.

A last and most important division of the Roman actions still remains for our consideration; that which arises from the method of proceeding which the judge was obliged to adopt for his rule, and the limits within which his authority was circumscribed. This division is that of actions into those "stricti

---

[126] Dig. xiii. 4.§1.

[127] Dig. xlvii. 1. De Negot.*Gest.*

[128] Dig. xiii. 1. 7.§1. xxv. 2. 21.§5.

juris" and "bonœ fidei"[129] The "stricti juris" were those in which the judge was bound by the severe letter of the law, not softened by any equitable consideration. The "bonœ fidei actiones," or as Cicero calls them the "arbitria," are those in which the judge was, on the contrary, bound to give full scope to those considerations of equity, without which law is very often only another word for the most odious and exasperating oppression. In mingling this element with their jurisprudence, the Romans did not think it necessary to establish two permanent tribunals, one of which should act in the same case, and on the same state of facts, upon principles directly hostile to those asserted by the other; one of which, where the same question was at issue, should be guided by written, while the other was bound to obtain oral, evidence; one of which was controlled by one set of maxims, which were abhorred, denounced, and on all occasions anxiously repudiated by the other.—Such was not the Roman notion of jurisprudence: their jurists made the nature of the cause the test of the proceedings to be adopted concerning it; and a cause intended for a legal, could not, in any part of it, be brought before an equitable, tribunal. In a "stricti juris actio," the formula directed the judge to decide according to the rigorous interpretation of the law. In the formula, on the other hand, to which the words "ex fide bona," or "quanti res est"[130] or "ut inter bonos agier oportet," were added, or "quod œquius melius," his decision was to be that of an equitable "arbiter," and to notice all the rights of the plaintiffs, as well all the "moyens" of the person named in the formu!a as the defendant. The plaintiff might recover less than he demanded, which in the "stricti juris actiones" was impossible, and the defendant might avail himself of every mode of defence which appeared to the "arbiter" reasonable and satisfactory. The "bonœ fidei contractus" were those of the

most frequent occurrence, "quibus vitœ societas continetur." The stricti juris actiones were those in which the obligation was unilateral. In order to decide on the stricti juris actiones; the

[129] Dig. iv. 6_§28. de Act.
[130] Savigny, System des heut. R.R., vol. v. p. 447.; Dig. ix. 2.1.2. 1. 27.§5. ad. Leg. ag. " quanti ea res fuit," " quanti id fuit."

judges must be taken from the album or official list; but for the "bonœ fidei actiones" any one was eligible.[131]

JURISDICTIO

Before we abandon the subject of Roman process altogether, it may be useful to make some remarks upon a topic which, as a recent discussion has shown, is very little understood among us, but which is extremely familiar, and indeed matter of elementary learning, to the jurists of other countries, that is, the division of jurisdiction into voluntary and contentious. The true principles on this subject, which has been much discussed by Voet, are laid down with admirable clearness by Merlin. The difference between these kinds of jurisdiction is explained in the Digest, De Officio Proconsulis. *(Tit.* 16. lib. i. 2.) "Omnes proconsules statim quam urbem egressi fuerint, habent jurisdictionem; sed non contentiosam, sed voluntariam, ut ecce manumitti apud eos possunt tam liberi quam servi, et adoptiones fieri." It follows from this passage that when a judge, in the exercise of his duty, ratified under the Roman law the adoption of a child, the emancipation of a son, or the enfranchisement of a slave, he performed an act of voluntary jurisdiction. It is manifest that in no similar case, under a free government, would the magistrate be permitted to exercise any choice as to the performance of his duty. Society requires that certain lawful acts shall be done under his superintendence, and authenticated by his signature, or by the records of his court; these acts he has no power to control, examine, or prevent. "L'officier de l'état civil ne doit faire aucune interpellation, ni recherche, ni inquisition sur les faits qui ne doivent pas être consignés, ni sur la verité des

---

[131] Cic. Top. c. 17. " In omnibus igitur iis judiciis in quibus ex fide bonâ est additam." De Off. iii. cc. 15. 17. Gaius, iv. 47. Seneca, De Ben. iii.§7. Dig. xii. 3. 5. " In actionibus in rem, et ad exhibendum, et in bonæ fidei judiciis." Dig. xviii. 5.§3. xxiv. 3.§21. xxx. 1. 84.§5. Dig. De Condict. Indebiti, xii. 6. 15. " condictio naturalis." Ibid. lxv. 4. " Ex bono et æquo habet repetitionem." Ibid. lxvi. " Ex bono et æquo introducta." Dig xxv. 2.§25. " Jure gentium condici puto posse res ab his qui non ex justâ causâ possident." Gaius, iv. 163.

déclarations faites par les parties; son ministére se borne à recevoir les déclarations lorsqu'elles sont conformés a la lot; il n'a le droit ni de les commenter, ni de les contredire, ni de les juger; si elles sont fausses, on pour-suivra les faussaires."[132] Voet (Dig. *Tit.* Jurisdictio, Tit. 3.) explains the subject as follows: "Jurisdictio contentiosa ea est quæ inter invites causæ cognitione intercedente, exerceri potest.... etiamsi non semper re ipsâ inter invitos, sed subinde etiam inter volentes locum inveniat, in judiciis præsertim divisoriis dum quisque communionis pertæsus, simul cum adversario ad judicem festinat, ad separationem contendit, ac post sententiam avide divisionis adjudicationisve effectum exoptatet executionem." Arg. L. 13. et L. 15. D. de Judiciis "At proinde sufficiat adesse cogendi potestatem casu quo quis reluctari velit et refractarius esse."

It follows, that whenever some magistrate is called upon to exercise his judicial duties in a matter not capable of contradiction at all, it is by virtue of a voluntary, and not of a contentious, jurisdiction; and not only are all the acts done by the judge with the consent of the parties whose consent was necessary, valid by virtue of this part of his office, but all the acts he does on the demand of one party, though no communication at all be made to another party (who may have a very strong interest, but no power to prevent it), must be ranged under the same category. Hence Pothier, improving the definition given by Heineccius and Voet of a voluntary jurisdiction, namely, that it is "*quœ inter volentes exercetur,"* has stated with greater accuracy that it is that "*quœ* in *volentes exercetur."* Such is the jurisdiction which by virtue of the 1007th article of the *Code Civil,* the president of a tribunal "*de première instance,"* is required to exercise in opening holograph and mystic testaments, the mandate ordering the registration of these acts by a notary, the emancipation of a child of fifteen[133], and the mandate which he is bound to give to the universal legatee, and which the latter must receive before he can be put into possession of the goods of the deceased. In

---

[132] Toullier, Droit civil Francais, t. i. p. 280. *Des Actes de l'élat civil.*

[133] Code Civil, 477.

all these cases, the duties of the judge are merely passive and ministerial. In the first, second, and third of these cases, no opposition whatever can be raised; in the last, no opposition can be raised to the act itself, but its consequences may be disputed. Whether an objection shall be taken to the ministerial act itself, or to its consequences, by him who wishes to dispute the result to which it leads, is a matter of form, which will vary according to the policy of various nations; and thus the cases which fall under the voluntary jurisdiction of a magistrate, will be essentially of two kinds — those which cannot, under any circumstances, be prevented; and those which either immediately, or in their consequences, are liable to dispute. "*Voluntaria Jurisdictio,*" says D'Argentrée, one of the great writers on French customary law, "*transit in contentiosam interventu justi adversarii.*" *So,* when the next of kin or the heir *ab intestat* resists the mandate by which the president puts the universal legatee in possession of the goods of the deceased, the "*contentious*" succeeds to the "*voluntary*" jurisdiction; so, too, under the Roman Law, when he who had been adopted in his infancy at a more advanced age protested against his adoption, the judge was bound to take his demand into consideration. "Nonnunquam autem impubes qui adoptatus est, audiendus erit, si pubes factus emancipari desideret. Idque causâ cognitâ per judicem statuendum erit."[134] There are moreover certain cases, as Voet proceeds to point out, of a mixed nature. "Sciendum tamen quædam esse quæ nec in universum ad voluntariam nec ad contentiosam satis apte retuleris, sed quæ velut medium inter utramque videntur obtinere. Talia sunt tutoris datio.... decreti interpositio de alienatione bonorum pupilli.... aliaque similia." In these the judge is obliged to do the act required; but he is bound to institute preliminary inquiries: so where the emancipator of the slaves was a minor, the second chapter of the "*Lex Ælia Sentia*" required the judge not to proceed till after examination.[135] It is, as has been stated, one general characteristic of a voluntary jurisdiction, that the person who is

---

[134] Inst. tit. Do Adoptionibus. Savigny, Ges. des R. Rechts, vol. i. p. 107., enumerates three cases particularly. " Bey grossen Schenkungen, bey der Verfertigung von Testamenten, und bey der Eröffnung derselben." Theod. Code, 3. 5. 1.§12. 1.

[135] Quibus manumittere non licet. Inst.

called upon to exercise it may fulfil his functions any where, whereas another judge can discharge his only within a certain territory; this principle of course admits exceptions, where publicity is required by solemn promulgation from a seat of justice, or where acts are to be done with a character of locality; and accordingly the Code Civil has pronounced, without making any distinction between voluntary and contentious jurisdiction, that. "tous actes et procès verbaux du ministre du juge seront faits au lieu où siège le tribunal." (1040.) Acts of voluntary jurisdiction might be done, on festivals, when ordinary transactions were forbidden. But an instance still more striking of the difference made by the Roman law, between acts of contentious and acts of voluntary jurisdiction, is that, whereas the magistrate was bound to abstain from the former, where he had any personal interest, he might perform the latter, not for his relations only but for himself. It follows, from all the analogies of law, that he could only thus act in cases when, according to the definition of Heineccius, he could be called upon to proceed "*sine cognitione causœ.*" A last difference may be stated, which is well pointed out by M. Henriot de Pansey, cited by Merlin, that in matters of voluntary jurisdiction the judge is called upon to interpose his authority, and in those of contentious jurisdiction to pronounce a sentence. The first is matter "*magis imperii quam jurisdictionis*;" the latter "*magis jurisdictionis quam imperii*;" hence it follows that it is annexed to the local and ordinary administration of justice, and can only appertain to any other judge by virtue of an express and positive delegation. So the "*Juges de Paix*" (being, in the words of the French Code, "*Tribunaux extraordinaires et d'exception"*) only possess the power of concurring in the nomination of tutors and acts of emancipation in consequence of the 416. and 477. articles of the Code Civil.

PROCESS OF THE LATER ROMAN LAW[136]

The formal proceeding in the time of Justinian, though free from the absurdities which infest our own, was not so judicious as that in force during the more flourishing period of Roman jurisprudence. The plaintiff delivered to the tribunal a libel (τὸ της αιτιάσεως βιβλιον), which was communicated to the defendant. This libel contained a short account of the nature and object of the plaintiff's demand, that the defendant might judge whether or not he should dispute it; — and if he did dispute it, that he might be aware of the complaint that he had to answer, "ut proinde sciat reus utrum cedere an contendere ultra debeat, et si contendendum putat, veniat instructus ad agendum cognitâ actione qua conveniatur." The object of the Norman lawyers, who contrived the system now in use among us, was directly the reverse of this; the intention of that method being to keep the defendant in the most profound ignorance of the real nature of the plaintiff's demand, whereby recourse to their assistance became necessary. The lawyers employed by Justinian were perhaps corrupt, but not barbarous, or legislating for barbarians. According to their system no particular form was necessary. The complaint was shaped according to the matter. The signature of the party (or, if he could not write, of a tabularius in his place, and who thereby incurred the whole responsibility of the proceeding) was essential. (Nov. 112. 2.) In addition to this he was obliged to give security, 1st, that he would within two months "*litem contestari,*" or repay the defendant twice the amount of the expence he had obliged him to incur: 2d, that he would continue the cause to a decision, and in case of failure pay the costs. These proceedings were followed by the act of the judge *(sententia interlocutoris),* who either admitted or refused the action. If the action was allowed, there issued a "*commonitio conventi citato*" to the defendant, which was served upon him by the officer of the court, to whom he gave an *ἀντιβιβλιον, libellus responsionis* (Nov. 53. 3. 2.) and a "*cautio judicio*

[136] Bethman Hollweg, Civil Process, p. 19., from which most of this is taken.

sisti." By this last the defendant bound himself to appear before the court at a certain time, and to abide its final judgment. Possessors of landed estates *"personæ illustres,"* and other privileged people, were allowed to give a *"cautio juratoria"* only. The amount of the security was fixed by the judge; if the defendant could not supply the amount he was placed in the custody of the officer of the court. Justinian (Nov. 53. c. 3.) prolonged the time allowed to the respondent to determine whether or not he would resist the action from ten to twenty days. If the defendant did not appear he was condemned for contumacy, *μονομερῶς*.. If he did, the proceeding was now technically called *cognitio, διάγνωσις,* and it was said to be carried on *cognitionaliter.* No particular form was necessary, the matter was managed entirely by the judge; and this method of proceeding, which in the time of Justinian had superseded every other, was faithfully borrowed from the *extraordinaria* of the old Roman law, at the time when the system *of formulæ* was generally adopted, and when, as the name implies, few cases were so conducted. When the defendant formally contradicted the statement of the plaintiff *"per narrationem propositam et contradictionem objectam,"* the "li*s"* was said to be *"contestata."*

1st. When the defendant admitted the plaintiff's claim, *"confessio in jure,"* which admission was followed by execution.[137]

2d. When the defendant put in a dilatory plea; *i. e.* if he objected to the competence of the judge.

But if he denied the plaintiff's right, or endeavoured to guard himself by an exception— if he, in short, applied himself to the matter contained in the plaintiff's libel, there was a *"litis contestatio."*

As there was *no formula,* if there were no dilatory exceptions either to the jurisdiction or to the complaint itself, the plaintiff first made out his case. The peremptory exceptions of the defendant, if he relied upon any such defence, were then

---

[137] Dig. xliv. 2. Cod. vii. 259.

heard. They might be brought, forward at any time, even in an appeal, until the case was ultimately decided. Of course, if the defendant succeeded in establishing them, the plaintiff was defeated; or if the defendant had no exception to maintain, he brought forward his witnesses to contradict the plaintiff's case. The Christian emperors have transmitted to us several rules of evidence, some of which are very arbitrary. Many of them relate to the "*onus probandi*;" but we have no means of knowing the manner in which the witnesses were brought forward, or the rules which governed their examination. A respite was sometimes granted to produce documents, "*dilatio instrumentorum causâ.*" The witnesses were heard after the statement of the contending parties. They were brought before the tribunal, at least in the passage in Symmachus, which will be cited. They were brought according to their rank, were sworn, and were examined by the judge, and a written copy of their evidence was delivered to each of the litigants. They were examined in the presence of the parties or their representatives. If they were examined by commission, their examinations were transmitted to the judge of the cause, and were by him delivered to the parties, who might except, for different reasons, to the testimony. After these objections had been made, and the protocol containing the evidence delivered, the opposite party could not strengthen his case by additional evidence.[138]

The party[139] producing documents was bound to prove them genuine by the oath of the public officer who registered,

---

[138] Nov. xc. 4.

[139] Hearsay was excluded by the Athenian law of Evidence,—ακὸην μαοτυρειν is the expression: ού γὰρ ἂν ειδειητ' ύμεῖς εἴτ' έστιν ἂληθη, εἴτε φευδή ä φασιν έκατεροι, εί μή τις καὶ τούς μάρτυρας παρέχοιτο. (Κατὰ Στεφ. Β.) ούδέ μαρτυρειν ἂκοήν εϖσιν οὶ νόμοι, ούδ' έπι τος πανυ φαύλοις έγκλήμασιν. (Πρὸς Εὐβουλ.) But if the witness, from illness or other adequate reason, was unable to appear, his deposition might be taken by commissioners appointed for that purpose, and read, when confirmed by the testimony of those commissioners, to the court. This deposition was *έκμαρτνρια.*. These commissioners were said *μαρτυρειν την εκμαρτυριαν.*. Demosthenes, Κατ. Λεωχ. 1097. Ό δΕ γε νόμς ακοην τϖν τετελεντηκοτων κωλυει διαμαρτυρειυ, &C., a corrupt passage, which Reiske, t. xi. 1488., explains thus, Ό *νομος κωλυει σε ζϖντος ετι του ατρος διαμαρτυρειν τα υπ' εκεινου πραχθεντα.* I think the meaning is rather, the law will not allow you, while your father is alive, to give evidence of what he said, as this is hearsay evidence; the Athenian law allowed hearsay evidence of

or of the witnesses by whom they were attested. Comparison of hands was resorted to only when other means of proof failed, as when the attesting witnesses were dead, and the result was spoken to by officers appointed for the purpose. The original document was required, and copies were inadmissible, nor could excuses be received. Where, however, the documents could not be produced, a commissioner was sometimes especially appointed to examine their authenticity.

The following description of a trial at that period is left us by Symmachus. (Cit. ap. Bethman Hollweg.) Symmachi lib. x. ep. 18.

"D. Theodosio semper Aug. Symmachus, Praef. urb.

"Quid possint justi principes culpare, praesentio. la causis etenim, quibus momenti reformatid postulatur, appellationes recipi non oportet. Sed consulto nunc objectum provocationis admisi, ut in examen clementiæ vestræ et invasionis indignitas et modus indicii perveniret, D. Imperator. Nam Scirtius vir perfectissimus ereptam sibi partem Cæsarianæ massæ crebra additione conquestus, cum integrationem status quern amiserat impetrasset, heredes Thesei qui reluctarentur objecti sunt. Turn vero Artemisius, Olibrii clarissimi atque illustris viri actor, executori, ut ipse professus est, obviavit. Et cum ad pernoscendum possessionis statum loci habitatores adesse jussissem, in injuriam legum Ruffino Officiali jussa curanti, qui deducebantur, abrepti sunt. Gesta indicabunt facti incivilis auctores. Interea distuli vindictam judiciorum et rursus officio negotium dedi, ut necessarios evocaret. Tune cessantibus actoribus clarissimæ domus ceterisque subtractis, ad contradicendum Thesei subrogantur heredes, uno tantum exhibito, qui se assereret libertum esse defuncti. Is interrogatus, quo abessent incolse prædiorum, delituisse nonnullos, Scirtii vero mancipia ad urbanam villam, quæ est clarissimi et illustris viri Olibrii, translata respondit. Cetera ut a liberto Thesei dicta prætercam, licet in eum præscriptio ista noil competat, cum a

pedigree. Isæus, ii. Του Κιρϖνος κλ. Τὰ μεν παλαι γεγενημενα (επιδειξω) λόγων ακοή, κ.τ.λ.

patre minorum beneficium libertatis acceperit. His ita positis Prænestini, in quorum finibus Cæsariana possessio jacet, missis apparitoribus exhibentur. Tunc demum viri clarissimi et spectabilis Olibrii procurator emergit. Adest etiam defensor minorum tandem cogentibus judiciis postulatus. Scirtio adversum duos pugna proponitur, quamvis patrocinia clarissimæ domus et successorum Thesei quadam specie dissiderent. Itur in quæstionem possessions, quæ partium variis agitata conflictibus, ad interrogationem testium jure transivit. Admoneri singulatim, ut mos est, jubeo Curiales nominum et dignitatis. Ab unoquoque posco responsa: tum locorum justos possessores requiro; dehinc percunctor, quis annuas functiones aut indicta persolverit. Cum secundum Scirtium testimonia cuncta procederent, atque eam possessionem cum Theseo tenuisse constaret, quando aut per quos dejectus esset, examino. Secundum fere vel tertium mensem manare consentiunt, ut eum clarissimæ atque illustris domus homines expulerint. Auditis optimatum testimoniis, denuo defensores admitto jurgantes: quæsita et responsa partibus intimantur. Ibi Sarpeius vir clarissimus, procurator illustris viri Olibrii, asseruit, ei sex uncias prædiorum Thesei morte quæsitas. Contra Scirtius de sex unciis, quas minores etiam se consentiente retinebant, non ibat inficias, nec sua interesse dicebat, actores clarissimæ domus, an heredes Thesei eadem parte fruerentur. Tune actionibus copulatis Scirtium urgere cœperunt, quod secundum mandatum clarissimæ feminæ Facianæ sex uncias Theseo per epistolam reddidisset, sex vero alias in ejus liberos contulisset spontanea largitate. Ad hæc Scirtius, idem litteris familiaribus, quod donationibus in Theseum vel parvulos transfusum esse, dicebat, ipsius petitu, ut actorum fides beneficium roboraret. Et revera cum posteriora gesta pro indiviso sex uncias massæ in eos collates esse testentur, intelleximus partem donatoris exceptam. Cur enim pro indiviso daret, si nihil resideret quod retineret? Sed hoc cum ad proprietatis causam dicerem pertinere, recitata est a defensoribus constitutio, quæ judicibus tribuit copiam, non impoait necessitatem, ut quoties de possessione successionis judicant, continuo, si casus tulerit, etiam de jure cognoscant. Qua actione confessi sunt, ad aliam causam se malle transire. Præterea non solus Scirtius proprietatis quasstione videbatur urgendus, cum ipsi quoque inter se super hac parte quodammodo dissiderent. Quare de possessione secundum docu-menta Scirtii et principalium testimonia judicavi, adversariis ejus sex unciarum retentione et jure firmatis. Principalem vero causam salvis allegationibus partium futuro examini reservavi. Et mox sontentiæ exemplum emisi, cum ejus editionem procurator spectabilis viri continuo postulasset. Tunc Scirtius obtulit sanctiones, quibus doceret, in reformatione momenti nullum esse appellationis locum. Postridie procurator clarissimi et illustris viri Olibrii ac defensor minorum, qui putabantur in judicio discrepare, concordiam suam junctis provocationibus indicarunt. Hæc omnis summa luctaminis. Nunc oraculum numinis vestri fortuna litis exspectat. Gesta et supplementa partis utriusque subjeci, quibus instructa perennitas vestra exempio unius causse securitati omnium dignabitur commodare."

CHAP. III.
PRÆTOR[140]

IN consequence of the increasing power of the republic, new magistrates became necessary. Among these, one was created of the utmost importance in the history of Roman legislation; this was the[141] *Prætor peregrinus qui inter cives et peregrinos jus dixit.* The function of this magistrate was to adjust the disputes which might arise between citizens and foreigners. Thus a new element found its way into Roman jurisprudence. In addition to the local and positive laws, by which their own society was regulated, it became necessary for the Roman judge to consider the fundamental principles of justice from which all law derives its obligation. These

[140] Beaufort, République Romaine. Savigny, Sys. des heut. R. R. vol. i. Dig.;. 11. Ibid. xxi. 1. Cod. xii. 2. Ibid. vi. 12. Ibid. i. 27. Ibid. i. 14. Giraud, Hist. du Droit Romain, 162. Mémoires de l'Ac. des Inscriptions, vol. xli. Mémoire de Bouchaud.

[141] The Athenian Πολέμαρχος. ειλκέμε προς τον πολέμαρχον έγοητας αιτω̃ν.—Isoc. Τραπεζ.§361.

principles, under the name of *"jus gentium,"* thus became familiar to the minds of Roman jurists, and exercised a considerable and happy influence over the institutions of Rome itself. Thus it was that the views of the jurist became more liberal and extensive; and the notion of a law, not dependent on climate or on caste, common to man on the banks of the Ilissus, of the Tiber, or of the Euphrates, a covenant, as it were, between earth and heaven, which no human authority could abrogate or supersede, from which all laws derive their controlling power, was transferred from the schools of Greece to the tribunals of Rome. It became every day more and more necessary to appeal to broader principles than those which the municipal institutions of any country could supply, and these were only to be found in the *"naturalis ratio,"* the principles implanted in man wherever he lived and however he was governed; and from these principles the consoling and sublime doctrine of a law eternal and imperishable followed as an irresistible corollary. Such was the law which existed before its principles were written on the Plank of the Judge at Athens, or cut into the Tablet of the Decemvir of Rome, or blazoned on the album of the prætor; of which all human laws, in so far forth as they are binding, are but paragraphs and transcripts, the fountain from which all our laws are drawn, which, when those laws are just, is their guarantee, and when unjust, their condemnation. It is to this law that the philosophers and moralists, whom God has sent among us to raise our species by their precepts, and adorn it by their example, sometimes to hallow it by their lives, sometimes to shame it by their deaths, have ever appealed against prevailing error and triumphant iniquity, on behalf of those who are trampled down and oppressed, on whom servitude has been imposed by violence, or settled by prescription. Were it not for this law the most enormous crimes, the foulest vices, might still be practised with impunity, or even inculcated as virtues, as they were once surrounded by all the sanctions that monarchs, and priests, and senates, and even popular assemblies could bestow. "Quod si populorum jussis, si principum decretis, si sententiis judicum jura constituerentur, jus esset latrocinari, jus adulterare, jus testamenta falsa supponere, si hæc suffragiis aut scitis multitudinis probarentur. Quæ si tanta potestas est stultorum sententiis atque jussis, ut eorum suffragiis rerum natura vertatur: cur non sanciunt, ut quæ mala perniciosaque sunt, habeantur pro bonis ac salutaribus? aut cur quum jus ex injuria lex facere possit, bonum eadem facere non possit ex malo? Atqui nos legem bonam a mala, nulla alia, nisi natura dijudicantur, sed omnino omnia honesta ac turpia."[142]

It was from the comparison between their own institutions and the laws of other nations, that the Romans

---

[142] Cic. De Leg. i. 16. I cannot resist the pleasure of enabling the reader to compare with this magnificent passage in Cicero two passages from modern writers almost equal to him in eloquence. The first is from Mr. Burke, answering the suggestion that arbitrary power had been delegated to Warren Hastings:—

"He have arbitrary power! My Lords, the East India Company have not arbitrary power to give him; the King has no arbitrary power to give him; your Lordships have not; nor the Commons; nor the whole Legislature. We have no arbitrary power to give, because arbitrary power is a thing which neither any man can hold nor any man can give. No man can lawfully govern himself according to his own will, much less can one person be governed by the will of another. We are all born in subjection, all born equally, high and low, governors and governed, in subjection to one great, immutable, pre-existent law, prior to all our devices, and prior to all our contrivances; paramount to all our ideas, and all our sensations, antecedent to our very existence, by which we are knit and connected in the eternal frame of the Universe, out of which we cannot stir. This great law does not arise from our conventions or compacts; on the contrary, it gives to our conventions and compacts all the force and sanction they can have; — it does not arise from our vain institutions." Burke's Works, vol. xiii. p. 165.

The second is from Malebranche, a greater philosopher than Cicero, and a more eloquent writer even than Burke: —

Recherche de la Vérité, liv. 3. c. 11. " Si je me demande, ou plutôt (puisque je ne suis pas à moi-même, ni mon maître, ni ma lumière) si je m'approche de Dieu, et que, dans le silence de mes sens et de mes passions, je lui demande si je dois préférer les richesses à la vertu ou la vertu aux richesses, j'entendrai une réponse claire et distincte de ce que je dois faire; réponse éternelle qui a toujours été dite, qui se dit, et qui se dira toujours, réponse qu'il n'est pas nécessaire que j'explique, parceque tout le monde la sait, ceux qui lisent ceci et ceux qui ne le lisent pas; qui n'est ni Grecque, ni Latine, ni Francaise, ni Allemande, et que toutes les nations concoivent; réponse enfin qui console les justes dans leur pauvreté, et qui confond les pécheurs au milieu de leurs richesses. J'entendrai cette réponse, et j'en demeurerai convaincu."

" Ignorance of the causes and original constitution of right, equity, law, and justice, disposes a man to make custom and example the rule of his actions, in such manner as to think that unjust, which it has been the custom to punish, and that just, of the impunity and approbation of which they can produce an example; or as the lawyers, which only use this false measure of justice barbarously term it, a precedent." Hobbes Ser. c. 11. How can this admirable passage be reconciled with the main doctrine of the author,?

derived their division of law into *jus civile* and *jus gentium.* Several of these institutions, and the principles by which they were governed, were common to both these divisions. Such, for instance, were the contracts usual in the intercourse of daily life — "*Emptio, venditio,*" "*Societas,*" most of the "*delicta,*" also, inasmuch as they carried with them the duty of compensation.

In order to obtain a correct idea of this subject, we should bear in mind that the meaning of the "*jus civile,*" when opposed to the "*jus gentium,*" is not quite the same as when it is opposed to "*jus prœtorium.*"

Jus civile, opposed *to jus gentium,* may be considered as the law of England opposed to the law of nations.

"*Jus civile,*" opposed to the "*jus honorarium,*" may be considered as the common law of England opposed to the law of Courts of Equity.

These examples are adduced to show the incorrigible ambiguity of language on such subjects, rather than as being in exact correspondence; but they sufficiently illustrate the different shades of meaning belonging to the words "*jus civile,*" when it is contrasted with the "*jus gentium,*" and when it is contrasted with the "*jus honorarium.*"

The "*jus honorarium*" is sometimes used to describe the "*jus gentium,*" as opposed to the Roman usage; and sometimes it is used in contrast with the "*jus gentium,*" to denote the Roman usage. "Si testamentum, quod resignaverit testator, iterum signatum fuerit septem testium signis, non erit imperfectum, sed utroque jure valebit, tarn civili quam prætorio.[143] Si quis autem constituent, quod jure civili debebat, jure prætorio non debebat, id est per exceptionem, an constituendo teneatur, quæritur. Et est verum, ut et Pomponius scribit, eum non teneri, quæ debita juribus non est pecunia, quas constituta est.[144] Sed hæc quidem verborum obligatio: dares, spondes? spondeo, propria civium Romanorum est. Ceteræ vero juris gentium sunt; itaque inter omnes homines, give cives

---

[143] Dig. xxviii. 1. 23.
[144] Dig. xiii. 5. 3. 1.

Romanes, sive peregrinos, valent, et quamvis ad Græcam vocem expressas fuerint."[145] Thus, if a Roman citizen and a foreigner litigated a question before a Roman tribunal, the dispute was settled by that portion of *the jus gentium* which was incorporated in *the jus honorarium.* If C, a Roman citizen, resisted a demand from D, another Roman citizen, from which demand C was equitably released, but which, according to the strict rules of the law *(jus civile),* was still binding on him, C had recourse to another branch of the *jus honorarium,* from which he obtained an *exceptio,* and so opposed an insuperable obstacle to the claim of D.

The *jus civile,* in both these cases, is opposed to the *jus honorarium,* and to two different branches of it; in the first, to that part of the *jus honorarium* which was a portion of the *jus gentium* — in the second, to that part of it which was not.

But, as will be seen afterwards, the principle of the *jus gentium* was extended to regular transactions of Roman citizens with each other.

If a Roman citizen, with a solid cause of complaint, for which the *jus civile* provided no remedy had recourse to the prætor's assistance, this was a part of the *jus honorarium* immediately connected with *the jus gentium.*

The early interpreters of the Roman Law had imbibed a very erroneous notion of the *jus prætorium* or *edicta magistratuum*[146], which soon became one of its most considerable branches, and contains some of its most luminous regulations. They considered the magistrate's edict as an encroachment on the constitutional rights of Roman citizens, and the exercise of a legislative power by the magistrate which gradually supplanted law, introduced for, arbitrary purposes, and tending, according to the capricious will of the Prætor or Ædile, to unsettle the ascertained principles of the constitution. It was no such thing. The greatest of the Roman lawyers speak

---

[145] Gaii Com. iii. 93.

[146] Even Cujacius, thie first of interpreters, has fallen into this error; and Heineccius has propagated it extensively.

of this portion of law with respect and veneration. Obedience to these edicts was inculcated by the civil law, and the obligation of publishing his edict was one which no Prætor could venture safely to neglect, and which, in fact, no Prætor did ever attempt to disregard. That strict separation of the executive and legislative functions which prevails among us, and which characterises most modern governments, is an invention of comparatively recent date: the shortness of the period for which the executive power was delegated among the Romans made such a precaution useless and impossible; the power of the magistrate during his year of office was almost unlimited, and so when that period had expired was his responsibility,[147] Nothing could be more natural than that a person so situated should, at the commencement of his year of office, endeavour to protect himself against future animadversion by solemnly proclaiming to his fellow-citizens beforehand the rules that were to govern his decisions, and the rules to which, during the continuance of his authority, all citizens might appeal. Accordingly, the preparation of the Prætor's edict was a task on which the erudition and abilities of the greatest jurists were employed, — the beneficial doctrines announced in one year were transmitted to the next, and became the inheritance of successive generations. By the Lex Cornelia[148] the Prætor was forbidden to change his edict during his year of office. It was valid for the year; hence the name of *edictum per-petuum,* which has been so much and so vexatiously misunderstood. It means only that the questions brought before the Prætor would be decided, not according to his caprice, but by fixed and published principles, which it was in the power of any one who

---

[147] Jura reddebant et ut scirent cives... *seque præmunirent* edicta proponebant, says Pomponius.

[148] A. U. C. 687. Dio. Cassius, 1. xxxvi. c. 23. says the prætors πολλάκις αύτà μετέγραφον.... προς χάριν ή kàι κατ' έχθραν... έσηήσατο κατ' αρχàς τà δικαια προλέγειν, και μηδέν άπ' αυτϖν παρατρέπειν. The study of the prætor's edict in Cicero's time had been substituted for that of the Twelve Tables, "quas jam nemo discit." De Leg. ii. 23. Hugo (i. 5.) compares the edict with the senatus consulta cameralia of the German law, and the arrêts de réglement of the French parliaments. "Rien ne ressemble plus aux edits, que les joyeuses entrées des dues de Brabant." Warnkœnig Hist. ex. du Droit Romain, p.86. Cicero proves Verres guilty of abusing the jus edicendi.

chose it to ascertain. The effect of this system was that a supply of actual opinions and customs were added to the Roman Law, and that Roman jurisprudence kept pace with the exigencies of the age and the progress of society. Obsolete doctrines were discarded (not by the ruin of some unhappy victim, in whose case they were for the first time questioned), and requisite alterations introduced. Improvement was always busy, and innovation always judicious. The law was constantly exposed to the salutary influence of public opinion; instead of stagnating into corruption and chicanery, it was governed by a salient active principle; it represented the wisdom of the age; it was not a dead letter but a living word, a merit well appreciated and happily described by the civilians when they use the phrase "*viva vox juris civilis.*"

The value of this *jus honorarium* was limited to the time and place of the Prætor's jurisdiction. If a Prætor disapproved the principles laid down by his predecessor, he might omit them in the succeeding year; and this in the early ages of the Republic, before these doctrines had been thoroughly sifted, and had acquired by reiterated adoptions a binding force and hold on the public mind, was no doubt an event not uncommon. Hence we find in the older writers[149] the distinction between *lex* and *quod legis vicem obtinet,*—between the law and that which in this particular case is to be so considered. The Prætor could only declare what he would consider as law, subject among other restraints to the liability of its future application to himself. The task of restoring and improving the old law, of supplying its omissions and mitigating its harshness, was thus left to him with almost unlimited authority. And thus, from the yearly succession of Prætors, the Roman system was perpetually renovated and refined by an infusion of doctrines, the utility of which had made them current among the people, and by discarding others which experience had shown to be pernicious and ill adapted to the service of the Commonwealth.

---

[149] Gaius, iv. 1. 1. 8.

CHAP. IV
LAW OF POSSESSION[150]

IT is extremely difficult to give any fixed and accurate definition of the "*Possessio*" of the Roman law. For as the intention to possess is necessary but not sufficient to constitute possession, as this disposition of the mind must be seconded by some visible act, and as the word, nevertheless, does not always imply direct physical contact, some circumlocution is necessary to explain, in all its senses, an expression of itself very easily understood in most cases, and even that circumlocution can hardly exclude all possibility of doubt and cavil: "Adipiscimur possessionem corpore et animo, neque per se animo neque per se corpore."

We have, therefore, to consider, first, what is meant by "*corpus;*" next, what is meant by "*animus.*"

1st.—By *corpus* is not meant direct contact; for the proof of which I cite the following passages: —

"Si jusserim venditorem procuratori rem tradere, cum ea in præsentia sit, videri (mihi) traditam Prisons ait: idemque esse, si nummos debitorem jusserim alii dare: *Non est enim corpore et actu necesse apprehendere possessionem, sed etiam oculis et affectu:* et argumento esse eas res, quæ propter magnitudinem ponderis moveri non possunt, ut columnas: nam

[150] Dornat, Loix Civiles, lib. iii. tit. 7. Code Civil, 549. 1141. 2279. 2229. Niebuhr, K. Geschichte, th. ii. p. 162. lenbruch, Doctrina Pandect, p. 224. Puchta, Instit. vol. ii. p.513. Dig. xli. 2. Cod. vii. 32. Schilling, Römische Rechtsgeschichte, vol.ii. 445. *Dig.* xliii. 17. Cod. viii. 6. Uti possidetis. Dig. xliii. 31. Utrubi. As an instance of learned extravagance in the anti-Livy school, I may quote the doctrine, cited by Savigny, p. 56. Recht des Besitzes, of a writer who maintains that the Romans or Ramnes, represented the *body,* and *therefore* were the authors of possession, and the interdict for its defence, and that the Quirites or Titians represented the *soul,* and *therefore* were the authors of right, of property, and its defence by action. As Malebranche, liv. ii. c.3, says of Tertullian, "Peut-on de sang froid et de sens rassis tirer de pareilles conclusions, et peut-on les voir tirer sans en rire?

pro traditis (eas) haberi, si in re prassenti consenserint; et vina tradita videri, cum claves cellæ vinariæ emptori traditæ fuerint."[151]

"Si venditorem, quod emerim deponere in mea domo jusserim, possidere me certum est, quanquam id nemo attigerit: aut si vicinum mihi fundum mercato venditor in mea turre demonstret vacuamque se possessionem tradere dicat, non minus possidere cœpi quam si pedem finibus in-tulissem."[152]

"Quod autem diximus, corpore et animo adquirere nos debere possessionem, non utique ita accipiendum est, ut qui fundum possidere velit omnes glebas circumambulet; sed sufficit quamlibet partem ejus fundi introire; dum mente et cogitatione (hac) fit, uti totum fundum usque ad terminum velit possidere."[153]

"Pecuniam quam mihi debes, aut aliam rem, si in conspectu meo ponere te jubeam, efficitur ut et tu statim libereris, et mea esse incipiat; nam turn quod a nullo corporaliter ejus rei possessio detineretur adquisita mihi, et quodam modo manu longa tradita existimanda est."[154]

Hence it appears, that the actual power of dealing with any object uninterrupted by any third person, whether that power be immediately exercised or not, is sufficient to constitute that ingredient of possession which is expressed by the word "*corpus*" in the passage first cited, and which is sometimes termed "*apprehensio*" by the civilians.

It remains to consider the second ingredient, the *animus,* a disposition of the mind.

This consists in the intention of the possessor to deal with the object in question as his own; this is the "*animus domini,"* and requires no further definition.

---

[151] Dig. xli. 2. 1.§21.
[152] Dig. xli. 2. 18.§3.
[153] Dig. xli. 2. 3.§1
[154] Dig. xlvi. 3. 79.

There are other cases in which possession may be parted with, though the property be retained; here the "*animus domini*" and the "*animus possidendi*" are distinct. In these cases a disposition of the possessor to deal with the article as his own is by the definition impossible, as it is the admitted property of another. Such were the *pignus* (not the *pignus causâ judicati captum)* and the *emphyteuta.* In these cases the holder had the "*jus possessionis.*"[155]

Possession, generally speaking. Can only be lost as it was acquired, by a disposition of the mind testified by some visible act.

"Quemadmodum nulla possessio acquiri nisi animo et corpore potest, ita nulla amittitur nisi in qua utrumque in contrarium actione est."[156]

But possession and its rights ceased where it was forcibly taken away, and all exercise of power by the former possessor over the object in question was physically impossible. "Naturaliter interrumpitur possessio, cum quis de possessione vi dejicitur, vel alicui res eripitur; quo casu non adversus cum tantum qui eripit interrumpitur possessio, sed adversus omnes."[157]

"Si autem, cum dominus veniret in possessionem, armati eum prohibuerunt, qui invaserant possessionem; videri eum armis dejectum.§ 9. Eum igitur, qui cum armis venit, possumus armis repellere, sed hoc confestim non ex intervallo; dummodo sciamus non solum resistere permissum ne dejiciatur, sed etsi dejectus quis fuerit, eundem dejicere non ex intervallo, sed ex continenti."[158]

---

[155] Dig.xli. 3. 16.—" Servi nomine, qui pigno ri datus est, ad exhibendum cum creditore, non cum debitore, agendum est: quia qui pignori dedit, *ad usucapionem tantum* possidet; quod ad reliquas omnes causas pertinet, qui accepit, possidet: adeo ut addici possit at possessio ejus, qui pignori dedit." id. de Usurp, i.§16, Lex.—" Qui pignori dedit, ad *usucapionem tuntum possidet quod ad reliquas omnes causas pertinet, qui accepit, possidet."* Id. de Poss. 1. xxxvi. " Qui pignoris causa fundum creditori tradit intelligitur possidere." Id. xv. 1. " Ad unam enim tantum causam videri eum a debitore possideri—ad usucapionem."

[156] Dig. 1. 17. 15.§3.

[157] Dig.xli. 3.§5.

[158] Dig. xliii. 16. 3.§8.

And here I would call the attention of the reader to one of those distinctions, to decide upon which the study of jurisprudence is necessary, and which nevertheless arise in the ordinary course of affairs.

Caius expels Titius from his possession.

Sempronius, a stranger to both, encroaches upon the possession of Caius.

Caius, as against Sempronius, is entitled to all the rights, remedies, and privileges of the possessor.

But Titius also sues Caius.

Caius against him is not entitled to any of those rights.

"Quod ait prætor in interdicto, *nec vi, nec clam, nec precario, alter ab altero possidetis,* hoc eo pertinet; ut si quis possidet vi, aut clam, aut precario; si quidem *ab alio* prosit ei possessio, si vero *ab adversario suo, non debeat eum propter hoc,* quod ab eo possidet, *vincere;* has enim possessiones non debere proficere palam est."[159]

"Justa enim an injusta adversus cæteros possessio ait, in hoc interdicto nihil refert; qualiscumque enim possessor, hoc ipso, quod possessor est, plus juris habet, quam ille qui non possidet."[160]

Sequens divisio interdictorum hæc est, quod quædam adipiscendæ possessionis causæ comparatæ sunt, quædam retinendæ, quædam recuperandæ.

Retinendæ possessionis causa comparata sunt interdicta uti possidetis et utrubi, cum ab utraque parte de proprietate alicujus rei controversia fit, et ante quæritur, uter ex litigatoribus possidere, uter petere debeat. Sed interdicto quidem uti possidetis fie fundi vel ædium possessione contenditur, utrubi vero interdicto de rerum mobilium possessione.

---

[159] Dig, xliii. 17. 1.§9.
[160] Dig. xliii. 17.§2.

Recuperandæe possessionis causa solet interdict, si quis ex possessione fundi vel sodium vi dejectus fuerit. Nam ei proponitur interdictum, unde vi per quod is qui dejecit, cogitur ei restituere possessionem," &c.[161]

"Usucapio est adjectio dominii per continuationem possessionis temporis lege definiti."[162]

"Fieri potest, ut alter possessor sit, dominus non sit, alter dominus quidem sit, possessor non sit; fieri potest, ut et possessor idem et dominus sit."[163]

We have next to consider how possession may be acquired by a representative. Paulus (Recept. Sentent. v. 2. 1.) says, "Possessionem adquirimus et animo et corpore; animo utique nostro, corpore vel nostro, vel alieno."[164]

The representative might either be in the power of the person for whom he acquired possession, or free.

1. But he must have intended to acquire possession for that person.

2. And the person for whom he acquired possession, must have been willing to receive it.

The *traditio* was an exception to the first rule, as the intention of the *tradens* in that case was alone important. "Qui mihi donatum volebat, servo communi meo et Titii rem tradidit; servus vel sic accepit, quasi socio adquisiturus; vel sic quasi mihi et socio. Quærebatur quid agere? Et placet, quamvis servus hac mente acceperit, ut socio meo, vel mihi et socio adquirat, mihi tamen adquiri. Nam et si procuratorio me hoc animo rein tradiderit, ut mihi adquirat, ille quasi sibi adquisiturus acceperit; nihil agit in sua persona, sed mihi adquirit."[165]

---

[161] Dig. xliii. 17.§§2. 4. 6., i. iv. 15. de Interdictis.
[162] Modestinus, in Fr. 3. Dig. xli. 3. de Usurp, et Usuc.
[163] Ulpianus in Fr. 1.§2. Dig. xliii. Uti possidetis.
[164] Dig. xliii. 16. 1.
[165] Dig. xxxix. 5. 13.

And the cases where the slave and unemancipated son, who were allowed a *"peculium,"* acted for the master or father, who might acquire possession unconsciously, were exceptions to the second. "Item adquirimus possessionem per servum aut filium qui in potestate est, et quidem earum rerum quas peculiariter tenent etiam ignorantes."[166]

In later times the possession of a free representative was the possession of his principal. "Per liberam personam veluti per procuratorem placet non solum scientibus, sed etiam ignorantibus vobis acquiri possessionem."[167]

Generally speaking, possession is independent of right[168]; society bestows on him who possesses certain privileges, because he *is* the possessor. These rights flow from the fact of possession, and exist, though by the law that possession may be subsequently taken away, or even punished.[169] Justa enim an injusta adversus ceteros possessio sit, in hoc interdicto nihil refert; qualiscunque enim possessor hoc ipso quod possessor

---

166 Dig. xli. 2. 5.

167 Dig. ii. 9. 5.§1.

168 The vices of possessio were three: it might be " vi," " clam," " precario." " Vi " denoted possession taken by violence, " vi possidere eum definiendum est qui, expulso vetere possessore, adquisitam per vim possessionem obtinet."— Dig. xliii. 16. 1.§28. " Clam" denoted possession, of which he who might have resisted it, was purposely kept in ignorance " Qui deceptio facit eo ad quem pertinuit non facere."—Dig. xliii. 24. 5. " Precario," the possession which was permissive. " Precarium est quod precibus petenti utendum conceditur quamdiu is qui concessit patitur."—Dig. xliii. 26. i.

169 Justa enim an injusta possessio sit *adversus ceteros* in hoc interdicto nihil refert, qualiscunque enim possessor hoc ipso quod possessor est plus juris habet quam ille qui non possidet." — Dig. xliii. 17. 2. " Omnis de possessione controversia eo pertinct ut quod non possidemus nobis restituatur aut, ad hoc ut possidere nobis liceat quod possidemus."—Dig. xliii. 17. 1.§4. Id. iv. 15. 4. " Commodum autem possidendi in eo est, quod etiamsi ejus res non sit qui possidet, si modo actor non potuerit suam esse probare, remanet suo loco possessio; propter quam causam, cum obscura sint utriusque jura, contra petitorem judicari solet." Dig. xliii. 17. 1. " Ait prætor: *Uti eas ædes guibus de agitur, nec vi, nec clam, nec precario alter ab altero possidetis, quo minus ita possideatis, vim fieri veto."* Dig. xliii. 3. 7.§1. " Prætor ait utrubi hic homo quo de agitur majore parte hujusce anni fuit, quo minus is eum ducat, vim fieri veto. Gaius, iv. 148—152. Dig. 1. 16. 156. Majore parte anni possedisse quis in-telligitur etiam si duobus mensibus possederit, si modo adversarius ejus aut paucioribus diebus aut nullis possederit." Paulus, v. 6. 1. " Retinendæ possessionis gratia comparata sunt interdicta, per quæ eam possessionem quam jam habemus, retinere volumus: quale est uti possidetis de rebus soli, et utrubi de re mobili."

est, plus juris habet quam ille qui non pos-sidet."[170] "Separata est causa possessionis et usucapionis; nam vere dicitur quis emisse sed mala fide quemadmodum qui sciens alienam rem emit, pro emtore possidet, licet usu non capiat."

The right of possession, then, is quite distinct from the right of property;[171] either may exist without the other, and each may be at the same time in different people; the *bona fide* purchaser of a horse from a thief was, the moment he acquired possession of the animal, entitled to the rights of its possessor; but the property of the horse was in the rightful owner. "Nihil commune habet proprietas cum possessione." "Nec possessio et proprietas misceri debent."

The peculiar rights which flowed from the mere fact of what the Roman law recognised as legal possession, were the right to the *interdicta* as the protection of such possession. "Formæ actionum quibus prætor aut jubebat aliquid fieri aut fieri prohibebat." These interdicts were called the *interdicta "retinenda aut recuperandœ possessionis causa."*[172] And, secondly, the right of acquiring a title by "*usucapio*" to the property possessed. According to the principles so clearly laid down in the Digest, "Sine possessione usucapio contingere non potest."

A mere act of violence, on the part of the rightful owner, entitled the possessor to these interdicts. But more than this was necessary to ground a title by "*usucapio,*" mere possession was not sufficient. It must be a possession grounded on "*bona fides*" and a "*justa causa,*" and a possession of that kind of property to which the "*usucapio*" was applicable. The origin of this remedy by interdict, may most undoubtedly be traced to the peculiar tenure by which many of the largest estates of the great Roman proprietors were held. The land from which they derived their income was, in reality, the property of the state, "*ager publicus,*" of which they (generally the patricians) were the usufructuaries. The state, meanwhile, was the legal proprietor

---

170 Dig. xli. 4. 2.§1.
171 Gaius, iv. 139
172 Dornat, Loix Civiles, lib. iii. tit. 7.

of these districts; and, if the occupation of those who actually possessed them was encroached upon, or interfered with, by private violence, the holders could not obtain redress by the remedies instituted for the protection of property. Hence, as these tenures were recognised by the state, and were liable to be disputed, it became necessary to introduce, under the name of "*interdicta,*" these possessory remedies. At last they were incorporated with the edict of the prætor, and their application was extended from the "*ager publicus*" to land held by the ordinary tenure, or the property of individuals.

1st. *Interdicta retinendæ possessionis.* These two edicts were called "*Uti possidetis* " and "*Utrubi.*" The first was employed for what was immovable; the latter, for what was movable. Under the old law was another difference, namely, that he prevailed under the "*Uti possidetis,*" who, at the time when application was made to the prætor for the interdict, could show that he possessed the immovable, as the Roman law expressed it, "*nec vi, nec clam, nec precario.*"

Whereas, when application was made for the interdict "*Utrubi,*" he prevailed who could show that, during the greater part of the current year, he had been in possession of the object sought, unexceptionably as concerned his adversary, and he was allowed, in this calculation, to add to the time during which the object had been in his own possession, the time during which it had been in that of him from whom he received it *(accessio temporis).* By the latter Roman law, however, this distinction was abolished, and the two interdicts were put exactly on the same footing,[173] The object of the interdicts was, of course, a recovery of the object, and compensation for the injury inflicted by loss of possession. Both interdicts were what the Roman law called "*duplicia;*" and therefore the plaintiff might be condemned to payment if it were found that the defendant was really the possessor, or that the plaintiff had obtained possession, *vi,* or *clam,* or *precario,* from the defendant. Both must be applied for within a year after the injury for which redress was sought. After that time, they could

[173] Inst. iv. 15. 4.§1.

only be used to recover the advantages which had since accrued to the defendant. "Ex quibus causis annua interdicta sunt, ex his de eo, quod ad eum, cum quo agitur, pervenit, post annum judicium dandum, Sabinus respondit."

2. Interdicta recuperandœ possessionis.[174] These were three:

1. Unde vi; which was only applicable to immovable property, and only in cases where "atrox vis " had been employed.

2. *De clandestina possessione.*

3. *De preeario.*

I cannot help considering the dispute which has been revived, as to whether possession be a right or a fact, as a mere logomachy.[175] Both parties agree that it gives rise to certain legal consequences, and entitles the possessor to certain legal benefits.

---

[174] Dig. xliii. 16. Th. C. iv. 22. Cod. viii. 4. Unde vi. Dig. xliii. 26. Cod. viii. 9. Inst. iv. 15. 6. Cic. pro Tull. 44. pro Cæc. 31. " Ad duas dissimiles res duo disjuncta interdicta sunt." Gains, iv. 154. He calls " vis armata," " vis quotidiana." Savigny, Recht des Bes. 459. " Prætor ait: Unde tu ilium vi dejecisti, aut familia tua dejecit, de eo quieque ille tune ibi habuit, tantummodo intra annum, post annum de eo quod ad eum qui vi dejecit, pervenerit, judicium dabo."

[175] Zeitschrift für geschichtliche Rechtswissenschaft. Rudorff, vol. vii. p. 93. Azo and Accursius began the dispute. It was taken up by Cujacius; and in modern times has been revived by Spangenberg, Zacharia, Lange, Ungeland, Uribaut and Savigny.

CHAP. V. LAW OF PROPERTY

DOMINIUM[176]

IN the oldest times of Roman history one kind of property alone was recognised, which was called, first, "*mancipium,*" afterwards "*dominium ex jure Quiritium.*"

Afterwards there arose another kind of property which was recognised by the law, and of which the owner was described by the phrase "*in bonis rem habere.*"[177] This latter property was modelled by the prætor's edict, and was protected by him alone, as the "*actiones juris*" only protected the Roman property. To possess the property *"ex jure Quiritium,"* the proprietor must have the "*commercium;*" this belonged, of course, to the Romans, to the "*Latini coloniarii*" as well as to the "*Juniani,*" but not to the "*Peregrini*" The right of property "*in bonis,*" and that *"ex jure Quiritium* "to the same thing, might be in different persons; e. *g.* if the seller of a "*res mancipi*" had omitted any of the requisite ceremonies in the transaction. The latter right, in contradistinction to the former, was called the *"nudum jus Quiritium."*[178] This division continued till the time of Justinian, who abolished it with all its consequences.

---

[176] Puchta, Instit. vol. ii.§233. Schilling, Römische Rechtsgeschichte, ii.§146, seq. Zeitschrift, für *G.* R. 8. Mayer " Duplex Dominium." Tigerström l. G. Muhlenbruch Doctrina Pandectarum,§245. Mareszoll, Instit.§89.§90. seq. Lerminier, du Droit, 84 Giraud, Histoire du Droit Remain.

[177] Gaius, ii. 14.

[178] Cod. de Nudo Jure Quiritium tollendo, vii. 25 Gaii Inst. Comment, i. 120. "Eo modo et serviles et liberæ personæ; mancipantur; animalia quoque quæ mancipi sunt, quo in numero habentur boves, equi, muli, asini; item prædia tam urbana quam rustica, quæ et ipsa mancipi sunt, qualia sunt Italica, eodem modo solent mancipari." 121. " In eo solo prædiorum mancipatio a ceterorum mancipatione differt, quod personæ serviles et liberæ, item animalia quæ mancipi sunt, nisi in præsentia sint mancipari non possunt, adeo quidem ut eum (qui) mancipio accipit, apprehendere id ipsum quod ei mancipio datur necesse sit; unde etiam mancipatio dicitur, quia mann res capitur. Prædia vero absentia solent mancipari."

The Roman *dominium,* in its narrower and more appropriate signification, answered to our right of property.[179] It expressed the exclusive power of the owner the *dominus legitimus* of the Twelve Tables over what belonged to him, as well as his right to call upon the assistance of the state to uphold him in the exercise of that power, to guarantee its continuance if menaced, and if infringed to punish its violation.[180] The *"dominium ex jure Quiritium"* was the phrase by which the Roman citizens expressed this right; such a property, so long as there were no provincial possessions, might be had in any thing. Its great peculiarity was, that the property,

---

Gains ii. 17. " Item fere omnia quæ incorporalia sunt, nec mancipi sunt, exceptis servitutibus prædiorum rusticorum; ' nam hæ quidem mancipi res' sunt, quamvis sint ex numero rerum incorpora-lium." 29. " Sed jura prædiorum urbanorum in jure tantum cedi possunt; rusticorum vero etiam mancipari possunt."

Whether pearls were " res mancipi" or not, has been the subject of fierce controversy. Those who take the affirmative side, rely on a passage in Pliny, Hist. Nat. lib. ix. c.35.:—" Lolliam Paulinam, quæ fuit Caii principis matrona, ne serio quidem aut solemni cærimoniarum aliquo apparatu sed me-diocrium etiam sponsalinm cœna, vidi smaragdis margaritisque opertam, alterno textu fulgentibus, toto capite, crinibus, spira auribus, collo, monilibus, digitisque; quæ summa quadringenties HS. colligebat: ipsa confestim parata mancupationem tabulis probare. Nec dona prodigi principis fuerant, sed avitæ opes, provinciarum scilicet spoliis partæ."..." Et hoc tamen æternæ prope possessionis est: sequitur hæredem, in mancipatum venit, ut prædium aliquod. Conchylia et purpuras omnis hora atterit, quibus eadem mater luxuria paria pæne etiam margaritis pretia fecit."

[179] Varro (De R. R., ii. 10. 4.) enumerates six modes of acquiring dominion: — "In emptionibus dominium legitimum sex fere res perficiunt: si hereditatem j ustam adiit; si ut debuit mancipio ab eo accepit a quo jure civili potuit; aut si is jure cessit qui potuit cedere et id ubi oportuit; aut si usucepit; aut si e præda sub corona emit, tumve cum in bonis sectioneve cujus publice venit. Ulpian (xix.2.):—Singularum rerum nobis dominia adquiruntur mancipatione, traditione, usucapione, in jure cessione, adjudicatione, lege." Gaius, i. 119.:— " Ut mancipatio imaginaria quædam venditio quod et ipsum jus proprium civium Romanorum est," &c.:—" Res mobiles non nisi præsentes tnancipari possunt, et non plures quam quæ manu capi possunt; immobiles autem etiam plures simul, ut quæ diversis locis sunt mancipari possunt. Ulp. Fr. 19.§6. " Nexum est, ut ait Gallus quodcunque per æs et libram geritur, idque necti dieitur quo in genere sunt testamenti factio, nexi datio, nexi liberatio."—*Festus,* v. *Nexum.* "Traditio propria est alienatio rerum, pec mancipi harum rerum dominia ipsa traditione ad-prehendimus, silicet si ex justa causa tradita sint nobis." — Ulp. Fr. xvii. 9. " In jure cessio hoc modo fit, apud magistratum populi Romani.... is cui in jure ceditur rem tenens ita dicit," &c.— Gaius, ii.§24. "Lege nobis adquiritur velut caducum, vel ereptitium ex lege Papia Poppæa; item legatum ex lege XII Tabularum, sive mancipi res sint, sive nec mancipi." — Ulp. Cod. 17.

[180] The phrase " *in bonis,"* to denote property not *"ex jure Quiritium"* is not used before the time of the emperors. Cicero ad Fam. xiii. 30. uses the word in a different sense. Hugo, torn. i. p. 122.

"ex jure Quiritium," might be reclaimed by the real owner, even from a *bonâ fide* possessor, and without any offer of compensation.[181] The application of this doctrine was extremely important with regard to slaves, for unless the forms required to transfer such property were complied with, the property in the slave long after his imperfect liberation continued in the master. It is, therefore, as Hugo has remarked in the law of slavery, that the most ancient, as well as the most recent traces of this doctrine are to be met with. The first great division of this property was into *"res mancipi "* and *"non mancipi;"* to the first class belonged, among other things, *"prœdia in Italico solo," "jura prœdiorum rusticorum," "jus viœ, itineris, actus aquœductus," "quadrupedes qua collo dorsove domantur," "sevvi,"* everthing else fell under the head of *nec mancipi.*

The *"res mancipi"*[182] could not be alienated by the *traditio,* and thus become the property *ex jure Quiritium* of another. To make them so the *"injure cessio,"* or the *"mancipatio per œs et libram,"* was requisite. The *"traditio"* made the thing delivered *"in bonis"* of the person to whom it was given. Every thing *"nec mancipi"* might be alienated by tradition only; it might also be alienated by the *in jure cessio,* but not by the *mancipatio;* that was confined to the *res mancipi* alone.

Mancipatio habet locum inter cives Romanes eosque peregrinos quibus commercium datum est.[183]

The form of the *"mancipatio"* bears, traces of the age when it was first employed — when coined money was

---

[181] See the Code de Nudo Jure Quiritium tollendo, vii. 25. Varro only uses the words " dominus legitimus" with reference to a slave. Hugo, torn. i. p.122.

[182] " Mancipium," like " obligatio," as Hugo observes, is employed to denote the fact and its consequences, that is the incorporeal right arising from it; so Lucretius says of life, that " mancipio nulli datur, omnibus usu." Seneca, in the spirit of the same philosophy, " Fortuna nihil dat mancipio," Ep. 72., and the corporeal object, so Horace, " Mancipiis locuples eget æris Cappadocum rex." Horace also alludes to this mode of acquiring property, Ep. ii. 2. " Si proprium est quod quis librâ mercatus et ære est." " Quædam si credis consultis, mancipat usus." Curio, Ep. Fam. 729. alludes to the " fructus" as opposed to the "mancipium," the *χρησις* and the κτησις.

[183] Ulp.c.ix.4

unknown. Five Roman citizens were convened, and the sixth ("*libri-pens*") held the balance. The sum paid was represented, at first, by a lump of brass, afterwards by an " *as,"* and the purchaser received the things sold, which, if a movable, was actually produced. The old word by which this proceeding was described is "*mancipium,"* and as such it is mentioned in the Twelve Tables. Another expression for the same proceeding, which also occurs in the Twelve Tables, is "*nexum,"* or *nexus.* The buyer took hold of the object of his purchase, *i. e.* when it was a movable, and uttered an appointed form of words.[184] He then struck the balance with the money, and gave it to the seller as the price. The conditions of the bargain *(lex mancipii)* were at the same time pronounced by the interested parties, and the Twelve Tables made them binding. Cicero de Oratore[185] alludes to this "*mancipii lex:"*— "Quum enim Marius Gratidianus ædes Auratæ vendidisset, neque servire quamdam earum ædium partem in mancipii lego dixisset; defendebamus quidquid fuisset incommodi in mancipio, id si venditor ecisset neque declarasset, præstare debere."

Cicero tells us, also, that a breach of these conditions was punished by a double penalty:— "Quum ex XII Tabulis satis esset ea præstari, quæ essent lingua nuncupata, quæ qui infitiatus esset, dupli pœnam subiret."[186]

The "*traditio*" was not necessarily connected with the *mancipatio,* where immovable property was concerned; but it was mentioned in cases where the object was to procure immediate possession.[187]

In the time of Diocletian, and even in the regulations of Constantine, we find "*mancipatio"* mentioned; but it had fallen into disuse, especially in the Eastern empire, where, as it was necessary to conduct the proceedings in the Latin tongue, its application became frequently difficult, and sometimes impossible.

---

[184] Gaius, i. 119.
[185] Lib. i. 3. 9.
[186] De Off. iii. 16.
[187] Gaius, ii. 204.

The "*injure cessio*" consisted in the surrender of property before an authorised magistrate. It required three persons: the "*injure cedens,*" that is, the proprietor; the "*vindicans,*" that is, the person who was to acquire the property; and the "*addicens,*" that is, the magistrate who pronounced the law; in Rome, the prætor. This mode of alienation, like the *mancipatio,* was instituted in the Twelve Tables, and extended to "*res mancipi*" as well as "*nec mancipi.*" The person to whom the property was to be transferred *seized* it, and uttered a certain form of words.[188] The magistrate asked the proprietor if he wished to vindicate; and if the latter was silent, or declined, the magistrate adjudged the property to the other.

Together with the "*mancipatio,*" and the "*in jure cessio,*" the "*usucapio*" is mentioned in the Twelve Tables, under the title "*usus auctoritas,*" as a mode of alienation. This "*usucapio*" supposes the person who was to profit by it already *"bona fide "* in possession of the object which he sought to make his own, but not, strictly speaking, its proprietor, on account of some legal defect, *"ex jure Quiritium."* If, for instance, a "*res mancipi*" had been transferred by the "*traditio*" only, but with the full consent of the original owner, the law allowed the purchaser, by the aid of this principle, after one year, if it was a movable, after two years, if it was a "*fundus,*" to possess it as his own "*ex jure Quiritium.*"[189]

Many things were, by the law of the Twelve Tables, expressly excluded from the operation of this law of "*usucapio,*" *e. g.* the *"forum"* of a grave, the place where a dead body was burnt, five feet round the boundaries of estates[190],

---

[188] Gaius, ii. 24.

[189] Goesius, Scriptores Rei Agr. p. 224. Dirksen über die gesetzliche Einschrunkangen des Eigen-thums nach R. R. Zeitschrift, sup. cit. vol. ii. p.413. Dionys. Hal.ii.7. *Festus* v. *Termino.*

[190] Cicero de Legibus, i. 18.:— " Ex hac autem non rerum sed verborum discordia, controversia nata est de finibus; in qua, quoniam usucapionem Duodecim Tabulæ intra quinque pedes esse no-luerunt, depasci vctcrem possessionem academiæ ab hoc acuto homine non sinemus: nec Mamilia lege singuli, sed ex xii. tres arbitri fines regemus. *Quinfus.* Quamnam igitur sententiam dicimus? *Marcus.* Require placere terminos, quos. Socrates pepigerit iisque parere. *Quintus.* Præclare, frater, jam nunc a te verba usurpantur civilis juris et legum, quo de genere expecto

things stolen, the "*res mancipi*" of a woman under the *tutela* of an *agnatus,* unless parted with by her, under the sanction of her guardian.

This principle of "*usucapio*" was adopted, enlarged, and refined by the prætor, and became a most valuable and characteristic part of the Roman law.

Those who had been long in possession of any property, might protect themselves by an *exceptio* against its former owners, and even against mortgage creditors. To the "*exceptio*" was added a right of action, as we learn from the Code (vii.39.8): — "Hoc enim et veteres leges si quis eas recte inspexerit, sanciebat." To be entitled to this, a "*justum initium*" of the title was requisite, and its uninterrupted continuance for a certain time. This "*longum tempus*" embraced, according to the law of the emperors, and without difference between movable and immovable property, a period of ten years, "*inter præsentes,*" and of twenty years "*inter absentes.*" To these was added by the Christian emperors a third species of "*usucapio,*" "*præscriptio triginta,* or *quadraginta annorum,*" which, before Justinian's time, only gave the possessor an "*exceptio;*" Justinian added to it a right of action for the *bona fide* possessor. But the changes he made in this part of the law, were still greater and more important. He made the "*usucapio*" applicable to the provinces, ordaining that for movables it should apply in three years, and for immoveables in two-and-twenty; and by this law and two other edicts, one of which put an end to the distinction between property "*in bonis*" and that "*ex jure Quiritium,*" and the other of which joined the effect of the "*vindicatio*" to the "*longi temporis præscriptio,*" the distinction between "*usucapio*" and "*longi temporis præscriptio,*" *so* far as immovable property was concerned, was substantially effaced.

Together with *mancipatio,* the *in jure capio,* and the "*usucapio,*" there existed many other means of acquiring property according to the civil law, as well in case of singular

---

disputationem tuam; nam ista quidem magna dijudicatio est, ut ex te ipso sæpe cognovi."

objects, as "*per universitatem.*" Besides those peculiar to the Roman law, there were others which, like the transmission of property by delivery, rested on natural right, and were engrafted in Roman jurisprudence. Such was the occupation of wild animals (the attempt to enforce which has been so savagely and is still so unjustly punished by our and other Gothic institutions), and spoil taken from the enemies in battle, so "*id quod per alluvionem nobis adjicitur,*" and others which are without any particular interest. With the increased civility of Borne the forms of the "*mancipatio*" became more irksome, and the property "*in bonis*" more important. As a protection for this last class of proprietors, the prætor Publicius invented a formula which anticipated by a fiction the benefit of the "*usucapio,*" and enabled the owner to vindicate his property against a wrong doer as effectually as if the *"jus Quiritium*" had belonged to him. "Datur hæc actio a qui ex justa causa traditam sibi rem nondum usucepit, eamque amissa possessione petit, nam quia non potest eam ex jure Quiritium suam esse intendere fingitur rem usucepisse"[191]; and so the natural, or, as he may be called, the equitable owner was protected against the Quiritarian, by an "*exceptio doli,*" or an "*exceptio rei venditce et traditœ.*"

"Si quis rem meam mandatu meo vendiderit, vindicanti mihi rem venditam nocebit hæc exceptio."

The prætorian edict created many kinds of property unknown to the early Roman law.[192] Many of its clauses were framed especially for the protection of the owner, and fictions were moulded to justify the use of particular remedies in their behalf: so Gaius (iii. 32.) tells us:—" Quos autem prætor vocat ad hereditatem heredes ipso jure fiunt, nam prætor heredes facere non potest." Again, new questions of law arose with reference to the *peregrini* in the Roman kingdom. They were

---

[191] Gaius, iv. 36.

[192] Dig. xliv. 4.4.§32.:—" Si a Titio fundum emeris, qui Sempronii erat, isque tibi traditus fuerit pretio soluto; deinde Titius Sempronio heres extiterit, et eundem fnndum Mavio vendiderit et tradi-derit: Julianus ait, æquius esse prætorem te tueri; quia et si ipse Titius fundum a te peteret, excep-tione in factum comparata, vel doli, mali summo veretur; et si ipse cum possideret et publiciana peteres, adversus excipientem, si non suus esset, replicatione utereris; ac per hoc intelligeret cum fundum rursum vendidisse, quern in bonis non haberet."

incapable of Roman property; but a certain property was, as has been said, nevertheless ascribed to them. A *peregrinus* might acquire a property by tradition, or any other legal means, in Rome or Italy. Here the prætor interfered (probably by a fiction) for his assistance, or he might possess movables in a province. Here he was protected by the provincial edict. Or, thirdly, it was the theory of the law that the soil of the provinces belonged to the Roman people; but practically the right of the proprietor was upheld, and the terms "*dominium,*" "*proprietas,*" and "*vindicatio*" were applied to it. After the edict of Caracalla[193], who gave the rights of citizens, for purposes of fiscal extortion, to all the inhabitants of the Roman empire, the two first cases we have been considering became comparatively rare; but the peculiarities arising from the rights of landed proprietors still continued to exist. Justinian put an end to them by the laws which have been mentioned; his laws abolished the distinction between the *"jus Quiritium*" and that "*in bonis.*" The importance also ceased of the "*mancipatio*" and the "*in jure cessio,*" which were replaced by the "*traditio;*" and as the "*vindicatio*" could be employed by means of the *"formula petitoria,"* the "*publiciana fictio*" became useless. Of course, in such a state of things, the "*exceptiones,*" which were invented to protect the equitable proprietor, were no longer of any consequence.

Another element of the law of acquiring property deserves some notice. Under the old system it was a principle that property could not be acquired by one person through another not within his power: "Ex his apparet per liberos

---

[193] Sueton. Calig. 41.: — " Vectigalia nova atque inaudita, primum per publicanos deinde, quia lucrum exuberabat, per centuriones tribunosque prætorianos exercuit: nullo rerum aut hominum genere omisso, cui non tributi aliquid imponeret. Pro eduliis, quæ tota urbe venirent, certum statutumque exigebatur: pro litibus atque judiciis ubicumque conceptis, quadragesima summæ de qua litigaretur; nec sine pœna, si quis composuisse vel donasse negotium convinceretur: ex gerulorum diurnis quæstibus pars octava; ex capturis prostitutarum, quantum quæque uno concubitu mereret, additumque ad caput legis, ut tenerentur publico, et quæ meretricitum, et qui lenocinium fecissent; nec non et matrimonia obnoxia essent Ejusmodi vectigalibus, indictis neque propositis quum per ignorantiam scripturæ multa commissa fierent, tandem flagitante populo, proposuit quidem legem, sed et minutissimis litteris, et angustissimo loco, uti ne cui describere liceret."

homines quos neque juri nostro subjectos habemus.... item per alienos servos... nequs justam possessionem nulla ex causa nobis acquiri posse." Hence arose a variety of rules as to the slaves who were the property of different owners. The new law allowed a free person, if employed as the agent of another, to represent him, and, as a consequence, to acquire property for him:— "Procurator si quidem mandante domino rem emerit, protinus illi acquirit possessionem."[194] With regard to the means by which property may be lost, there is one which, on account of its connection with the doctrine of *postliminium,* deserves attention. If property was taken by an enemy and afterwards returned to the Roman, the right of the first proprietor revived; but if the property had been ransomed by another, not until the price had been repaid.[195] "Si quis servum captum ab hostibus redemit, protinus est redimentis: quamvis scientis alienum fuisse, sed oblato ei pretio quod dedit postliminio redisse aut receptus esse servus credetur."

Property is the creature of positive law, and is therefore subject to any modification that society may impose. The question is, what regulations contribute most to the welfare of the community, and this is the sole test by which the laws concerning it must be tried. To talk of any abstract right that exists independently of this consideration, will appear ridiculous to any one who considers that the right of property is founded on the good of society alone, and that (except during the prevalence of that shocking combination of cruelty, superstition, and absurdity, which is known by the name of the feudal system, when nations were divided between a few tyrants and herds of slaves) those rights have never been the same in any two civilised nations. No stronger proof that they are of a secondary nature can be imagined. This, however, is not the view of them which is taken in the infancy of society. Much reflection and long experience is requisite to teach mankind that property exists only for the sake of society, and that its enjoyment must be authorised by the public interest. The laws of all primitive and isolated nations punish any violation

---

[194] Inst. ii. 9. 5.; Cod. vii. 32.1.
[195] Dig. xlix. 15. 12.§7.

of property with the utmost severity. The English law, till within a very few years, was modelled on that of Draco; and the right of the proprietor to dispose as he pleases of what belongs to him, is looked upon as absolute. Such was, for many centuries, the spirit of the Roman law. Every proprietor might raise his walls as high as he pleased, though he deprived his neighbour of light, and he might drain for his own purposes the spring that irrigated his neighbour's field.[196]

The limitations imposed upon this right before the time of the emperors, arose from religious feeling or absolute necessity. Such were the five feet of the *finis,* which have been already mentioned[197]*;* and the law which obliged the proprietor to bury a corpse thrown upon his field,[198] But the first serious interference with the exercise of the proprietor's discretion is the law of the "*fundus dotalis,*" of which the "*Lex Julia de adulteriis,*" intended to check the frequency of divorce, forbade the alienation. Tacitus tells us, also, that Nero, after the conflagration of Rome, forbade the erection of party walls,[199] Augustus assigned seventy, Trajan sixty, feet as the greatest height of buildings[200]; and the neighbour acquired a right of preventing any change that might obstruct his established enjoyment. Suet. Octav. 89. He who allowed his buildings to remain in a dilapidated condition, could be called upon by his neighbour to give security against the anticipated evil *(cautio damni infecti)*; and if he refused, the prætor gave the plaintiff possession of the building[201]: and he was bound to give the same security who threatened to undermine, by digging on his own estate, the buildings of his neighbour.[202] A still more direct

---

[196] Cod. de *Æd.* priv., viii. 16. 12.§4.

[197] Dig. de damn. infect. Lex, 24.; Lex 26. de aqua et aquæ pi. 1.§12. D. ne quid in loco publ. Lex. 2.§13.; Id. 21.

[198] Intra quinque pedes æterna auctoritas esto; so the Actio de tigno juccto.

[199] Dig. ii.§§2. 7. de Religios. 43. Cod.

[200] Annal. xv. 43. Communio Parietum.

[201] Dig. xxxix.§2.

[202] Dig. xxxix. 2. 24.§12.

interference with the proprietor, however, was the law by which the proprietor of land containing minerals might be compelled to allow mines to be dug for them[203], on receiving security for the tenth part of their produce.[204]

CHAP. VI.
LAW OF CONTRACTS

OBLIGATIO[205]

OBLIGATIO in the Roman law denoted that legal tie which enforced from one person the discharge of a certain duty towards another.

"Obligatio est juris vinculum quo necessitate astringimur solvendæ alicujus rei, secundum nostræ civitatis jura."

The essence of the obligation was — that, of the persons between whom it existed, one was bound to give something, or to do some action, or to abstain from a certain action.

"Obligationum substantia non in eo consistit ut aliquod corpus nostrum aut servitutem nostram faciat, sed ut alium nobis obstringat ad dandum aliquid vel faciendum vel præstandum."

That the first class of legal obligations rested on the strict *"jus civile,"* corresponds exactly with the idea of the Roman

---

203 The instances of railroads and canals will, of course, occur to every reader. Let us hope, for the sake of national honour, that the present House of Commons, if called upon to exercise its authority in such matters, will display more good sense and impartiality than its. predecessor.

204 Cod. de Metall.(xi.6.)iii6.

205 Savigny, Geschichte des h. R. R., vol. iii. 300. v. 482. R. R. vol. iii. Hugo, Histoire du Toullier, Droit Civil Francais, vol. vi. Walther, Gesch. des R. R., vol. ii. Marezoll, Inst. Schilling, Ges. Des R. R. Vol. Iii. Hugo, Histoire du droit Romain, vol. i. Gaius. iii.§85. Ipst. iii.§13. Dig. 44.§7. Cod. iv.§10. ii.§14.

law, which is suggested by an attentive examination of its history. From such an obligation arose, in the strict sense of the word, an "*actio;*" and accordingly we find that, at first, the "*obligationes et actiones*" are reciprocal — that an "*obligatio*" confers an "*actio,*" and every "*actio*" supposes an "*obligatio.*" In the course of time, however, another class of "obligations," dependent on equitable principles, was recognised — "*jus naturale et gentium.*" These, in contradistinction to the "*civiles,*" were called "*naturales,*" They differed from the first class of obligations in the cause from which they arose, and especially in giving the creditor no right of action.[206] But they gave him an "*exceptio.*" He might keep the property of his debtor, which had come into his hands, and place his defence on the "*naturalis obligatio.*" The "*naturalis obligatio,*" no less than the "*civilis,*" might be the origin of the "*depositum,*" "*pignus,*" "*novatto,*" and so forth. Moreover, the narrow list of "*civiles obligationes*" was enlarged; and many "*obligationes,*" which had been formerly considered merely as belonging to the class of "*naturales,*" were incorporated with the others, and conferred a right of action. This was accomplished by the interference of the prætor, and hence the division of the "*obligationes*" into the "*civiles* and *honoraria.*" At the same time, and by the same means, many of the "*obligationes civiles*" were neutralised by the prætor's "*erceptio,*" which sometimes abrogated them altogether, and sometimes reduced them to the level of a "*naturalis obligatio.*"

Two different sources from which obligations may arise, occur to the mind at once. An obligation may arise from an engagement entered into by the free will of the debtor, and assented to by the creditor; or an obligation may arise against the will of the debtor, in consequence of his illegal act, by which he has inflicted upon another an injury that entitles the party aggrieved to compensation.

---

[206] " Nuda pactio obligationem non parit, sed parit exceptionem. Quinimo interdum format ipsam actionem, ut in bonæ; fidei judiciis. Solemus enim dicere, pacta conventa inesse bonæ fidei judiciis. Sed hoc sic accipiendum est, ut, siquidem ex continenti pacta subsecuta sunt, etiam ex parte actoris insint. Ex intervallo non inerunt, nec valebunt, si agat; ne ex pacto actio nascatur." Dig. ii. 14, de Pactis.

When the Roman system of obligations was complete, they endeavoured to adjust each obligation to its origin. For this purpose they divided obligations into those which arise from the consent of the parties concerned, which they called "*ex consensu,*" and into those which arise without their consent, which they called "*ex delicto.*" To these divisions they added a third, which they called "*ex variis causarum figuris.*" This last class was again divided into two, which they called "*quasi ex contractu,*" and "*quasi ex delicto*". The "*obligationes,*" which arise "*ex contractu*" and "*ex delicto,*" are obvious. Of those which arise, "*quasi ex contractu*" and "*quasi ex delicto,*" Justinian has left the following account: —

QUASI CONTRACTU

"Igitur cum quis absentis negotia gesserit, ultro citroque inter eos nascuntur actiones, quæ appellantur negotiorum gestorum; sed domino quidem rei gestæ adversus eum qui gessit, directa competit actio, negotiorum autem gestori contraria. Quas ex nullo contractu proprie nasci, manifestum est; quippe ita nascuntur istæ actiones, si sine mandate quisque alienis negotiis gerendis se obtulerit, ex qua causa hi, quorum negotia gesta fuerint, etiam ignorantes obligantur. Idque utilitatis causa receptum est, ne absentium, qui subita festinatione coacti, nulli demandata negotiorum suorum administratione, peregre profecti essent desererentur negotia, quæ sane nemo curaturus esset, si de eo, quod quis impendisset, nullam habiturus esset actionem, Sicut autem is, qui utiliter gesserit negotia, habet obligatum dominum negotiorum, ita et contra iste tenetur, ut administrationis rationem reddat; quo casu ad exactissimam quisque diligentiam compellitur reddere rationem; nec sufficit talem diligentiam adhibuisse, qualem suis rebus adhibere solet, si modo alius diligentior commodius administraturus esset negotia.

"Tutores quoque, qui tutelæ judicio tenentur, non proprie ex contractu obligati intelliguntur (nullum enim negotium inter tutorem et pupillum contrahitur); sed, quia sane non ex maleficio tenentur, quasi ex contractu teneri videntur.

"Item si inter aliquos communis sit res sine societate, veluti quod pariter eis legata donatave esset, et alter eorum alteri ideo teneatur communi dividundo judicio, quod solus fructus ex ea re perceperit, aut quod socius ejus in eam rem necessarias impensas fecerit: non intelligitur proprie ex contractu obligatus esse, quippe nihil inter se contraxerunt; sed, quia ex maleficio non tenetur, quasi ex contractu teneri videtur. Idem juris est de eo, qui coheredi suo familias erciscundæ judicio ex his causis obligatus est.

"Heres quoque legatorum nomine non proprie ex contractu obligatus intelligitur. Neque enim cum herede, neque cum defuncto ullum negotium legatarius gessisse proprie dici potest. Et tamen, quia ex maleficio non est obligatus heres, quasi ex contractu debere intelligitur.

"Item is, cui quis per errorem non debitum solvit, quasi ex contractu debere videtur. Adeo enim non intelligitur proprie ex contractu obligatus, ut, si certiorem rationem sequamur, magis (ut supra diximus) ex distractu, quam ex contractu possit dici obligatus esse. Nam qui solvendi animo pecuniam dat, in hac dare videtur ut distrahat potius negotium quam contrahat. Sed tamen perinde is qui accepit, obligatur, ac si mutuum illi daretur, et ideo condictione tenetur."[207]

---

[207] Just. Inst.§§1—6. i. iii. Qy. de Obligat. quasi ex Contractu. Just. Inst. iii. iv.§3. Cod. De Neg. Gestis, ii. 19.§20. Dig. iii. v.§41.

"Certains engagemens se forment sans qu'il intervienne aucune convention ni de la part de celui qui s'oblige, ni de la part de celui envers lequel il est obligé."—Code Civil, tit. iv. Liv. iii.§1370.

"Les uns résultent de l'autorité seule de la loi, les autres naissent d'un fait personnel à celui qui se trouve obligé.... Les engagémens qui naissent d'un fait personnel à celui qui se trouve obligé, résultent ou des quasi contrats, ou des délits ou quasi délits." —§§1371,1372, 1373,1374,1375.

"Tout fait quelconque de l'homme qui cause à autrui un dommage oblige celui par la faute duquel il est arrivé à le réparer "—§1382.

"Chacun est responsable du dommage qu'il a causé non seulement par son fait mais encore par son imprudence ou par sa negligence." —§1383. Can any Englishman compare this simple and lucid statement of *principles* with the decisions in *Meeson* and *Wellsby*, 15vols., and the gibberish of our acts of parliament, without feeling his cheek glow with blushes? "Quousque tandem *σμικρολογια* abutere patientiâ nostrâ? When shall we be persuaded that ermine and black letter, and the royal

QUASI EX DELICTO

"Si judex litem suam fecerit, non proprie ex maleficio obligatus videtur. Sed, quia neque ex contractu obligatus est, et utique peccasse aliquid intelligitur, licet per imprudentiam, ideo videtur quasi ex maleficio teneri, et in quantum de ea re æquum religioni judicantis videbitur, pænam sustinebit.

"Item is, ex cujus cœnaculo, vel proprio ipsius vel conducto, vel in quo gratis habitabat, dejectum effusumque aliquid est, ita, ut alicui noceretur, quasi ex maleficio obligatus

---

arms, and criers, and sheriff's officers (even in the most gorgeous liveries), and assize sermons, do not make the law, and that it must be looked for " somewhere else "? See Motifs du Code Civil, vol. i. p. 426. vol. ii. p. 507. &c. Ed. Didot, 1838.

There can be two sources only of moral obligation; the command of God and the law of man. The law of the strongest is an absurdity; it is that by which the robber with a pistol at your throat, is entitled to your money. No law that man could make could justify the giving of Norway to Sweden, or the power of Austria over Lombardy, or that of Russia over Poland. All the rulers, ministers, and generals in the world could not make the infamous treaty of Vienna binding on the people whom it delivered over like sheep to unmixed despotism, in the name of those who called themselves with such loathsome hypocrisy the liberators of Europe, even though England stooped to be the instrument of these acts which cast the worst usurpations of Napoleon into the shade, and famished a free people into surrender to a foreign yoke. The doctrine so happily applied by De Thou is false: —

"Excidat ille dies ævo, ne postera credant
Sæcula, nos certe taceamus, et obruta multâ
Nocte tegi nostræ patiamur crimina gentis."

Rather should such deeds be blazoned for the warning of posterity.

Where the law enforces obligations like those of the quasi contractus and quasi delicta, to which the parties have not assented, it is by virtue of that higher law according to which the will of every citizen of *a free* state is bound up in that of the community to which he belongs.

Domat, Loix Civiles, "Engagemens qui se forment par les cas fortuits."

Donellus (Comment, de Jure Civili, lib. xv. c. 14.) defines the quasi contractus: — " Factum non turpe quo, aut is qui fecit alteri, aut alter ei, sine consensu obligatur." A definition not unworthy of Papi-nian. So Code, 651. mentions the duties of vicinage.

Toullier, Droit Civil Francais, vol. ii. p. 1. seq.

The principle, on which the doctrine which Justinian has confused rests, is de reg. terris, Dig. L. 206. " Jure naturæ; æquum est neminem cum alterius damno fieri locupletiorem."

Heineccius (Inst. Comm. 966.) grounds it on a presumed consent.

"Si negotia absentis et ignorantis geras, et culpam et dolum præstare debes," Dig. iii. 5. 11., agreeing with the French law. S0, ib. 21.§2., "Si vivo Titio negotia ejus administrare cœpi, intermittere eo mortuo non debeo."

Dig. ix. 3. de his qui effuderint vel dejecerint.

intelligitur. Ideo non proprie ex maleficio obligatus intelligitur, quia plerumque ob alterius culpam tenetur, aut servi aut liberi. Cut similis est is, qui ea parte, qua vulgo iter fieri solet, id positum aut suspensum habet, quod potest, si ceciderit, alicui nocere, quo casu pœna decem aureorum constituta est. De eo vero, quod dejectum effusumve est, dupli, quanti damnum datum sit, constituta est actio.

"Item exercitor navis, aut cauponæ, aut stabuli, de dolo aut furto, quod in nave aut in stabulo factum erit, quasi ex maleficio teneri videtur, si modo ipsius nullum est maleficium, sed alicujus eorum quorum opera navena, aut cauponam, aut stabulum exerceret. Cum enim neque ex contractu sit adversus eum constituta hæc actio, et aliquatenus culpæ reus est, quod opera malorum hominum uteretur, ideo quasi ex maleficio teneri videtur. In his autem casibus in factum actio competit, quæ heredi quidem datur, adversus heredem autem non competit."[208]

"Ex maleficiis servorum, veluti si furtum fecerint, aut bona rapuerint, aut damnum dederint, aut injuriam commiserint, noxales actiones proditæ sunt, quibus domino damnato permittitur, aut litis æstimationem sufferre, aut hominem noxæ dedere. Noxa autem est corpus quod nocuit, id est, servus; noxia ipsum maleficium, veluti furtum, damnum, rapina, injuria.

"Animalium nomine quæ ratione carent, si quidem lascivia, aut fervore, aut feritate pauperiem fecerint, noxalis actio lege Duodecim Tabularum prodita est; quæ animalia, si noxæ dedantur, proficiunt reo ad liberationem, quia ita lex Duodecim Tabularum scripta est; puta, si equus calcitrosus calce percusserit, aut bos cornu petere solitus petierit. Hæc autem actio in his quæ contra naturam moventur, locum habet. Ceterum, si genital is sit feritas, cessat actio. "[209]

In every obligation we find two parties — one who owes, and another to whom something is due. But, though this

[208] Inst.§§3. 1. iv., 5. de obligat. quæ quasi ex delicto nasc.

[209] Pr. i. iv. 9., si quadrupes pauperiem fecisse dicetur.

definition includes the greater portion of obligations, there are others which form an exception to it in one sense; as, instead of one debtor and one creditor, they comprise several. These are the "*obligatio plurium pro rata*" In such cases, many creditors are entitled to demand, and many debtors are responsible for, the fulfilment of particular contracts. Sometimes every creditor may claim the whole, sometimes every debtor is liable for the whole. If, however, any creditor has received, or any debtor has paid, the entire debt, the other debtors are discharged. "*Uno solvente reliqui liberantur.*" Such *obligationes* are termed" *correales;* "such creditors, "*correi,*" "*plures rei stipulandi*" (credendi); such debtors, "*correi,*" "*plures rei promittendi.*"

The rigour of these correal obligations was mitigated by Adrian, who introduced or extended the "*beneficium divisionis.*"

Justinian, by the 99 Novell, c. 1., which, by the way, strongly marks the decrepitude of jurisprudence, provides, that although several debtors had, in express terms, made themselves responsible for each other, each should, nevertheless, be bound only for that portion of the debt which he had himself contracted.[210]

The word contract is not to be found in the Twelve Tables.

The Roman lawyers, after this period, annexed a sense to it synonymous with that of "*obligatio*" and "*vinculum,*" as well as that of "*nexus;*" and they employ it only to denote those transactions, the paramount object of which is the existence of a compact.

They divided contracts into two kinds —"*pacta*" and "*conventa.*" The "*pacta*" were mere agreements between the parties, without the conditions required by law to confer the right of action.

---

[210] 1. "Qui stipulatur, reus stipulandi dicitur; qui promittit, reus promittendi habetur."
2. "Cum duo eandem pecuniam aut promiserunt, aut stipulati sunt, ipso jure et singulis in solidum debetur, et singuli debent; ideoque petitione et acceptilatione unius tota solvitur obligatio." — Dig. i. ii. 45.2.

The conditions which the early Roman law required, in order to found an action, were:—

First, in contracts (re) the delivery of the thing, or the performance of the act, which were the objects of the convention. This delivery of the thing, and this performance of the act, were what the Roman civilians called the "*causa,*" or, as we should say, the consideration of the contract.

Secondly, They gave an action to the contract *(verbis)* in which certain words were used. This was the "*stipulatio.*"[211] It was nothing more than a question and answer. *Dari spondes? Spondeo.—Dabis? Daho.—Promittis? Promitto.—Fidepromittis? Fidepromitto.—Fidejubes? Fidejubeo.—Facies? Faciam.*

It is the origin of the form now used in baptism. The Romans thought it afforded some security that the agreement was entered into with forethought and deliberation. Where it was not employed, they looked upon the transaction as unsettled; and, unless in some particular cases, refused an action to support it.

The "*stipulatio*" was the most important of all the "*stricti juris actiones:* "it was the only form of contract in the Roman law, which, if employed, gave a right of action to every kind of agreement; and by means of which, be its subject-matter what it might, any covenant might become binding and imperative. In this respect it differed from all other contracts: from the "*emtio venditio,*" "*mandatum,*" &c., which were applicable to a defined and particular object; and from the "*expensilatio,*" which, though its object was indefinite, was, nevertheless, limited to pecuniary transactions, and was inapplicable to cases in which labour, or a specific action, was involved.

---

[211] The civilians were bad etymologists. Festus has given the real derivation of stipulatio. Isidore, like the civilians, derives it from stipula. " Stipem esse nummum signatum, testimonio est et id, quod datur stipendium militi, et quum spondetur pecunia, quod stipulari dicitur." *Festus* v. *Stipem.* So, "soldat," from solidum, in which the troops were paid. Hénault Abrégé Chr. de l'Hist. de France, vol. ii.

Valerius Maximus (2. 8. 2.) has preserved a curious instance of the purposes for which the *stipulatio* was employed. In the A. U. C. 512, the consul Lutatius won a great victory over the Carthaginian fleet, for which a triumph was awarded him. The prætor Valerius asserted that the chief merit of the victory was due to him; and, in order to procure a judicial decision of the fact, he entered with the consul into a *sponsio*[212] *(sponsione lacessere),* which was decided by an ordinary judge.

The convention, neither as yet executed by either of the parties, nor clothed with the formalities of the "*stipulatio,*" was "*pactum nudum;*" that is, a contract which, though it might furnish matter of defence, could not be the ground of an action.

Some of the more necessary proceedings in the intercourse of ordinary life, were soon exempted from these formalities. "Quæ pariunt actiones, in suo nomine non stant, sed transeunt in proprium nomen contractus, ut emptio venditio, locatio conductio, societas, commodatum, depositum, et ceteri similes contractus."[213]

These contracts were called "*consensu.*" To these others were added at a later period, founded on written documents, which Gaius has pointed out to us. These were the contracts "*litteris.*" Hence the enumeration of the civilians, "*aut re contrahitur, aut verbis, litteris, consensu.*"

1. *Re.* The most important of these contracts was the *mutui datio.* It gave rise to an action called *certi condictio* or *mutui datio,* which arose from the loan of silver money; or, as is expressly said in the *Lex de Gallia Cisalpina,* of Roman money, "*pecunia certa credita signata formâ publicâ populi Romani.*"[214]

These contracts, in which the performance by one of the parties of his share of the agreement gave a right of action, were called *contractus innominati;* and were divided into four.[215]

---

[212] Gains, I.§494.
[213] Dig. xxvii. 14. 7. 1.
[214] *S. f.* p. p. R Hugo Civilist. Mag. 2. 447. 484.
[215] Dig. xix. 5.2.

"Aut enim do tibi ut des, aut do ut facias, aut facio ut des, aut facio ut facias,"[216]

2. *Consensu.* This contained the *"emtio venditio," "locatio conductio," "societas," "mandatum;"* in all of which the consent of the parties alone was necessary. Sufficit eos qui negotium gerunt, consensisse.[217]

3. Litteris.[218] The "nomina transcriptitia," and the obligations "chirographis et syngraphis, id est, si quis debere se aut *daturum se scribat, ita scilicet, si eo nomine stipulatio non fiat"*[219]

4. *Verbis.* The *stipulatio* we have already considered. The Emperor Leo abolished all the solemnities of the *stipulatio,* and provided that a mere question and answer should be sufficient,[220] To this was added, in later times, the promise of a dowry.[221] And the *receptum* of an *argentarius,* and of the *nautæ, caupones, stabularii.*[222]

As exceptions to the general rule that the *pacta,* unless clothed with the *stipulatio,* were not actionable, may be

---

[216] Among the consensual contracts was the commodatum, in which there might be occasion to consider the dolus, culpa, diligentia, custodia. This contract, besides an actio directa, was the basis of an actio contraria. Besides these were the depositum and the pignus.

Under this head also may be ranked a contract not unlike the one on which so much of modern commerce depends. Dig. xix. 5.5.§4. Nam si pacti sumus, ut tu a meo debitore Carthagine exigas, ego a tuo Romae... in priore specie mandatum quodammodo intervenisse videtur, sine quo exigi pecunia alieno nomine lion potest."

"Quæ (scil. juris gentium conventiones) pariunt actiones, in suo nomine non stant, sed transeunt ill proprium nomen contractus, ut emtio venditio, locatio conductio, societas, commodatum, depositum, et ceteri similes contractus."

[217] Gaius, iii.§136.

[218] " Olim scriptura fiobat obligatio, quæ nominibus fieri dicebatur quæ nomina hodie non sunt in usu.—Just. Inst. i. iii. 21. de literarum obligationibus."

[219] Gaius, iii.§§128. 134. These were established by the books which, in the time of the republic, were kept by every citizen who stood in need of such evidence. One, the book in which every thing was written indiscriminately, "adversaria;" the other, the book into which the contents of the former were methodically transcribed, " Codex," or " tabulæ expensi et accepti." — Gaius, iii. 128. Seneca, ii. 23. De ben. iii. 15.

[220] Cod. viii. 38. 10. Inst. iii. 15. 1.

[221] Dig. xxiii. 3. 6.§1. vii.§3.

[222] Dig. iv. 9.

mentioned—the *pignus, de pignoris jure, honoraria nascitur ex pacto actio*[223]; the *de pecunia constituta*[224] these were called "*pacta prœtoria.*"[225] "In re hypothecæ nomine obliligatæ ad rem non pertinet quibus fit verbis sicuti est et in his obligationibus quæ consensu contrahuntur, et ideo et sine scriptura, si convenit ut hypothecæ sit et probare poterit, res obligatæ erunt de quo conveniunt.[226] And the *arbitrii receptum.*[227] "De receptis qui arbitrium receperunt ut sententiam dicerent."[228]

CHAP. VII.
LAW OF INHERITANCE

THE law which regulates the succession of the dead, is one of the most important among those by which the rights of man, as a member of society, are governed; and it is the subject which, perhaps more than any other, illustrates the genius and character of Roman policy and jurisprudence. In its changes and varieties, in its principles no less than in its departure from those principles, the reader will discover, not only much that flings light upon the workings of our common nature, but the conflict of those opposing elements which have already been mentioned as eliciting the most peculiar and instructive lessons of Roman history,[229] The power of disposing of property by will marks a state of society not altogether primitive.[230]

---

[223] Dig. ii. 14. 17. 2.
[224] Dig. xiii. 5. 1. Gaius, iv.§171.
[225] Dig. xx.§1. Cod. viii.§4.
[226] Dig. xxii.§494.
[227] Dig iv.§8.
[228] Cod. ii. 56.
[229] Marezoll. Lehrbuch der Institutionen, p. 422. Puclita, Institutionen, 3 Band, p. 217. Walter, Geschichte des Römischen Rechts, vol. ii. p. 241. Hugo, Histoire du Droit Romain, vol. i p. 150. Gaius, Comment, ii. Jus. ii. 3. Dig. xxix. 2, 3. Tigerström, p. 590. Inn. Gesc. des R. R. Gaius, Erbrecht, vol. ii. Montesquieu, Esprit des Loix, liv. xxvii. Motifs du Code Civil, lib. iii. tit. 1.
[230] "L'ordre de succession ayant été établi en conséquence d'une loi politique, un citoyen ne devoit pas le troubler par une volonté particuliére; c'est-à-dire que, dans

Originally the child or children, or those nearest to him at his death, succeeded to the inheritance of the deceased. The right of succession depends on the principle of consanguinity. It is, says D'Aguesseau, "Une invention du droit des gens, autorisé par le droit civil." Among the German tribes wills were unknown: — "Hæredes sui cuique liberi, et nullum testamentum." In Greece the appointment of an heir was an act of adoption; and in Rome, before the law of the Twelve Tables, the heir was the next of kin in the male line. This, of course, was a patrician principle.[231] The absolute power of bequest, conferred on every citizen by the Twelve Tables, was a concession to the people. The transfer of property by will at this time being an event which, in a small state, might materially affect the well being of the community, was an act of legislation to which publicity was requisite. The oldest forms of wills were those of the "*testamenta*" made "*in procinctu,*" and those made "*in calatis comitiis.*" As the *comitia calata* for ratifying testaments, were held at considerable intervals, the necessity for more frequent opportunities of obtaining that privilege occasioned the "*testamenta in procinctu,*" in which we find the germ of those advantages that were so constantly granted to the soldier by the warlike Romans. The "*testamentum in procinctu*" was the declaration by the soldier of his will before battle, in the presence of the assembled host, which was supposed to represent the state.[232] Cicero[233] has preserved a striking application of this ceremony by a great orator:— "Reprehendebat igitur Galbam Rutilius, quod is C. Sulpicii Galli, propinqui sui, Q. pupillum filium, ipse pæne in humeros suos extulisset, qui patris clarissimi recordatione et memoria fletum populo moveret, et duos filios suos parvos tutelæ populi

---

les premiers temps de Rome, il ne devoit pas être permis de faire un testament." — Esprit, des Loix, liv. xxvii.

" Et chaque testament fut en quelque facon un acte de la puissance legislative."—Ib.

" L'héritier est le successeur universel de tous les biens et tous les droits d'un défunt." — C. Civil, 724, 725. 745. Domat, vol. ii. p. 306.

[231] "Si nullus agnatus sit, eadem lex XII. Tabularum gentiles ad hereditatem vocat." — Gaius. iii. 47.

[232] Liv. x. 29. 26—11. *Æn.* vii, 612. Cicero (De Nat. Deorum, ii.§3) says that it had ceased in his time, nulli viri vocantur ex quo in procinctu testamenta perierunt.

[233] De Oratore, i. 53.

comendasset, ac se, *tanquam in procinctu testamentum faceret, sine libra atque tabulis;* populum Romanum tutorem instituere dixisset illorum orbitati."

The "*testamentum calatis comitiis*" was made by an appeal to the legislative power of the people, assembled in the "*comitia curiata,*" which were held twice a year for this especial purpose, to ratify and attest its contents. The close resemblance between this proceeding and that before the Athenian *φρατρια,* in which the will of a citizen was registered, has been pointed out by Niebuhr, and can hardly fail to attract the reader's consideration. The *curia,* like the *phratria,* was the guardian of the religious rites and traditional worship of the races whom it included. As the *phratria* was intended to perpetuate the names, origin, and worship of the tutelary deities of different families, so the *curies* were the original elements of the Roman state; and each *curia* had its particular rites and usages. It is, therefore, probable that as the Athenian testament was, in fact, the adoption of an heir to carry on the "*sacra*" of the race, and to introduce him to the *phratria,* so the testament of the *calata comitia* was to announce to the *curia* the relation between the testator and his heir, and to point out the person by whom, when the former died, the rites of his family would be celebrated, and his duties as a citizen fulfilled. To illustrate this opinion, I shall quote two passages from the history of Rome at the close of the republic; one from Cicero:

"Quid Crassum inquam illum censes, istius Licinæ filium, Crassi testamento qui fuit adoptatus?[234] The other from Suetonius: "In ima cera C. Octavium etiam in familiam nomenque adoptavit."[235] Again: "Post reditum in urbem a M. Gallio Senatore testamento adoptatus hereditate adita, mox nomine abstinuit, quod Gallius adversarum Augusto partium fuerat."[236]

---

[234] Brutus, 58.

[235] In Julio, cap. 83.

[236] In Tiberio, cap. 6. I think Gaus, Erbrecht, vol. ii., has made out this point most satisfactorily, notwithstanding the objections of Lerminier, Histoire du Droit, p. 866. He has not quoted Horace:—

"Milesne Crassi conjuge Barbarâ

These testamentary adoptions were, no doubt, the remnant of the ancient usage, when the heir was named *calatis comitiis*. The form and publicity became obsolete, but the right and principle were preserved. The only memorials of them which we possess are derived from the latter days of the republic, and the beginning of the empire. It cannot, however, be supposed, with any shadow of probability, that they came first into use during that period.

The next form, which, probably, was introduced by the decemvirs, was the *"testamentum per œs et libram."* The principle of the Twelve Tables was that of implicit obedience to the will of the testator. "Uti legâssit super pecunia tutelave suæ rei, ita jus esto.[237] Uti legâssit suæ rei, ita jus esto.[238] Uti (quisque) legassit suæ rei ita jus esto," is their emphatic language. The state, the ties of blood, the duties of kindred were nothing: the single question was the purpose of the testator. Even in Cicero's time we find the question raised, whether or

---

Turpis maritus vixit; et hostium
Proh *curia!* inversique mores
Consenuit, socerorum in arvis."

Savigny, über die sacra privata der Römer. Zeitschrift f. G. R. W. vol. ii. p. 362. Cicero de Leg. ii. 19,20, 21.

"Publica sacra, quæ publico sumptu pro populo fiunt, quæque pro montibus, pagis, curiis, sacellis. At privata, quæ pro singulis hominibus, familiis, gentibus fiunt."—*Festus* v. *Publica sacra.*

Niebuhr, R. G. p. 229. Th. 1.

Pliny mentions the sacra Serviliæ Familiæ, Hist. Nat. 35. Macrobius the sacra fam. Corneliæ Juliæ, Claudiæ. Sat. i. 16. dul. Gaius, v. 19. Livy, v.§52. an gentilitia, sacra ne in bello quidem intermitti, publica sacra, et Romanes deos etiam in pace deseri placet? But the most remarkable passage is that pro lege Maniliâ, c. 12., ridiculing the special pleaders of his day. Cicero says, — " Mulieres omnes propter infirmitatem consilii majores in tutorum potestate esse voluerunt; hi invenerunt genera tutorum, quæ potestate mulierum continerentur. Sacra interire illi noluerunt; *Jiorum ingenio senes ad coemtiones faciendas, interimendorum sacrorum causa, reperti sunl.* In omni denique jure civili æquitatem reliquerunt, verba ipsa tenuerunt; ut quia in alicujus libris, exempli causa, id nomen invenerant, putarunt, omnes mulieres, quæ coemtionem facerent, Caias vocari." An heiress who wished to set herself free from the hereditary sacra of her estate, agreed " in manum convenire" to some old man, who took her, the estate, and the sacra. Immediately afterwards, by " remancipatio," he separated from her, and gave her back the estate, without the burden of the sacra. Cie. Top.§4., cum mulier viro in manum convenit omnia quæ mulieris fuerunt, viri fiunt, dotis nomine.

The age of the man showed that the proceeding was formal. Gellius, 15. 27.

[237] Ulp.xi. 14. i. 120.Dig.50.16.

[238] Inst. ii. 22.

not a son must be disinherited by name; and, though the making of a will was still called a branch of public law (testamenti factio non privati sed publici juris est)[239], and though the use of the word *quirites* still remained as a vestige of the ancient form of proceeding[240], *it* had, in reality, assumed a character strictly private, and altogether arbitrary. The testator, observing the forms of the "*mancipatio,*" transferred his property, in the presence of five witnesses, to the *"families emptor,"* who was originally his heir. This soon ceased to be necessary; and, instead of transferring the *familia* to him, the testator, in later times, produced a written instrument, which he declared to be his will, and which was signed by the five witnesses. This form, which consisted of two parts—the apparent sale and the *nuncupatio testamenti, i. e.* the declaration of the will—existed under the emperors. Before the time of Cicero, however, another less complicated form of proceeding had become common, which depended on the edict of the prætor. When a written instrument was produced, corroborated by the seals of seven witnesses, in which an heir was mentioned, the prætor gave the heir possession of the testator's property, "*secundum tabulas bonorum possessionem.*" At first the appointment of the heir was the essence of the Roman testament; and it is a conclusive proof of the arbitrary principle, which prevailed at the time of the "*testamentum per œs et libram,* that the words declaring the heir were imperative, "*titius hœres esto;*" and that, if a less peremptory form was employed, the will, even in the

---

239 Dig. xxviii. 1.

240 Five witnesses were requisite besides the " libripens," ail of whom must have the testamenti factio. Gains, ii. 104. "Eaque res ita agitur; qui facit, adhibitis sicut in ceteris mancipationibus V testibus civibus Romanis puberibus et libripende, postquam tabulas testamenti scripserit, mancipat ali-cui dicis gratia familiam suam; in qua re his verbis familiæ emptor utitur; familiam pecuniamque tuam endo mandata tutela custodelaque mea (recipio eaque) quo tu jure testamentum facere possis secun-dum legem publicam hoc sere, et ut quidam adjiciunt, æneaque libra esto mihi empta. Deinde sere percutit libram idque æs dat testatori, velut pretii loci; deinde testator tabulas testamenti tenens ita dicit: hæc ita; ut in his tabulis cerisque scripta sunt, ita do, ita lego, ita tertor, itaque vos, quirites, testi-monium mihi perhibetote. Et hoc dicitur nuncupatio, nuncuparo est enim palam nominare; et sane quas testator specialiter in tabulis testamenti scripserit, ea videtur generali sermone nominare atquo confirmare."

time of Gaius, was invalid; "*illa non est comprobata, titium hœredem esse volo.*"

None but they who could be witnesses to an ordinary act of *mancipatio,* could be witnesses to the *testamentum per œs et libram.*[241] "In testibus autem non debet is esse, qui in potestate est aut familiæ emptoris aut ipsius testatoris, quia propter veteris juris imitationem totum hoc negotium, quod agitur testamenti ordinandi gratia, creditur inter familias emptorem agi et testatorem; quippe olim, ut proxime diximus, is qui familiam testatoris manciple accipiebat, loco heredis erat, itaque reprobatum est in ea re domesticum testimonium.[242] Unde et si is qui in potestate patris est, familiæ emptor adhibitus sit, pater ejus testis esse non potest; at ne is quidem qui in eadem potestate est, velut frater ejus.[243] De libripende eadem quæ et de testibus, dicta esse intelligimus: nam et is testium numero est." The witnesses in this ceremony represented the Roman people in the *comitia calata,* and were addressed by the testator as quirites. The first restraint on the arbitrary principle of the Twelve Tables was an obligation, imposed on the testator, of naming his son whom he meant to disinherit. This doctrine was afterwards extended by the præter, who required that all children, whether "*sui hœredes,*" or emancipated, or posthumous, with the exception of those actually adopted into another family, should be by name either instituted as heirs, or excluded from the inheritance. If they were passed over in silence, he gave to them *"contra tabulas honorum possessionem."* So the birth of a posthumous child, for whom no provision was made, and who was not "*nominatim exhœredatus,*" annulled the testament. There was also a class entitled to be considered "*posthumorum loco.*" So the wife of the husband, "Cui post factum testamentum in manum conveniat, vel quæ in manu fuit, nam eo modo filiæ loco esse incipit, et quasi sua est." The son who, after the first or second emancipation, came back to his father's power, or who unexpectedly returned from captivity, *"jure post liminii,"*

---

[241] Gaius, ii.§105.

[242] Gaius,§106.

[243] Gaius,§107.

cancelled the will which had been made before, any of these occurrences.

During the next period of the Roman law concerning wills, the principle already remarked upon became more prominent and decisive. This was at the close of the republic, when the still repose of despotism had succeeded to the tempests that had so long distracted the community, and the feelings and charities of domestic life exercised in consequence a less divided empire over the business and bosoms of mankind. We find that the centumvirs formally recognised the "*querela inofficiosi testamenti"* In consequence, the will of the testator was set aside if he did not leave to certain near relations, "*liberis et parentibus,"* a portion, *"pars legitima,"* which, by the Falcidian law, was fixed at a fourth of the whole property. The brother and sister to whom a "*turpis persona"* was preferred, might complain on this ground; but the privilege belonged to no more distant relative. Such was the law before the time of Justinian,[244]

The written testament was not alone known to Roman jurisprudence, even for persons not entitled to any special privilege.[245] The prætor gave the *possessio bonorum* to a

[244] By the 115 of Novell., Justinian ordained, not only that the testator must leave the *pars legi-tima* to his ascendants as before, but that he must, except for certain specified causes, institute them as his heirs.

"Sancimus igitur, non licere penitus patri vel matri, avo vel aviæ, proavo vel proaviæ, suum filium, vel filiam, vel ceteros liberos præterire, aut exheredes in suo facere testamento, nec si per quamlibet donationem, vel legatum, vel fideicommissum, vel alium quemcunque modum eis dederit legibus debitam portionem; nisi forte probabuntur ingrati et ipsas nominatim ingratitudinis causas parentes suo inseruerint testamento. *Sed,* quia causas, ex quibus ingrati liberi debeant judicari, in diversis legibus dispersas et non aperte declaratas invenimus,—ideo necessarium esse perspeximus, eas nominatim præsenti lege comprehendere, ut præter ipsas nulli liceat ex alia lege ingratitudinis causas opponere, nisi quæ in hujus constitutionis serie continentur."

"Sancimus, non licere liberis, parentes suos præterire, aut quolibet modo a rebus propriis, in quibus testandi habent licentiam, eos omnino alienare, nisi causas, quas enumeravimus, in suis testa-mentis specialiter enumeraverint."

"Si autem hæc omnia non fuerint observata, nullam vim hujusmodi testamentum, quantum ad institutionem heredum, habere sancimus, sed, rescisso testamento, eis, qui ab intestate ad hereditatem defuncti vocantur, res ejus dari disponimus, legatis videlicet, vel fideicommissis et libertatibus et tutorum dationibus, seu aliis capitulis suam obtinentibus firmitatem." — Justinianus in Nov. 115. cap. 3. et 4.

[245] Dig. 37. 11. 8.§4.

nuncupatory testament attested by seven witnesses, and this continued to be the law; in the time of Valentinian—a testator also might register his will in the public archives of the city, or consign it to the governor, or deposit it with the *curia;* but among all these various exceptions, those in favour of the soldier's will were the most numerous and remarkable. An entirely new form of will, called the *holograph,* was introduced 446 A. D., by Valentinian III.[246] These privileges, which rendered all formal objections unavailing if the will could be ascertained, continued for a year after the soldier's discharge, till they were limited by Justinian to the time of actual service.

TESTAMENTI FACTIO

The *peregrini* could not make a will, as they had not the *commercium;* neither could the "*Latinus Junianus,*" or "*is qui in deditiorum numero est.*" The first, because he was forbidden by an express law; the second, because he belonged to no community[247], "*quoniam nullius certœ civitatis civis esf.*" But the *Latini* had the *testamenti factio.*

All Roman citizens, "*patres familiarum, puberes,*" in full possession of their faculties could make a will. By the fiction of the Cornelian law, the will of a prisoner among enemies was valid, if it was made before his captivity. The *filius familias* could only make a will "*de castrensi et quasi castrensi peculio.*"

The *impubes* could not make a will; and a will made before puberty was invalid, even if the maker died after he had attained that age.

The deaf, the dumb, the *prodigus,* and the *furiosus* could not make a will. The dumb, because he could not utter the *verba nuncupationis;* the deaf, because he could not hear *verba familiœ emptoris.* But a will made by the *furiosus,* before his

[246] Nov. Val. iii. tit. 26. de test. c. 2.
[247] Ulp. Fr. 20.§14.

disorder began, or in a lucid interval, was valid, as was the testament of the prodigal made before he was interdicted.

The loss of the right to make a will, was inflicted as a punishment on those guilty, "*læsœ majestatis,*" on traitors and their sons, on those condemned "*ob carmen famosum,*" on all convicted of a capital offence, on the parties to an incestuous marriage, and, when the church became powerful, on apostates, and certain classes of heretics.

Si quæratur an valeat testamentum imprimis advertere debemus, an is qui id fecerit habuerit testamenti factionem; deinde, si habuerit, requiremus an secundum juris civilis regulam testatus sit.[248]

[248] Gaius, ii.§114.

THE HEIR[249]

The appointment of an heir was essential to the validity of the Roman testament, "*caput atque fundamentum intelligitur*

---

[249]"Et unum hominem, et plures in infinitum, quot quis velit, heredes facere licet.

"Hereditas plerumque dividitur in duodecim unciæ, quæ assis appellatione continentur. Habent antem et hæ partes propria nomina ab uncia usque ad assem, utputa hæc: uncia, sextans, qua-drans, triens, quincunx, semis, septunx, bes, dodrans, dextans, deunx, as. Non autem utique semper duodecim uncias esse oportet. Nam tot uncias assem afficiunt, quot testator voluerit. Et si unum tan-turn ex semisse verbi gratia heredem scripserit, totus as in semisse erit. Neque enim idem ex parte testatus, et ex parte intestatus decedere potest, nisi sit miles.

"Si plures instituantur, ita demum partium distributio necessaria esl, si nolit testator eos ex sequis partibus heredes esse. Satis enim constat, nullis partibus nominatis, ex æquis partibus eos heredes esse."—§§4—6. 1.11. 11. de Heredibus instituendis.

"Neque enim idem ex parte testatus ex parte intestatus decedere potest." — *Inst.* ii. 14.§5.

"Nihil aliud est hæreditas quam successio in universum jus quod defunctus habuit. Bona autem hic, ut plerumque solemus dicere, ita accipienda snnt, universitatis cujusque successionem, qua suc-ceditur in jus demortui, suscipiturque ejus rei commodum et incommodum. Nam sive solvenda sunt bona, sive non sunt, sive damnum habent, sive lucrum, sive in corporibus sunt sive in actionibus, in hoc loco proprie bona appellabuntur." — De Bonorum Possessionibus. — *Dig.* xxxvii. 2.§3.

"Heredes aut necessarii dicuntur, aut sui et necessarii aut extranei. Necessarius heres est ser-vus lieres institutus. Ideoque sic appellatur, quia, sive velit, sive nolit, omnino post mortem testatoris protinus liber et necessarius heres fit. Unde, qui facultates suas suspectas habent, solent servum suum primo, aut secundo aut etiam ulteriore gradu heredem instituere, ut, si creditoribus satis non fiat, potius ejus heredis bona, quam ipsius testatoris a creditoribus possideantur, vel distra-hantur, vel inter eos dividantur. Pro hoc tamen incommodo illud ci commodum præstatur, ut ea, quæ post mortem patroni sui sibi adquisierit, ipsi reserventur.

" Sui antem et necessarii heredes sunt veluti filius, filia, nepos, neptisve ex filio, et deinceps ceteri liberi, qui in potestate morientis modo fuerint. Sed sui quidem heredes ideo appellantur, quia do-mestici heredes sunt, et vivo quoque patre quodammodo domini existimantur. Unde etiam, si quis intestatus moriatur, prima causa est in successione liberorum. Necessarii vero ideo dicuntur, quia omnino, sive velint, sive nolint, tarn ab intestate, quam ex testa-mento, ex lege duodecim tabularum heredes front Sed his prætor permittit volentibus abstinere here-ditate, ut potius parentis, quam ipsorum bona similiter a creditoribus possideantur.

"Ceteri, qui testatoris juri subjecti non sunt, extranei heredes appellantur. Itaque liberi quoque nogtri, qui in potestate non sunt heredes a nobis instituti, extranei heredes videntur." — *Inst.* 2.§§1, 2, 3.§19. de Heredum Qualit. et Differentia.

"Sed his (suis et necessariis heredibus) prætor permittit abstinere se ab hereditate, ut potius parentia bona veneant. Idem juris et in uxoris persona, quæ in manu est, quia filiæ loco est, et in nurus, quæ in manu filii est, quia neptis loco est.

"Quin similiter abstinendi potestatem facit prætor etiam mancipato, id est, ei, qui in causa man-cipii est, cum liber et heres institutus sit, cum necessarius, non etiam suus heres sit, tamquam servus."—*Gaii Comm.* xi.§§158— 160.

totius testamenti hæredis institutio."[250] This could only be done by a testament which was revocable during the testator's life, and became binding by his death,[251] The other dispositions of the testament might be modified, or changed by a codicil; but the heir could be named in the testament only. The instrument by which an heir is legally nominated, is the formal definition of a Roman testament. The inheritance might be divided among several heirs.

The heir must be a person capable of succeeding. The following persons were incapable.

1. *Peregrini.*

2. Slaves of the testator not emancipated when the will was made. But Justinian held that such an appointment was emancipation.

3. *Intestabiles.*[252]

4. *Latini Juniani.*

5. According to the Voconian law, no woman could be the heir of one "*qui centum millia œris* census *esset."* In order to evade this law, parents kept out of the census. " C. A. A. mortuus est... cum haberet unicam filiam neque census esset... fecit ut filiam bonia suis hæredem institueret."[253] Or they left their property to a trustee, with an entreaty that he would give it to the daughter; an entreaty which, before the days of Augustus, was often disregarded. Cicero has preserved a remarkable instance of this breach of faith,[254]

---

[250] Inst. ii. 20.§34.

[251] "Ambulatoria est voluntas defuncti usque ad vitæ supremum exitum." —*Dig.* xxxiv. 4.§4.

"Stipulatio hoc modo concepta si hæredem sui non feceris tantum dare spondes, inutilis est."—*Dig.* xlv.§61.

"Ante heredis institutionem legari non potest quoniam et potestas testamenti ab heredis insti-tutione incipit."—*Ulp.Frag.xxiv.§*1—8.

"Hæres quandoque adeundo jam tum et morte successisse intelligitur." —*Dig.* xxix. 2.§54. De Acq. Hæred.

"Hæres in omne jus mortui... succedit." — Ib.§37.

[252] Dig.xxviii. 1.§§18—26.

[253] In Verr. i. 41.

[254] Cicero, De Fin. ii. 17. 55.

6. *Incerta corpora,* i. e. bodies with only a legal existence.

7. *Incertæ persona,* e. g. he who shall first be prætor after my death. Such an appointment as this, however, "*ex cognatis meis si quis filiam uxorem duxerit,*" was valid. Justinian abolished this restriction.[255]

8. P*osthumi,* not *sui.*[256]

There were different ways of appointing another heir, in the event of any failure in him who was first nominated. This proceeding was called "*substitutio.*"

" Titius hæres esto (institutus), si T. hæres non erit Mævius hæres esto (substitutus), si Mævius non erit Sempronius et Gaius hæredes sunto (substitutus substituti)."

This was called "*vulgaris substitutio.*"[257]

In the case of minors, who were the "*sui hœredes*" of the testator, a particular effect was given to the *substitutio* — each might be appointed heir in succession, if the one named before should die a minor. This was called the "*substitutio pupillaris.*"

---

[255] Just. ii. 20.§27.

[256] Gaius, ii.§242.

[257] Code Civil.

"896. Les substitutions sont prohibées."

"Toute disposition par laquelle le donataire, l'héritier institue, ou le légataire, sera chargé deconserver et de rendre à un tiers, sera nulle, même à l'égard du donataire, de l'héritier institue, ou du légataire."

Exceptions.

"1048. Les biens dont lea péres et méres ont la faculté de disposer pourront être par eux donnés, en tout ou en partie, à un ou plusieurs de leurs enfans, par actes entre-vifs ou testamentaires, avec la charge de rendre ces biens aux enfans nés et à naître, aux premier degré seulement, des dits donataires.—C. Capacité, 906. s. 1050.; Disp. par cont. de m., s. 1081.

"1049. Sera valable, en cas de mort sans enfans, la disposition que le défunt aura faite par acte entrevifs ou testamentaire, au profit d'un ou plusieurs de ses fréres ou sœurs, de tout ou partie des biens qui ne sont point réservés par la loi dans sa succession, avec la charge de rendre ces biens aux enfana nés, et à naître, au premier degré seulement, des dits frères ou sœurs donataires.—C. 897. 906.1050.1081." —*Domat, Loix Civiles, 5. 3. 7.*

The two kinds of *substitutio* were sometimes mixed, as *"filius hares esto; si intra pubertatem decesserit — tum Gaius hœres esto."*

To pass over some persons in silence, *prœteritio,* was not sufficient. They must be disinherited by express words, *"exhœres esto."* Justinian ordained that all the "*sui hœredes"* must be excluded by an *exhœredatio nominatim facta.* The law and its changes on this point have been already touched upon.

The *hœres* might either be "*directus,"* or *"fidei commissarius."* By the "*senatus consultant Trebellanium,"* in the time of Nero, a "*utilis actio"* was given against him, "*cut ex fidei commissi causâ restituta esset hœreditas,"* as if he had been the heir. By the "*Senatus consultum Pegasianum*" the trustee who was asked to restore all the inheritance might retain one fourth. Justinian ordained that he might keep "*quadrantem bonorum,"* and that he should be responsible for no larger proportion in actions against the inheritance. Justinian virtually abolished the "*Lex Falcidia"* by allowing the testator to prohibit its application.

By the "*Senatus consultum Trebellianum*" the *"fidei commissarius*" of the inheritance was treated as the universal successor, and his right was guarded by a *"fidei commissaria hœreditatis petitio."*

BONORUM POSSESSIO[258]

Closely connected with the right of inheritance, we find another institution. — The heir takes the place of the deceased. But nevertheless the testator may confer on persons, who are not his heirs, portions of his estate. This may be done by the "*legatum*" and "*fidei commissum.*" Here the struggle between the "*jus civile,*" and the "*jus pratorium,*" is conspicuous. At first, there is but one *hereditas,* that recognised by the "*jus civile.*" But the prætor conferred the inheritance upon those who were not heirs according to the "*jus civile:*" he could not, indeed, make them heirs; "*prœtor hœredem facere non potest;*" but he could give them possession of the property of the deceased, "*secundum tabulas bonorum possessionem,*" if the written testament was attested by the seals of seven witnesses. They were called "*bonorum possessores,*" and the right given by the prætor was called "*bonorum possessio.*" The "*bonorum possessio*" was to the "*hœreditas*" what the "*in bonis*" was to the "*dominium.*" *As* the principles of inheritance were extended, the doctrine of the *bonorum possessio* became less important — but it formed a part even of the latest Roman Law.[259]

---

[258] Gaii Comment, ii.§123. Inst. ii.§13. Dig. xxviii. 2. xxxvii. 4. Cod. vi.§§12. 28. "Sui heredes instituendi sunt aut exheredandi."—*Dig.* xxii.§14. Ulp. F. " Emancipates liberos cum jure civili neque heredes instituere neque exheredare necesse sit, tamen prætor jubet si non instituantur heredes exheredari....

Alioqui contra tabulas bonorum possessionem eis pollicetur."—*Ulp.* F. xxii.§23.

aius, iii. 25. Dig. xxxvii. 1. Inst. iii. 9. Cod. vii. 9. Dig. xliii. 2. Cod. viii. 2.

"Jus bonorum possessions introductum est a prætore."—*Inst.* iii. 9. 1.

"Habemus etiam alterius generis fictiones in quibusdam formulis, veluti cum is, qui ex edicto bonorum possessionem petît ficto, se herede agit. Cum enim prætori, se jure et non legitimo succedat in locum defuncti, non habet directas actiones, et neque id, quod defuncti fuit, potest intendere suum esse, neque id, quod defuncto debebatur, potest intendere dari sibi oportere. Itaque ficto se herede intendit." — *Gaius,* iv.§34.

[259] And is inserted in the Basilica, notwithstanding the 115. Novell.; so the 38th Dig. was not superseded by the 118. Novell.

LEGACIES[260]

"Legatum est delibatio hæreditatis, qua testator ex eo, quod universum hæredis foret alicui quid collatum velit."[261]

The Roman law recognised two kinds of legacies; the *legatum,* and the *fidei commissum,* which was the growth of a later age.

There were four kinds of the *Legatum.*

1. That per *vindicationem, "Stichum do," "lego,"* or *"sibi habeto," "capita."* This gave the *rei vindicatio* to the legatee.

2. *Per damnationem.* "Hæres meus Stichum servum meum dare damnas esto." This created an obligation between the legatee and the heir; the former had "*in personam acfio ex testamento,"* if the heir denied it "*in duplum."*

3. Sinendi modo. "Hæres meus damnas esto sinere L. Titium, hominem Stichum sumere, sibique habere." This gave an *actio in personam.*

4. *Per præceptionem.* "L. hominem Stichum præcipito." The Proculeians held the syllable *præ* superfluous. The Sabinians thought the expression tantamount to *præcipuum sumere.*

The legatee must have the "*testamenti factio."* A legacy could not be left to one who was in the power of the heir.

Or to one in whose power the heir was.[262]

The Furian law forbade, with some exceptions, all legacies of more than a thousand asses.

This was abolished by the Falcidian law.[263]

---

260 Inst. ii.§23. Dig. xxxvi. Cod. vi. 49.§§36. 43. 50. Gaius, ii.§247. Dig. xxxiv.§4. xxix.§7. xxx.§32. xxxv.§§2, 3. Gaius (ii.§224.) gives an outline of the history of the different laws. " Tulit apud majores nostros legem C. Furius de testamentis, tulit Q. Voconius de mulierum hereditatibus." Pro Balbo, viii.§21. In Verr. i.§42.

261 Dig. xxx. 1. 116.

262 Gaius, ii.§246.

263 A. u. c. 714.

By this law the heir was entitled to one fourth of the estate—and, if necessary, deductions were made *pro rata* from each legacy.

THE FIDEI COMMISSA[264]

In consequence of the restraints on legacies, it became usual for testators to impose certain burdens on the heir — whom they entreated to do a particular action, or to give a particular sum, *"non civilibus sed precativis verbis."* The heir was called *"fiduciarius;"* the person for whose benefit the charge was given, *"Jidei commissarius;"* at first the piety or honour of the *fiduciarius* was the testator's only security. But afterwards, these trusts were the subject of an "*evtraordinaria cognitio*" under Augustus, and a "*prœtor fidei commissarius*" was appointed to enforce their execution.

No particular form was required in the *"fidei commissa."*

They might be given orally, in writing, or even by a sign, "etiam nutu relinquere fidei commissum, in usu receptum est."[265] It was not necessary that the person for whose benefit they were intended should have the *"testamenti facfio."* Afterwards they were assimilated by Justinian to legacies, "per omnia exæquata legata fidei commissis."[266]

The sons of Constantine abolished the necessity of particular forms for legacies.[267]

---

264 Domat, Loix Civiles, lib. 5.
265 Ulp. xxv. 3.
266 Dig. xxx. 1.§1. Cod. vi. 43. Inst. ii. 20.§36.
267 C. vi. 23.15.

THE INHERITANCE OF AN INTESTATE[268]

By the law of the Twelve Tables, the succession of one who died intestate was given, first of all, to the "*sui hœredes,*" "*liberi,*" "*aut qui in liberorum loco sunt.*" In default of such heirs, it went to the "*consanguinei fratres et sorores ex eodem patre.*" In their default, "*ad reliquos agnates proximos.*" Women, beyond the degree of sisters, could not inherit; but this severe law was mitigated by the prætor, who, by his edict, "*unde liberi,*" "*unde legitimi,*" "*unde cognati,*" pointed out the three first classes of those whom he called to share the property of the deceased. He conferred it not upon the "*agnati*" only, but upon the "*cognati*" to the sixth and seventh degree. Sometimes before, sometimes simultaneously with, sometimes after, the *agnati.* In the fourth class, "*ex edicto unde vir et uxor,*" the intestate's property, in default of these relations, was given to the survivor of husband and wife. The later civil law was framed in a similar spirit: though in the main it adhered to the rule of preferring the *agnati,* yet by the "*Senatus consultum Tertullianum, Orphitianum,*" and several imperial constitutions, it conferred upon certain of the *cognati* a limited right of inheritance. The law of inheritance to an intestate was in this state of perplexity and embarrassment, when Justinian drew up the 118th Novell. A. D. 543, which, from his days to our own, has been the rule of countries governed by the Roman law. To this, important additions were made by the 127th Novell. A. D.547.[269]

The right to succession is grounded in part upon relationship, with regard to which the cognati were placed on an equal footing with the agnati, as was the relation of husband and wife. Mere affinity gave no title to any inheritance. All capable of inheriting were divided into particular classes and particular orders. Each particular order, and each particular

[268] Inst. tit. 1—6. lib. 3. *Dig.* xxxviii.§§6, 7, 8. 16. 17. Cod. vi.§§14, 15. 55. Dig. xxviii.§§3,4. Inst. ii. 17. " Si nemo hereditatem adierit nihil valet ex his quæ testamento scripta sunt." — *Dig:* xxvi.§§2. 9. Domat, Loix Civiles, lib. iv.

[269] The law did not, except as to the portion which came to the " liberi naturales," attempt to fix the share of these heirs.

class, excludes the more remote. Sometimes even in the same class of relationship, the nearer excludes the more distant in degree. With regard to the immediate relations of the deceased, the descendants, ascendants, and collateral relations, are put apart from each other, though it does not always happen that each belongs to a distinct class. In the first class are the descendants of the deceased, without reference to age, paternal authority, or even their proximity to the ascendants capable of inheriting. In the second class, are the ascendants; but if they are severed, only those nearest in degree. Together with these are placed the brothers and sisters of the whole blood of the deceased, and the sons and daughters of those deceased relations. In the third class are the half brothers and sisters of the deceased, and the sons and daughters of those deceased relations. The fourth class includes the remaining collateral relations of the deceased, without regard to the whole or the half blood, who are called to the succession in the degree of their proximity. As to the succession of husband and wife, the widow, according to the latest civil law, was entitled, even though the husband left relations able to succeed, if she were poor, and unendowed, and if her husband died in easy circumstances, to claim a portion, generally a fourth part, of his estate. The distribution of the intestate's property among the different classes of his relations took place sometimes *in capita,* sometimes *in stirpes,* according to their various degrees of proximity, and not according to any principle applicable to all alike.

CHAP. VIII.
LAW OF IMPEACHMENT

As the power of Rome increased, corruption became more extensive and more formidable; remedy after remedy was tried, sometimes from mere impatience, sometimes from deliberate policy, and tried in vain. The history of these changes, of the straggles by which they were brought about, and of the abuses by which they were rendered ineffectual, gives a peculiar interest to the study of the criminal law in Rome during the latter ages of the commonwealth. For, the administration of that law in cases of impeachment was then the battle-field of party, on which the cause of liberty was lost and won, and lost again for ever.[270] From the fourth to the sixth century of the republic, there were in Rome three tribunals, if I may be allowed the expression, to which great political offenders were amenable. The *comitia centuriata,* by which alone, since the Twelve Tables, capital punishment could be inflicted on a Roman citizen. The *comitia tributa,* and the senate, part of the functions of which consisted in punishing crimes, and malversation in office, perpetrated beyond the precincts of Rome, and thus exercising a paramount control over the municipal magistrates of Italy, and the governors of the provinces. Nothing could be more according to the analogy of the Roman proceeding, than the delegation of this judicial authority, on particular occasions of difficulty and importance, to a single person, assisted by a council; or as we should call it a jury chosen as in the time of Polybius[271], exclusively from the senators. The inquiry was called a "*quæstio,*" and the president, quæstor, whose functions were altogether different from those

---

[270] Dig. de 0. T. ii.§23. " Quia, ut diximus de capite civis Romani, injussu populi non erat legi permissum consulibus jus dicere, propterea quæstores creabantur a populo qui capitalibus rebus præessent, hi appellabantur quæstores parricidii quorum etiam meminit lex. xii Tab. "

[271] Polyb. v. 17. Livy, xliii. 2.

of the "*quæstores ærarii*" Sometimes this quæstor was a magistrate, consul for instance, or prætor; sometimes, as in the case of Scaurus[272], a private person; there is also an example of a "*dictator quæstionibus exercendis*[273]," nominated by the senate. Sometimes the commission was instructed what precedent it was to follow, and what form it was to observe. "Senatui placere quæstionem de expilatis thesauris eodem exemplo haberi, quo M. P. Prætor triennio ante habuisset." In the sixth century, these commissions become frequent; sometimes they are named by the people, sometimes by the senate. Laboulaye cites two remarkable examples; the one in the impeachment of Scipio Asiaticus, the other[274] in that of M. Popilius.

---

[272] Sallust, Jug. 40.

[273] Livy, xxxi. 12.

[274] Livy, xxxviii. 55. xlii. 21. Laboulaye, Essai sur les Lois Criminelles des Romains. Geib. Geschichte des Römischen Crim. Process. A very useful book, but it would have been a better if the writer had dared to draw his own inferences, and to speak his own thoughts. Appian, De Bello Civ. Beaufort, République Romaine. Cicero, In Verrem, passim.

Mr. Burke warns against a similar error, when he points out the absurdity of choosing " the breakers of law in India for the makers of law in England."

"Les chevaliers étaient les traitants de la République; ils étaient avides, ils semaient les malheurs dans les malheurs, et faisaient naitre les besoms publics des besoins publics. Bien loin de donner à de telles gens la puissance de juger, il aurait fallu qu'ils eussent été sans cesse sous les yeux des juges... Lorsqu'à Rome les jugemens furent transportés aux traitants, il n'y eut plus de vertu, plus de police, plus de lois, plus de magistrature, plus de magistrals." — *Esprit des Loix,* ii.§18.

" Une profession qui n'a, et ne peut avoir, d'objet que le gain — une profession qui demandait tonjours, et à qui on ne demandait rien; une profession sourde et inexorable, qui appauvrissait les richesses et la misère même, ne devait point avoir à Rome les jugemens." — Ib. The history of other countries, as well as of our own, especially in its East Indian annals, exemplifies the truth of these remarks. Nothing is more unscrupulous than a corporation. No passion is fiercer and more savage than the love of gain, when thwarted and interfered with. Q. Mucius Scævola, sent as prætor into Asia, round the province bleeding at every pore from the cruelties and extortions of the knights (the traitans). As they were certain of impunity, their wickedness was unbounded. Scævola put a stop to their exactions, and forced them to restore their plunder.

Tà τϖν δημοσιωνϖν άνομήματα διορθώθατο... καί τάς μέν άργυρικάς βλάβας, τοϊς ήδικημένοις έκτινειν ήναγκαξεν. — Diod. Sicul. vol. iv. p. 610. The knights, infuriated by this justice, accused Rutilius, the friend and deputy of Scævola, of corruption. Rutilius was a man of spotless purity; " Quod specimen habuit hæc civitas innocentiæ," in the words of Cicero: but he was of course condemned, " Quo judicio penitus convulsam esse rempublicam scimus." — *Brutus.*

Thus a jurisdiction which was originally vested in the comitia or the senate, or in commissions established for a particular investigation under the control of particular magistrates, was transferred to a standing tribunal continually renewed, which, as the edict of the preetor was called "*edictum perpetuum,*" was called "*quœstio perpetua:*" by this mode of trial a jury was selected from the people, and a limited number of citizens discharged the duties of the assembly.

L. Calpurnius Piso, the author of this innovation, was probably not aware of the mighty change which he had brought about. The possession of this judicial power became the great object on which the contests turned between the different orders who contended for the administration of the republic. It became the guarantee and criterion of supremacy. Gracchus took it from the senate and gave it to the knights. Sylla, the most determined and implacable enemy of the popular party, restored it to the senate. After his death, it was divided, by a sort of compromise, between the senate and the knights, till the triumph of arbitrary power under Augustus. It was in the year of Rome 604, that L. Calpurnius Piso (Frugi), tribune of the people, carried his law concerning peculation. Though corruption was far from having reached the height to which it afterwards arrived, its progress was so rapid and alarming, that the necessity of some more powerful restraint was obvious. Piso, though a tribune, was not by any means a violent or exclusive champion of the popular part of the constitution; he was, on the contrary, disposed to support the authority of the senate; and the people, who, in gratitude for his law, conferred upon him the surname "Frugi," forgave him his opposition to Gracchus, the best and greatest of their champions. Cicero tells us over and over again that the law was instituted for the protection of the confederates. It is a mistake to suppose, on the other hand, that it was intended to strengthen the aristocracy. By exempting the allies from the necessity of appearing as suppliants before the senate, and by enabling them to apply, through the intervention of the manager of their cause (patronus) at once to a prætor, it tended very much to circumscribe its influence. In this mode of proceeding, the forms of a civil action were preserved; but though the accused, if guilty, was condemned only to pecuniary restitution, he was branded with a certain degree of infamy, and became incapable of holding certain offices. Simple restitution was the punishment inflicted by the Calpurnian law. The Junian law followed the "*Lex Calpurnia;*" the date of it is unknown; it still bore the character of a civil proceeding. But the *"Lex Servilia"* enabled the injured provincials to demand double, and the *"Lex Cornelia "* four-fold the value of what they had lost, from the guilty party, as compensation. In the meantime it should be recollected that the establishment of a "*quœstio perpetua,"* did by no means oust entirely the jurisdiction of the senate and the people; it was a concurrent remedy. Subsequently, for instance, to the Calpurnian law, we find that Tunius Silanus was accused before the senate by the Macedonians. But the accusations brought before the prætor were far more numerous. L. Aurelius Cotta, Livius Salinator, and M. Aurelius, the plunderers of Asia, were respectively impeached within the space of fifteen years before this tribunal by the most upright and illustrious of their contemporaries. But these proceedings served only to illustrate the miserable corruption of the senate. Though the guilt of the accused was proved by evidence the most cogent and irresistible, and though Scipio Æmilianus was his accuser, the judges of Cotta adjourned the cause seven times[275] for further information; and finally acquitted him. In like manner, Salinator and Aquilius, accused by Lentulus, escaped the punishment of their crimes. It was not by judges, or rather a jury, chosen from the senators eager for the opportunity of enriching themselves by the same means as the accused, that the conviction of a senator, however flagrant his guilt, could be expected. While the public indignation, which these repeated mockeries of justice had excited, was at its height, Caius Gracchus succeeded in carrying a law which transferred to the knights the judicial power that such reiterated instances of prevarication had shown the senators altogether unworthy to possess. If Rome could have been saved, it would have been by the Gracchi. They were eloquent, magnanimous, and solely

---

[275] was the just retribution of such enormous guilt.
Val. Max. viii. 1. 11.

bent on the regeneration of their country. The means they employed were, in spite of the slavish attempts to blacken their memory, as literally constitutional, as the end they sought to attain was legitimate and noble; they were not, like Cleon or Hyperbolus of Athens, boisterous and ignorant demagogues, but men who, in a time of general corruption, endeavoured to awaken the best and purest feelings of their countrymen. Like Mirabeau, gifted with extraordinary eloquence, and of a descent that might well be called illustrious, they maintained that unsullied purity of character which, unhappily for his fame, Mirabeau was without, and which the slightest taint of pecuniary corruption is sufficient to destroy. They were summarily assassinated by the Roman aristocracy, and the servitude of that aristocracy. Tiberius, the elder brother, had a two-fold object — one to create a body of independent citizens, the other to insure the integrity of the judges. He endeavoured, by an Agrarian[276] law, to attain the first; and by a law that enforced the responsibility of the judges, to insure the second of these noble ends. Opposed by a venal colleague in his attempt to wrest from the nobility the vast possessions which, without the shadow of justice, they had usurped from the community, he called upon the people to exercise their inherent, unquestionable, and constitutional right, and to depose the functionary by whom they were betrayed. For this he was murdered in cold blood by Scipio Nasica, armed with the formula which enabled the aristocracy to get rid of so many patriot citizens. C. Gracchus, ten years afterwards, came forward in the same cause; he proposed, in the language of Paterculus, to make Rome include the Alps; in other words, to give the right of citizenship to all the inhabitants of Italy — a wise and comprehensive policy, which, if adopted in time, would have saved Rome from the social war that shook the foundations of her power, and brought her to the very verge of ruin. He also proposed to distribute corn at a nominal price among the people — a pernicious measure, evidently dictated

---

[276] An Agrarian law was not a distribution of the property of the rich among the poor; it was dividing the lands of the state (which the rich held at a nominal rent, and cultivated by their slaves,) among the poor at a higher rent.

by the desire to conciliate the favour of the multitude, as well as other enactments tending to break the power of the senate, and to check the rapacity of provincial governors. But the law by which he endeavoured to wrest from the aristocracy the dagger which they had employed to destroy so many famous patriots, was the *"Lex Sempronia de capite civium Romanorum,"* which in terms forbids any measure affecting the life of any Roman citizen without the express assent of the Roman people. The Valerian and Porcian laws gave an appeal to the people in capital cases; but the Sempronian law took away from the consuls, the senate, or any jury of senators, all cognisance of such offences under the severest penalties. This law was retrospective. As long as it prevailed, Nasica, Rupilius, and Popilius sought refuge in exile from the justice of an injured country. The vengeance of Caius Gracchus limited itself to them. The magistrates whom the constitution invested during the period of their office with almost unlimited power, were, after its expiration, alone attacked. The senate by whom they were supported was permanent and irresponsible. This sketch of some of the laws of Caius Gracchus was necessary, in order to give the reader an idea of the actual condition of Rome when he brought forward his great measure to transfer judicial power from the senatorial to the equestrian body; in other words, to select from the knights those by whom impeachments under the "*quœstio perpetua*" were to be determined. Appian (i.§ 21.) tells us that when the law was passed, Caius Gracchus exclaimed that he had overthrown the power of the senate; and the event justified the prediction: but, though the abuses to which the combination of judicial and executive power in the same hands gave rise were so notorious that any change was acceptable, the remedy of Caius Gracchus did but change the instruments of corruption. The class to which he assigned the judicial power was that from which the farmers of the revenue in the different provinces were selected, and it therefore became the interest of the governors of the provinces by every means to conciliate their support. Thus all the extortions of the *"publicani"* were connived at by the governor in order to secure his own impunity; a league was made between those who were responsible and those who were to enforce the responsibility of which the unhappy provinces became the victims. The evil became deeper and more inveterate than before. Meanwhile, the senate had murdered Caius Gracchus — had revived, as far as was within its power, the *mos majorum* which his law abolished, and had abrogated his laws in favour of the multitude, whom it was easy, especially when confounded by the death of their leader, to intimidate and seduce. But the *publicani* (the knights) were not so easily to be managed. The power which G. Gracchus lodged in their hands could not be wrested from them without a struggle, which would convulse society; they were, therefore, suffered to retain it; nor is it improbable that the indifference with which they beheld the death of Gracchus, ought to be ascribed to some compromise of this sort. This authority was not long without employment; the venality of the generals employed in the Jugurthine war revived the indignation of the people. Albinus Scaurus, the first of the senators, and Opimius, the assassin of Gracchus, dishonoured the Roman name and arms by selling to the perfidious tyrant, whom they were appointed to subdue, the inactivity of the legions which they commanded. Memmius, the tribune of the people, and the declared enemy of the nobles, endeavoured to chastise this treachery. In the speech which Sallust has put into his mouth we may discover the bitter hatred and deep indignation with which the infamy brought upon the Roman name, by the cruelty and avarice of the senate, had inspired every virtuous citizen. Many of his efforts were rendered unavailing by the intercession of his colleague. But the same measure was afterwards renewed by C. Mamilius Limetanus, and at his proposal the people named the Commission to try the peculators. Opimius was the first victim of this proceeding. Three senators of consular rank, and among them Bestia who, while tribune, had encouraged P. Popilius the assassin, were condemned. The law *Servilia Cœpionis* 647, *A.U.C.* was intended to restore the judicial power to the senate, whether it ever passed or not is a matter involved in some obscurity. Thus much, however, is certain, that Servilius Glaucia carried a law by which judgments on matters of corruption were confined exclusively to the knights. By this law "*Servilia,*" the prætor peregrinus was ordered to prepare every year a list of 450 names, from which all senators, their fathers, brothers, and children, were excluded, as well as all magistrates who were not senators. This law was far more severe (*acerbissimâ Lege Serviliâ)* than either of the Calpurnian or the Junian laws. Among other enactments it provides that the provincial, on whose accusation a corrupt magistrate is condemned, shall become a Roman citizen. This measure, carried by a profligate man, might, nevertheless, have been beneficial, had not the class from which the judges were taken been as corrupt as that which they were appointed to control. The alterations of Sylla, who carried into effect the worst projects of a corrupt aristocracy, all bear the same stamp, and tend to the same object. The confiscation of property, the division of Italy among the 120,000 veterans, the right of citizenship conferred on 10,000 slaves, the annihilation of the influence of the knights, the political disability which he imposed on the children of his victims, a measure which Cicero, to his eternal disgrace, was time-server enough to defend — nay, the very proscription which soaking the soil of Italy in blood, surpassed the worst horrors of the French Revolution, and almost equalled the abominable cruelties which, amid the indignation of shuddering Europe, were inflicted by the Emperor Nicholas on the Poles— these measures, frightful as they were, and vast as was the amount of contemporary suffering which they entailed, were none of them perhaps attended with any very durable or prolonged results; but the new law, as passed by Sylla during his dictatorship, completely changed the constitution, and destroyed the effect which two centuries of an almost perpetual struggle had not been more than able to produce. Sylla deprived the tribunes of the right to assemble the "*comitia tributa,*" thus stripping them at once of all judicial and legislative power. He even forbade them to harangue the people; and as if to insure the degradation of those who filled that office, he rendered them ineligible to every other. His laws with regard to judicial power turned on three points. He abrogated, as we have seen, the popular power; he established standing commissions of inquiry, "*quæstiones perpetuæ,*" in a new form; and he confined the judicial functions exclusively to senators. Of the *quæstiones perpetuæ* established by Sylla, the names of five are still remaining:—

"Lex de Sicariis et Veneficis."

"Lex de Parricidio."

"Lex de Falsis (testamentaria)"

"Lex Peculatus," } i. e. against corruption in

"Lex de vi publicâ Majestatis," } magistrates and treason.

But though Zacharia gives the two last names, and the matter to which the laws relate is certain, the ground on which he asserts the title is but slender. To provide chiefs for these tribunals the number of prætors was increased to eight[277] and the number of quæstors to twenty.

What the laws were by which these magistrates were made responsible, cannot now be ascertained; that they were, however, useless is attested by almost every page of subsequent history. The control of the senate over the crimes of its own order, was of course illusory; but from a passage in Cicero's speech against Piso, and others in that against Cluentius, it seems that the "*Lex Cornelia majestatis*" comprised almost every offence against the constitution of Rome, and against the majesty of the people represented by the senate. A clause of this law obliged every governor to leave his province thirty days after the arrival of his successor. Another forbade every governor to leave his province without the consent of the senate. The crime against *majestas* was incurred by those who employed their official power to the detriment of the Roman people, or who obstructed a magistrate in the exercise of his functions. Sylla, also, in the cautious spirit of an aristocracy, provided that there should be between two consulships an interval of two years, and that no one should hold the office of prætor till he had filled that of quæstor, or that of consul till he had passed through that of prætor. Such is the outline of the

---

[277] Tac. Ann. xi. 22.

changes intended by Sylla to consolidate the power of an aristocracy; changes which entirely destroyed the balance of the Roman constitution; and by taking from the same class the magistrate and the judge to whom the magistrate was responsible, insured impunity to the foulest crimes, and was the cause of a portentous and unrestrained corruption. The evil was so enormous that, after the death of Sylla, to maintain things in their actual state became impossible; the people loudly demanded the restoration of the tribunitian power and efficient judges. The first of these measures was conceded by a law restoring the authority of the tribunes, which was proposed by Pompey and supported by Cæsar; the second by a law of L. Aurelius Cotta, who remodelled the constitution of the judicial body. By the law of Cotta the judicial power was divided between the senators, the knights, and the *"tribuni ærarii."* Who the *"tribuni ærarii"* were is uncertan; but Laboulaye, who combines the deep erudition of a German, with the sagacity and penetration of his own country, thinks that they were, in all probability, citizens of the first class, rated in the census below the knights: and I incline to this opinion. The *"Lex Amelia"* then established three *decuriæ* of judges; the first comprising the senators; the second, the knights; the third, the tribunes of the *ærarium.* In what manner these judges, of whom an uneven number was appointed, voted is uncertain. By the Fufian law (A. *U. C.* 694) they were required to vote separately, so that the opinion, if not of each judge, of each *decuria* at least, was ascertained; but this regulation did not affect the principle of the law, and the condemnation or acquittal of the accused was decided by the majority of suffrages.

A law of Pompey (A. *U.* C. 698) made a change still more considerable. Up to this time the judges were selected by the prætor, and he might of course take care that they were subservient to his designs. To remedy this evil, which has tainted, and continues to taint, trial by jury in other countries besides Rome, Pompey established a rule of eligibility, according to which the prætor's option was taken away; it is in allusion to this law that Cicero says *(In Pisonem):* "Ecquid vides, ecquid sentis lege judiciariâ latâ quos judices simus habituri? neque legetur quisquis voluerit, nec quisquis noluerit non legetur: nulli conjicientur in ilium ordinem, nulli eximentur; non ambitio ad gratiam, non iniquitas ad simulationem conjicietur. Judices judicabunt ii quos lex ipsa non quos hominum libido delegerit."

Thus were destroyed, as to two most essential points, the reforms by which Sylla endeavoured to unite two things so irreconcileable as justice and the government of an aristocracy. But though the class from which the judges were taken ceased to be the same, the commissions he established as the instrument of attaining justice were suffered to continue even under the empire, and the jurisdiction of the tribunes, as well as of the people, fell into oblivion and disuse. The trial of Rabirius before the centuries, that of Gabinius, and the decree by which Cicero was driven into exile, are the only popular decisions of this period; and indeed after the inhabitants of Italy were admitted to the rights of citizens, four hundred thousand people might have claimed the right to act as judges in the case of every public male-factor. It was therefore necessary that the judicial power should be delegated to a limited number of citizens, and the abolition of this part of Sylla's system was impossible. In the time of Augustus, the object of the right of impeachment was altogether changed. It ceased to be exercised by men in a private station; it ceased to be a means of acquiring reputation; it ceased to be a guarantee for the integrity of magistrates or the privileges of the people. The laws of Augustus, the *"Lex Julia ambitus,"* the "*Lex Julia majestatis,"* the *"Lex Julia de vi,"* remodelled, in some degree, but did not apparently change, much less did they violently overthrow, the institutions of the republic. Augustus well knew that the forma of a free, and the ends of an arbitrary government were perfectly compatible. He aimed his blow, not at the branches, but at the root; he flung his poison, not into the channel of the stream, but into the fountains from which it sprung; he allowed the letter to save, but he made the spirit kill. Thus the laws "*Cornelia*" and *"Julia*" remained during the empire. But exceptional trials took the place of the regular methods of proceeding — fines were aggravated into exile, exile into relegation, and relegation into death.

The senate was substituted for the old tribunal; and at last, when this flimsy veil was thought no longer worth preserving, the emperor for the senate. Such was the tenure by which the once free Roman came to hold his fortune, his personal dignity, and his life. Such were the scars of servitude branded upon a people, to whom the name of king was once intolerable, and which was now marked out by Heaven for successive ages, as a warning to mankind against the government of one.

Hitherto[278] we have considered the laws which were intended to chastise the rapacity and oppression of provincial governors.; but there was another evil which preyed upon the heart of the republic, and against which positive laws were ineffectually directed: the same evil which now menaces England—the venality of voters, and the unscrupulous ambition of candidates — "*respublica venalis,*" that worst and most incurable of public misfortunes, when high and low, rich and poor, electors and elected, form together one tainted mass of indiscriminate corruption.

Rome was the market in which provinces and kingdoms, "*uno calamitatis jure,*" were sold to the highest bidder; in which the pillage of Spain, Sicily, the Gauls, Africa, was the reward that, as Varro tells us, the universe was convulsed to gain. The traffic in seats of parliament among us — a numerous assembly where the influence of no individual is irresistible — leads to no such consequences. The evil was soon discovered. Livy tells us of a law (A. U. C. 321) — "Ne cui album in vestimentum addere petitionis liceret causâ,"[279] which appears to him in the same light as the homely declamations of Latimer do to us. In the year A. U. C. 395, C. Pætilius[280], a tribune of the people, brought forward another law, by which the canvass of suffrages in places of public resort was especially prohibited. In the A. U.

[278] Laboulaye, p. 282.
[279] Liv. iv. 25.
[280] Liv. vii. 15.

C. 439, C. Mænius, who has been already mentioned as the dictator "*quæstionibus exercendis,*" and whose duties struck the nobles with the greatest terror, declared "*coitiones honorum adipiscendorum causâ facias, contra rempublicam esse.*"[281] This exasperated the nobles, who combined against him, claiming the highest places in the state as their patrimony, and accusing the dictator of the crime, as inexpiable in the eyes of the patricians of Rome as in those of the patricians of Great Britain, that he was "*novus homo.*" Mænius defied and baffled the malevolence of these interested enemies. The next law on the subject was that passed A.U.C. 572, and called the *Cornelia Bœbia.* Another law for the same purpose was passed A.U.C. 594. In the year A.U.C. 614, a law was passed, the *Lex Gabinia,* the subject of which is among us at this day the topic of frequent and acrimonious discussion. This law was the vote by ballot. Cicero contradicts himself so repeatedly in speaking of this law, that it is difficult to ascertain his real opinion. One thing, however, is certain, that it was forced upon the people by the violence and corruption of the aristocracy. "Quia non sentit tabel-lariam legem omnem auctoritatem optimatium abstulisse? Quam populus liber nunquam desideravit, *idem oppressus dominatu ac potentiâ principum flagitavit.*"[282] Cicero in this passage admits that the law which Atticus condemns, was necessary and effectual. Again, in the third book of his Laws, Cicero says, how consistently with himself is not now the question: "Ne quis tabellam inspiceret, ne rogaret, ne appellaret, quibus legibus studia suffragatorum sublata esse." Calpurnius Piso, the consul who had narrowly escaped the consequences of an accusation of *ambitus* himself, carried a law of great severity against those guilty of that crime. Under this law, Autronius Pætus and Cornelius Sylla were condemned; and Cicero brought forward another law, still more searching and comprehensive. But this law was equally unavailing with its predecessors. In A.U.C. 693, Pompey[283] purchased openly the

---

[281] This may remind the reader of the " undertakers " who engaged to pack the House of Commons for James I.

[282] De Legibus, iii. 16. Vote by ballot is insisted upon by Demosthenes, II. *Пαρα.,* as a motive for judicial purity.

[283] Ad Att. i. 16.

consulship for his creature Afranius, one of the vilest and most contemptible of mankind, as great men's creatures usually are. To consider Pompey as the champion of Roman freedom is ridiculous: he was the fit representative of a corrupt aristocracy, composed in part of men of low extraction and without education, who had acquired colossal fortunes by sordid arts, who were anxious for power without any one qualification for it, and who, more than any other class, accelerate the ruin of countries when the measure of their degradation and iniquity is complete.

It was not, however, inveterate corruption only that threatened the stability of the constitution during the last days of the republic. Open violence was employed to intimidate those whom money could not seduce. Blood was shed where gold was impotent. The "*Lex Plautia de vi,*" which preceded the year A. U. C. 690, was followed by the "*Lex Licinia de sodalitiis,*" which was carried by M. Licinius Crassus, A. U. C. 698. These associations, to corrupt and terrify, were called "*sodales,*" "*collegia sodalitia.*"[284] The distribution of the people was called "*tributes decuriare.*" Under the *Lex Licinia,* a citizen might be accused "*ambitus,*" if he had purchased individual votes; "*sodalitatis,*" if he had employed the emissaries or "undertakers" we have described; "*de vi,*" if he had used direct violence. Vatinius, Plancus, Milo, Messala, were accused under this law (Mito before three distinct tribunals), while the streets of Rome were drenched with blood, and Crassus, the friend of Pompey, was extorting the consulship by violence from the nobles who despised and the people who abhorred him. During the elections of the year A. U. C. 700, the interest of money rose from four to eight per cent.[285] Instead of the splendid eloquence of the Gracchi, the Roman forum echoed to the yells of the hired gladiators and assassins, by whom the election of

---

[284] Cic. ad Q. F. ii. 3.: " Eodem die senatus consultum factum est ut sodalitates decuriatique discederent," &c. Pro Plancio: " Ego Plancium habuisse" in petitione multos cupidos sui gratiosos dico, quos tu, si sodales vocas officiosam amicitiam nomine inquinas criminoso, jam, ut ego doceo gratiosum esse tribulibus Plancium, sic tu doce sequestrem fuisse... tributes decuriâsse."

[285] Ad Att. iv. 15.: " Ardet ambitus, σημα δε τοι έρέω, foenus ex triente Id. Quint, factum erat bessibus."

consuls was now decided—a just retribution on the Roman nobles, who were slaves to the refuse of humanity. The ruffians of Clodius preceded only by a few years the murders of Tiberius. The last laws of Pompey were two, intended for the punishment of Milo: one *"de vi,"* the other *"de ambitu;"* the first special, the latter permanent. Milo, Gabinius, Hypsæus, Sextus, Memmius, were its victims; but Memmius, availing himself of a provision in Pompey's law, which gave impunity to the criminal who convicted another of *ambitus,* impeached Pompey's father-in-law, L. Scipio; Pompey, in open violation of his own law, *"suarum legum auctor et subversor,"* canvassed on Scipio's behalf, and tore him away from punishment.[286] This law of Pompey irritated the people, and precipitated the struggle, with Cæsar. His arms ended what the injustice of the nobles had begun, and when Caligula's horse became a consul the Gracchi were avenged.

---

[286] Appian ii.§24.: Μέμμιος δέ αλούς έπι δεκασμϖ, κ.τ.λ. Val. Max. ix.5.: "Pompeius non erubuit. P. S. socerum suum legibus noxium quas ille tulerat, muneris loco a judicibus deposcere."

PART III

EXTERNAL HISTORY OF THE ROMAN LAW

CHAP. I.
EXTERNAL HISTORY OF THE ROMAN LAW

THE history of the Roman law may be divided into four periods. The first, extending from the foundation of the city to the time of the decemvirs; the second, from the time of the decemvirs to that of Augustus; the third, from Augustus to the time of Diocletian; the fourth, from the reign of Diocletian to the period when Justinian, by sanctioning the compilations which have made his name immortal, insured to mankind an inheritance, the value of which with all its mutilations it is impossible to overrate. If we examine the characteristics of the first of these epochs, we shall find the law in a primitive condition, among a people drawn together from different races, inhabiting a city which is the seat of empire, and to which, for a considerable time, their dominion was almost limited — a circumstance to which the municipal character, apparent in all the monuments of Roman policy, may probably be attributed. During this time, law and religion are almost identical. The law is a kind of religious mystery, and its application is carefully concealed from the multitude by the pontiff. Most of the institutions during this age are of Tuscan origin. The government, though nominally regal, is mainly in the hands of an aristocracy, which, after the expulsion of the Tarquins, obtained for a time an unrivalled and complete ascendency. I do not, however, think it necessary, in a treatise of this nature, to enter into any long detail concerning the first of these periods. However interesting as matter of liberal speculation, its history has but little relation to the later Roman law. This period, which is involved in considerable doubt and obscurity, has afforded opportunity for many learned and ingenious speculations, some bearing an aspect of probability, others utterly extravagant and setting at defiance all the common rules of historical evidence.[287] The name of Niebuhr is alone sufficient to remind the reader of the examination which this portion of history has undergone, and of the theories that it has suggested. Let it not be considered in any way inconsistent on my part with the most profound respect for the memory of that distinguished writer, if I say that his erudition and acuteness were not always sufficiently within his control, or always balanced by views sufficiently comprehensive and impartial; and that, like the youthful champion of Ausonia, he has been sometimes hurried, by the charm of hoped-for triumph and in the flush of anticipated victory, into a contest with antagonists superior to him, as well as into a disregard of the most authentic and conclusive testimony. His investigations are of great value, but to turn them to their proper use, much caution is requisite, and the incessant exercise of a chastised and sober judgment. When a writer of the present century, however surprising his acuteness, and however deep his erudition, calls upon his readers to set aside as utterly insignificant the constant, unbiassed, unequivocal testimony, direct and indirect, not of

---

[287] The yoke of Niebuhr has been shaken off by several recent writers. Amongst others I may cite *Laboulaye,* a disciple worthy of Montesquieu; and Carl. Peter, Epochen der Verfassungsgeschichte der Römischen Republik. " Tite Live," says the former, "nous donne sur la constitution Romaine et l'organisation judiciaire des notions parfaites, et il s'en faut de beaucoup que l'eloquence de l'écrivain fasse tort à son exactitude." Peter, after mentioning an hypothesis of Niebuhr's, adds (p. 2.): "Welcher nach meiner Aussicht durchaus unbegründet ist, und welcher als der Hauptquellaller der zahlreichen zu kühnen Hypothesen seines Urhebers im Verlauf der Entwickelung der Verfassungsgeschichte anzusehen ist, jener Hypothesen welche statt das Gregebene und Factische zu erklären, welches immer als das Hauptkennzeichen einer guten Hyputhese betrachtet worden ist, zu einer Verwirrung aller Auctoritäten, *und zu einer Vernichtung der klärsten und bestimmtesten Zeugnisse geführt haben."* And see Tigerström, Aeussere Ges. des R.R., in which, after quoting one of Niebuhr's theories, he says, p. 17., with great truth: " Die Quellen selbst enthalten das gerade Gegentheil."

such writers only as Livy and Dionysius Halicarnassensis, but of Cicero, Varro, the authors of the Digest, and Tacitus, not to one fact but to hundreds, while they were writing on subjects interwoven with the laws, history, and constitution of their own country, he makes, I think, very much too large a demand on the submission and even on the patience of his disciples.[288]

[288] Cicero mentions the name of Romulus in his works certainly not less than thirty times. De Rep. ii. 2.4. xxviii. 50. De Leg. i. 1.3. De Divin. i. 12. 20. ii. 20. 45. Tusc. i. 12. 28 (where he quotes Ennius's line upon him.) De Divin. i. 47., i. 48.: Ille Romuli auguratus pastoralis non urbanus fuit, *nec fictus ad opinionem imperitorum sed a certis acceptus etposteris traditus."* De Nat. D.: " Romulus auspiciis, Numasaeris constitutis fundaments, jecit nostræ civitatis." In Vatinium. In Cat i. De Off. iii. 10. 41. Pro Balbo, referring to the incorporation of the Sabines with the Romans, he distinctly points out the date of Romulus, and denies that he rules over barbarians. De Rep. i. 37. He gives the month of the eclipse at the death of Romulus. Ib. xvi. He mentions Numa about as often; says that he was not a Pythagorean, that he was a foreigner,- that he was elected by a " lex curiata." De Rep. ii. 13. 15.25. 28. He says Numa preceded Pythagoras by nearly two centuries. Quotes his institutions. De Or. iii. 19. His system of intercalation, De Leg. ii. 12. He mentions Tullus Hostilius about four times. De Rep. ii. 17. He states whom he succeeded, how he was elected, his peculiar qualities and institutions. De Nat.. D. ii. 3. 9., he mentions Servius Tullius several times; De Rep. ii. 21. 37., enters at great length into his measures, says that he was a contemporary of Solon and Pisistratus; shows that he was spoken of in several histories: " Quæ historia non prodidit? " He mentions Ancus Martius, De Rep. ii. 18. 33. 3. 5.; and Tarquinius Prisons, De Rep. ii. 20. 15. Tarquinius Superbus is spoken of about twenty times; once *in a letter to Atticus.* De Leg. i. 1. 4.: "Male Tarquinius, qui Porsenam, qui Oct. Marn., contra patriam excitavit." Now, if Porsena and Tarquinius are mythical persons, this is as if Lord Bolingbroke writing to Pope were to say, " I think the conduct of the Lady of the Lake in destroying Merlin quite unjustifiable," in a grave letter on moral conduct; or as if Berwick, in the War of the Succession, were in a letter to Louis XIV. to illustrate his conduct at the battle of Almanza, by citing Orlando's behaviour at Roncesvalles. Again, he says: " Unius importunitate et superbia Tarquinii nomen huic populo in odium venit regium." " Tarquinio exacto mirâ quâdam exuliavit populus insolentiâ libertatis tum exacti in exilium innocentes." De Rep. i. 40., exactly corresponding with Livy. De Fin. iii. 22.: " Tarquinius nec se nec suos regere potuit. Tarq. Sup. cum restitui in regnum nec Veientium lice Latinorum armis potuisset Cumas se contulisse dicitur, inque eâ urbe senio et ægritudine esse nonfectus." Jus.i. 36. Pro Rab. Parad. i. 2. 11. Sextus Tarq. is mentioned: De Rep. ii. 25., where the story of Lucretia is told. The elder Brutus is mentioned still more frequently, with every sort of allusion to his life and his death. Atticus, who was a great antiquarian, deduced the pedigree of M. Brutus from Ahala by the mother's, and Jun. Brutus by the father's side. Cicero alludes particularly to his removal of Collatinus. De Off. iii. 10.: " Cum Collatino collegæ imperium abrogabat, id erat ita honestum ut etiam ipsi Collatino placere deberet." Ad Att. xiii. 40. 1. Coriolanus is often cited. Once in a letter to Atticus, " Impie egit Coriolanus qui auxilium petiit a Volcis." Ad Att. ix. 10., to which my remarks on Tarq. apply; " *Ei et Themistocli* adjutor contra patriam inventus est nemo, itaque mortem sibi Uterque conscivit." Lælius, xii.42. If Coriolanus was mythical, nay, if

there existed the least doubt as to his reality, the propriety of coupling him with Themistocles would be on a par with such a phrase as this in a grave treatise: " Amadis of Gaul and Frederic the Great, both defeated vast armies, with very inconsiderable numbers." Brut. x. 41. " Porsena." Ad Att. 9.10.: " Eum C. Mucius interficere conatus est." Pro Sextio: " Ejus necem tentavit Mucius." Parad. i. 2. 12. Tacitus in the very first sentences of his Annals, corroborates the fact of Rome having been governed by kings, and says that Brutus expelled them. He mentions Tarquinius Prisons, and in such a way as to show his utter ignorance of our modern discoveries. He says the mons Cælius was so called " a Casle Vibennâ, qui dux gentis Etruscæ... sedem earn acceperat a Tarquinio Prisco, seu quis alius regum dedit nam scriptores in eo dissentiunt (which of these scriptores have those who reject the authority of Cicero, and Tacitus, and Varro, examined?) *cœtera non ambigua sunt."* Hist. iii. 27. Speaking of the conflagration of the Capitol, he says: " Id facinus! luctuosissimum populo R. accidit... Sedem Deis.. conditam *quam non Porsena* (it is clear he believed such a person to have existed) deditâ urbe, neque Galli captâ, temerare potuissent furore principum exscindi... voverat Tarquinius Priscus Rex bello Sabino, jeceratque fundamenta... mox Servius Tullius sociorum studio, deinde Tarquinius Superbus... hostium spoliis, extruxêre." They know little of that immortal writer who think that he would have exposed the energy of his concentrated indignation to doubt or even ridicule by interweaving the expression of it with *myths* and fabulous traditions. Annal. iii. 27., he gives a concise and rapid sketch of Roman history from Romulus, naming " Numa qui divino jure populum devinxit," Tullus, Ancus, Servius Tullius,Tarquinius, the decemvirs, the Gracchi, Sulla, Pompeius suarum legum auctor et sub-versor, who, " quæ armis tuebatur, armis amisit." Nor is there the least reason to suppose that he disbelieved the existence of one more than of the other. Such is a very scanty portion of the evidence we are asked to disbelieve; evidence absolutely uncontradicted, concerning which no ancient writer hints a doubt; that satisfied Cicero, and Tacitus, and Varro (for I might have quoted many passages from this last writer in support of my opinion); evidence broad, obvious, and explicit, minute, circuitous, and oblique, given in private letters, in public speeches, in histories, in philosophical treatises, in solemn edicts, stamped upon the thoughts, colouring the opinions, guiding the judgments, of those who lived at an age when abundant materials of scepticism, had any existed, must have been within their reach; conveyed to us in every form, and without a hint of contradiction: for, the narrative, the argument, the expostulation, the dialogue, the illustration, the panegyric, the invective, the pleasure and the pain, the wrath and the gratitude, the earnest and the jest, of some of the greatest writers that ever lived, on the laws, constitution, history, and usages of their own country, assume as unquestionable the facts we are required by those who are inferior to them in all respects (and especially in having come into the world, eighteen hundred years later), dogmatically to reject. " Sed tu vera puta." Livy, whom, to agree with modern theories, we must consider not as Quintilian did, but as a sort of Archbishop Turpin, and Dion. Hal., I have put aside. Yet in the words of the best treatise on evidence in our language (Horse Paulinas), I may say these works establish " the substantial truth of the narrative, and substantial truth is that which in every historical inquiry ought to be sought after and ascertained: it is the groundwork of every other observation;" and, again, " the character of truth and originality is undesignedness." However, the extravagance of a doctrine insures to it a certain number of proselytes; or, as La Bruyere says, " Quand il s'agit des choses si claires on est sûr de ne pas convainere.".

The worst of this credulous scepticism is, that it provokes a host of writers, who resemble their model in nothing else, to imitate the defects of a great man, and by caricaturing his exaggerations to aim at a reputation for genius and originality. For instance, I must consider the attempt to represent the patricians and plebeians of Rome, as belonging, like the Normans and the Saxons, to two different stems, the former being the Etruscan and the victorious, the latter the Latin and the vanquished caste, as a ludicrous proof of submissive incredulity. This is directly at variance with all which the evidence of every ancient writer that bears at all upon the subject, teaches us. On the contrary, there are the most unanswerable reasons to believe that there was an exact resemblance in the language, manners, and worship of the inhabitants of ancient Rome. There is, as it appears to me, no reason whatever to disbelieve the fact attested by so many writers, that Rome was an Alban colony, and that at first it was governed by no settled law. "*Omnia manu a regibus gubernabantur.*"

A body of law, however, grew up under the Roman kings in some degree adequate to the exigencies of the state. These laws, the authors of the Digest tell us, were collected by Sextua Papirius, a contemporary of Tarquin the younger, whose book *was extant under the emperors,* and on this book Granius Flaccus wrote a commentary in the days of Cæsar.

Up to the time of Servius Tullius the legislative power was exercised by the *comitia curiata* which were composed of the different *gentes* into which the community[289] was divided. I certainly think that this was a democratical institution: it is so spoken of by Tacitus, and Cicero. Niebuhr[290], however, affirms, without any authority of any kind, that the plebeians were excluded from them altogether, though he admits that the votes were given, not by the heads of races only, but "*viritim.*" While others who maintain Niebuhr's doctrine, perceiving how

---

[289] Tac. xi.§22. A. G. 15.27.

[290] "So," says Hegel, speaking of Niebuhr, " is the plainest and most decisive evidence of history overthrown." Phil. der Geschichte, 294.

untenable this proposition is, assert that the plebeians were members of the "*comitia curiata,*" but that the head of each "*gens*" alone had a right to vote. The school of Niebuhr is thus driven to the paradox that the measure of Servius Tullius, by which the Romans were distributed according to their wealth into the *comitia centuriata,* and by which, in reality, the whole legislative power was flung with such dexterity into the hands of the opulent, was to strengthen the plebeian interest, notwithstanding the obvious reason of the thing, and the positive testimony of Cicero, "*Curavit Servius quod semper in republicâ*[291] *tenendum est ne plurimum valeant plurimi.*" It may be mentioned here that the very first measure of Brutus after the expulsion of the Tarquins was to convene[292] the "*comitia curiata*" (this oligarchical assembly, as, for opposite and mutually destructive reasons, the school of Niebuhr affirm it to have been), in order to ratify the banishment and deposition of Tarquin; and at the same time a law was passed transferring the election of the consuls to the *comitia centuriata:* thus appealing to the people, whose consent was necessary to a change of constitution, in the one assembly, and securing the power of the aristocracy by vesting the election of the highest magistrate in the other. The *comitia curiata,* after the *comitiâ tributa* fell into disuse, were convened only for the sake of the auspices, and were represented by the thirty lictors who once convened each *curio.:* "*comitiis illis ad speciem atque usurpationem vetustatis per triginta lictores auspiciorum causa adumbratis.*"[293] Should it be asked, why, if the "*comitia curiata*" were an assembly constituted on popular principles, the tribunes of the people should have taken the right of election from them to transfer it to the *comitia tributa,* the answer is, that the calling of this assembly was mixed up with the superstitious notions which are so conspicuous in all the early Roman usages; that three augurs must be present whenever a "*lex curiata* " was passed; and that any augur might put an end to the meeting by saying, "*alio die*" when it was convened, and pretending that the auspices were

---

[291] De Rep. ii. 22.
[292] Dion. Hal. b. iv.
[293] Cic. De Leg. Ag.ii.§12.

deficient — a circumstance which, so long as the augurs were patricians, must considerably impair the efficiency of any popular convention.

"Every time," says Dion. Hal., "that the votes of the people were given in the *comitia curiata,* the vote of the poor man was equivalent to that of the rich; and as there were more poor voters than rich, the poor generally prevailed. Servius Tullius perceiving this, hit upon a means of making the rich the stronger; for, whenever it was requisite to elect magistrates or to pass a law, or to declare war, instead of convening the people, according to the *curia,* he convened them by centuries," Can any passage be more decisive than this, which there is no counter authority to balance, and no counter evidence to contradict? and is not the attempt to give a directly opposite character to the measure of Servius Tullius to make the *comitia curiata* an oligarchical, and the *comitia centuriata* a democratical assembly, in defiance of such a passage, a proof of the errors into which the most learned and acute plunge headlong when deserting common sense, and anxious only to support a theory, they give the reins to fancy and conjecture. Had the passage been directly the reverse of what it is, the hypothesis of the Niebuhr school would have had some authority in its favour; had it been, equivocal, there might have been some opportunity for cavil and some scope for ingenuity: but standing as it does, supported by all probability, and confirmed by overwhelming testimony, I know not if it had been the intention of the writer to refute Niebuhr by anticipation, what words he could have used more direct, conclusive, and irresistible.[294]

In the *comitia centuriata,* the people voted by centuries. They were divided into classes, and each class contained a certain number of centuries. The first class, consisting of all citizens whose wealth exceeded 100,000 *asses,* contained more centuries than all the rest together. It comprised 100.

---

[294] Gaius, xvi. 10.

The second class contained twenty centuries, into which the citizens whose property amounted to 75,000 *asses* were distributed.

In the third class, also of twenty centuries, the citizens were put whose property amounted to 50,000 *asses.*

The fourth class also contained twenty centuries; its voters possessed each property to the value of 25,000 *asses.*

The fifth class contained thirty centuries; each voter had property to the value of 11,000 *asses.*

The last class, which contained the greatest number of citizens, had only one century, and was so insignificant that many authors omit it altogether. Its members were called "*capite censi*" and "*proletarii.*" Afterwards it was divided into three centuries, the first two of which were enrolled and served in the legions; the last only served in the marine till the time of Marius.

The *comitia centuriata* could not give the "*imperium*" or military command. That could only be done by the "*comitia curiata,*" even in the last days of the republic, and when they were represented by the thirty lictors. The consuls, the prætors, the proconsuls, and proprietors, after their election by the suffrages of the tribes, were invested with military authority by the formal proceeding before the "*comitia curiata,*" and were forced to go through the ceremony of this second election. "Consuli, si legem curiatam non habet, attingere rem militarem non licet," are the words of Cicero. Though in general these proceedings were mere form, it sometimes happened that they were abused for party or personal purposes by the augurs, any one of whom could obstruct them; and we find a remarkable instance of this in Cicero's letters,[295] Appius Claudius, consul in

---

[295] " Jove tonante cum populo agere nefas," was a maxim of Roman constitutional law, and a very useful one to the patricians. Without suggesting any resemblance between a Roman augur and an English bishop, it may be observed that this opposition to Appins, which Cicero calls " calumnia legia curiatæ," may be compared as an instance of the abuse of forms with the opposition to Dr. Hampden, and an attempt of the same kind against Dr. Rundle—the " Rundle has a heart " of Pope. He was accused of being an Arian, and therefore was not made Bishop of

A.U.C. 699, was so tormented by an hypocritical (for religion was the pretext) and factious opposition of this sort, that he resolved to take possession of his government of Cilicia without the sanction of the *lex curiata.*

After the expulsion of the Tarquins, the royal power was conferred on two patricians, elected for a year under the name of consuls. By the "*rogationes Valeriœ,*" an appeal was given from their determinations to the *comitia.* Internal discord and foreign war made changes necessary; one of these was the appointment of a dictator in great emergencies. His power was absolute. The senate decided when the election of a dictator was necessary, and the consuls named the person who should fill the office.

Another institution was that of the tribunes. This was a concession to the people after their secession to the "*mons sacer.*" The *tribuni plebis* were created A. U. C. 260. Their persons were inviolable (for which reason Augustus took the office). Their houses were open day and night, each of the plebeian tribes had a tribune; two of these tribunes were chosen annually to assist the deliberations of the senate. The tribunes had no "*imperium,*" but each had a "*veto*" by which he could suspend the measures he disapproved. At first their power was rather negative than active, their office was one of jealous controul and superintending vigilance; as, however, their character as representatives of the people, became more and more developed on different emergencies, their functions, like those of our House of Commons, in the place of which they stood, became more significant. They could call together the plebs in the "*comitia tributa,*" over which they presided; and thus was instituted the third class of *comitia,* the importance of

---

Gloucester, but Bishop of Berry. The Lord Chancellor (Talbot) of that day, said, "if the Bishop of London refused to consecrate he would incur a premunire." Hervey's Memoirs, vol. i. p. 451. With regard to Appius, see Cic. ad Att. iv. 16.: "Appius, sine lege, suo suinptu in Ciliciam cogitat." Ad Fam. i. 9. 25. Ad Q. Frat. iii. 2. 3.: " Appius sine lege curiata confirmat, se Len-tulo nostro successurum. Gabinium accusavit majestatis." (A sort of Roman premunire.) Gabinius, who had stirred up the opposition, was, though an augur, a most pernicious sycophant. Without the " lex curiata" the quæstor could not defray the expenses of the prætor from the public purse.

which increased with the prosperity of the empire. Besides these offices the plebeian ædiles were created; their duty was to take care of the markets, the public edifices and shows. To these may be added the military tribunes, and the quæstors, who took care of the archives and treasure of the state.

During the fierce struggle between the patricians and the plebeians, the civil law is scarcely mentioned, while the constitution expands itself by successive alterations. There are, however, three capital points in which the transition from public law into the institutions by which the intercourse of private life was regulated may be remarked; and these as Vico has observed, are the "*connubium,*" the "*patria potestas,*" and the "*nexus,*" the triple source of Roman jurisprudence. Meanwhile, the terrible weapon in the hands of the patricians, was the rigour and obscurity of the law. When the kings were expelled, the laws were carefully concealed from the knowledge of the people, every thing relapsed into confusion, "iterumque cœpit populus Romanus incerto magis jure et consuetudine ali quam per latam legem." It became therefore necessary to build upon a new foundation. The nobles, like the church in the dark ages, and our lawyers in the reign of George III., offered the fiercest resistance to the introduction of any fixed or regular system of ascertained law; ξηλουντες, says Dion. Hal., τὰ τῶν τυρὰννων ἐθη. It appears to me (and many learned German writers concur in the opinion), that without setting at defiance evidence above all suspicion, and far more cogent than that on which it is usual to rely with implicit confidence, it cannot be disputed that the senate, with the assent of the people, did appoint three commissioners to travel into Greece, in order to acquire a knowledge of the Athenian law. In the year A. u. c. 302, after their return, ten patricians were appointed to prepare a code of laws which were produced in the same year. That these laws were drawn up by the assistance of an Ephesian exile, named Hermodorus[296], is to my

[296] Cic. De Legibus, ii.§23., says, quoting the law of the Twelve Tables on funerals, in which the word "lessum" is used: " Lessum, quasi lugubrem ejulationem, ut vox ipsa significat, quod eo magis judico veram esse quia *lex Solonis* id ipsum vetat." This is as if Blackstone, explaining the meaning of the word Exchequer, were to

understanding as certain as that Solon was a citizen of Athena. Two more tables were added to these and (305) published by L.

---

quote the grand coûtumier of Normandy in support of his opinion. Blackstone would take the Norman Conquest for granted, just as Cicero does the embassy to Athens. Now Cicero had in his hands a commentary written during the reign of the kings of Rome (c. 5. Pro Rab.). Besides, Papirius immediately after the expulsion of the kings, collected their laws in six books; and Granius Flaccus in the time of Cicero wrote a commentary on this treatise. It is therefore clear, that all the records of the state were not destroyed by the Gauls. Is Cicero, then, profoundly versed as he was in the usages and history of his own country, and a complete master of Grecian eloquence, with Solon's laws and the Twelve Tables, their commentators, the records and annals of the state before him, even if, instead of being supported by the testimony of every writer on the subject, near his own age, they had been silent, a superior authority to Nicbuhr? There can be no doubt as to what Cicero thought of Nicbuhr's myths. Is he a competent witness?, or has there ever existed a man whose opinion on such points, where he had no party to serve, was entitled to more consideration?—and, observe, the evidence is not about a minute point of antiquarian learning, but on the origin of laws which he learnt by heart, or a fact just as notorious, and just as likely to be believed without foundation in his time by educated men, as the Norman conquest in our own.

Dion. Hal. x. 26. Livy, iii. 33. Tac. iii. 27. Plinius Maximo (1. viii. ep. 24.): — " Habe ante oculos hanc esse terrain quæ nobis miserit jura— quæ leges non victa acceperit sed petentibus dederit—Athenas esse quas adeas;... quibus reliquam umbram et residuum libertatis nomen eripere durumest." Direct testimony in a grave exhortation. *Οἵ Ρωμαῖοι..... τρεις ἄνδρας εις τήν 'Σλλάδα, διά τουςνὸμουςεθη πεπόμφασι.* Zonaras, Ann. vii. 18. p. 66. ed. Bonnæ. Cicero says in terms, ii.§23. De Legibus: "cætera in XII Tab.... translata de Solonis fere legibus." De Rep. ii. 36. Pliny the Elder says, lib. xxxiv. c. 5. p. 219, ed. Lipsiæ: "Fuit Hermodori Ephesii in comitio, leguni quas decemviri scribebant interpretis, publice dicata." He goes on to corroborate another *myth:* " Horatii Coclitis statua quæ durat hodic, quum hostes a ponte sublicio solus arcuisset." No proposal that I know of has yet been made for a statuo to Guy of Warwick in the new Houses of Parliament. A. Gell. (xi. 18.) points out where the decemvirs modified Solon's laws: " Incisas sint leges Duodecim Tabulis et publice sere præfixo jura præscripta sunt." Cyp. Op. p. 4. ed. Par. 1726, ad Don. E. p.7. "PopulusRomanus,.. decemviros legibus scribendis creavit, qui eas ex libris Solonis translates in duodecim tabulis exposuerunt." Aurelius Victor de Vir. 111. c. 22. Amm. Marcell. 22. c. ult. Varro mentions the Commentarii Consulares, lib. vi. 88., the " Literæ Antiquæ," lib. v. 143. Strabo, lib. xiv. p. 951. ed. Amtel. (p. 642. ed. Paris.) speaking of Hermodorus, says: *SoKtl St* twrog o *avi'fp- i^ofir/v^* Ttvcn; *'PwfJtaiois ovyypd*-4-ni. I forgot to add the testimony of Gains to the evidence ad Legem Duodecim Tabularum, lib. 4. Sciendum cat. in actione filiium l"e-giiiidi>riiiii illud observandum essu quod *ad œxemplum ejus legis quodam modo scriptum est quam Athenis Solon* dicitur tulisse, nam illic ita CSt: *fdv rts* at^MfTi'a irap* *d\\orplf{i ^(wpiffi opvyrj* J— *ri}v 'upov fil} Traf.af3iti-veiv—^at/Tef^lov -n-oSa mro^i-ireiv— tw5e c^KTjfJLn* 5uo TroScfcs, fc. *r.* A. What evidence, especially if the date of the law be considered, can be more direct? One of the greatest Roman jurists, commenting on the Twelve Tables, says, " such a law is taken from Solon's," which he quotes: and against this is to be set the hypothesis of an ingenious Prussian in the nineteenth century, — " malo, mehercule, meorum negligentiam."

Valerius and M. Horatius. These were suspended in the Forum. In these Twelve Tables were incorporated:—1. Positive laws of other countries. 2. Some of the laws of the ancient kings of Rome. 3. Many of the unwritten Roman customs which had hitherto supplied the place of law. Some of the laws of the kings not actually incorporated with the Twelve Tables, were still considered binding commentaries on these laws, existed in the days of Cicero; certainly, when[297] it is considered that after the law of the Twelve Tables, the intermarriage of patricians and plebeians was looked upon almost as incestuous, and the latter were debarred from all access to the highest and most important offices of the state, it is surprising to find writers asserting that the Twelve Tables were a treaty of reconciliation between the two orders.

According to the most judicious writers, the order of the Twelve Tables was as follows. First, the process (tab. 1.); then private law; law of things — of obligations; family law; law of inheritance (tab. 2-5.), to which there was an addition (6.). Table seven is supposed to have related to offences. Tables eight and nine to public law. Table ten to *the jus sacrum.* The last tables were;added by the second decemvirs, and they contained an expressive law forbidding the marriage of patricians and plebeians. Vico has dwelt upon some of the points of resemblance pointed out by Salmasius, Petit, and Gothofredus, between the Athenian and Roman law. He thinks they may be accounted for by accident, and similiarity of purpose. Some of them, perhaps, may be so explained; others can hardly be adjusted to such an hypothesis. But how can the "*deductio quœ moribus fit,*" mentioned (page 27.), and its strict resemblance to the *ἐξαγωγή* of the Athenians, be accounted for otherwise than by the fact that one was borrowed from the other? Again, there is the passage in Plato (Noμ. xii. p. 202., ed. Bipont.), in which the Roman proceeding called the *furtum per lancem et licium concipere,* cited above, p. 24., is in terms described. Besides the different means of acquiring property,

---

[297] How Livy paints the state of parties, and how well he describes the spirit of an aristocracy! " Quicquid libertati plobis caveretur id suis decedere opibus credebant." iii. 55.

mentioned in the Twelve Tables, the four *contractus re,* and the four *contractus consensu,* bear no relation to the primitive institutions of Rome, and are clearly borrowed from a people more refined, and accustomed to the exigencies of a more complicated state of society. The exclusively Roman modes of acquiring property, *mancipatio, in jure cessio,* and *usucapio,* are enumerated, The *usucapio* changed simple possession into the *dominium quiritarium,* in the case of what was immoveable *(fundus)* after the possession had continued for two years, in the case of what was moveable, after a possession of one. "Lex[298] usum et auctoritatem fundi jubet esse biennium, et utimur eodem jure in ædibus quæ in lege non appellantur." "In lege[299] ædes non appellantur, et aunt casterarum rerum quarum annuus est usus."

The law of persons distinguished the freeman from the slave, and the *civis* from the *veregrinus.* Women were always under the *tutela* of some *agnatus,* till they became the property of the husband "*in manum mariti.*" There were three forms of marriage: the patrician *(confarreatio);* the plebeian *(coemptio);* and uninterrupted cohabitation for a year, which was prevented by the *trinoctium usurpatio (usus).*[300]

The son is the *hœres suus* of the father. As to constitutional law Livy tells us—" In XII Tabulis legem esse ut quodcunque *postremum* populus jussisset ill jus ratumque esset."[301]

I am extremely glad that I can fortify my opinion on the value of Livy's authority and as to the reckless arrogance of scepticism in the school of Niebuhr, by the authority of the greatest philosopher of his day, and a man as remarkable for strong direct sense as for his prodigious capacity and power of thought, I mean Hegel (Philosophic der Geschichte, p. 291.). He censures the attempt by Niebuhr to substitute philology for

---

298 Pro Cæc. 19. Hugo, vol. i. p. 140.

299 Top. I.

300 Aul. Gell. iii. 2.

301 Liv. vii. 17.

history, and to narrow, instead of enlarging, the intellectual view.

The domain of history, he says, has fallen to the lot of mere learning, which always extends itself most widely where there is least to be got. He adds the striking remark, that the early Grecian ages are indeed mythological and the creatures of a brilliant imagination, but that nothing can be more unlike the Roman character; and that the remains we possess of what is really transmitted to us as authentic Roman history are, on the contrary, sober, precise, and marked by an air of reality and truth.[302] This prosaic character, he continues in great disdain, "dieses prosaische verlangt man als *etwas mythisches* anzusehen, und dem biaher als geschichtlich aufgenommenen sollen Epopoen zu grunde legen." And again he says most truly: "Ueberhaupt muss Niebuhr's Geschichte als eine Kritik der Römischen Geschichte betrachtet werden, denn sie besteht aus einer Reihe von Abhandlungen die keineswegs die Einheit der Geschichte haben." (p. 296.) So Peter, Römische Verfassung, p. 2. It is so far from being the case, as has been said to justify the wild chimæras put forward on this part of the Roman history, that no records of Rome were left after the invasion of the Gauls, that appeals are constantly made to them by Cicero; that a *lex regia*[303] is cited in the Digest; that a work on Roman law,

[302] Hor. Ep. ii. 1.:
" Sic fautor veterum, ut tabulas
peccare vetantes,
Quas bis quinque viri sanxertint,
fœdera reguni
Vel Gabiis vel cum rigidis
æquata Sabinis,
Pontificum libros, annosa vo-
lumina vatum,
Dictitet Albano Musas in monte
locutas."

In this passage, Horace, had there been any such ballads as Niebuhr supposes, could no more have avoided all allusion to them than Dr. Percy could have helped citing Chevy Chase, in his Old English Ballads.

[303] And a very remarkable one. " Negat lex regia mulierem quæ prægnans mortua sit, humari antequam partus ei eximatur; qui contra fecerit spem animantis cum gravidâ peremisse videtur."—*Dig.* xi. 8.§3. " Imprimis fœdera et leges (erant autem ese Duodecim Tabulæ, et quædam regiæ leges) conquiri jusserunt.. vetus lex regiá

written before the Gallic invasion, was actually extant in the age of Augustus; and that Polybius[304] points out especially the time of the *decemviri,* i. e. thirty years after the invasion of Greece by Xerxes, as that when the prosperous period of the Roman constitution began: ought not this to outweigh whole volumes of modern speculation? Would the most careful, accurate, and judicious of historians have written gravely of a period concerning which no authentic documents were extant, where there were no records to guide him, or any thing but mythological tradition?[305]

quæ; simul cum ipsâ urbe nata esse videtur.... quod secundum est a decemviris ad condenda jura creatis in Duodecim Tabulis scripta."— *Livy,* xxxiv. 6.

[304] Frag. Vat ed. Maii, vi. 57.

[305] Niebuhr gravely argues that Livy is translating a ballad, because the words, "Tace inquit, Lucretia! Sextua Tarquinius sum, ferrum in manu est: moriere si emiseris vocem," can be made into Saturnian verses: so, I will answer for it, might half Cicero. Did Tacitus copy from a poem because his Annals begin with a regular hexameter quite as harmonious as some of those written by Father Ennius? —

"Urbem Romæ a principio reges habuere."

Can any man build grave arguments on such fantastic accidents? These theories are destitute alike of the attractive graces of fiction, and the severe dignity of truth.

CHAP. II.
FROM THE TWELVE TABLES TO AUGUSTUS[306]

BY these laws of the Twelve Tables a new character was impressed on Roman jurisprudence; here, however, as in so many instances which occur in Roman history, we may trace the narrow views and baneful influence of an oligarchy. No longer able to conceal from the people the words of the laws which were to regulate their proceedings, they contrived to make this knowledge nugatory, by attributing to themselves exclusively the interpretation of those laws, and by encumbering their method of proceeding with so many forms and ceremonies, any error in which was fatal, that the necessity of having constant recourse to them became more urgent and inevitable than before. These proceedings were called "*actus legitimi,*" because it was supposed that they were founded in the law of the Twelve Tables — in such a compilation there were, of course, many obscure and many doubtful passages. To

---

[306] Warnkönig, Histoire Externe du Droit Romain. Hugo, vol. i.: " Sextum Ælium etiam Ennius laudavit, et extat illius liber qui inscribitur Tripertita, qui liber, velut cunabula juris, continet. *Tripertita autem dicitur* quoniam lege Duodecim Tabularum præpositâ, jungitur interpretatio—dein subtex itur legis actio." The whole of the 2. tit. lib. i. of the Digest ought to be read as a most elegant summary of legal and constitutional history. It is taken from Gaius's Commentary on the Twelve Tables, and where it contradicts Niebuhr is, unless all the usual rules of evidence be utterly cast aside, entitled to the preference. It furnishes one striking proof of Niebuhr's love of paradox. Niebuhr has suggested that Brutus the Elder was a plebeian (by the way, on his principles, why does he allow that such a person ever existed? he rejects much stronger evidence): to say nothing of the unanimous language of all history and all probability. Gains tells us:—" Quod ad magistratus attinet, initio civitatis hujus constat reges omnem potestatem habuissa; iisdem temporibus et tribunum Celerum fuisse constat. Is autem erat qui equitibus præeratet *veluti secundum locum a regibus* obtinebat, quo in numero fuit Junius Brutus, qui auctor fuit reges ejiciendi." This is Niebuhr's plebeian! As Archbishop Whateley has shown, in his admirable argument against the existence of Napoleon, if you keep out of sight the collective force of the arguments in favour of a cause, and insist upon the probabilities against it (some of which, in the nature of things, are almost always to be found), you may make a plausible case in favour of any proposition. This is very well explained by Sir James Macintosh in his decisive refutation of the notion that Charles I. wrote the " Eikon Basilike."

explain and limit these was the peculiar task of the nobles; and without the assistance of some one among them, redress was hopeless. They invented forms, ceremonies, and distinctions, which they guarded with the utmost rigour; they assigned a particular meaning to certain words, and calling religion to their aid, they appointed certain days on which all legal proceedings were forbidden. The knowledge of all these pernicious usages they reserve exclusively to themselves, and thus maintained an ascendancy over the people till an event happened by which the spell of their dominion was dissolved. About the year of Rome 449, Cnæsus Flavius, who had been secretary to Appius Claudius Cæcus, probably with the sanction and assistance of his patron, published a collection of these *formulæ:,* with a list of the days on which judicial proceedings were permitted, and thus communicated to the people what had so long been withheld from them by the selfish jealousy of the nobles. This collection was called *Jus Flavianum;* and in spite of the cabals and intrigues of the nobles, the grateful people conferred on its author the dignity of Curule Ædile.

That a people like the Romans, even at this early period of their history, should submit to a system so pernicious and absurd, may appear surprising to those who do not reflect that in the nineteenth century of the Christian sera, England is governed by a system of law equally irrational in its technicality, and even more oppressive from its accumulation. The patricians of Rome, like other monopolists, were not easily to be overcome. They set about inventing new forms and technicalities, in order to keep the people in dependance; but in rather more than a century after the publication of Flavius, this other web of their iniquity was unravelled by Sextus Ælius[307], who, A. *U. C.* 552, published a collection of these later forms, and thereby put an end for ever to their mystery. This collection was called "*Jus Ælianum.*" In the year A. u. C. 500, Tiberius

[307] Instit. cursus, vol. i. Puchta Gewohnheitarecht, vol. ii. Tigerstrom, Aeussere Ges. des R. Rs. Giraud, Hist. du Droit Romain. Beaufort, Rép. R. c.

Coruncanius, the first plebeian who had obtained the pontificate, taught the science of law openly at Rome.[308]

After this, the sense of present and the recollection of past oppression led to a new mode of proceeding, which was introduced by the *Lex Œbutia,* and confirmed by the *Leges Juliœ,* of which I have already spoken (p. 34.). The first of these laws abolished the *legis actiones* in most cases, and the formulas, of which a full account is given in the fourth book of Gaius, and which Valerius Maximus tells us[309] the prætors consulted the ablest lawyers to determine, continued in force, till the days of Diocletian.

Roman law during this period may be divided under two heads. Positive Law, *Jus Scriptum,* and Customary Law, *Jus non Scriptum.* The former consisting of the *Plebis cita* and *Senatus Consulta,* the latter of the *Edicta Magsitratuum,* and the *Responsa Prudentium.*

The measures proposed by a magistrate, who was a member of the Senate, and adopted by the whole Roman people, were called laws, "*Lex est quod populus Romanus senatorio magistratu constituente velut consule constituebat.*" After the force of law had been given to the "*Plebisscita,*" the "*leges*" were rather directed to matters of public order than to questions of private concern, and controversies between man and man. During this period several changes took place in legislation: some relating to the form in which the laws were cast, others to the authority from which they emanated. Formerly it had been usual to comprise in a single law the most opposite and heterogeneous subjects. This was called "*leges per saturam ferre,*" and of course was liable to great abuse. During the period we are now speaking of, it was prohibited, and every law was limited to a specific and single object. The "*comitia tributa*" were also substituted in numerous instances, for the "*comitia centuriata,*" and the vote by ballot, for that given in

308 "AnteTiberium Coruncanium publics professum neminem traditur, cæteri autem ante hunc vel in latenti jus civile retinere cogitabant, solumque consultatoribus vacare potius quam discere valen-tibus se præstabant."—*De Orie. J.* ii.§35.

309 Val. Max. b. viii. 2.

public. Particular forms were required in the preparation of the law. First came the "*præscriptio,*" in which was specified the magistrate who had convened the *comitia* and proposed the law. Then came the *præceptum, i. e.* the enacting part of the law; and, lastly, the *cautio,* or penalty by which its provisions were enforced. The laws were often divided into several chapters. They were sometimes named after the proposer, and sometimes from their object, e. *g. "leges sacratæ, somtuariæ, cibariæ, agrariæ, tabellariæ judiciariæ."* The expressions *"rogari," "abrogari," "derogari," "subrogari," "obrogari,"* were respectively employed to denote the abolition, partial or total, the addition to, or the change of, any particular law.

The *Plebisscita* were the laws passed at the *comitia tributa,* where the vote of every man was equal.[310] According to the form of government established by Romulus, the votes of the people were taken at the *comitia curiata,* where the same principle was in force. But as the *comitia curiata* could only be presided over by a patrician magistrate, and the auspices were taken there, it was in the power of the patricians to interrupt them whenever they thought proper. Again, it was requisite that the *comitia centuriata,* as well as the *comitia curiata,* should be authorised by a decree of the senate; and though the tribunes at first submitted to this law for the *comitia tributa,* they were not long in shaking off so pernicious a restriction. This great victory over the oligarchy was gained A.U.C. 468; at least, it is from this date only that the validity of decrees passed at the *comitia tributa* was acknowledged by the nobles: *"ut quod tributim populus jussisset populum teneret."* The contest began in the year A.U.C. 304, when this concession was made to bring the people back from Mount Aventine. In order to escape from its consequences, the nobles at first maintained that the word *populus* did not bind them. This evasion was encountered by the law *"Ut plebiscita omnes Quirites tenerent."*

The tribunes[311] also succeeded in procuring a law that the tribunes of the people and the other plebeian magistrates should

---

[310] Dig. i. 2. Dion. Hal. lib. ix. vii. Livy, ii. A. Gell. 13. 15., and Livy, 38. 40.
[311] Livy, iv. 41.

be elected at these assemblies. The power of the Roman people exerted in the *comitia tributa* was supreme. It was tantamount to an act of the legislature with us; and thus the conduct of Tiberius Gracchus, in depriving his colleague of a trust that he abused, was strictly constitutional. It was just as much in the power of the *comitia tributa* to depose a tribune, as it would be in the power of the Queen, Lords, and Commons, in this country, to depose a judge[312]; and the patricians frequently applied to the *comitia tributa* for governments which they knew the senate would refuse. Marius, Julius Cæsar, Pompey, Crassus, all obtained commands from this authority, which no one ever questioned till it was exerted on behalf of the people, against a perfidious servant and contemptible renegade to their cause. The causes tried at the *comitia tributa* were never capital. If any one accused of a capital offence did not appear before the *comitia centuriata,* his exile was confirmed by a vote of the tribes.

Among the most remarkable of the laws during this period were, as to persons: —

The *Lex Canuleia,* which, by making the marriages of patricians and plebeians lawful, broke down the great rampart of the aristocracy,[313]

428.The *Lex Pœtilia Papiria* "De nexis ob *æs* alienum;" "Pecuniæ creditæ *bona* debitoris non

corpus obnoxium esse."[314]

---

[312] Ib. xxv. 4. xxvi. 3.

[313] Livy, iv. 1—6.

[314] This principle has at last, after the indignant eloquence of our greatest writers had been long employed in its behalf, forced its way into the English law, and mitigated its savage and useless provisions. See Burke's " Letter to the Sheriff of Bristol." They who read the account of the way in which a debtor was tortured to death in the Fleet prison, by the warden and his servant, about the middle of the last century, with perfect impunity *(State Trials, Higgins & Arne, Life of Lord Hardwicke,* vol.ii.), while men were constantly hanged for fowl-stealing, will be less shocked by the provision of the Roman law, " De inopi debitore in partes dissecando " *(Oell.* xx. 1.), " Tertiis nundinis secanto." This horrid murder, the details of which are too revolting for insertion, under the eye of the law, and almost with its sanction, for the murderers were both allowed to escape, led to no alteration or improvement of the law. When we reflect on the abuses, inconsistencies, and abominations of the English law, down to a very recent period, the antipathy to

557.The *Lex Atilia,* which related to the tutela conferred by the magistrate.

The *Lex Licinia Mucia,* as to the right of citizenship.

The *Lex Plœtoria* or *Lœtoria.* It related to the obligations contracted by persons under the age

of twenty-five, and allowed such persons, when sued, to bring an action against their creditors, the object of which was to deprive the creditor of certain political rights. It is to this decree that the appointment of a curator for the *prodigus* and *furiosus* is mainly to be ascribed.

664. *Lex Julias, de civitate cum hostibus commumcandâ.*

Lex Atinia, de rerum furtivarum usucapione.[315] By this law the *usucapio* of stolen property was forbidden. It was only a re-enactment of a law in the Twelve Tables. On the same subject were the

663. *Lex Plautia* and the *Lex Julia* of Julius Cæsar: *de rebus vi possessis non usucapiendis."*

571. *Lex Furia Testamentaria,* restraining the power of leaving more than a certain sum from the heir. *"Furia testamentaria plus quam mille assium legatum mortisve causa prohibet capere."*[316]

585. *Lex Voconia,* the object of which was to exclude women from succession *"ab intestate,"* and to limit the bequests that could be made to them by will. It was urged by Cato, *"magnâ voce et magnis lateribus;"* and had a vast influence on the Roman law. Hence, as has been stated, sprung the doctrine of *fidei cummissa.* It has given rise to innumerable discussions in modern times. It was *"ne cuiquam plus legaret quam ad hœredes perveniret."*[317]

---

reform in this free country appears like judicial infatuation, in every sense of the word.

[315] Inst. ii. 7. 5.

[316] Ulp. Fr. i.§2.

[317] Gaius, ii. 226.

672. *Lex Cornelia Testamentaria: "de testamentis captivorum qui apud hastes discesserunt,"*[318]

589. *Lex Manilla* relates to the boundaries of fields.

589. *Lex Roscia and Lex Fabia* relate to the same subject.

Lex Licinia prohibits alienation by a co-proprietor.

Lex Scribonia abolishes the *usucapio* of servitudes.

LAW OF OBLIGATIONS

This is the portion of law which underwent the most thorough change during the time of which I am speaking.

488. *Lex Aquilia de damno injuriâ data.*[319]

550. *Lex Cincia de donis ac muneribus.*[320]

659. *Lex Furia.*[321]

673. *Lex Cornelia.*[322]

Lex Publicia.[323]

PROCESS

673. Lex Pinaria.[324]

510. Lex Silia.

513. Lex Calpurnia.[325]

Lex Marcia.[326]

---

[318] Dig. xlix. 15.§22.
[319] Dig ix.§2. Budæus in Pand. p. 5.
[320] Tacitus, Ann. 11. Budæus in Pandect, p. 46.
[321] Gaius, iii.§122.
[322] Ibid. iii.§124.
[323] Ibid. iii. 127.
[324] Ibid. iii.§13.
[325] Ibid. iv.§18.
[326] Ibid. iv. 23

589. Lex Manilia. (De finibus agrorum).

520. Lex Æbutia.[327]

708. Leges Juliœ Judiciariœ.

PENAL LAWS

605. Lex Remnia.

635. Lex Marcia.

648. Lex Servilia.

Lex Julia.

Lex Apuleia.

664. Lex Servilia II.

665. Lex Plautia.

673. Leges Corneliœ.

695. Lex Julia (repetundarum).[328]

599. Lex Pompeia.

BEQUESTS

714. Lex Falcidia.[329]

Among the monuments of Roman law, during this period, which are still extant, may be mentioned the *Lex Thoria Agraria*[330] A. *V. C.* 647, and *Lex Servilia repetundarum* A. U. C. 654. All that remains of either consists of seven fragments of a large tablet, which contains the *Lex Servilia* on one side, and the *Lex Thoria* on the other. Another most important remnant of

---

[327] Ibid. iv.§30. Aul. Gell. xvi. 10.
[328] Cæsar, v. in Pison.
[329] Dig. xxxv.§2. Cod. vi.§50.
[330] Rudorff, Z. für G. W. cit. *infra.*

law is the *Lex de Galliâ Cisalpinâ*[331], a plebiscitum, probably carried about the beginning of the seventh century. It relates to the municipal authorities and to the rights of the inhabitants of Cisalpine Gaul, it was found 1760, and is now in the museum at Parma. The twentieth to the twenty-second chapters, and part of the nineteenth and twenty-third chapters, are alone preserved. The *Tabula*[332] *Heracleensis* must also be assigned to this period, as it belongs undoubtedly to the time of the Republic. This also is a *plebiscitum* which relates to the Roman policy and municipal government: a fragment of it was found A. D. 1732, and was brought to Naples. It was the continuation of another fragment brought to England 1735, and carried to Naples 1752. It was first published in twelve chapters by Mazochi[333], with a commentary 1816, and has since been published by Hugo, with a German translation and notes. Savigny considers it a "*Lex Julia Municipalis,"* or a law binding on all municipalities of Roman citizens. The *Senatus consultum de Bacchanalibus* was discovered A. D. 1640, in a village in Calabria, written on an iron tablet which is now at Vienna.

EDICTA MAGISTRATUUM

The change in the Roman constitution by the expulsion of the kings was one which affected the duration, not the nature of the supreme authority. To check or controul one power by another, was at first too refined a principle for so primitive a people; and, indeed, such a doctrine never seems to have been

---

331 Hugo, Civ. Mag. vol. ii. p. 423. art. xx. It was published first by Carli Antichità Italiche, 1788. It was discovered thirteen years after the Tabula Alimentaria of Trajan was dug up, and within fifteen braccia of the same spot: it was published by Marini without a word of explanation, 1796. " Gli Atti e Monumenti de Fratelli arvali." Tigerström, J. Gaius, p. 96.

332 Savigny, Z. für Ges. It. cit. *infrà.*

333 Hugo, Civ. Mag. Art. xix. vol. iii. p. 340. The second fragment was bought by Mr. Brian Fairfax, and published by Maittaire, 1735. The first was found in the bed of a rivulet (Salandra) that runs from Basilicata (Lucania) into the Gulf of Tarentum. Ib. 342. It was a tablet with a Greek inscription on one side and a Latin inscription on the other. The Greek *jus* was a psephisma of the town Heraclea concerning a plot of ground sacred to Bacchus. Tigerström, J. G. p. 97.

thoroughly incorporated with the Roman system, even when that people had arrived at the greatest height of power and reputation. The power of the tribune was almost the only instance in which the office of controul was called into operation. Every magistrate, within the sphere of his functions, appears to have possessed an absolute and unlimited authority, for the abuse of which he was, when the term of office had expired, responsible to the community. The Romans looked for their security against unconstitutional and oppressive violence, not to the scanty power of their magistrates, but to the shortness of the time for which that trust was delegated. Whatever evils may have flowed from this system, it cannot be denied that it communicated an extraordinary degree of energy to their administration, and enabled them to combine the vigour of a free people with the despatch and secrecy usually supposed peculiar to despotic governments.

Each of the higher magistrates, as they were successively created, were invested with the full authority of the state, and their edicts, while they were in office, had the force of law. So we find mentioned edicts of the tribunes; edicts of the priests; edicts of the censor; edicts of the curule ædiles, which are referred to in the Digest. But by far the moat comprehensive and important of these edicts was the edict of the prætor. The first prætor was created 388 A. U. C.: "Concessum a nobilitate plebi de consule plebeio, a plebe nobilitati de prætore uno qui jus in urbe diceret ex patribus creando."[334] The præætor peregrinus was created A. U. C. 408; the number of those magistrates increased with the dominion of the state. Two were added after, when Sicily and Sardinia became provinces, A. U. C. 526; two more for Spain and Provence, 556. A. U. C.; four more on account of the *quœstiones publicce,* introduced by Sylla; two more by Julius Cæsar. As the *edictum prœtoris,* and its effect on Roman jurisprudence, has been the subject of a particular discussion, it is here sufficient to mention, as an important circumstance in its history and the history of the Roman people, the "*Lex Cornelia,*" 687 A. U. C.; *ut prœtores*

---

[334] Livy, vi.§42.

ex edictis perpetuis jusdicerent. The edict was composed by each prœtor on entering office. That part of the former edict which has been incorporated with the actual edict was termed *edictum tralatitium* (the addition, *edictum novum).* Before the *Lex Cornelia,* the prætor might make an "*edictum repentinum;*" an edict for a particular occasion. Afterwards such an exercise of caprice became impossible. After the edict had been read to the people by the "præco," it was exposed on a white board (in *albo).* The form in which the prætor gave his judgment was "*dabo judicium,*" "*servabo,*" "*interdico,*" "*restituam,*" "*prœtor judicetur*"

To the influence of the prætor in Roman jurisprudence may be ascribed —

1. Many new actions.

2. Exceptions.

3. The necessity of giving sureties and guarantees;" *Cautiones."*

4. The giving possession under certain circumstances of disputed property. *Possessiones bonorum;* "*missio in bona."*

5. The "*interdicta."*

6. The "*restitutiones in integrum."*

7. The *"fictiones,"* which have been already mentioned, by which technical obstacles to justice were put aside.

8. And the *Octavian Formula*[335] must not pass unnoticed. This was a *formula* by which any one might be compelled to restore, "*quod per vim aut metum abstulisset,"* and was inserted in the prætor's edict by L. Octavius. It is expressly mentioned in the Verrine Orations (iii.§ 61.): "C. Gallius senator postulavit a L. Metello ut ex edicto suo judicium daret in Apronium quod per vim aut metum abstulisset, quam formulam Octavianam et Romas Metellus habuerat et habebat in provincia." Metellus

---

[335] Dig. iv. 2. 9. 7. (quod metus); iv. 4. 4. 4.§33. (de doli excep.); iv. 4. 15. 3. (de dolo); iv. 2. 14. 13. "Eum qui metum fecit et de dolo teneri certum est; et consumi alteram nctioiiem ner alteram exceptione in factum opposita."

refused on the pretext "*prœjudicium se de capite Verris nolle fieri.*" Now, as the connection with Apronius was itself, if proved, the condemnation of Verres, Cicero says: "Hoc miror quomodo de quo homine prœjudicium fieri noluit per recuperatores, de hoc ipso non modo judicarit verum gravissime ac vehementissime judicarit."

Servius Sulpicius, Antistius Labeo, and A. Ofilius wrote commentaries on the Edict; of the last we are told that "*edictum prœtoris primus diligenter composuit.*"

MORES

As language preceded grammar, custom preceded law. But custom is rather the symbol of law than its origin; the foundation of that custom must be, to use a German phrase, the " Bewusstseyn," or, as we may call it, the way of thinking and acting, peculiar to the people among whom it exists,[336] This customary law is the mirror in which the peculiarities of a people are reflected. Besides the great and unquestionable principles which take the shape of positive institutions, there will be usages less comprehensive in their object, to which frequent habit will give validity; and where legislative genius and the power to generalise are, as among us, the qualities in

[336] The law of custom is, of all laws, the most imperious. It call make the most indifferent action criminal, and turn the most ordinary words into a reproach, only to be washed away by the blood of the speaker. For instance, an English farmer would not be offended it" any one said that he had bred mules, or had sown clover and wheat in the same field; but such imputations might have cost an inhabitant of Palestine his life: or an English husband, if he were asked whether his wife was at home; in Turkey, the inquirer would be put to death, and the lady sown up in a sack after mutilation. The subject is extremely well illustrated by Mr. Hume, in his dialogue of Fourli. The *rerum perpetuo similiter judicatarum auctoritas* was evidence of custom by the Roman law. Confined within this definition the maxim is sound and unexceptionable. But I know not if the evils of narrow minds and vulgar habits of thought were ever more unhappily exemplified than by the English system, under which, case law, or, as the French call it, the *jurisprudence des arrêts,* is the rule of the empire, and the sole study of those who, under the garb and guise of judges, are, in fact, its very incompetent and *ex post facto* legislators; and so long as we have no code— that is, so long as their opinion is thought conclusive on a matter wholly beyond their province, will continue to be so.

which a nation is most deficient, it will be long before such usage is circumscribed within certain rules, and assumes the shape of definite law.[337] To this want must be ascribed the barbarous state of law in this country. Custom is particularly displayed in the symbolic forms of legal proceeding, and in the decisions of popular tribunals, as opposed to those of learned bodies, like the parliaments in France. Such were the German Schöffen; and, as the prætor was changed every year, the "*res judicatœ*" of the Romans, who, however, owed their admirable system to the principle diametrically opposite to that which prevails among us: "*non exemplis, sed legibus judicandum.*" "L'identité[338] entre les lois d'une nation et les lois qui les

---

[337] It may be ascribed also to the mistaken view lawyers take of their own interest, and to the power it gives the judges by making them legislators in nine cases out of ten; being exactly the office for which they are most eminently, and, by their pursuits, disqualified. With a weak or partial judge the counsel who has most weight with him is, *pro tempore,* legislator; a code would prevent all this. But when I reflect that Romilly was opposed by all the judges, and almost all who wished to be judges, and when I look to the supine indifference, and even aversion, of all governments, to legal improvement, and the wretched ludicrous patchwork which is called legal reform, I can hardly think any such blessing is in store for my contemporaries. The general reader will recollect Montaigne's judge, who wrote:

"Questions pour l'ami " opposite every moot point. The name of these moot points in the English law is legion. On this subject, I may refer to the able, learned, and well-written treatise of Mr. Herbert Broom—Selection of Legal Maxims. If more law books were constructed with the same method and arrangement as Mr. Broom's, the profession of the law would, perhaps, become less mechanical, or, as the Germans contemptuously say, less of a Brodwissenschaft (Anglieé, trade), p. 712. 2d edit.

[338] "Cum de consuetudine civitatis vel provinciæ confidere quis videtur; primum quidem illud explorandum arbitror, an etiam contradicto aliquando judicio consuetudo firmata sit." — L. 34. *Ulp.* iv. de Off. Proc.

"Præses provinciæ, probatis his quæ in oppido frequenter in eodem controversiarum genere servata sunt, causâ cognitâ statuet. Nam et consuetudo præcedens, et ratio quæ consuetudinem suasit, custodienda est. Et, ne quid contra longam consuetudinem fiat, ad solicitudinem suam revocabit præses provinciæ."—L. I. *cod. quæ sit longa consuet.* Pothier. Pandectæ Justin. vol. ii.

Savigny, System des R. R. vol. i. b. i. c. iii.§§12. 18. 29.

Eichhorn, Grundsätze des Kirchenrechts, vol. ii. b. iv. c. i. Cap. quæ sit longa consuetudo, L. ii. cap. ii. 6., an unreasonable custom is exemplified. " Non putamus illam consuetudinem consonam rationi quod ab officiali episcopo, ad eundem episcopum valeat appellari," &c.

Eichhorn, D. Staat und Rechts G. vol. i.§75. Walter, Lehrbuch des K. R. 5. de consuetudine, He calls it with great propriety, "Eine Ergänzung des geschriebenen Rechts."

Rédaction Officielle des Coûtumes, Klimrath, torn ii. p. 135. Sismondi, Hist. des Francais, viii. 16. ix. 347, 348. " L'expérience, l'habitude, et une sorte de

constituent, ou qui en sont l'expression, est si réelle, que les écrivains qui ont décrit l'état des peuples barbares n'ont jamais songé à les distinguer les unes des autres. Il n'a fallu souvent, pour donner le nom de lois aux phénomènes qu'on désigne sous le nom des mœurs, qu'en avoir trouvé une description plus ou moins authentique.... ainsi de ce que plusieurs des nations dont j'ai à décrire l'état social ne connaissent ni livres, ni archives, il ne faut pas conclure qu'elles ne sont soumises à aucune loi; il n'y a pas beaucoup de siècles que la plupart des nations de l'Europe étaient dans le même cas, et cependant elles étaient régies par des lois auxquelles nous avons donné le nom de coûtumes."[339] All we know of the Romans leads us to believe that they were a nation over which custom and tradition would have great influence. Accordingly, this head of law is especially mentioned by Cicero[340], and we find it at a later period appealed to in the Digest,[341] "Moribus apud nos receptum est," says Ulpian; "ne inter virum et uxorem donationes valerent." And again: "De quibus causis scriptis legibus non utimur id custodiri oportet quod moribus et consuetudine inductum est.... Inveterata consuetudo pro lege non immerito custoditur, et hoc est jus quod dicitur moribus constitutum, nam cum ipsse leges

---

jurisprudence, formèrent à la longue, dans chaque tribu, des règles communes, que chacun connaissait, et dont le souvenir était conservé par l'usage."—*Pardessus, Loi Salique,* p. 416.

"L'antiquité convient à la religion, parceque souvent nous croyons plus les choses à mesure qu'elles sont plus reculés; car nous n'avons pas dans la tête des idées accessoires, tirées de ces temps-là qui puissent les contredire."—*Montesquieu, Esp. des Lois,* 26.§2.

"The rule of the canon laws was " si inducatur consuetudo præter jus sufficit tempus 10 annorum; si contra jus canonicum opus est quod consuetudo præscripta sit 40 annis." So Dig. 39. 3.§ult. " Si tamen lex agri non inveniatur vetustatem vicem legis tenere (ait Labeo), in servitutibus hoc idem sequitur, ut ubi servitus non invenitur imposita, qui diu usus est servitute, neque vi, neque clam, neque precario, habuisse *longâ consuetudine, vel ex jure, impositam servitutem* videatur.".For the canon law see Eichhorn, Grundsätze des Kirchenrechts, bd. ii. 36. Walter, Lehrbuch,§57. The most uninterrupted ecclesiastical usage in temporal matters is, that of the persecution of the sect not supported by the power of the state by the sect invested with it. This prescription reaches from the law of Constantine to the five mile act, and even later.

339 Comte, Traité de Législation, iii. 16. Puchta, Gewohnheitsrecht, i. 163. Communis Opinio.

340 Topic, 5.

341 Dig. xxiv. 1.

nullâ aliâ ex causâ, nos teneant quam quod judicio populi receptæ sunt, merito et ea quæ sine ullo scripto populus probavit tenebunt omnes, nam quod interest suffragio populus voluntatem suam declaret an rebus ipsis et factis? "So wrote and so reasoned the jurists of ancient Rome, even amid the contagion of servitude; and these are the writers which are neglected, as it too plainly appears, by the framers of our acts of parliament. The dignified language of this extract shows that among the jurists of Rome, "manebant etiam turn vestigia morientis libertatis."

RESPONSA PRUDENTÛM[342]

The influence of jurists on the Roman law, was considerably before the time of Cicero. They were called *juris periti,* and their answers were termed *"responsa prudentûm."* The law, so pronounced, was described as *"auctoritas prudentûm.* Cicero[343] covers the still remaining forms, that soon after his time became obsolete, with the happiest ridicule, but his respect for the character of a jurist is very great.

The *"substitutio pupillaris,"* the *"stipulatio Aquiliana,"* the *"regula Catoniana,"* the *"usucapio œdium,"* the meaning of the words *"hœredes necessarii,"* the *"fidei commissa,"* belong to this branch of law. Among the controverted points, we may enumerate the questions as to the *"partus ancillœ,"* between Brutus and Manilius, as to whether the *"substitutio vulgaris"* was implied in the *"substitutio pupillaris,"* and the famous discussion as to the *"jus postliminii,"* all of which are mentioned by Cicero. Appius Claudius Cæcus was the first

---

[342] Dig. lib. i. tit. iii. c. 32.

[343] But Cicero's wit would have found far more fruitful topics among us. He never heard of a plea amounting to the general issue, of a " negative pregnant," of " certainty to a common intent," of " giving colour[343]," of "the casual ejector," of objections that could be taken " on special demurrer " only, of a double summons for jurors (the first answering no earthly purpose but that of inflaming the expense of an English law suit.); nor did any Roman judge in his day condemn a party to lose his cause because he said he was " ready " instead of saying that he was " ready and willing" to do a particular act. See Appendix.

commentator on the law of the Twelve Tables; his speech on Pyrrhus was extant in Cicero's time. Sextus Ælius Pœtus wrote the "*Tripertita Juris civilis.*" Cato, the censor, wrote "*Commentarii,*" and "*Responsa, Juris civilis.*" M. Junius Brutus wrote seven books on the civil law; Manilius, three. Among other famous names in the history of Roman law, are Scævola, consul, A. U. C. 659; and Cicero's contemporaries, Servius Sulpicius, Lætius Felix, and C. Aguilius Gallus, who framed the "*formulœ de dolo malo,*" and the *stipulatio Aquiliana.*

CONDITION OF SUBJECTS AND CITIZENS

In the seventh century[344] after the foundation of Rome, all the inhabitants of Italy were subject to its dominion. The relations, however, in which the different regions of this country stood towards the metropolis were extremely various. A great number of colonies were spread over the soil, as so many garrisons to ensure the supremacy of the parent state. Some were *civium Romanorum,* some were *Latinos;* in the former, citizens, at first, were alone incorporated; the latter consisted of Romans and of Latins, but the Romans lost their rights as citizens, and the colony was reckoned among the Latin communities.

I shall reserve for another chapter an account of the *jus Italicum* and the Roman system of taxation; at present I mean

---

[344] Savigny, Zeitschrift für G. W. ii. 301. Cicero, Pro Balbo, Pro Archia. Gellius, iv. 4. 16. 13. Yell. Pat. ii. 16. Appian, i. 49. Roth says of Romulus (p. 1.), that " aspernatus pravam aliarum gentium consuetudinem quæ devictos hostes aut internecione deleverunt ut Judæi aliæque orientis nationes barbaræ, aut ut Helotas Lacedœmonu in miserimam servitutem detruserunt, non incolumitatem modo superatis gentibus finitimis sed ctiam Romanam civitatem plerisque tribuit." Cicero (Pro Balbo) has pointed out the happy effects of this policy. Some future historian will show, in the conduct of this country towards Ireland, America, and India, the malignant effects of an opposite policy: see a very learned and able work on the government of dependencies, by George Cornewall Lewis, p. 256. Dion. Hal. lib. ii., Tac. Ann ii. 24., iv. 73., and the admirable speech of Cerealis, " *nihil separatum clausumve:* proinde pacem et urbem quam victi victoresque *eodem jure* obtinemus, amate, diligite." Compare this with the condition of Ireland in the last century, or of Hindostan in this. The rule of the Mahometan emperor was not so blighting or oppressive as that of the English merchant. Shore, Government of India.

only to consider the Municipia, the Colonies, the Condition of the Socii, and the Classes of Roman subjects not reduced to servitude at the close of the Social War. It was a principle of Roman law that no Roman citizen could be the citizen of any other community distinct from that of Rome, and governed by different institutions. The first city[345] admitted to some of the privileges of the Roman commonwealth was Cære, A. U. C. 365. Hence the expressions *"jus Cœritum," "in Cœritum tabulas referri,"* applied to those whom the censors deprived of the right of suffrage, but who still continued Roman citizens. The towns which the Romans thus admitted to a share in their rights were termed *municipia.* I think Roth[346] is right in supposing that *all* the *municipia* were *"fundi,"* and that the adoption of the Roman laws was a preliminary condition, without assenting to which no town could become a *mvnicipium.* In each of these towns the political privileges of each citizen, as member of the Roman state, were different from his rights as an inhabitant of a particular town. The former could be exercised only at Rome, and in concurrence with other Romans; the latter were peculiar to the members of each separate municipality. Thus, Cicero was a citizen of Arpinum, and Milo was dictator of Lanuvium when a candidate for the consulship at Rome.[347] Maffei remarks that the Romans (before the Social War) took care, in conferring a right of suffrage upon an extensive district, to place the voters from each town in a separate tribe. By thus spreading their suffrages over a wider surface they diminished their effect. For instance, he says, in the territory of the Veneti, Aquileia voted in the Veline tribe, Concordia in the Claudian, Padua in the Fabian, Aste in the Romilian, Verona in the Popilian, &c.[348]

A *senatus consultum,* or a law ratified by the people, was necessary to establish a colony. It was the profound policy of the Romans to confiscate a portion of the conquered territory,

---

[345] Liv. v. 50. The Emperor Leo, who abolished the authority of the senate, annihilated the last vestige of the Municipium (Novell. Leon. 46.) about 1200 years after the privileges of a Municipium had been first conferred on Cære.

[346] De Re Municipali Romanorum. Beaufort, Rep. R. vol. v. p. 214. Liv. xxxvi.§36. Juv. x. 99.

[347] Maffei, Verona Illustrata, lib. iv.

[348] Beaufort, Rep. R. vol. v. p. 264.

and to occupy it with their own citizens, thereby at once[349] increasing, ultimately, their own population, providing for the more indigent citizens, and riveting the chain around the vanquished. Before the Social War, the colonies were not on a level with the municipal towns; they were not admitted to a full participation in the rights of Roman citizens: as soon as the decree authorising the settlement had passed, commissioners were appointed — Triumviri, Quinqueviri, &c. for its execution. That this office was esteemed highly honourable, we know from the fact that Julius Cæsar offered Cicero the place of one of the commissioners for the colonisation of Campania[350], and though Cicero not approving the law, declined the office, it was accepted by Pompey and the first citizens of Rome. There were, during the republic, Roman colonies and Latin colonies. That the first were distinct from the second we know from Livy[351], who mentions a deliberation of the senate, whether the colony of Aquileia should be Roman or Latin. The former, no doubt, enjoyed more extensive privileges, but neither had the right of suffrage. Cicero, in a very luminous passage (Pro Cæc. 35.), says that Sylla, who deprived the inhabitantsof Volterra of their right of suffrage, left them still all the rights of the most favoured colonies. Again, Dio Cassius[352] tells us that Julius Cæsar, after the defeat of Pompey's sons, granted different privileges to the different towns in Spain; to some the rights of Roman citizens, to others those of a Roman colony; the same

---

[349] "C'est une puerilité dans les chefs d'une nation à s'imaginer qu'elle s'affaiblit par de telles émigrations quand elles sont bien conduites. Nul état florissant n'a cessé de l'être pour avoir donné naissance à des colonies florissantes. Tyr, Athénes, Corinthe, ne parvinrent à leur plus grande puissance qu'aprés avoir enfanté plusieurs grandes cités. Les provinces d'Espagne d'où sortirent les aventuriers qui conquirent le Mexique furent toujours les plus populeuses. II y a une isle en E'cosse (L'isle de Skye), qui n'a pas douze lieues de long. Elle comptait, en 1755, plus de 11,000 habitans; dans les années qui suivirent elle en perdit 8000, qui allèrent s'établir soit aux E'tats Unis, soit dans les parties basses de l'E'cosse. Vous pourriez croire qu'après ces émigrations il ne lui resta que 3000 habitans, elle se trouva en avoir au delà de 14,000," This is the opinion of by far the greatest modern writer on political economy. Say, Cours Complet, &c. tom. ii. p. 193.

[350] Dio Cassius, xxxviii. Ad Att. ii. 16. Quinet. xii. 1. Suet. Aug. 4. Tib. 4. Cic. de Leg. Ag. ii.§13.

[351] L. xxxix. 55.

[352] Dio Cassius, xliii.

distinction is made by Pliny,[353] Probably the Roman colony had the *connubium* and the *commercium,* the Latin colony the *commercium* only.

Thus the Italian nations might be divided into two classes, the one consisting of those who *were* incorporated with the Roman state, the second of those who, under the name of allies of Rome, were, in fact, her tributary vassals.[354] The first class, again, might be divided into those who had the rights of Roman citizens, and those who had not. The *civitas* sometimes included all the rights of a Roman citizen, and sometimes was incomplete *(sine suffragio).* The general, indeed the universal condition of all these alliances was, the virtual surrender by the Socii of the right to make peace and war, and their engagement to supply Rome with troops and money according to certain fixed proportions. Their internal government was independent; they chose their own magistrates in the assemblies of the people, which among them, as at Rome, exercised the supreme authority. If it happened that one of these states became a *municipium* of Rome, it, as we have seen, at first preserved its internal administration. Latterly, however, and at the period we are speaking of, magistrates were sent from Rome for the purpose of administering justice, "*præfecti juri dicundo*" The relations of each community with Rome were regulated by its own specific treaty. Such was the state of Italy and such the different condition of its inhabitants, when, in the middle of the seventh century, the long smouldering hatred of so many oppressed communities broke out into the fierce flame which torrents of blood were required to quench, and by which it seemed, at one time, as if the stately fabric of Roman grandeur,

---

[353] Pliny, Ep. 3. 2.

[354] The jus civitatis cum suffragio was given and taken away by the people in the comitia. Cic. Pro Sulla, 7. Livy viii. 21., xxxviii. 36., xxvi. 33., xlv. 15. So the people confirmed Cæsar's grant to Cadiz. Dio Cassius, 41. δ δῆμος ἐπεκύρωσε. No one was compelled to accept it. Livy, ix. 43., Cic. Pro Balbo, 13. Tacitus says that the wife of Drusus " seque ac majores ac posteros municipali adulterio fœdabat." " Roma communis omnium nostrum patria." Dig. 1. 4. Cic. de Leg. ii. 1. "Ego, mehercule, et illi (Catoni) et omnibus municipibus, duas esse censeo patrias, unam naturæ, alteram civitatis.... Itaque cum ortu Tusculanus esset, civitate Romanus, habuit alteram loci patriam, alteram juris." Cato was " citoyen de Rome, bourgeois de Tusculum."

raised by so much toil, and cemented by so much wisdom, must inevitably be consumed. This was the Social War. The Romans, however, were wise in time; they knew when to hold out, and when to yield. The *Lex Julia,* A.U.C.664, gave to the cities of the "*nomen Latinum*" and the "*socii*" who had not taken up arms, the rights of Roman, citizens. In the following year most of the confederates laid down the arms, and the *Lex Plautia Papiria* bestowed the same privilege on them. At last the Lucanians and Samnites consented to accept the same conditions. The incorporation of so vast a number of foreigners would have completely changed the character of the state, and the original Romans have been reduced to comparative insignificance, had it not been for the expedient of flinging all these new members of the community into eight tribes, which were added to the preceding thirty-five. These states retained the independent administration of their own affairs: at the head of each was an assembly of the people. There were two, or, at most, four, magistrates, "*duumviri* or *quatuorviri,*" who held an office analogous to that of the Roman prætor, or consul, and were chosen by the popular assembly every year. Their chief duty was the administration of justice. Each city had the care and management of its own revenues, and the duties of the Roman censor were discharged by the local authorities.

It was a condition annexed to the grant of Roman citizenship, that the city accepting it must become "*fundus.*" The meaning of *fundus* is explained by Festus, "fundus dicitur populus esse rei quam alienat hoc est auctor." However strange it may seem, that the communities who had taken up arms to become Roman citizens should hesitate in accepting the privilege when it was offered to them, if we recollect that the new citizens were flung into eight new tribes, and thus deprived of all political importance,—that they lost the right of self-government, and that the pecuniary burdens, in all probability, were much augmented, the fact will appear less extraordinary.

It was long before the valley of the Po, the great plain between the Alps and Apennines, was known by the name of Italy. When the Social War broke out it was a Roman province, and governed, like other provinces, by a proconsul. The

Rubicon, between Rimini and Ravenna, was the northern limit of Italy towards the Adriatic, and the Macra, not far from Carrara, towards the Mediterranean. This district was divided by the Po into Gallia Cis and Transpadana; — at the time of the Social War Gallia Cispadana contained the colonies Placentia, Bononia, both Latin—Parma and Modena, both Roman.

Gallia Transpadana contained Cremona, Aquileja, both Latin, and Aporedia, uncertain.

In the year A. U. C. 665, the same year in which the *Lex Plautia* was passed, Cneius Pompeius Strabo, in order to reward the fidelity of the Transpadani (for neither they nor the Cispadani had taken any part in the Social War,) conferred upon them, by a particular law, the *"jus Latii."* That is, the Transpadani were raised from the condition of mere *peregrini* to an intermediate class, which brought them nearer to the state of Roman citizens. To express this position, the word *Latini* was chosen, which had described communities in a similar situation, on which communities the *Lex Julia* had conferred, as has been stated, the rights of Roman citizens.

This is the *jus Latii* which soon comprehended many cities and many people, which Vespasian extended to Spain, and which the *Lex Junia* conferred upon freedmen. The word was now employed to denote particular legal rights and relations, and lost altogether its original meaning of a particular tribe in a particular district.

The two facts, that the *jus Latii* ceased, after the *Lex Julia,* to apply to a certain race, and that a new *jus Latii,* in another signification, was used to describe first the relations of the Transpadani, and afterwards those of other countries, to Rome, are incontestable. How much of the first *jus Latii* was included in the second, is a question of greater difficulty. The new Latins acquired the rights of Roman citizens by filling certain offices in their native cities. The old Latins[355] acquired it by fixing their domicile in Rome, if they left children to carry

[355]"Lex sociis ac nominis Latini qui stirpem ex sese domi relinquerent dabat ut cives Romani fierent."—*Liv.* iv. 1. 8.

on their race at home. Niebuhr has, with admirable sagacity[356], seized upon this fact to fill up the defective passage in Gaius[357], in which the first *jus Latii* is called *majus,* and the second, *minus Latium.* The new Latins had not the *connubium,* but had the *commercium.*

This Latinity was by the *Lex Junia Norbana* extended to a numerous class of freedmen. The precise date of this law is unknown. The "*Latini coloniarii,*" mentioned by Ulpian, relate to the communities out of Italy which had acquired the right of Latinity.

The same law which gave the Transpadani this new Latinity, gave the Cispadani the rights of Roman citizens. In the *A. U. C.* 689, Cicero says in a letter to Atticus, "videtur in suffragiis multum posse Grallia," i. 2. To conciliate the Transpadani became a great object for the leaders of the Roman factions. In A. U. C. 688, Cæsar, then Quæstor in Spain, left that country before the proper time to agitate the Transpadani; in the year *A. U. C.* 703, Cicero writes to Atticus that there was a rumoured[358] intention of making the Transpadani citizens, and that he dreaded the consequences, "quod si ita est, magnos motus timeo." In A. U. C. 705, when Cæsar had crossed the Rubicon, he made the Transpadani citizens.[359]

---

[356] "*Majus Latium vocatur, cum quicunque Romæ munus faciunt, non his tantum qui* magistratum gerunt, civitatem Romanam consequuntur; minus Latium est cum hi tantum qui vel magistratum vel honorem gerunt ad civitatem Romanam perveniunt."—*Gaius,* i. 96. Ad Att. v. 11." Marcellus fœde de Comensi, etsi ille magistratum non gesserat, erat ille transpadanus." — *Ulpian,* Fr. L. R.§3. We know that twelve Latin colonies had the commercium as a distinction, from the Pro Cæcina,§35.: " Sulla ipsc ita tulit de civitate ut non sustulcrit horum nexa et hereditates; jubet enim eodem jure esse quo Ariminenses, quos quis ignorat 12 coloniarum fuisse, et a populo Romano, hæreditates capere potuisse?" Liv. viii. 14.: " Cæteris Latinis populis connubia, commerciaque et concilia inter se ademerunt." Cicero, Ad Att. xiv. 12. uses the word Latinitas in the sense of "jus Latii." "Multa illis (Siculis) Cæsar, neque me invito, etsi Latinitas erat non ferenda." Tacitus uses Latium in the same sense, Hist. iii. 55.: " Vitellius... fœdera sociis Latium externis dilargiri." Appian, ii. 26. Savigny, Ueber die Enstehung der Latinität, Zeit. für Ges. Recht. vol. v. p. 231.

[357] Gaius, i. 96.

[358] Ad Att. v,§2.

[359] Dio Cassius, xl. 36.

Thus, at the close of the period we are now considering, and to the time of Ulpian, the free inhabitants of the countries under the government of Rome might be divided into three classes.

CIVES. — LATINI. — PEREGRINI

Each class is distinguished by its share of civil and political rights.

The *civis* is entitled to every privilege of a Roman citizen.

The *peregrinus* is excluded from all the rights arising from the peculiar character of Roman law. He has neither the *connubium* nor the *commercium.* But he is competent to perform, to engage to perform, and to bind others to perform, all that is recognised by the *jus gentium;* such as the *emptio, venditio, locatio, conductio,* and other contracts.

The *Latinus* stands between the *civis* and the *peregrinus.*

Like the first he has the *commercium* — he may hold property *ex jure Quiritium,* and may perform the actions which arise from it, — those which relate to the "*vindicatio,*" "*cessio in jure,*" "*nexum.*"

So he has the *testamenti factio;* he may make a will according to the Roman method; he may be made the heir in a Roman will, or he may be made the witness of one.

Like the second, he is without the *connubium* — and the rights arising from it, the *agnatio* and the paternal authority.

Such is the inference from these passages in Ulpian.

"Tit. v.§4. Connubium habent cives Romani cum civibus Romanis: cum Latinis autem, et Peregrinis ita, si concessum sit."

"Tit. six.§4. Mancipatio locum habet inter cives Romanos et Latinos colonarios, Latinosque Junianos, eosque Peregrinos quibus commercium datum est."

"Tit. xx.§8. Latinus Junianus et familliæ emptor, et testis, et libripens fieri potest; quoniam cum eo testamenti factio est."

"Tit. xi.§16. Latinus habet quidem testamenti factionem."

The Cincian and Agrarian Laws require distinct notice.

LEX CINCIA[360]

"Multi effuderunt patrimonia inconsulte largiendo,"[361] hence the Cincian law. "M. Cincius quo die legem de donis ac muneribus tulit." "Suasor legis Cinciæ de donis ac muneribus." Such is the manner in which Cicero has noticed the Cincian law, and its author; but it appears to me not unlikely, that the Cincian law might be partly intended to check the evasion of the Licinian law, which will be hereafter mentioned[362], and to make the nominal gifts of large estates by the opulent to their relations invalid.

The first clause of this law was, "Ne quis ob causam orandam pecuniam donumve accipiat."[363]

Another clause forbad all gifts above a certain sum; afterwards exceptions were engrafted on it for particular persons, for instance, "ei qui aliquem a latrunculis vel hostibus eripuit, in infinitum donare non prohibemus."[364] So Ulpian, in a passage explained by Savigny, says, "*exceptis quibusdam cognatis.*" So the Theodosian code mentions the "*exceptas Iegi Cinciœ personas.*"

---

[360] Livy, xxxiv.§4. Festus v. Muneralis. Savigny, Zeits. für Ges. R. vol. iv. p. 1. Gothof. (Codex Theod. viii. 12. 4.) says "Varia capita hujus legis fuere." Cujacius, Obs. 6. 18. lib. xxix. Quæst. Papin. Fr. p. 786. ed..Neap. Dig;. xxxix. 5. 9.1. Cod. Jus. viii. 54.§§29. 31.

[361] De Off. ii. 15.

[362] Infra, 202.

[363] Tac. Ann. ii. 5.

[364] Paulus, v. 11. 6.

Another clause provided that all gifts above a certain sum, (or, as was the law afterwards, not made to the persons above-mentioned) should be invalid, unless actually delivered or made over to the object of the giver's bounty. Such is the policy of our Mortmain Act. Improvidence is less probable where the privation is immediate. The traditio was requisite for the "*res nec mancipi;*" emancipatio for "*res mancipi,*" or the "*in jure cessio,*" which applied to both. "In jure cessio communis alienatio est et mancipi rerum et nec mancipi."[365] This law is illustrated by Pliny[366]: "Mater Romani liberalitatem sestertii quadringenties quod conferre se filio codicillis.... professa fuerat nondum satis *legitime peregerat,* quod postea fecit admonita a nobis, nam et *fundos emancipavit,* et cetera.[367]... consummavit." Tacitus[368] says that Otho, to corrupt Cocceius Proculus, who was entangled in a boundary dispute, bought the whole field and gave it him, "agrum suâ pecuniâ emptum — dono dederit." Now Suetonius (Otho, 4.) speaking of the same transaction, says, "agrum redemit *emancipavitque.*" Still more conclusive is the language of legal monuments. In three constitutions of Constantine and his sons, comprised in the Theod. Code, mancipation or tradition are required[369], "ut donatio inter extraneos minus firma judicetur, si jure mancipatio et traditio non fuerit impleta." Theod. 2. requires tradition. Justinian[370] mentions that tradition had been necessary.[371] He abolishes part of the form: "Verba... quæ in donationibus poni solebant, scil. sestertii, nummi unius, assium quatuor, penitus esse rejicienda censemus;" these were the words used in the *manicipatio,*[372] and the *Lex Romana Burgund.* (Papian) Tit. 22. says: "De animalibus, vestibus, gemmis, vel quocunque metallo, vel aliis quæ pondere, numero,

---

[365] Ulpian, tit. xix.§9.
[366] Pliny, Epist. x.§3.
[367] This from a mother to a son shows that the Lex Cincia had no exceptions.
[368] Hist. i.§24.
[369] Cod. Theod. viii. 12.§§4, 5, 7.
[370] Nov. 162.§1.
[371] In Cod. viii. 54.§37. " De donationibus animum advertimus ad Cinciæ legis veteris legisla-tionem."
[372] Cujac. Obs. 10. 37.

mensurâ constant, omnem donandi solemnitatem in solâ traditione posse constare."

Antoninus exempted parents and children, and the nearest collateral relations from the Cincian law. Constantine confined the exemption to parents and children only. But in his time, or in the time of his father *(pater nosier voluit nullam liberalitatem vâlere,* &c.)[373], the law was changed, and a gift was invalid unless declared before a court of justice, drawn into a protocol, and "insinuated" among its records. The Theodosian code mentions the amount[374] *"ducentorum solidorum,"* as that for which such insertion was necessary, reckoning the aureus at 25 denarii, or 100 sesterces, this would make the sum of 20,000 sesterces, about 125 l. of our money, the requisite sum. Cujacius thinks this the original amount; and that this was expressed in later times in "aurei," and after the time of Constantine, in "solidi."

AGRARIAN LAWS[375]

The contests to which the Agrarian Laws gave rise during the seventh century of the Roman era were at first limited to those districts of Italy which in the A.U.C. 621, when Tiberius Gracchus proposed them[376], were the property of the commonwealth. The laws in question in no way aimed, as was

---

[373] Cod. Th. iii. 5. 1.

[374] Cujacius assumes erroneously that 1000 sesterces make an aureus or a solidus; 100 is the right calculation. Cuj. ad 1. i. Cod. de dolo malo, Obs. 19. 17. Pauli Rec. Sen. iii. 5.§10. Gaius, iv. 46. De in jus voc. 1. 24. in eum qui adversus ea fecerit 50 aureorum judicium datur (Ulpian). Ib. 25. (Modestinus). That the aureus, whatever change might be made in its size and weight, was equal to 100 sesterces, there is the evidence of Tacitus, Hist. i. 24., compared with Suet., Otho 4. The former says, " cohort! excubias agenti viritim centenos nummos divideret: " the latter, "Aureos excubanti cohorti viritim dividebat." Dio Cass. 55.: Χρυσόν γὰρ καὶ?γώ τὸ νμσμα τὸ τὰς πέντε καὶ εἴκοσι δραχμὰς δυνάμενον κατὰ τὸ επιχώριον ὀνομάζω. Zonaras, 2. 167. says: *δυνανται παρὰ Ρωμαιοις αι εἴκοσι* καὶ πεντε δραχμὰὶ χρυσούν νομισμα έν. Pliny, v. 21.

[375] Zeitschrift für Ges. Wiss. vol. x. p. 40. Rudorff, Niebuhr, ii. 146. (I think his most successful effort.)

[376] Cic. De Leg. Ag. 2. Pro Sextio, 48. Plutarch, Tib. Grace. 9. Velleius Pat. ii. 2. Appian, i. 18. &c.

long supposed, at any interference with private property, or any resumption of lands actually granted to communities or individuals, — nay more, many of the most fruitful districts, such as that of Capua, were by name excluded from their operation, and reserved for the exigencies of the state. The territories which it was the object of those laws, from the time of their first proposal by Tiberius Gracchus, to the time when C. Gracchus was murdered, to distribute among the people, or at least to turn to the advantage of the state, were those which were scattered in vast domains over Samnium, the country of the Sabines, Picenum, Etruria, and other districts of Italy, which had been won by Roman blood and treasure, and ceded to the state by its vanquished enemies. This public domain was now engrossed by a few great families, who held it almost for a nominal rent, and employed their slaves sometimes in its cultivation, sometimes in tending the countless herds that were spread over its surface. A system more adverse to the public weal, in more impudent defiance of undisputed right, and more oppressive to agriculture (the only branch of industry it should be recollected that the Roman could pursue without degradation), can hardly be imagined. "Latifundia," says Pliny, "perdidêre Italiam." To put an end to it was the duty of every wise and patriotic citizen. It was proposed to take from these enormous proprietors some portion of this undoubtedly national property, and to distribute it at a higher rent among the poorer citizens. In this way it was thought not only that vast numbers of distressed families might be provided for, but also that some check might be offered to the prodigious multitude of slaves, which was alike dangerous to public peace, and destructive to all private industry. The tenure of these proprietors is thus stated by Cicero:

"Qui agrum Recentoricum possident, vetustate possessionis se, *non jure,* miserlcordia senatus, non *agri conditione,* defendunt, nam ilium agrum esse publicum fatentur;" this is not the language of violated right.

In order to attain his object, Tiberius Gracchus, with the advice probably of Mucius Scævola, appealed to the Licinian law[377], A. U. C. 387. By this law, no citizen was allowed to possess more than five hundred acres (jugera). The law, like all sumptuary laws, was useless; but as the advocates of a pedantic adherence to the letter of the law (which in struggling against ancient abuses is often impossible, especially when the law is made by those who have grown great and opulent by those very abuses), are those who attack the reputation of Tiberius; it is well to show that the form and letter of the law happened to be as much on his side, and against his adversaries, on this occasion, as the principles of justice and the genius of a free government. The law had been evaded, as our qualification for members of parliament has been. Appian tells us that colourable transfers of estates were made to their sons by the great proprietors, "*τήν γήν ες τούς οικειουςέπι ύποκρίσει διένεμον.*" The Sempronian law, besides the five hundred acres of the Licinian law, allowed two hundred and fifty acres for every son. The value of the land above this quantity was to be paid for by the state; and the land conferred by the law on each of the poor citizens was to be unalienable. Three commissioners were to be chosen every year from the five and thirty tribes to superintend its execution. It was not till he was exasperated by the opposition of M. Octavius Cæcina, the hired tribune of the oligarchy, that Tiberius Gracchus withdrew the proposal for compensation to the actual holders of the lands belonging to the community. He extended his plan to the inheritance of Attalus, which had been bequeathed to the Romans. The money he proposed to distribute among the new proprietors. The territory he intended to dispose of by a plebiscitum. After the destruction of Tiberius Gracchus, the senate endeavoured to get rid of this measure, which it did not dare at once to abrogate, by taking away the authority it conferred from the original triumvirs (C. Papirius Carbo, M. Fulvius Flaccus, and C. Gracchus) and transferring it to the consul C. Sempronius Tuditanus, then engaged in the Illyrian war. This was virtually to cancel it, and the resentment of the people probably cost Scipio Africanus, by whom the transfer of

[377] A. G. vii. 3. Livy, vi. 35. 7. 16. 10. 13. 83. 42. 34. 40. Plutarch, Tib. G. c. 1. Appian, i. 7. 8. Niebuhr, iii. 13—23.

power was proposed, his life. That no inquiry was ever instituted into the death of the most illustrious citizen of the commonwealth, proves the fear of the patricians, and the bitter hatred of those whose expectations had been so cruelly defeated and put aside.

After the untimely end of Tiberius Gracchus, the efforts in the same cause of Fulvius, consul in A. U. C. 629, were easily disappointed. Those of Caius Gracchus were irresistible. He restored the Sempronian Law, which, in defiance of the constitution, the nobles pretended that a resolution of the senate had modified, as has been stated, in an essential part. Many *plebiscita* were passed for this purpose, by which the poorer citizens were settled in different districts of Italy, where the "*ager publicus*" was situated. In order to deprive Caius Gracchus of the popular favour, the patricians had recourse to the most dishonest artifices. They caused their creature Marcus Livius[378] Drusus to outbid him for the favour of the people, by the most extravagant proposals utterly incompatible with the true welfare of the state. According to one of these the land assigned to the colonists was to be entirely rent free; according to another, twelve colonies, each consisting of 3000 families of the lowest citizens, were immediately to be settled in the lands of the Republic. At the same time the senate contrived, to send Caius Gracchus away from Rome, on pretence of establishing a colony in Africa. At his return, he was put to death. The nobles flushed with victory, pursued their adversaries with the most unrelenting ferocity. They proscribed their persons, and repealed their laws. But they exacted from the wealthy possessors of the lands of the state a trifling tax which they[379] distributed among the poor. Even this law was afterwards repealed, and in fifteen years after the death of the younger Gracchus, all the advantages which he and his brother had won for the people by their lives and by their deaths were

---

[378] Not to be confounded with the Drusus mentioned afterwards in this chapter. Cic. Do Orat, iii. 1.2. Brutus, 28. De Finibus, iv. 24.

[379] Appian, 1. 27.: Σ. β..... εισηγησατο νομον τήν μέν γην μηκέτι διανέμειι, αλλ' ειναι των εχοντων και φορους υπέρ αυτης τφ δημψ κατατιθεσθαι, καιταδε τα χρηματα χωρειν ες διανομας.

annihilated.[380] "Illa quidem," says Sallust by the mouth of Memmius, "piget dicere his annis quindecim quam ludibrio fueritis superbiæ paucorum, quam fœde quamque inulte perierint vestri defensores." But the spirit of freedom was not yet extinguished. The power of the nobles was struck at by the Memmian law A. U. C. 644, and by the Mamilian law A. U. C. 644. Again, L. Philippus Marcius A. U. C. 650, in the second consulship of Marius, proposed an agrarian law, which he enforced by saying that there were not in the whole Roman state 2000 families in easy circumstances,[381] This law was given up. But in the sixth consulship of Marius a law was carried A. U. C. by which 100 acres of land in Africa were given to each of the veterans of Marius. A more terrible precedent was never sanctioned. Every member of the senate was required within five days after it was passed, to swear to its observance. To avoid this oath, Q. Metellus Numidicus, "ille ille vir cui patriæ; salus dulcior quam conspectus fuit," went into voluntary exile. But the utmost limit of the agrarian project was attained by Marcus Livius Drusus, who proposed the immediate distribution of all the lands belonging to the state, rent free, among the people, boasting "nihil se ad largitionem ulli reliquisse, nisi quis aut cœnum dividere vellet, aut cœlum."[382] As much of the land which it was proposed to distribute was in the occupation of the confederates, the prospect of becoming Roman citizens was held out to reconcile them to the loss. The first measures of Liv. Drusus were carried on in concert with the senate[383]; but he incurred the suspicion of the nobles and was killed, *domi sues interfectus est,* under pretence that his measures were at variance with the Cæcilian and Didian laws, and according to that neverfailing resource of the aristocracy that they were against the auspices, they were abrogated by the senate. "Decrevit senatus in Drusi legibus populum non teneri[384]; and the disappointment which his death occasioned among the confederates, who saw their hopes of Roman

[380] Appian, i. 27.
[381] De Off. ii. 21.
[382] Florus, iii. 16.
[383] De Nat. De. iii. 32.
[384] Pro Domo, 16.

citizenship indefinitely postponed, was one principal motive, and perhaps the immediate cause of the Social War.[385]

[385] "M. Livius Drusus cum partes senatus... suscepisset, idem vero postea volens gratificari sociis et Latinis civitatem Romanam promisset, ad extremum ejusdem pollicitationis implendæ desperatione præventus in atrio domus suæ, incerto quo percussore confossus est." —*Schol. Bob. pro Milone,* cit. on Tullian, p. 358. Orellius et Baiterus.

EXTERNAL HISTORY OF THE ROMAN LAW

CHAP. III. FROM AUGUSTUS TO DIOCLETIAN

AFTER[386] the battle of Actium the power of Augustus was secure. Antony was the last rival who opposed his greatness, and who fell a victim to his treachery. The Republic was at an end. The submission of the Romans was henceforth inevitable. For not only had their new ruler poured out the blood of their best and noblest citizens to cement his usurped authority; not only was their submission the reward of corruption, of indiscriminate confiscation, of cold calculating cruelty, of clandestine murder, of open and premeditated massacres; but Augustus was destitute even of those specious qualities, which if they cannot atone (as what can atone) for national servitude, at least, diminish its disgrace. A hypocrite, notorious for personal cowardice, wielded the Roman legions at

---

[386] "Non fu sì santo ne sì benigno
Augusto,
Come la tromba di Virgilio
suona;
L'aver avuto in poesia buon
gusto
L'iniqua proscrizione gli per-
dona."

After all, when Augustus wrote to ask Horace if he thought that it would disgrace him to be known by posterity as his friend, he was nearer the truth than he supposed. The intimacy of Horace with Augustus is a disgrace to him (Suet. in Vit. Hor.), even though Augustus did not bring Scribonia, whom he abandoned, before the Roman House of Lords.

his will, and governed the conquerors of the civilised world, as the great historian has told us in one of those passages where every word glows with its own deep indignant meaning, "Militem donis, populum annonâ, cunctos dulcedine otii pellexit, insurgere paulatim, munera senatus, magistratuum, legum in se trahere, nullo adversante, cum ferocissimi per acies aut proscriptione cecidissent, cæteri nobilium, *quanto quis servitio promptior, opibus et honoribus extollerentur ac novis ex rebus aucti*[387], tuta et præsentia quam vetera et periculosa mallent;" and by a last act of consummate wickedness, which cast into the shade all his former crimes, he appointed Tiberius for his successor.

During the reign of Augustus, the magistrates continued to exercise the same functions, and to be named formally in the same manner as under the Republic, "*eadem magistratuum vocabula,*" one new magistrate the "*præfectus urbi,*" was created at Rome. This office was only known formerly in time of war, but was now made permanent. To consider the forms and appearances by which the servitude of the Roman people was made plausible, is a painful and not a very profitable task. It appears from Gaius that[388] a law was actually passed by which the emperor was invested with absolute authority. This may remind the reader of a passage in our own history, when by a parliament calling itself the representative of a free people, the arbitrary caprice of Henry VIII., that fury of lust and blood, the most detestable tyrant that has existed since the downfal of the Roman empire, was invested with the force of law. In the reign of Tiberius the election of magistrates and jurisdiction in

---

[387] The old excuse of despotism and its satellites. It was constantly used to justify the government of Prussia before the late events. So Horace —

"Tutus Bos rura perambulat."

No doubt, but Cicero could not. The Bos did not interfere with tyranny, nor did men who resembled it; so in Germany they endeavoured to cheat the people by encouraging men of science. " Les sciences naturelles, physiques, et mathématiques... sont plus difficilement contestés, leur investigation ne blesse aucun intérêt, on peut étudier la physique dans les états Autrichiens sans alarmer le prince, les grands, ni le clergé."—*Say. EC, Pol. 5.* The King of Prussia rewarded mineralogists; and the Emperor of Russia, while endeavouring to make a Poland of Circassia, affected to patronise geology.

[388] Gaius, i. 2.§6. Dig. i. 4§1.

criminal matters, were transferred from the people to the senate. The senate was the instrument of imperial will. Its members were named by the emperors, who employed it in the improvement of legislation. The power of the consuls became nominal. They served as a calendar to denote the year. The number of prætors was increased to eighteen, and the tribunes were the executive ministers of the senate in matters of police. The *prœfectus prœtorio,* originally the commander of the guards, soon became one of the most important functionaries of the empire. Papirius, Ulpian, Paulus, Modestinus, all filled this office, the holder of which presided over the *consistorium principis,* or ordinary council of the emperor, and the supreme court of appeal, in all cases civil as well as criminal: most of the imperial orders were drawn up by this assembly.[389] In the towns of Italy the election of magistrates was vested in the municipal council. Their authority was restrained, and their jurisdiction limited to a certain sum; magistrates (like our judges of assize) were sent to administer justice in the towns of Italy under the government of Adrian and Marcus Aurelius, and a magistrate clothed with the same powers, resided at Alexandria.[390]

LIST OF EMPERORS.

1 Augustus	31 B.C.	4 Claudius	41 A.D.
2 Tiberius	14 A.D.	5 Nero	54 A.D.
3 Caius Caligula	37 A.D.	6 Galba, Otho, Vitellius	

[389] Tigerström, Aeuss. Ges. des R. Rs., De ordine. Dig. Gibbon, Hist. vol. i. 2. Warnkœnig, Hist. externe du Droit Romain. Theod. Codex, ed. Ritter. Schlosser, Geschichte der alten Welt. Zimmern, G. vol. iii. Hugo, Hist. du Droit Romain, vol. ii.; Mackeldey traduite par Poncelet. Walter, Geschichte des R. R. vol. ii. Hist. du Droit Romain par C. H. Giraud. Hegel, Philos. der Geschichte, p. 382. Marezoll, Lehrbuch der Institutionen. Zeitschrift für Ges. Rft. Savigny, &c. Civilist. Mag. Hugo. Puchta, Institutionen, vol. i.

[390] Digest, i. 26.: " Adoptare quis apud juridicum potest quia data est ei legis actio." Digest, i.§2.: "Juridico qui Alexandriæ agit datio tutoris... concessa est."

	A.D.		A.D.
7. Vespasian	70	22. Gordianus	237
8. Titus	80	23. Philippus	244
9. Domitian	83	24. Decius	247
10. Nerva	96	25. Gallus	251
11. Trajan	97	26. Valerianus	253
12. Hadrian	117	27. Gallienus	260
13. Antoninus (Pius)	138	28. Claudius	268
14. Marcus Aurelius	161	29. Aurelian	270
15. Commodus	180	30. Tacitus	275
16. Pertinax, Didius,		31. Probus	276
Julianus.		32. Carus	282
17.Septimius Severus	193	33. Carenus	283
18.Antoninus Caracalla	281	34. Diocletian,	
		Maximian,	284
19.Macrinus et		Galerian,	
Heliogabalus	222	Constantine	
20.Alexander Severus	235	Chlorus	306
21.Maximian		35.Constantine	

LEX JULIA AND LEX PAPIA POPPŒA[391]

These laws are as important with regard to the civil law as any that were passed after the Twelve Tables; the most eminent jurists of the day were employed by Augustus in their preparation; they bear the different names of Lex de Maritandis Ordinibus, de Caducis, de Pœnis Cœlibatus et Or-bitatis.

The *"Lex Julia"* declares that every person above twenty and under sixty years of age, if a man, or fifty, if a woman, shall be reputed *cœlebs;* no such person can receive any thing by the will of a stranger, nor even of the affines. The exception, and the only exception to this rule, is in favour of an individual, who being unable to contract a suitable marriage, cohabits with a concubine "*liberorum quœrendorum causâ.*"

The "*Lex Papia* " declares that every individual above twenty-five and under sixty, who has no children, either of his own or by adoption, shall be "*orbus.*"

That no *orbus* shall receive from the will of a friend more than half of what is bequeathed to him.

That neither the husband nor the wife, to whom this epithet is appropriated, shall receive more than the tenth of what the deceased consort has bequeathed to the survivor; added in the case of the husband to the usufruct of a third part of the wife's property, and in the case of a wife to the value of her dowry.

Where, however, a particular relation existed between husband and wife, known by the name "*solidum capere,*" *or*

---

[391] Cujacius, vol. x. ed. Neap. p.1. Ausonius:—
"Jurisconsulto cui vivit adultera
conjux,
Papia Lex placuit, Julia dis-
plicuit."
Tacit. Ann. iii. 28. Juvenal, ix. 87.:—
"Jura parentis habes, propter me
scriberis hæres,
Legatum omne capis, necnon et
dulce caducum"

"*libera testamenti factio,*" the survivor, even though childless, might inherit all that was bequeathed by the other's will. But when the will of a stranger was in question the "*Lex Voconia*" deprived the wife who was not the mother of three or even four children, of any advantage from the bequest. The father of one child might not only take the bequest but the caducum; or that bequest, which had been left by the same will under which he himself claimed as heir or legatee, to some other person who was unable to profit by it. By the Papian law also the Latinus, who was the father of one child, became a civis, and the wife who was the mother of several, was liberated from the oppressive *tutela.* The relations between the freedman and his patron were also affected by the same circumstance. By this law, also, was regulated the disposition of the bequests, all of which were forfeited by the *cœlebs,* and one half by the *orbus,* as well as the part taken away from the surviving consort.

These bequests were termed sometimes caduca, sometimes quasi caduca (in causa caduci). Caduca, when the heir or legatee died after the testator, but before the event on the arrival of which he was to inherit quasi caduca, when the heir or legatee died before the testator. In these circumstances the law gave the property (jus antiquum in caducis) to such of the children or relations of the testator as are appointed heir by the will; if there were none, to such of the heirs or legatees named in the will who had children; and lastly to the public treasure. They who gave information to the public treasury of such bequests received a portion as a reward. The burdens to which these bequests were liable followed them into whatever hands they fell.

Those who were absent on public service, reipublicæ causâ, and those who had obtained a special privilege from the people or the emperor, were exempted from these obligations. This was called "*Jus liberorum impetrare.*"

The *"Lex Junia Velleia"* allowed the nomination of posthumous children as heirs, and thus *multos casus rumpendi abstulit.*[392]

The Laws *"Juliæ Judiciariæ"* have been already spoken of; one of them belongs to Augustus.

The *"Lex Julia Norbana"* was passed under Tiberius, by which the condition of those slaves, who were emancipated from actual servitude alone, was regulated. They became *"Latini,"* but with some restrictions, one of which was that they had not the *"testamenti factio"* hence the name *"Latini Juniani."*

SENATUS CONSULTUM SILANIANUM[393]

Deprived the heir of the right of inheritance, and forbad the prætor to grant *bonorum possessionem.* The occasion seems to have been the murder of the master of a family under circumstances which gave cause to suspect his slaves, or those who were to profit by his death. *"Quum afamilia necatus esse diceretur;" "Qui posthumus hœredes instituerat."* This decree seems to show that Juvenal does not exaggerate.

Among the enactments of Augustus, that which forbids the father to disinherit a son who is a soldier, has been already noticed. But the binding force which that ruler gave to the *"codicils"* and *"fideicommissa*[394]*"* was a still more material

---

[392] Dig. xxviii. 2. 29.§6.

[393] Dig. xxix. 5.

[394] " Sciendum est, omnia fideicommissa primis temporibus infirma *esse,* quia nemo invitus cogebatur præstare id, de quo rogatus erat. Quibus enim non poterant hereditates vel legata relinquere, si relinquebant, fidei committebant eorum, qui capere ex testamento poterant. Et ideo fidei commissa appellata sunt, quia nullo vinculo juris, sec tantum pudore eorum, qui rogabantur, continebantur. Postea primus divus Augustus, semel iterumque gratia personarum motus, vel quia per ipsius salutem rogatus quis diceretur, aut ob insignem quorundam perfidiam, jussit consulibus auctoritatem suam interponere. Quod, quia justum videbatur et populare erat, paulatim conversum est in assiduam jurisdictionem tantusque favor eorum factus est, ut paulatim etiam prætor proprius crearetur, qui de fideicommissis jus diceret, quem fidecommissarium appellabant" — Inst.§§1. 11. 23. De Fideicommissariis Hereditatibus.

alteration of the Roman law. Up to this period, the enfranchisement of a slave belonging to another[395], the delay of the time when the heir was to enter into possession, or a condition imposed upon the heir on which his right was to cease, an obligation imposed upon the heir of restoring anything after his death, any duty or burden annexed as the condition of a legacy, were invalid. These conditions, if imposed by will, were nugatory, and no obligation that was not in the will, was at this time, under any circumstances, binding on the heir. The gratitude and probity of the heir were the sole security of the testator. Trebatius is supposed to have recommended this alteration of the law.

The changes made by Tiberius in the civil law were few compared with those introduced by Augustus. He extended the punishment of celibacy by the *Senatus consultum Persicianum,* and inflicted penalties on those *qui sibi ascribunt testamento* by

---

"Fideicommissum est, quod non civilibus verbis, sed precative relinquitur, nec ex rigore juris ci-vilis proficiscitur, sed ex voluntate datur relinquentis.

"Verba fideicommissorum in usu fere sunt hæc; fideicommitto, peto, volo dari, et similia. Etiam nutu relinquere fideicommissum, in usu receptum est.

"Fideicommissum relinquere possunt, qui testamentum facere possunt, licet non fecerint. Nam intestatus quis moriturus fideicommissum relinquere potest. Res per fideicommissum relinqui possunt, quæ etiam per damnationem legari possunt.

"Fideicommissum et ante heredis institutionem, et post mortem heredis, et codicillis etiam non confirmatis, testamento dari potest, licet legari non possit. Idem Græce scriptum non valeat.

"Fideicommissa non per formulam petuntur, ut legata, sed cognitio est Romæ quidem consulum, aut prætoris, qui fideicommissarius vocatur, in provinciis vero præsidis provinciarum." — *Ulpiani Fragm.* tit. xxv.§§1—5. 8, 9. et 12.

"Ante Augusti tempora constat jus codicillorum in usu non fuisse. Sed primus Lucius Lentulus, ex cujus persona etiam fideicommissa cœperunt, codicillos introduxit. Nam cum decederet in Africa, scripsit codicillos testamento confirmatos, quibus ab Augusto petiit per fideicommissum, ut faceret alt-quid. Et cum divus Augustus voluntatem ejus implesset, deinceps reliqui, auctoritatem ejus secuti, fideicommissa præstabant, et filia Lentuli legata, quæ jure non debebat, solvit. Dicitur Augustus convocasse prudentes, inter quos Trebatium quoque, cujus tune auctoritas maxima erat, et quæsisse, an posset hoc recipi, nec absonans a juris ratione codicillorum usus esset. Et Trebatium suasisse Augusto, quod diceret, utilissimum et necessarium hoc civibus esse propter longas et magnas peregrinationes, quæ apud veteres fuissent, ubi, si quis testamentum facere non posset temen codicillos posset. Post quæ tempora, cum et Labeo codicillos fecisset, jam nemini dubium erat, quin codicilli jure optime admitterentur."

[395] Hæreditas ex die vel ad diem non datur. Inst. ii. 23. 1. De fideicomm. hær. Ib. ii. 25. De codicillis. Heineccius, Elementa J. Civ. (658.)

the *Senatus con. Libonianum,* a subject which Justinian inserted in his code.[396] Besides this, was the *Lex Vitellia.*

Under the reign of Claudian we have the *Lex Claudia,* which provided that a free woman should not be the ward of her heir; the *Senatus consultum Velleianum,* on the obligations of married women; the *S. C. Macedonianum,* the name of which is taken from the criminal it was intended to control; a constitution, forbidding masters to expose, or to kill, their sick slaves. The marriage of a brother's daughter was made lawful by a *S. C.* 802.

Under Nero we find the S. *C. Trebellianum*[397], on the law of *fideicommissa.*

The S. *C. Memmianum;* on adoptions.

The *S. C. Neronianum;* as to the form of legacies.

The *S. C. Calvisianum;* regulating marriage.

Under Vespasian: —

The *S. C. Pegasianum,* which applies the principle of the *Lex Falcidia* to *fideicommissa;* and an edict, that no embassy from any city should consist of more than three *legati.*

Under Titus: —

An edict on *delatores,* and another on the wills of soldiers.

Under Domitian: —

A law on the castration of men.

A law on the immodesty of women.

The *S. C. Surpillianum.*[398]

Under Nerva: —

---

[396] ix. 23.

[397] It put the cestui que trust on a level with the heir, as to the right of bringing actions, and liability to them.

[398] Dig. xlviii. 3. 2.§1.

A law forbidding castration.

A law forbidding marriage with a brother's daughter.

A law, forbidding the *status* of a person to be litigated five years after his death.

A law on the *Peculium castrense,* and the testaments of of soldiers.

Under Trajan: —

A law *vectibulici.*[399]

A *S. C.,* giving an action against the municipal authorities of a city if they neglected their duty as *guardians.*

Mandata to the different functionaries, commanding them to observe the will of a soldier who died in actual service, however it was expressed, and notwithstanding any disregard of form.

An edict, cited in the Digest, on *Stateræ Adulterinæ.*

An edict, cited in the Digest, on *Delatores* and the height of buildings.

The *Tabula alimentaria,* to insure the support of children whose fathers were free, called *Obligatio Prædiorum.*

The use of the word *obligatio* to denote the deed by which land is bound, and the publicity of mortgages, are the most important topics of information which this monument of antiquity supplies, but it has no peculiar value in a history of Roman law.

Under Adrian, we find in Gaius and Ulpian, a number of *Senatus consulta, auctore Hadriano,* which bear sufficient testimony to his activity in legislation. One of these decides that the enfranchisement of slaves, "*fraudandorum creditorum causâ,*" shall be invalid; another gave the right of citizenship to the children of a Latinus and a Roman woman; a third related to the "*pro hœrede usucapio,*" which it ordained should not

[399] Relative aux affranchissements des villes. Hugo, ii. 63.

interfere with the action for the *"petitio hœreditatis;"* another cited[400] relates to the restitutions which the *"bonœ fidei possessor"* of an inheritance may be compelled to make.

An edict of Adrian allowed the heir by will to obtain speedy possession of the inheritance. By an *epistola* he introduced, the practice of dividing the debt among the different *fidejussores* of the same debtor. He allowed soldiers, after they had left the army, to dispose of the *"peculium castrense."*

Under Antoninus Pius was enacted the *S. C. Tertullianum*[401], following in the steps of the *"Lex Julia"* and the *"Lex Papia Poppœa"*[402]; it enabled the mother who had the *"jus liberorum "* to share in the inheritance of her children who died intestate. The *"Lex Falcidia"* was applied to the estate of an intestate, *"propter fideicommissa;"* an *"actio utilis"*[403] was given at once without a formal cession to the *"emptor hereditatis,"* and he gave the *"exceptio doli mali" to* him who had by will *"bonorum possessionem."*

M. Aurelius: — the *S. C. Orphitianum*[404] was added to the *S. C. Tertullianum;* the *S. C.* forbade the guardian to marry a woman who had been his ward, and also it enacted, that a marriage, where the rank of the parties was utterly disproportioned, might be set aside.

A *S. C.* of this ruler also limited the cases in which an alimentary pension bequeathed, by will, might be redeemed.

An epistola laid down the principle that an individual might cause an inheritance to be adjudged to him solely to to preserve the liberties of those enfranchised by it.[405]

---

[400] Dig. v. 3. 20.§6.

[401] Dig. xxxviii. 17. Cod. 6. 56.

[402] Dig. xxxv. 2. 18.: "Dixi Legem Falcidiam inductam esse a Divo Pio in intestationem succes-sionibus propter fideicommissa."

[403] Dig. ii. 14. 16.: "Ex quo rescriptum est a Divo Pio, utiles actiones emptori hereditatis no-cere."

[404] Dig. xxxviii. 17.

[405] Inst. iii.§11.: "Si ii qui libertatem acceperunt a domino in testamento, ex quo non aditur hæ-reditas, velint bona sibi addici libertatum conservandarum causâ, audiuntur," &c.

He enacted also that a prescription of five years should vest property received from the treasury in him who received it, even though it should belong to a third party, that a *compensatio* might in an action "*stricti juris*" be pleaded as an *exceptio.*[406] He determined also the consequences of what is designated as *"pro hœrede gerere."* He established the "*accusatio expilatœ hœreditatis,"*[407] that the heir guilty of it, where there were several heirs, should be taken to have acted for the benefit of the co-heirs[408], and should not acquire himself even by "*usucapio"* any property in what he seized. M. Aurelius also is the author of the act known as the "*Decretum Divi Marci,"* by which a magistrate is forbidden to be at the same time a member of several colleges.[409]

PERTINAX AND SEPTIMIUS SEVERUS

The decrees of Septimius Severus, collected by Paulus *(decreta* or *imperiales sentential in cognitione probates)* were long reckoned among the most important treatises on Roman law. The decision of Septimius Severus in the case of a "*taciturn fideicommissum,"* contributed mainly to the doctrine that interest was not due on the "*fructus"* of what was retained even in "*fraudem legis.*" "Divus Severus bonorum tacite relictorum citra distinctionem temporis, fructus duntaxat deberi, non etiam usuras eorum benigné decrevit, quo jure utimur."[410] He also laid down as a general rule, "si non fuit evidens diversa voluntas," that the "*substitutus*" of a testator was bound to the performance of the same conditions as the "*institutus,"* "videri[411].repetita a substituto quæ ab instituto fuerint relicta."

---

[406] Inst. iv. 6. 30.: "Et in stricti juris judiciis, ex rescripto Divi Marci, oppositâ doli mali ex-ceptione, compensatio inducebatur."
[407] Dig. xlvii. 19. 2.§1.
[408] Dig.§4.
[409] xlix. 19. 1.§1.: "Si quis in duobus fuerit rescriptum est, eligere eum oportere in quo magis esse velit."
[410] Dig. xxxiv. 9. 18.
[411] Dig. xxx. 74.

CARACALLA

Caracalla was more than indifferent[412] to the welfare of his people. The pleasure of adding to their misery seems to have been the sole gratification which the satiety of unbounded caprice allowed him to enjoy. Instead of a twentieth, he exacted a tenth of all legacies and inheritances. He appropriated the "*caduca,*" which had been the privilege of parents. He diminished the immunities granted by the "*Lex Papia,*" and in order to make the liability to his taxes universal, he conferred the right of citizens on all the inhabitants of the empire. Doubts have been hinted by Wachsmuth, a writer entitled to the greatest respect on this fact, which nevertheless Spanheim and Burman, and Schlosser and Savigny, and Hugo, as I think, on sufficient evidence, believe. From this reign also may be dated many of the privileges granted to the Treasury, as well in the case of insolvent debtors, as under other circumstances. Haubold is of opinion, and his explanation seems to reconcile the apparent contradiction between Ulpian and Dio Cassius, that the edict of Caracalla applied only to the generation in being, and did not include the future subjects of the Roman empire.

Many of these fiscal edicts were cancelled by his successor, Macrinus.

Alexander Severus was distinguished for his wise and vigorous government, but he added little to the civil law. An edict by him, applying to a "*donatio in fraudem legis*" the principles of a "*testamentum inofficiosum*" is, however, cited in the Digest,[413] He reduced the tributes to the twentieth part of the sum levied at his accession.[414]

---

[412] Gibbon, c. vi.

[413] Dig. xxxi. 87.§3.: " Si liquet tibi, Juliane, aviam intervertendæ inofficiosi querelæ patrimo-nium suum donationibus in nepotem factis exinanisse, ratio deposcit id quod donatum est quo dimidiâ parte revocari."

[414] " He who paid ten aurei was charged with no more than half an aureus."—*Gibbon,* c. vi.

The evils inseparable from all governments but those founded on a popular basis, began, after the death of Alexander Severus, to show themselves with extraordinary virulence. Of sixteen emperors who were raised to the throne between his reign and that of Diocletian, scarce one died a natural death.

EDICTUM PRATORIS

This portion of the Roman law became the object of assiduous study during this period. The "*Lex Cornelia,"* and the labours of Servius Sulpicius had imparted to it a more durable character, and made it the object of more attentive examination of Ofilius, the friend of Julius Cæsar. We are told of him that "edictum prætoris primus diligenter composuit." Under Augustus, Labeo wrote a treatise upon it, and others, following in his track, made it the topic of very elaborate commentaries. Thus, as the science of the law advanced, the difference between the *jus civile,* and the jus *honorarium* became less marked and positive. The efforts of Roman jurists were successfully directed to reconcile and adjust their respective doctrines. Till the time of Hadrian and Marcus Aurelius, the edicts by which different provinces of the Roman empire were governed, and which it may reasonably be inferred from the genius of Roman legislation, bore a close resemblance to each other, were formally separate. Put after these reigns they were amalgamated. Adrian divided all Italy into the city of Rome and four districts. The jurisdiction of the Roman prætor and the Roman magistrates was limited to the former, and officers under the names at first of consulares, in the time of M. Aurelius, under that of juridico were appointed governors of the latter. A measure of great and lasting importance was connected with this change in the administration. Salvius Julianus, by command of Adrian (who assigned to him the same powers that Justinian afterwards conferred upon Tribonian), composed an edict drawn from the edicts of the *prœtor peregrinus,* of the *œdiles,* and the *edictum provinciale.* The edict thus composed became the rule of law at Rome, and in the provinces. Adrian forbade any alteration in it without the express assent of the sovereign; and deprived the prætors of their legislative power A. D. 131. The edict thus prepared, was no longer confined to the *jus honorarium.* It was a code of Roman law. The pandects are, in fact, little more than extracts from dissertations on matters contained in the edict. The law created after Hadrian is contained in the code and the constitutions of the emperors; nor is there remaining any illustration of, or commentary upon it. The order of the code of Justinian corresponds exactly with that of the fragments in the Digest, taken from the writings of the commentators on the edict. The edict of Hadrian was, of course, the subject of constant commentary, as well by Julian himself, in his "*Libri Digestorum,"* as by Pomponius, who wrote eighty-three books upon it; Ulpian, who wrote the same number; Paulus, who wrote thirty; Gaius, who wrote thirty-two; Callistratus, who wrote six; Furius Antheanus, who wrote five; and Hermogenian.

SOURCES OF POSITIVE LAW

Even to the time of Adrian instances are to met with of the "*leges populi*" and *"plebiscite."* They were but the names under which the emperor signified his pleasure; the last resistance which it cost the emperor any difficulty to overcome was that encountered by Augustus in carrying laws so repugnant to the genius of the age and the feelings of the people, as the *"Lex Julia"* and the *"Lex Papia Poppœa,"* The *Senatus consulta* disappear after the reigns of Septimius Severus and of Caracalla. They were also mere names to disguise the commands of the prince, signified sometimes by an *oratio* or a *libellus.*

After this period the *constitutiones*[415], *"placita," "decreta," principum* are the chief sources of law. They are

---

[415] "Constitutio principis est quod imperator, vel decreto, vel edicto, vel epistola, constituit, nec unquam dubitatum est quin id legis vicem obtineat, cum ipse imperator per legem imperium acci-piat."—*Gaius,* i.§5.

extremely various in form and matter. Sometimes they relate to matters.of administration, sometimes to judicial, sometimes to legislative questions; sometimes they are decisions given in the first instance, sometimes they are given on appeal; sometimes they are answers to the inquiries put by others; sometimes they are resolutions taken in the cabinet of the emperor; sometimes they declare new laws, sometimes they enforce old ones. There were also *constitutiones personales,* which were different from all these, and which contained a special clause prohibiting their use as precedents.

They may be divided into the following classes: —

1. Edicta, edictales leges, generales leges.

2. Rescripta, by Epistolœ.

———Subscriptiones.

———Sanctiones Pragmaticœ.

3. Mandata.

4. Decreta.

"Quodcunque ergo imperator per epistolam constituit, vel cognoscens decrevit, vel edicto præ-cepit, legem esse constat. Hæc sunt, quæ constitutiones appellantur. Plane ex his quædam sunt personales, quæ nec ad exemplum trahuntur, quoniam non hoc princeps vult. Nam quod alicui ob meritum indulsit, vel si quam pœnam irrogavit, vel si cui sine exempio subvenit, personam non transgreditur. Aliæ autem, quum generales sint, onmes procul dubio tenent."—§6. 1. 1. 2. De Jur. Nat.

RESPONSA PRUDENTUM[416]

"Responsa Prudentium sunt sententiæ et opiniones eorum quibus permissum est jura condere. Quorum omnium si in unum sententiæ concurrunt, id quod ita sentiunt legis vicem obtinet; si vero dissentiunt, judici licet quam velit sententiam sequi." This power of declaring the law was conferred by Augustus, first upon certain selected jurists; of course this privilege did not interfere with the right of private interpretation. After Augustus, a standing council of the most eminent jurists was appointed by the emperors to decide the questions which were constantly submitted to them. This *Concilium Principis* was enlarged under Adrian by the addition of the *præfecti.* Hence the extraordinary wisdom and sagacity which characterises the decrees, sometimes of the most flagitious emperors. This measure had a most important influence on the progress and improvement of the Roman law. Many distinguished writers under Augustus devoted themselves, some to explain the principles of law in scientific treatises, others to impart to their fellow-citizens the knowledge of that sound and enlarged theory, without which the mere practice of law, by whatever name it may be dignified, or whatever wealth or honours it may procure, degenerates into

---

[416] "Responsa Prudentium sunt sententiæ et opiniones eorum quibus permissum eat jura condere. Quorum omnium si in unum sententiæ concurrunt, id quod ita sentiunt legis vicem obtinet; si vero dissentiunt, judici licet quam velit sententiam sequi. Idque rescripto Divi Hadriani significa-tur."—*Gaius Comm.* i.§7.

"Responsa Prudentium sunt sententiæ et opiniones eorum quibus permissum erat de jure respondere. Nam antiquitus constitutum erat, ut essent qui jura publice interpretarentur, quibus a Cæsare jus respondendi datum est, qui jurisconsulti appellabantur. Quorum omnium sententiæ et opi-niones eam auctoritatem tenebant, ut judici recedere a responsis non liceret; ut est constitutum."—§8. 1.1. 2. De Jure Nat.

"Et, ut obiter sciamus, ante tempora Augusti publice respondendi jus non a principibus dabatur, sed qui fiduciam studiorum suorum habebant, consulentibus respondebant. Neque responsa utique signata dabant, sed plerumque judicibus ipsi scribebant, aut testabantur, qui illos consulebant. Primus divus Augustus, ut major juris auctoritas haberetur, constituit, ut ex auctoritate ejus responderent, et ex illo tempore peti hoc pro beneficio cœpit. Et ideo optimus princeps Hadrianus, cum ab eo viri prætorii peterent, ut sibi liceret respondere, rescripsit eis, hoc noit peti, sed præstari solere, et ideo, si quis fiduciam sui haberet, delectari se, populo ad respondendum, se præpararet." — *Pompon,* in fr. 2.§47. *Dig. i.* 2. de Orig. Jur.

mere chicane, and becomes a routine as illiberal as the trade of a shopkeeper, or the drudgery of a mechanic; more mischievous to the moral character, as contracting in its effect upon the intellect, and not nearly so beneficial to society.

Labeo[417], the disciple of Trebatius, and the son of a jurist who fell at Philippi fighting against Cæsar, and Ateius Capito, the pupil of Ofilius, are constantly classed together by Pomponius as the great jurists of the Augustan age. Capito, the first of the too numerous race of servile lawyers, was the parasite of Augustus, and of course the enemy of his country. His sordid character provoked the just indignation of his contemporaries, and obtained the highest honours that his master could bestow; he was made consul, A. *U. C.* 759.

Labeo, his rival, was a Roman of masculine sense[418], deep learning, of enlarged and generous views, and therefore,

---

417 The hostility between Labeo and Capito may remind the English lawyer of that between Lord Mansfield and Lord Camden. Lord Mansfield was as superior to Lord Camden in the knowledge of jurisprudence, as he was inferior to him in magnanimity and probity. Nothing shows more complete ignorance than the attack of Junius on Lord Mansfield. Lord Mansfield no doubt was the enemy of freedom in any shape, and probably he is in some way answerable for much of George the Third's bigotry; but this is not, as Junius absurdly says, to be ascribed to the study of the " Roman Code," which is a system of private law. " By such treacherous arts " (i. *e*, by citing the Roman Code) " the noble simplicity of our Saxon laws was first corrupted. The Norman Conquest was not complete until Norman lawyers had introduced their laws." This last clause is true, but it unfortunately happened that the Norman lawyers, like their successors, pertinaciously rejected all improvement, and especially the Roman Code. So an old savage, who was (22 Ed. 3.) chief baron of the Exchequer, politely exclaimed on hearing the civil law cited, " in ceux paroix 'contra inhibitionem novi operis' ny ad pas entendement." Nolumus leges, &c., has been the war-cpy of chancellors, crown lawyers, and judges, with very few exceptions, from the earliest time to the makers of the new rules and the advocates of old chicane in the Exchequer. Junius says, still more absurdly, " It is remarkable that the laws you understand best nourished in the decline of a great empire, and are *supposed to have contributed to its fall." So* thoroughly and so justly did Junius rely on the ignorance of all connected with the Roman law in this country. So too he abuses Lord Mansfield for *not* upholding the law which was Norman, and in the same breath says the Norman law was a system of slavery.

418 One of the many learned pensioners of despotism on the banks of the Spree, censures Labeo for his republicanism. He should recollect that the feelings of a Roman in the days " crudi adhuc servitii et libertatis iniprospere repetitæ are not to be measured exactly by those of a Prussian employé, A. D. 1846, the inhabitant of a country where, in spite of royal promises and pledges, before the glorious events which have ennobled the year 1848, the faintest shadow of constitutional freedom was unknown. Even the " fæx Romuli" was better than the πολιτεια of Fred.

of course, (as were our own Sydney, and Milton, and Harrington, in the most glorious period of English story,) an earnest and inflexible republican. He never obtained any office higher than the prætorship. The following is a list of the successive champions of the sects founded by Labeo and Capito, and continued by Cassius and Proculus:—

Proculeians	Cassians, or Sabinians.
Labeon, disciple of Trebatius	Capiton, disciple of Ofilius.
Nerva, the father.	Massurius Sabinus.
Proculus	Gaius Cassius Longinus.
Nerva, the son	Cælius Sabinus.
Pegasus	Priscus Javolenus.
Juventius Celsus, the father	Aburnus Valens.
Celsus, the son.	Tuscianus, or Tuscius Fuscianus.
Neratius Priscus	Salvius Julianus.

Julian and Pomponius nourished under Adrian; the former was the pupil of Javolenus; his performance as the author of the Edict has been already mentioned. Pomponius, who wrote the Fragment de Origine Juris, was the contemporary of Julian. He wrote also upon the Edict. Gaius, or Caius, followed him. The best opinion is that he was born under Adrian, and wrote under the Antonines; he wrote on the *Edictum Provinciale* and the *Dodekadelton,* on the Twelve Tables. To him also we owe the commentaries which were discovered by Niebuhr at Verona, on a palimpsest, in 1819, and which were published in 1820. This invaluable work may serve to prove the loss mankind has sustained by the destruction of the great bulk of the writings of the Roman jurists. Its merit in point of style, as an elementary treatise, it is, I think, impossible

---

William IV. If, by the "Labeone insanior," Horace really alluded to this illustrious man, it is the most striking proof extant of his servility.

to exaggerate[419]; and its discovery has been to the students of Roman law, what the law of gravitation was to astronomers. It has explained what was obscure, settled what was doubtful, and if we would profit by what it contains, might enable us English to correct the scandalous barbarity of our proceedings. After the time of Gaius to the end of the reign of Alexander Severus, we find the following distinguished jurists: — 1. Sextus Cæcilius Africanus; 2. Junius Mauricianus; 3. Volusius Mæcianus; 4. Claudius Saturninus; 5. Venulejus; 6. Papirius Justus; 7. Æmilius Macer; 8. Ulpius Marcellus; 9. Ælius Marcianus; 10. Florentinus; 11. Thryphoninus; 12. Pedius; 13. Callistratus; 14. Servidius Scævola.

But the other glories even of Roman jurisprudence grow pale before four names of transcendant reputation. These are — Æmilius Papinianus; Julius Paulus, Domitius Ulpianus, and Herennius Modestinus.

Papinian was the friend of Septimius Severus, who, on his death-bed, recommended his two sons Geta and Bassianus (Caracalla) to his care. Caracalla, after the murder of Geta, required Papinianus to compose his vindication. A rhetorical sophist justified the son and assassin of Agrippina. But though Seneca was the apologist of a parricide, Papinian would not become the accomplice of a murderer.[420] He was executed by command of the tyrant whom he refused to obey, and exemplified by his death the sublime doctrines that he inculcated during his life. "Quæ facta lædunt pietatem, existimationem, verecundiam nostram, et, ut generaliter dixerim, contra bonos mores sunt, *nec facere nos bonos posse,* credendum est."[421]

Papinian was considered by the ancients the first of jurists. His writings were explained to the students of law in the

---

[419] It has been compared to Littleton!! (see Arnold's Correspondence — not by Arnold), to which it bears about the same resemblance that the story of the Seven Champions does to the Iliad.

[420] Baronius might have recollected this in his attack on Papinian, who was no doubt, as he says, like the other great jurists, an enemy to the Christian faith Baronius, ad Ann, 214.§3.

[421] Dig. xxviii. 7. 15.

third year, who were then called Papinianistæ. The extracts from them in the Pandects consist of the *Quæstionum Libri* 37, in the order of the edict; the *Responsorum Libri* 19; and the *Definitionum Libri* 2. Cujacius has devoted a folio volume to a separate commentary on the extracts of his works in the Pandects.[422]

Paulus and Ulpian were contemporaries, both "*præfecti prætorio,*" and friends of Alexander Severus. One third of the Pandects consists of extracts from Ulpian's work, and one-sixth of extracts from those of Paulus. Their commentaries on the Edict are the chief source from which the compilers transcribed, and are the basis of the Digest.

Paulus was born at Padua. Besides the fragments of seventy-eight works cited in the Pandects, we possess the "*Receptæ Sententiæ,*" in five books, preserved in the laws of the Visigoths, and in the "*Collatio Legum Romanarum et Mosaicarum.*" A long extract was also found with Gaius.

The *Receptæ Sententiæ* was sanctioned by the Emperor Constantine, "Pauli quoque sententias valere semper præcipimus." It became the law among the Visigoths in Spain, among the Burgundians and in the south of France, until the introduction of the compilations of Justinian.

Ulpian, as he tells us himself, was a Phœnician. He wrote under the title "*Leges,*" the work which was explained in the schools of law during the three years of study. Besides the extracts in the Pandects we possess a fragment of an abridged work of his, under twenty-nine heads; it is quoted under the title *Fragmenta Ulpiani;* and has not been altered by any barbarian. It was first published, 1549, and Hugo has since published an edition taken from the original MSS., which was discovered in the Vatican. Ulpian was the champion of law, and the enemy of the insolent and ignorant soldiers. They murdered him at the feet of Severus, who vainly strove to cover him with the purple.

---

[422] Cujacius, vol. iv. ed. Neap.

Modestinus was the pupil of Ulpian. There are in the Pandects, 345 fragments of his works. He wrote in six books the "*Excusationum Libri,*" the beginning of which is cited in the 27th book of the Digest.

JUS ITALICUM

Connected with the matter discussed in the preceding chapter, and belonging to the period of Roman history, we are now considering another head of Roman law, which, like almost every other subject that he has written upon, Savigny has elucidated with equal erudition and acuteness, and which now requires examination, I mean the *Jus Italicum.*

The *Jus Italicum* is mentioned in the following passages: — Plin. Hist. Nat. lib. iii. cap. 3. 21. where it is ascribed to several cities in Illyria and in Spain.

In the Digest. 1. 15.: "Sciendum est esse quasdam colonias Juris Italici ut est in Syriâ Phœnice," &c., in which several cities are enumerated as possessing it.

Cod. Theod. xiv.§ 13. De Jure Italico Urbis Constantin.[423]

Cod. Justin. xi.§ 20: Urbs Constantinopolitana, non solum juris Italici sed etiam ipsius Romæ veteris prærogativâ lætetur.

In all these places the *Jus Italicum* is ascribed to cities not to individuals. Moreover, Ulpian, who divides the inhabitants of the Roman empire into three classes, Cives, Latini, and Peregrini, does not assign to any of them the "*Jus Italicum,*" as a distinction; again, as Savigny remarks, the "*Jus Italicum*" must have merged had it been the privilege of a class of individuals, in the condition of the Civis or the Latinus; whereas the *Jus Italicum* is often combined with the "status" of the Civis and of the possessor of Latinity. Pliny after telling us

---

[423] Ritter, torn. v. p.238.

that Vespasian had conferred upon all Spain the right of Latinity, remarks as a peculiar right of two Spanish cities that they have the *Jus Italics.* Again, although Caracalla gave to all the cities of the empire the right of citizenship, this *Jus Italicum* is mentioned long after Caracalla as the right of a particular district. Lastly, although long before Justinian's time, all Latin cities had ceased to exist, constant mention occurs in his code of the *Jus Italicum.* Such are the arguments of Savigny.[424]

It seems, then, a fair inference from the passages cited above, that the "*Jus Italicum*" was common to all the cities of Italy, but not unless by express grant to provincial communities. The *Jus Italicum* consisted of three privileges.

1. The right of a comparatively free government.

2. Immunity from taxation.

3. The legal character of the soil, which could be held *ex jure Quiritium.*

1. The Right of a comparatively free Government.[425] "Est et Heliopolitana quæ a Divo Severo, per belli civilis occasionem, Italicæ coloniæ *rempublicam* accepit."[426] "Laodicea in Syria, et Berytos in Phœnice, juris Italici sunt, *et solum eorum,"* whence it is evident that the *Jus Italicum* implied other rights besides those connected with the soil.

Servius, in his commentary on Virgil, Æn. iv. 58. "Patrique Lyæo," says: "Qui, ut supra discimus, apte urbibus libertatis est Deus; unde etiam Marsyas minister ejua, per civitates in foro positus, libertatis indicium est, qui erectâ manu testatur nihil urbi deesse."

And, again (Virg. Æn. iii. 20.), the same commentator remarks: "Quod autem de Libero diximus, hæc causa est ut signum sit liberæ civitatis; nam apud majores aut stipendiariæ aut fœderatæ aut liberæ. Sed in liberis civitatibus simulacrum

---

[424] Zeitschrift für Ges. R. vol. vi. p.250.
[425] Dig. 1. 15. 1.§2.
[426] Dig.1. 15. 8. 3.

Marsyæ? erat, qui in tutela Liberi Patris est." Now, a Silenus[427], standing with uplifted hand is to be found on the coins of many cities. Most of these can be proved to have had the *Jus Italicum,* and there is no reason to suppose that any of them were without it.

2. Immunity from Taxation. After the establishment of the empire, an uniform system of taxation had been introduced in the provinces. Every proprietor paid a land tax, and every other proprietor a poll tax. Italy was liable to neither of these taxes, and, therefore, after even the shadow of a free municipal government had disappeared, and after property had ceased to be held "*ex jure Quiritium,*" this immunity from burdens which pressed heavily on the rest of the empire, accounts for the mention of the *Jus Italicum* in the Justinian law. So, again, when Pliny distinguishes the "*colonia immunes*" from the cities with the "*Jus Italicum,*" he shows that in his day it included something more than the immunity from taxation, which was its final characteristic.

3. The legal Character of the Soil. By this is meant the exclusive peculiarity that it could be held *"ex jure Quiritium."*

Every sort of moveable property might be held *ex jure Quiritium;* but, unless by special grant, land out of Italy could not. The law affecting the soil varied extremely in different provinces. Where the right of conquest had been exercised in all its rigour, the property in the soil was vested in the Roman

---

[427] Eckhel, Doctrina N. V. vol. iv. p. 493.: " IV. Silenus stans d. clata, 5. utrem humero injectum." "Occurrit hæc imago in nummis coloniarum:
Alexandriæ Troadis.
Beryti Phœniciæ.
Bostræ Arabiæ.
Cælæ munie. Thraciæ.
Damasci Cœlesyriæ.
Deulti Thraciæ.
Laodiceæ Syriæ.
Neapolis Samariæ.
Parii Mysiæ.
Patrarum Achaiæ.
Sodonis Phœniciæ.
Tyri Phœniciæ."

people and excluded all private right[428]: "In provinciali solo placet plerisque solum religiosum non fieri, quia in eo dominium populi Romani est aut Cæsaris;" which proves by the way how gross the usurpations of the nobles were, to which the Gracchi endeavoured to put an end. Therefore, the *"fundus ltalicus"* was *"res mancipi,"* which the *"fundus provincials"* was not. "Illud quæro, sintne ista prædia censui censendo: habeant jus civile: sint, necne sint, mancipi?"[429] " prædia quæ et ipsa mancipi sunt... qualia sunt Italica." So the *"fundus Italici juris,"* might become *"ex jure Quiritium"* property by a possession of one year or two years, through the *usucapio*[430]; whereas[431], "provincialia prædia usucapionem non recipiunt."[432] This distinction was put an end to by Justinian, who finally abolished the tenure *"ex jure Quiritium."* So by the *Lex Julia de fundo dotali,* the *fundus dotalis Italicus* could not be alienated. No inference can be drawn as to the *Jus Italicum* of a town from the condition of its citizens; not only the Latins, but cities with the right of citizenship, might be without the *Jus Italicum.*

This was the golden age of Roman jurisprudence[433] Driven from every rational and generous pursuit, the Roman

---

[428] Gaius, ii. 7.

[429] Pro Flacco, 32. Gaius, iii. 120

[430] Cod. vii. 31.

[431] Inst. de Usucap.

[432] Gaius, ii.§46.

[433] Haubold, Ueber den eigen. Geist des Röm. Rechts,§16.

"Dixi sæpius, post scripta Geometrarum nihil exstare, quod vi ac subtilitate cum Romanorum jureconsultorum scriptis comparari possit; tantum nervi inest tantum profunditatis..... Nec uspiam *juris naturalis præclare exculti* uberiora vestigia deprehendas."— *Leibnitz,* torn. iv. pp. 3. 267.

"Ego Digestorum opus, vel potius auctorum, unde excerpta sunt, labores admiror, nec quid-quam vidi, sive rationum acumen, sive dicendi nervos spectes, quod magis accedat ad mathematicorum Tandem Mira est vis consequentiarum, certatque ponderi subtilitas."—*Leibnitz, Epist.* 119. Ad Dio.

"Sunt quædam in Europa gentes, quæ non judicant res ex Romanis legibus, sed vernaculis. Et. tamen, qui ibi res publicas gesturi sunt, fere Romanas leges apud exteros discunt, qui, ut.accipio, interrogati, quid, quum nostrarum legum non sit apud eos usus, in lis cognoscendis tantum operæ ponant, respondere solent; animam se spiritumque legum (sic enim loquuntur) excipere, hoc est, sequitatis vim ac naturam hinc decerpere, ut de patriis legibus rectius judicent. Laudo prudentissimam vocem, qua significant, omnia rectius perspexisse summos illos viros nostri juris auctores, et neminem satis instructum esse ad civitatem regendam, qui non in his cognoscendis tirocinium fecerit. Quid? quod in his jureconsultorum litteris bona pars antiquitatis reliqua est? Veteres mores, sermonis Romani

intellect concentrated its strength on the study and improvement of the law. The arts of Greece which had been transplanted with so much care, and cultivated with so much success, had withered at the root. Poets, orators, historians, had past away. Military discipline itself, the tenure by which Rome held dominion over the civilised portion of the universe, was falling fast into oblivion. The legions terrible at home were no more invincible abroad. The savage hordes from which they were recruited, soon learnt the vices of Romans, and lost their courage, though they retained and exasperated their ferocity. The ominous sound of barbarous voices was heard on a contracting frontier. The Iong gathered cloud of approaching war cast its shadow over the empire. But while every thing else bore the stamp of decrepitude, and rapidly advancing ruin, while nations were pillaged, and the state, drained by an insatiable soldiery, was not relieved — while the miseries of exhausted provinces were attested by the increasing clamours which the most absolute power could not stifle, nor the most habitual servility prevent — amid all these hideous forms of corruption, distress, imbecility, oppression, barbarity, and despair, there is still one monument of ancient wisdom on which the eye can rest, one fact that makes the past history of Rome not incredible,

"One great seamark saving those that eye it — "

there is the Roman law, it stands alone the symbol of former glory, while the deluge of barbarians spreads itself over

---

plerasque figuræ, quas nisi hi explicarent, in aliæ scriptoribus nonnumquam non aliter atque in luto haireremus nec intelligi aptimorum auctorum plerique insignes loci possent. Quod si historia, si alias veterum litteræ nobis, ut debent, curæ sunt, quum his passim Iucem adferant jureconsuiti, vel a Grammaticis et Rhetoribus eorum commentarios adservari oporteret. *Itaque nisi simul omnibus litteris bellum indicemus, et plane in belluas degenerare juvabit, non permittendum est, ut situ ac senio Romanœ leges emoriautur."* This remarkable passage is from Melancthon, Oratio de Legibus. Strassburg, ed. vol. ii. p. 500. The last lines seem intended to describe England in this *golden* age. Schlosser (John George) Hugo, Civ. Mag. vol. i. p. 41. Ueber das Studium des reinen Römischen Rechts. " You see this people, until Justinian flung its system into disorder, everywhere true to itself, everywhere consistent, and that having once established a *principle,* it never departed from it without adjusting this deviation to a rule equally sure and solid." "This spirit of order, and these established doctrines drove the Romans into many subtilties." But we have ten thousand times the number of subtilties without any order or principle.

the world — the ark, in which are preserved the precious seeds of policy and justice; and when that tide of ruin has subsided and ebbed away — the harbinger of future refinement and civilisation.

The more we study the works of the ancient jurists, the greater pleasure do we derive from their perusal. If Reason were to speak[434], she would use their language. The wonderful propriety of diction, the lucid structure of the sentence, the exquisite method of the argument, give to the performances of these writers, a charm peculiarly their own. Terms used with mathematical rigour in an unvarying signification, the clearest reasoning, the most refined distinctions, the most powerful analysis, and, above all, the most fruitful and luminous analogy, these are the heirlooms which the Roman jurists transmitted long inviolate, from one generation to another.[435] If you turn from a page of Seneca, nay, I would even say of Tacitus, and compare the style of either of these great masters of thought and language with the text of the civilians, how striking is the contrast between the effort, art, and epigrammatic antithesis of the one, and the ease, simplicity, and transparent clearness of the other; and it should be remarked as explaining much that is singular in the destiny of the Roman law, that as it survived, it anticipated refinement. The order is inverted, but the consequence is the same; for, as in ancient Rome jurisprudence was at its meridian height long after the sun of literature had set, and when the darkness was becoming thicker and more profound in every part of the horizon, so in modern Europe the study of jurisprudence revived, while ignorance on other points was universal, and before that darkness had been succeeded by the dawn. In both periods it stood upon a higher level than any

---

[434] If learned Folly could speak, if unlearned, she would take that she would borrow Lord Coke's, or of our acts of Parliament; indeed,

"Facies non omnibus una, Noc diversa tamen, qualem decet esse *sororum,"*

Lord Coke, with a sentence from a classical writer, is like the Swiss boor who picked up the great jewel after the Battle of Nancy, which he employed to buy a shillings-worth of beer.

[435] "Le Livre des Digestes est admirable et des plus beaux que je connoisse, et qui peut aider beaucoup même pour les recherches du droit naturel." — *Leibnitzii Commercii Epist. selecta,* Hanover, 1805, p.145.

other pursuit. It was the link between the ancient and the modern world, like the evening of a summer sun which keeps the twilight long within the skies. Nothing could be more effectual to lay the foundation of modern policy than the system by which the ancient world had so long been held together. The fragments of the Digest exemplify the union of sound practice and enlightened theory, of comprehensive principle and accurate detail. There are no mere subtilties, no scholastic arbitrary distinctions, no affected parade of mischievous technicalties, no defiance of common sense; every division we can trace has a distinct object and an obvious application. The writers, it is evident, have drawn deeply from Grecian fountains. They are not ashamed to quote, even in the scanty extracts which we possess, Plato, Hippocrates, Demosthenes, and Homer, to illustrate a custom, to embellish a maxim, or to enforce an argument. The two characteristics of their style are precision and simplicity; in both, but especially in the former, by which I mean the art of expressing much in few words without obscurity, they are, so far as I know, without competitors.[436] Their weak point is etymology, many of their derivations are not only untenable, but in reality preposterous. They are fond of the triple division, which Kant has so much employed, e.g. *Jus naturale, gentium, civile;* the law of persons, things, and actions. But they follow most frequently the arrangement of the edict. They are great dialecticians, and have been accused of excessive subtilty; but it should be recollected, that in following out principles with rigour, and deducing long inferences, some subtility is inevitable; there must always be under every system of jurisprudence, some questions "*inter apices juris,*" that call for refined distinction and subtle reasoning, it is only when the subtilty is shown for wanton ostentation, and as a proof of technical knowledge, when it is dragged forward on all occasions, and insisted upon at all hazards, without regard to substantial justice, or the misery of the ruined suitor, that it becomes a scourge and a snare, provokes indignation where it does not incur ridicule, and often

---

[436] Except, perhaps, in the authors of the Code Napoléon.

inflicts more lasting evils on society, than the most blundering stupidity or even than direct corruption.

The Roman jurists were deeply read in the lessons of the Stoics; Cujacius was[437], I believe, the first to remark this in illustration of their doctrines. Though disbelief of the Roman religion had long prevailed among the inhabitants above the condition of the lowest vulgar, if even that exception is to be made, the emperors imagined that it might be rendered subservient to their purposes as it had been to those of the old aristocracy.[438] This attempt must not be confounded with the mistaken, indeed, but unquestionably patriotic design of the

---

437 Cujacius has enumerated some of the traces of the Stoic doctrines, Observ. lib. xxvi. p. 760. vol. Iii. ed. Neap.: —

" Ex eadem familia est usurpatio substantiæ pro materia, ut docui ad Africanum in 1. 36. de *ususr.* ex eadem *ἄποροι όγι* 1. qui cccc. *Ad legem Fulcidiam,* in qua et Dialectici, id est, Stoici et acervi Chrysippei definitio quam Julianus prodidit noster; et ex eodem Chrysippo definitio legis; ex Zenone, a quo primum Stoici profecti, definitio libertatis; ex eodem, de re quæ nusquam extat ex-emplum quo juris auctoribus uti amicum et familiare est Hippocentauri. Ilia quoque sunk Stoica, τὸ Ἐμβρυον non esse animal, et esse tamen matris partem, futura neque vera esse, neque falsa: Hominum causa omnia comparâsse naturam, quibus et natura Deus, sive τὸ δημιουργικον ημϖν αιτιον, quæ omnia etiam leguntur in juris auctorum libris. Et quæ de disjunctivis et subdisjunctivis orationibus Proculus in 1. *hæc verba, de verborum significat.* Adde quod legitur in 1. *proponebatur, dejudic.* Philosophos dicere ex quibus particulis minimis consisteremus, eas cottidie ex corpore nostro decedere aliasque extrinsecus in earum locum accedere, non de Epicuro, vel Democrito, vel Leucippo, et atomis ex quibus tradiderunt effici, quæ sunt quæque cernuntur omnia: neque de aliis philosophis quam Heraclitiis et Stoicis excipiendum est, qui corpora nostra rapi dixerunt fluminum more, et in adsidua deminutione atque adjectione esse, ut Seneca ait *Epist.* 58., nec quemquam eundem esse mane, qui fuit pridie. Omne momentum mortem prioris habitus esse: qua de re et Plutarchus scripserat *in Symposiacis* cap. *περι του μη τοις αυτους διαμενειν ημας αει της ουσιας ρεουσης.* Sed scriptum ejus hac de re disperiit. Ex Stoicis etiam est quod censent, eum, qui impatientia doloris aut tædio vitæ et adversarum rerum aut pudore æris alieni, vel pudore, et luctu perditæ summæ rei, pudore magis quam necessitate vim vitæ suæ attulit, extra noxam esse; nec eum quoque, qui conscientia criminis capitalis puniendum esse, quod sponte sumpserit mortem, sed quod capitis reus fuerit. Quin et suspendiosi, quamvis eorum, mors sit omnium maxime turpis, et ασχημονες αγχοναι μεταρσιοι, ut Euripides ait in *Helena,* si modo non in reatu capitali suspendio vitam finierint, non puniuntur, 1. 3.§*idem rescripsit, de bon. eor, qui mor. sibi consc.* Justa tantum eis non fiunt, neque lugeri solent, 1. 11.§*non. solent, de bis qui not. infa.* Varro *apud* Servium, suspendiosis justa fieri jus non esse."

438 There is a curious vestige of heathen worship in the Capitularies of Charlemagne, lib. i.§64. Lindenbrogii Codex, p. 839. ed. Frankfort, 1713: " Item de arboribus vel fontibus vel petris ubi aliqui stulti luminaria vel alias observationes faciunt ut iste pessimus usus... tollatur."

emperor Julian at a later period. The object of the emperors was not to improve the moral condition of their subjects, or to appeal to any noble principle of our nature, but to rivet tyranny by superstition. Augustus restored the ancient authority of the augur, and the former practice of divination; but the jealous vigilance of Tiberius required that the proceedings of the augur should be public. Claudius sanctioned these impostures by all means in his power. Alexander Severus gave a salary to the auspices. The emperors were like the patricians formerly, at the head of the state religion, and were anxious, like their predecessors and successors, to turn their office to the best advantage; but the real motive which animated them was too transparent to be concealed, and the mere circumstance that religion was enlisted on the side of despotic power, and was encouraged by despotic sovereigns, would hurry every patriot into incredulity. But such patriots saw around them nothing but motives to despair; they turned aside from the revolting scenes around them to find consolation in their own hearts. Freedom was now impossible, and they sought in philosophy[439] the lessons which would insure to them a resolution that no violence could shake, and a tranquillity that nothing external could disturb. Those sublime and lofty doctrines that had amused the leisure, or exercised the ingenuity of the Grecian philosopher in the garden or the porch, were now realities that directed the conduct and fortified the courage of the noble Roman, and prepared him to encounter whatever the malice or caprice of irresistible power might inflict. The doctrines of Chrysippus and Epicurus[440] were the religion of the few great citizens who lived during this dreadful period.

"Vain wisdom all, and false philosophy,
Yet with a pleasing sorcery could charm
Pain for awhile and anguish; or excite
Fallacious hope, or arm th' obdurate breast
With stubborn patience, firm as triple steel."

---

[439] "Non disputandi causa sod ita vivendi."
[440] Seneca quotes more from Epicurus than from any other writer.

"It alone," says Montesquieu, speaking of the sect of Stoics, "it alone made great citizens; it alone made great men; it alone made great emperors; while the Stoics looked upon wealth and greatness, and pain and grief, and pleasure, as vanity, their only object was to labour for the happiness of mankind, and to fulfil the duties of society." There can, indeed, be no more conclusive proof of the desperate state of mankind than the fact that none of these virtuous and magnanimous emperors endeavoured to restore the republic, or to awaken a sense of freedom. They did, indeed, put a stop to the abuses which prevailed; they checked the rapacity of provincial governors; they lightened the burdens of the miserable people; they endeavoured to controul the insolence of the legions; but they did no more. To restore public spirit to the inhabitants of Rome was a task beyond the power of Trajan, and the benevolence of the Antonines.

During the period at which we have now arrived, the system of Roman law, so far as its formal character was concerned, underwent an almost total revolution. The right of the party to choose his judge, the system of formulæ, the limited authority of the magistrate, which had been among the most essential features of the system, were altogether changed, and by the absolute authority of the judge, those principles which, during the flourishing period of Roman jurisprudence, had been considered as the most important guarantee for the fair administration of justice, were altogether annihilated. This was part, and not the least considerable part of that frightful degeneracy, corruption, and decay, which preceded the dissolution of the Roman empire, the last forms which bore the impress of a republic; the last traces of wisdom and justice disappeared; an Oriental despotism was substituted in their place, while the evils inseparable from a court, its servile arrogance, spurious distinctions, and ridiculous pageantry, the idea of honour annexed to menial functions[441], and frivolous

[441] " Quand on voit l'importance attachée par les plus hauts seigneurs à la présentation au roi de la chemise, de la serviette, du bougeoir, à la place réservée debout derriére lui à la messe, à la distinction du fauteuil et de la main, à la préséance dans les cérémonies entro dues et pairs, *daprès des crêations toutes récentes,* aux

employments about the person of the sovereign, above all the sway in temporal matters of insolent and hypocritical bishops, gave the last strokes to the finished picture of Roman degradation.

If to the inroads of the barbarians on the eastern and north-western provinces, and their incessant marches into the very heart of the empire, be added the evils of famine and of pestilence, the outrages of a savage and uncontrouled soldiery, duties so irksome, and taxes so oppressive imposed on the middle and upper classes, that their flight to the barbarians in order to avoid them was a common event[442]; we may fairly doubt whether the history of the world exhibits a scene of more entire and hopeless misery. To complete the draught we must remember that the mild doctrines, the simple creed, the elevated morality, the glorious hopes and liberal spirit of Christianity, were at the same time corrupted and profaned by time-serving and avaricious priests, and perverted to sanctify the worst

---

nominations pour les voyages de Marly, à la chévalerie du Saint-Esprit, aux distinctions entre Ies princes Iégitimes ut les princes illégitimes, entre les princes étrangers, les dues et pairs et les dues à brevet; quand on remarque l'*extreme insolence melêe* à *la bassesse de ces prétentious,* on sent que ee n'est plus *parmi do tels hommes* que peuvent naître les grands généraux, les *grands négociateurs,* les *grands ministres,* que avaient fait la gloire du commencement de ce règne." — *Sismondi, Histoire des Francais, Louis XIV.* vol. xviii. p. 347.

442 " Inter hæc, inquit, vastantur pauperes, viduæ gemunt, orphani proculeantur, in tantum, ut multi eorum et non obseuris natalibus editi, et liberaliter instituti, ad hostes fugiant, ne persecutionis publicæ afflictione moriantur, quærentes scilicet apud Barbaros Romanam humanitatem, quia apud Romanes Barbaram inhumanitatem ferre non possunt. Et quamvis ab his, ad quos confugiunt, discrepent ritu, discrepent lingua, ipso etiam, ut ita dicam, corporum atque indusiarum barbaricarum fœtore dissentiant, malunt tamen in Barbaris pati cultum dissimilem, quam in Romanis injustitiam sæ-vientem. Itaque passim vel ad Gothos, vel ad Bagaudas, vel ad alias ubique dominantes Barbaros migrant, et commigrâsse non pœnitet. Malunt enim sub specie captivitatis vivere liberi, quam sub specie libertatis esse captivi. Itaque nomen civium Romanorum aliquando non solum magno sesti-matum, sed magno emptum, nunc ultro repudiatur, ac fugitur, nec vile tantum, sed etiam abominabile pæne babetur. Et quod *esse* majus testimonium Romanæ iniquitatis potest, quam quod plerique, et honesti, et nobiles, et quibus Romanus status summo et splendori esse debuit et honori, ad hoc tamen Romanæ iniquitatis crudelitate compulsi sunt, ut nolint esse Romani? Et hinc est, quod etiam hi qui ad Barbaros non confugiunt, Barbari tamen esse coguntur; scilicet ut est pars magna Hispa-norum, et non minima Gallorum. Omnes denique, quos per universum Romanum orbem fecit Ro-mana iniquitas jam non esse Romanos." — *Salvianus de Cub. Dei,* lib. v.

crimes of the most odious tyrants; for, as the church was invested with secular wealth and power, its salutary influence diminished, and the growth of those evils, unknown to the ancient world, of which, in its perversion, it became the instrument, kept pace with the opulence and worldly splendour of its rulers.[443]

The period we are now entering upon was marked by four events of extraordinary social and political importance: 1. The Establishment of Christianity as the religion of the state, and the overthrow of Pagan worship; 2ndly, the Transfer of the Seat of Empire from Rome to Constantinople, and the exchange of military despotism for the still more odious despotism of a court, composed of the women, eunuchs, priests, sycophants, and courtiers, who could gain the royal ear, and obtain by clandestine means those honours which had once been the reward of merit; 3rdly, the Division of the Roman State into the empires of the East and of the West; 4thly, the Invasion of the Barbarians.

In the space of fifty years, immediately preceding the reign of Diocletian, sixteen rulers had been chosen and put to death; and at one time twenty-nine competitors were lacerating the empire. Diocletian, A. D. 284, raised to the throne by the army at Chalcedon, put a stop to these calamities; he introduced a new system of manners and administration. The danger was imminent, and he encountered it by remedies as extraordinary. The east was partly in open rebellion, the Saxons and Franks invaded Belgium, the Marcomanni were pressing upon Swabia; a "*Jacquerie,*" a bellum servile, had broken out in Gaul[444], where the people, under the name of Bagaudæ, rose as they did from the same motive in the 14th century in France and England, and Germany in the 16th century, against the intolerable oppression of the governments, the nobles, and the clergy. Up to this time, though the imperial power had been shared, the empire itself had been indivisible. But in the third

---

[443] If there be any one truth inculcated by history, it is, that no ecclesiastic ought to be trusted with the shadow of a shade of temporal authority.

[444] Gibbon, c. 13. One of his happiest passages.

year of his reign he conferred upon Maximian the title of Augustus, and consigned to him the north-western portion of the empire, even this was not sufficient; in the year 291 two Cæsars were nominated Constantius and Galerius. To Constantius were given the provinces of Gaul beyond the Alps; the coasts of Illyria and Roman Europe (Italy excepted) to Pontus; Italy and Africa fell to the share of Maximian, and the rest to that of Diocletian.

The change in manners was no less remarkable. Under Heliogabalus the Romans had been, indeed, insulted by the pageantry of a court. A woman called Soamis presided over its forms, and issued rules, which even the contemptible writer who chronicles the annals of that contemptible society, ventures to call ridiculous, about the dress and precedence of court ladies.[445] Alexander Severus had restored the less degrading habits of his predecessors. The contrast between the real power, and the simple exterior of the emperor was again remarkable. But Diocletian, either from vanity, or as is more probable in a man of so clear and strong an intellect, in order to accommodate every thing to a new system, surrounded himself with oriental pomp, and introduced the manners of the Persian court into his own. Diocletian wore the diadem, and adorned his person with jewels. Con-stantine went even beyond his predecessor[446], and the Byzantine court[447], with Its ranks and orders, and splendid vassalage of titled menials was established. Constantine created a new rank of princes of the blood, or those who were to be on a level with them, whom he called "*nobilissimi.*" Gratian, Valentinian the younger, and Theodosius, declare that of all things in the state, the arrangement of ranks is most important.[448] Thus the personal

---

[445] Ælius Lamprid. c. 4.: " Sœmitica facta sunt senatus consulta ridicula de legibus matronalibus."

[446] " Caput exornans perpetuo diademate."—*Victor, Epit.* 41. 14. Vanity was a very prominent part of the character of Constantine:— " Ultra quam æstimari potest fuit laudis avidus."

[447] The kings and emperors of the barbarous tribes who settled in Europe imitated the Greek court, and, as usual, going beyond their pattern in folly, made titles hereditary.

[448] Cod. Theod. lib. vi. tit. v.

favour of the sovereign came to supersede every other consideration, and honour and estimation to depend on the cabals of courtiers. It never occurred to former emperora that any rank independently of public office or service could exist; but at the end of this period the hierarchy of baseness has extended itself into twelve degrees, besides those of the nobilissimus[449] and the emperor.

Constantine, the murderer of his friends, of his captives, of his father-in-law, of his brothers-in-law, of his youthful and innocent nephews, of his wife, and of his son, was nevertheless in the beginning of his career, before he figured in church controversies, and became dizzy with episcopal adulation[450], an active, politic and valiant prince. He saw clearly what a much greater, a much better, and in most respects *a* much wiser man, Julian, did not see, that some new force was wanted to reanimate the sinking empire, and that it never could be extorted from the marrowloss skeleton of Paganism. He appealed to Christianity, and the Christians flocked under his banners. He did more. He bad Christianity lift her mitred front in courts and palaces. He made it a state religion. He established that union of the throne and altar which is so necessary to the religion of the fancy and the senses, and so dangerous to the religion of the understanding and the heart, which has so often made the ruler lawless, and the church intolerant, which has hazarded the purity of the one to defend the excesses of the other, and to which some of the blackest crimes, as well as some of the meanest and most odious vices that disfigure the history of our species must be attributed.

---

449 " Consules, 1; patricii, 2; præfecti prætorio, 3; præfecti urbis, 4; magistri militum, 5; præ-positi eubiculi, 6; quæstores, 7; magistri officiorum, 8; comites sacrarum largitionum, 9; comites rerum privatarum, 10; primicerius notariorum, 11; Magistri scriniorum, 12."

450 One instance of this, though no reader is easily amazed on such points, is really almost incredible. In celebrating the begining of the third ten years of his government, one bishop told Constantine that he was blessed, as having been appointed by God to rule all men in this world, and to rule conjointly with the Son of God over the next. Και τψ μιλλοντι συμξααιλεοειν μελλοι τψ νιψ τςν θιοř. —Eusebius, D.V. Con. iv. 48. The only parallel to this blasphemous flattery is Archbishop Whitgift's telling James L.!! at the Hampton Court conference, " that undoubtedly his majesty spoke by the special assistance of God's spirit."

Whether what at first, beyond all question, was policy on the part of Constantine, ever became serious conviction on his part, has been much disputed.[451] Why the enemies of Christianity should wish to deprive her of such a proselyte, or why her partisans should struggle for him with so much vehemence, it is not easy to discover.

The rapacity of Constantine is as indisputable as that of Henry VIII. A grosser act of unprincipled spoliation than his seizing upon all the corporate revenues of the different municipalities can hardly be found in history; and Julian deserves the highest honour for restoring them: this he did by an edict, A. D. 362. "Possessiones publicas civitatibus jubemus restitui, ita ut justis æstimationibus locentur quo cunctarum possit civitatum reparatio procurari."[452] Nor let it be supposed that Constantine bestowed any considerable share of his plunder on the church. Though every one of his crimes added to

---

[451] Julian, Zosimus, and Sozomen, the last a Christian writer and ecclesiastical historian, 1. 5., ascribe the conversion of Constantine to the refusal of Sopater, a philosopher and a follower of Plotinus, to undertake his purification after the Murder of his nearest relations and his son. Sopater affirming that he knew of no expiation for such crimes; on this refusal he applied to the Christian bishops, who undertook the task which Sopater declined. If this be so, I see in it no reproach to Christianity or its teachers. " When the wicked man turneth away from his wickedness and doeth that which is lawful and right, he shall save his soul alive," is a doctrine which so frail a being as man can never venture to reject. Eusebius tells us that Constantine was without any religious faith at all till the war with Maxentius. But that he then set himself to deliberate on the choice of a God. " Ingenue nec ut opinor falso," is Mosheim's comment on this passage in Eusebius.

[452] Cod. Theod. x. 3. 1. Amm. Marc.: " Liberalitatis ejus (of Julian) testimonia plurima sunt et verissima; inter quæ vectigalia restituta civitatibus cum fundis." And Libanius: προσφνητικϖ, και το αις πολεσιν επανρθϖσαι την πενιαν εξεληλαμεαις αρχαιων τε και δικαιων κτηματων δ μεν (Constantine) τους ιδιους οικους μεγαλους εποιησε τοις δε κονοις περιεχεεν αμορφιαν. And Sozomen, lib. v. Eccl. Hist. cap. 5., says that Julian restored to the cities what Constantine had taken away and given to the clergy.

The noble character of Julian continually displays itself. To call him an apostate is even more absurd than to call Constantine a Christian, or Henry VIII. a member of the English church; and, if we wanted any proofs of the character of the ecclesiastics of the day, if Gregory Nazianzen had not left us an account of them, if they had not in terms told us that it was the duty of a Christian to lie for the church, their abuse of Julian and praise of Constantine would supply them. When Julian was told by the prefect, Modestinus, that he would undertake to extort the arrears of the capitation, Julian replied that he would sooner perish than allow such oppression. " Animam prius amittere quam hoc sinere fieri memorabat." Amm. Max. lib. xvii.§3. This was when Julian was the delegate of Constans, and responsible to him.

the wealth of the church, and to the influence of its obsequious rulers, his religion did not stand more in the way of his interest than of his cruelty. He lavished large sums upon his favourites and courtiers. "Sicut in nonnullos amicos dubius, ita in reliquos egregius nihili occasionum prætermittens quo opulentiores eos præstaret," says Eutropius: "Proximorum *fauces* aperuit primus omnium Constantinus," is the vigorous and picturesque phrase of Ammianus.[453] About the same time that Constantine incorporated the church with the state, he divided the civil authority from military command.[454]

His anxiety to conciliate the troops[455] appears evidently from the purport of two laws which he enacted in the year A. D. 320, probably during the time of his campaign against the Franks. They exempt every one who is dismissed after service, from all civil burdens; they permit him, if he is disposed to agriculture, to occupy land free from taxes. They give him the right to cattle, seed, and stock for his farm. But if these edicts show the desire of Constantine to win the favour of the legions, they show also the miserable condition to which the military discipline of the Romans was reduced, and the efforts that were made to avoid the duties of a soldier. From the second law, tit.

---

[453] Ammian. xvi. 8. 12. the expression is worthy of Paul Louis Courier himself.

[454] Gibbon, c 17.

[455] "Constantinus A. dixit: Cum nune munificentia mea omnibus veteranis id esse concessum perspicuum sit, ne quis eorum ullo munere civili, neque in operibus publicis conveniatur, neque in ulla collatione, neque a magistratibus, neque vectigalibus. In quibuscunque nundinis interfuerint, nulla proponenda dare debebunt. Publicani quoque, ut solent agentibus supercompellere, ab his veteranis amoveantur; quiete post labores suos perenniter perfruantur.§1. Fisco nostro quoque eadem epistola interdiximus, ut nullum omnino ex his inquietaret, sed liceat eis emere et vendere, ut integra beneficia eorum sub sæculi nostri otio et pace perfruantur, et eorum senectus quiete post labores perfruantur.§2. Filios quoque eorum defendant decertationes, quæ in patris persona fuerunt, quosque optamus florescere sollicitius, ne si contumaces secundum eosdem veteranos comprobari potuerint, decimentur his sententiis, eum præsidali officio adjungentur probabilius, jussionem meam. Curabunt ergo stationarii milites cujusque loci cohortis, et parentes eorum desperationem, et ad sanctimoniam conspectus mei sine ulla deliberatione remittere, ut sint salvi, cum sævas consequuntur pœnas indulgentiæ."— *Cod. Theod.* vii. 20. De Veteranis.

22. lib. vii.[456] it appears that those liable to service mutilated themselves to escape from it: —

"Non his juventus orta parentibus

Infecit æquor sanguine Punico."

Neither the hope of profit, nor the dread of punishment, could make the coward brave, or animate the base with a sense of duty.

LEGISLATION[457]

In the years 321 and 327, Constantine published two decrees; the first ordered the destruction of all the notes of Ulpian and Paulus on Papinian.

The second confirmed the authority of the other writings of Paulus, and especially of his Receptæ Sententiæ. In the year 428. Valentinian III. promulgated his famous law of citations, by which the authority of law was given to the writings of Papinian, Paulus, Gaius, Ulpianus, and Modestinus, and to those of the jurists which they cite. If these authorities differ, the decision is to follow the majority; if the numbers are equally balanced, the casting vote is given to Papinian; if Papinian is silent, the judge is to decide for himself.

A compilation of the edicts and rescripts of the emperors, but principally of those of Constantine, was made probably in the age of Constantine, not, of course, before the fourth century; this was the Codex Gregorianus. Another compilation was made soon afterwards by Hermogenian, this was termed the Codex Hermogenianus, and was produced probably in the latter half of the fourth century. Fragments of these codes have been preserved in the Breviarium Alarici, by the author of the

[456] There is another law, Cod. Theod. vii. 13. 5, inflicting a penalty still more terrible " Si quis ad fugienda sacramenta militiæ fuerit inventus, truncatione digitorum damnum corporis expedisse, et ipse flammis concremetur."

[457] Théorie des Loix Politiques de la Monarchie Francoise. Mdlle. de la Lezardière, vol.i.

Comparison between the Mosiac and the Roman law; by the Consultatio Veteris Jurisconsulti; by the Papiani Responsa; by St. Augustine, and the scholiasts of the Basilica;: of the Gregorian code sixty-three fragments, of the Hermoginian thirty, are remaining. But in the year A. D. 438., a code was published by Theodosius II., which is of far greater importance to the study of jurisprudence, both inasmuch as it has been transmitted to us in a state comparatively perfect, and as a most patient, acute, and learned commentator exhausted the labour of thirty years in its illustration.[458] The commentary of James Godefroy is a mine in which all who desire to gain information as to the manners, usages, opinions, and laws of the period from Constantine to Theodosius must dig; but its value is by no means limited to that epoch. Godefroy's edition was published at Lyons, 1665, in six volumes folio, after the death of its indefatigable editor. A second edition was published by Ritter at Leipsic, in six folio volumes also, between the years 1736 and 1745. The text alone of the Theodosian code was published by Beck, 1815, at Berlin, as part of the *jus civile ante Justinianum.* Since that, new fragments of the code have been brought to light; some were discovered by Clossius, at Milan, some by the Abbé Peyron, at Turin. These fragments incorporated with the former text of the five first books of the code, have been published, with an admirable commentary by Wenck, at Leipsic, 1825. Wenck's notes to Gibbon sufficiently prove the sagacity and erudition of the writer, and the cruel blow which his death has inflicted upon literature.

I do not think that Godefroy, in ascribing to the Theodosian code an importance superior to that of the code of Justinian, was betrayed into any exaggeration of its utility. The compilers of the Theodosian code were not invested with such arbitrary powers as those conferred on Tribonian and his colleagues, by Justinian, and therefore the edicts which they

---

[458] Savigny, in his admirable work, Ges. des R. Rs., has left this code rather out of sight. He seems to reckon the Pandects and Code only as the Roman law; now there is a passage in William of Malmesbury, who died A.D. 1142, which distinctly mentions " leges quas Theodosius a temporibus Constantini... coegit," &c. Selden ad Fletam, c. 7. p. 507. 4to ed. 1685.

have preserved are more authentic, and transmitted to us with far more fidelity than those which Tribonian was allowed to mutilate and reform; and the Theodosian code marks, in characters not to be mistaken, the transition from Roman to Christian civilisation. It belongs to a period of decrepitude, but a period from which all traces of the traditions of Roman jurists were not effaced, as they are from the code of Justinian.

The first part in preparing the Theodosian code was entrusted to Antiochus, who had fifteen colleagues, among whom we find the names of Eubulus and Theodorus. The work was completed in three years, and promulgated as law in the Eastern empire. The authority of the imperial constitutions, since the days of Constantine, was limited to those included in this work. Theodosius sent it in the year of its promulgation, A. D. 438, to his son-in-law Valentinian, by whom it was made binding on the West, and published amid the acclamations of the Roman senate. Like the Hermogenian and Gregorian codes, the Theodosian code followed as far as was possible the arrangement of the prætor's edict. It consisted of sixteen Books — each book is divided into titles — and the edicts under those titles are arranged in chronological order. To each constitution is prefixed the name of the ordaining emperor, and the name of the person to whom it is addressed. At its close it states the consulship and the year. It is an infallible mark of the low condition of jurisprudence, that the first five books only, and those, especially from the second to the fourth, enter on subjects connected with private law. The rest relate to public law and ecclesiastical subjects. The books relating to the church, are at the end (instead of being, as Justinian has placed them, at the beginning,) of the work. We possess only the greater part of the work, namely, from the latter part of the sixth to the sixteenth book complete. The remaining fragments are extracts from the "Breviarium Alaricianum; " and (as has been observed) in our days, fragments from the five first, as well as from the later books, have been added to our former stock of knowledge. This code exercised very great influence over the later collections which appeared in the Roman empire, the *Edictum Theodorici,* the *Breviarium Alaricianum,* and the *Lex*

Romana Burgundiorum as well as over the Justinian code. And neither did the three German compilations, nor the Justinian codes, entirely abrogate the authority of the Theodosian either in the Eastern or Western empire. Other edicts called "*Novella Constitutiones,*" of later emperors, divided into six books, are annexed to the Theodosian code. The desire of Theodosius II. that the emperors of the East and of the West should each of them receive, and after making such alterations as might appear to him desirable, should publish the edicts of his colleague, is reiterated in the Theodosian code; and the interchange and communication of edicts, in conformity with tins wish, and the name "*Novella Constitutiones,*" referring to the Theodosian Code, lasted to the dissolution of the Western empire.

ALTERATION OF THE ORDO JUDICIORUM

The frequent inroads of barbarians had caused an alteration in the authority and number of the provincial rulers — the civil and military powers were now distinct. Under Alexander Severus we find mentioned[459] the "*limitanei duces,*" to whom the special charge of repelling the barbarians from the frontier was confided.[460] Lactantius complains of the brutal and illiterate leaders who were let loose *(immissi)* upon the provinces. It was a main object of imperial policy to weaken and divide the power of those whom they were obliged to invest with authority; it is the curse of tyranny that it cannot trust its own instruments. The provinces were broken up into smaller districts. Constantine divided the empire into four prefectures

[459] Lamprid. 58. Vopiscus, Aurelian, 13. " Provinciæ in frusta concisæ." Lact. de Morte, Pers, p. 7.

[460] Lands were assigned to soldiers, milites limitanei, on military tenure, and called " agri limitanei," " agros etisim limitaneos universes cum paludibus.... quos limitanei milites... ipsi curare... atque arare consueverant ab his.. detineri... volumus." Nov. Theod. tit. 32. vol. vi. p. 14. Lam-pridius says of Alexander, " sola quæ de hostibus capta sunt limitaneis ducibus et militibus donavit ita ut eorum ita essent si hæredes eorum militarent nec unquam ad privatos pertinerent." This is a very curious passage, as it is a description of a fief — though no conceit would be wilder than to imagine that the feudal tenures arose from those, or were in any way connected with them,— and see Theod. Cod. vii. tit. 15. and ib. tit. 13.§7.

— each prefecture was divided into several dioceses, governed by the *vicarii* of these prefects, who were excluded from all military command. A complete picture of this system of administration, is to be found in the "Notitia Dignitatum omnium tam[461] Civilium quam Militarium in Partibus Orientis atque Occidentis:" to that I refer. The old republican offices are omitted from it altogether. Meanwhile, the provinces became more and more helpless. The very idea of self-government had disappeared; every thing rested upon the emperor and his officers. They were multiplied to an incredible degree. Constantine invented dignities merely nominal, or, to borrow a word too familiar to English ears, sinecures, to enable his courtiers to escape from their share in the public burdens; and Eusebius, in the true spirit of a court bishop, praises him for this ingenious and convenient discovery. Thus the despotism of the emperor divided and subdivided itself into endless forms and ramifications, proceeding on through an endless labyrinth of offices, till, as Lactantius tells us, the governors were more numerous than the governed, and those who were supported by the public purse than those who contributed to it.[462] One of the chief signs of this state of things was the abolition of the old "*ordo judiciorum,"*[463] and especially of the *"judicis datio,"* the characteristic feature of the system. The proceeding *(extraordinem)* had become more and more frequent — "*status quœstiones* " had long been especially reserved for it, and the old republican method of proceeding was at last irreconcilable with the institutions of the empire; for, as the spirit of the citizen decayed, all share in public affairs was avoided as irksome, if not dangerous. The task of judge was avoided, or so

---

461 Gibbon, c. 18.

462 Lact. de Morte, Pers. p. 7.

463 I may here remark that, of all the writers on Roman Law, before the discovery of Gaius, which have fallen in my way, Pilati de Tassulo is the one who has the most accurate notions of the Roman civil process. The old Ordo Judiciorum: — "Ce qu'd y a de plus remarquable dans cette procédure c'est que l'on commencoit foujours par fixer l'état de la question, et qu'après il n'étoit plus permis de s'en éloigner; que cette disposition préliminairo se faisait devant le préteur avant que l'affaire fut portée devant les juges; enfin que la contestation de la cause etoit exposée en peu de mots où les longueurs des débats et les chicanes n'avoient pas lieu." All this is exact and luminous.

ill-performed, that, in all probability, it was rather an advantage than an injury to the public, when, towards the end of the third century, it was finally taken away. The duties of Judge were given to public functionaries; the only law which we possess on the subject is that relating to the provinces. It imposes upon them the same regulations which had probably been introduced before in Rome and the municipal towns of Italy. By this law, which is quoted in the note, the *præses,* in cases formerly referred to the "p*edanei judices,"* is bound to try the cause himself; if overwhelmed with business he may appoint particular judges, but this he is never to do in cases which, under the system, would have been *"extra ordinem."*[464] This was followed by a second edict, which allowed the nomination of *"pedanei judices"* in all trifling cases *(negotia humiliora).* That the corruption[465] of the age had extended itself to its courts of justice, is manifest from the frequent rescripts which attest the magnitude of the abuse, and the inefficacy of all attempts to restrain it. Constantine reiterates threats of the most savage punishment[466], with all the impotent violence of despotism; for

---

[464] Cod. Just. iii. 3.§2. " Impp. Diocletianus et Maximianus AA. et C C. dicunt: Placet nobis, præsides de his causis, in quibus, quod ipsi non possent cognoscere, antehac pedaneos judices dabant, notionis suæ examen adhibere, ita tamen, ut, si vel propter occupationes publicas, vel propter causarum multitudinem omnia hujusmodi negotia non potuerint cognoscere, judices dandi habeant potestatem. Quod non ita accipi convenit, ut in his etiam causis, in quibus solebant ex officio suo cognoscere, dandi judices licentia permissa credatur. Quod usque adeo in præsidum cognitione retinendum est, ut eorum judicia non deminuta videantur, dum tamen de ingenuitate, super qua poterant etiam ante cognoscere, et de libertinitate præsides ipsi dijudicent. Dat. xv. Kal. August. Cæss. Conss. [294—305.]"

[465] Cod. Theod. ix. 2. commands a second hearing in public; — " Ut judicibus immodice sæviontibus freni quædam adtemperies adhibita videatur," A. D. 326. What an idea of the age does the edict give which so describes men who are allowed to continue judges. Consul Mamertinus, in his panegyric of Julian, says, "Aliæ quas a vastitate barbaricâ terrarum intervalla distulerant *judicum nomine* a nefariis latronibus obtinebantur, ingenua indignis cruciatibus corpora lacerabantur nemo ab injuriâ liber — ut jam barbari desiderarentur, ut præoptaretur a miseris fortuna captorum." *Bouquet, i* 271.

[466] "Cessent jam nunc rapaces officialium manus, cessent inquam; nam si moniti non cessaverint, gladiis præcidentur. Non sit venale judicis velum, non ingressus redempti, non infame licitationibus secretarium, non virio ipsa præsidis cum pretio; æque aures judicantis pauperrimis ac divitibus reserentur. Absit ab inducendo ejus, qui officii princeps dicitur, deprædatio. Nullas litiga-toribus adjutores eorundem officii principum concussiones adhibeant; centurionum aliorumque officialium, parva magnaque poscentium, intolerandi impetus oblidantur, eorumque, qui jurgantibus acta restituunt, inexpleta aviditas temperetur. Semper invigilet industria

where such menaces are necessary, they are sure to be unavailing. The severity of the punishment attests the impunity of the crime. Such are the outlines of the system of legal administration, which was substantially unaltered in the West till the downfal of the empire at the close of the fifth century, and which in the eastern empire, continued till the legislation of Justinian.

CONSTITUTIONS PRINCIPUM[467]

The Rescripts of Diocletian and Maximian, with those of their colleagues, make up nearly a fourth of the Justinian Code. The legislation of Constantine is especially directed to insure the triumph of Christianity. Particular privileges are conferred on ecclesiastics. Christian (orthodox) churches are allowed to receive bequests, become heirs, &c. — a most important law, which the growing rapacity of the clergy obliged a Christian

---

præsidalis, ne quicquam a prædictis generibus hominuin de litigatore sumatur. Qui si de civilibus causis quicquam putaverint esse poscendum, aderit armata censura, quæ nefariorum capita cervicesque detruncet, data copia universis, qu concussi fuerint, ut præsidum instruant notionem. Qui si dissimulaverint, super codem conquerendi vocem, omnibus aperimus apud comites cunctos provinciarum aut apud præfectum prætorio, si magis fuerit in vicino, ut his referentibus edocti, super talibus latrociniis supplicia proferamus." — *Cod. Theod.* 1—16.§7. See also Ammian. Mar. xxx. 4. And another law, with an inconsistency which pervades Constantine's legislation, inflicts very severe punishments on the appellant who fails in making out his case. So Constantine retains the office of high priest, and makes laws against auspices. He becomes a Christian and refuses to be baptised. He belongs to the orthodox church, and when he dies Athanasius is in exile, and Arius in favour at Constantinople. It seems as if he was bewildered and confounded by the sense of guilt, and unable to find repose from his tormenting conscience in any creed or worship. " Ilæ sunt impiorum furiæ, hæ flammæ, hæ faces." All the subtilties of controversy and unintelligible disquisitions on subjects beyond human reason, and speculations, useless to all but a few interested priests, all the opiates of his mitred parasites could not restore tranquillity to a mind corroded by the incessant pangs of an ulcerated conscience. Such a state, as South says somewhere, " is not to be laid down, or put off; it is an emblem of hell, irksome and perpetual." All the waters of Jordan (which, Eusebius tells us, he delayed his baptism to bathe in, thereby showing that he thought such delay required some explanation,) could not wash away the blood of his nephew, his wife, his colleagues, and his son; he could not wash in them and be clean. Yet Constantine was not without good impulses, and almost great qualities.

[467] and fifty times in the code of Justinian; and, moreover, thirty-four of his laws are Hugo, vol. ii. Tigerström, Aeuss. Ges. Bethman Hollweg.

emperor to repeal; natural children cannot be made heirs; Constantine ordered the inhabitants of towns to cease on Sunday from their labours[468], but allowed and even enjoined agriculturists to continue their work on that day. Slaves may be emancipated in the church. Divorce and concubinage are forbidden; and the penalties against the celibacy encouraged by the Christian faith removed.

The "*Edictales Leges* " are so numerous under his reign, that his name is cited two hundred to be found among the fragments of the Theodosian Code. He did not abolish or mitigate slavery, even in favour of the Christians; every slave, however, who had enjoyed liberty for sixteen years, was free. He decided that slaves and beasts of draught, necessary for agriculture, should not be hypothecated. The "*Lex Commissoria,*" by which, in case of non-payment in a given time, the debtor forfeited at once his property in a pledge, which had been often recognised and was rigorously enforced, *was* totally abolished by a constitution which had a retro-active operation. The savings of the son employed in the palace of the emperor, were to be considered as a "*castrense peculium.*" It is characteristic of the period, that the "*bona vacantia*" were extremely frequent and conferred by the emperor on his favourites. The possession of five years made such property unquestionable. The tribunal of the bishop, "*episcopalis audientia,*" "*episcopale judicium,*" was established; but the "*miserabiles personœ,*" as they are repeatedly called, who refuse to embrace the Christian faith, might appeal to the emperor himself. It appears that the practice of addressing rescripts to the litigant parties from the emperor, had given rise to gross abuses, for there are a great number of constitutions on this matter only; sometimes the judges refer matters to the emperor himself. The party who appeals on frivolous grounds is liable to severe punishment; no appeal lies against an

[468] Cod. lib. iii. tit. 12. De Feriis,§3.: " Imp. Constantinus A. Helpidio. Omnes judices ur-banæque plebes et cunctarum artium officia venerabili die solis quiescant. Ruri tamen positi agrorum culturæ libere licenterque inserviant, quoniam frequenter evenit, ut non alio aptius die frumenta sulcis aut vineæ scrobibus commendentur, ne occasione momenti pereat commoditas cœlesti provisione concessa."

interlocutory judgment, before the definitive sentence is pronounced.

The most famous edict of the sons of Constantine is that by which the *"juris formulæ"* are abolished.[469] At this time also we find traces of the numerous impediments to marriage, founded on the difference of religion and the degrees of kindred, of which so many instances abound in subsequent constitutions. Marriage was forbidden between Jews and Christians, between brother and sister-in-law, uncle and niece. The rigorous form of instituting an heir was abolished. Forty years was an immemorial prescription. The property of a soldier, who died without kindred and without a will, were given to his regiment *(vexillatio),* instead of the treasury. Though Julian had abjured Christianity, Theodosius and Justinian did not venture to omit all mention of his edicts. But his reign was short, and most of his edicts were intended to remove or check the innovations of Constantine.

Jovian made very few edicts,[470] Valentinian abolished the law of Constantine allowing the church to inherit; he, his

[469] Théorie des Loix Pol. vol. i. Hugo, vol. ii.

[470] How presumptuous it is for monarchs to undertake alone the task of legislation the following edicts may serve to show. Cod. Theod. ix. 14.§*3.* If anyone has conspired to put to death any of the "virorum illustrium qui consiliis et consistorio nostro intersunt," he is to be put to death, his goods confiscated, his children, who are allowed to live by a stretch of imperial clemency, " quibus vitam imperatoriâ specialiter lenitate concedimus—paterno enim debent perire supplicio," adds the enlightened jurist, are to lose every inheritance—" a maternâ vel avitâ omnium etiam proximorum hæreditate ac successione habeantur alieni, testamentis aliorum nihil capiant, sint perpetuo egentes ac pauperes, infamia eos paterna semper comitetur.... sint, postremo, tales ut his perpetuâ egestate sordentibus sit et mors solatio et vita supplicio." This might almost furnish a hint to Nicholas himself. In this country, where all the excesses of the people are cut in brass, and all the crimes of despotism are written in water; where the crimes of a deluded populace in the last century are expatiated upon, and nobody ever talks of the massacres in Paland or Gallicia, or the slow, cruel, obtuse tyranny under which Italy has groaned so long; where the Emperor Nicholas was received with respect, not with abhorrence; where all the maxims for which our fathers shed their blood are out of fashion, and the very name of a patriot is a jest; it may be well to show that despotism has its evils, as well as a republic. Again, " Disputare de principali judicio non oportet, sacrilegii enim instar est dubitare an in-dignus sit quern elegerit imperator." Cod. Just. ix. 29.§3. " Si quis sacrilegii vitem falce succiderit aut feraciam ramorum fœtus hebetaverit quo declinet fidem censium (what a state of society!) mox detectus capitale subibit exitium." Cod. Theod. xiii. 11.§1. " Nullus omnino cui

brother Valens, and his sons Gratian and Valentinian II., deprived the Manicheans of all right of citizenship, and prohibited marriage with the barbarians. It is singular that the Visigoths should have kept this law, and that it should have been rejected by Justinian. Theodosius forbad first cousins to marry under penalty of being burnt alive,—here the interference of the church is sufficiently visible. It was under his reign that a law was passed, which strongly shows the depopulation of the empire — as it confers the property of an "*ager desertus*" on the occupant after two year's possession. A *decurio,* without a formal permission, is forbidden to alienate his slaves or his immovables. This prohibition was often repeated; the sale of a child by the father gave no right to the purchaser. Arcadius and Honorius put an end to gladiatorial spectacles, and punished a divorce from insufficient motives with great severity. If the divorce had been pronounced on sufficient grounds, the woman could not marry again for five years. Theodosius II. and Valentinian III. issued many laws, as well before as after the Theodosian Code. They determined the grounds of divorce, and established the "*legitimatio per oblationem curiœ.*" Under the reign of Valentinian and Martian, dower was enforced in all cases, and put on the same footing as the *donatio ante nuptias.* Leo I. enacted, that every creditor, with a mortgage ratified by an authentic public deed, should be preferred to the creditor whose mortgage rested only on a private contract between the

---

nescientibus nobis fidicularum (iron hooks) tormenta inferantur militiæ, vel generis, vel dignitatis defensione uti prohibeatur, *exceptâ tanturn majestatis causâ,* in quâ solâ omnibus æqua conditio est. " Cod. Just. ix. 8.§4. " Civitatum tabulariis erit flamma supplicium, si *cujusquam* fraude.... injusta profiteretur immunitas" (Cod. Theod. xiii. tit. x.§8.) *i. e.* if a public officer was imposed upon, and allowed any one who was not entitled to it to escape taxation he was burnt alive. Few officers of the revenue err on the side of indulgence, even without so strong; a motive to barbarity. Constans inflicted the same punishment on the adulterer, the poisoner, and the murderer, i. *e.* burning alive or sowing up in a sack. What would Bossuet have said, if any one had shown him the law condemning Louis XIV. to the same stake with Madame de Brinvilliers. Even in the last thirty years there are countries where such a law would hardly have been consistent with the respect due to the person of the sovereign, unless *men* had been exempt from its operation, and then perhaps some chancellor would have supported it. Cod. Theod. xi. 36. 4. " Oportuerit te... confessione detectos — punire ut manifestis probationibus adulterio pro-bato... tanquam *manifestos parricidas* insuere culleo vivos, vel exurere judicantem oporteat."

parties, though in writing. Leo suppressed the dowry and the *donatio ante nuptias.* He abolished all the forms of the *"stipulatio"* and declared a contract binding where none of them had been observed. He determined the authority before which the formal declaration of a donation was to be made. The person to whom the treasury gave or sold any thing, acquired an irrefragable title to it, and the original proprietor was allowed only four years within which to bring his action against the treasury. He made a special contract of the Emphyteosis. Anastasius allowed the divorced wife to marry again in a year. A prescription of forty years was valid in all cases. Justinian abolished the law forbidding marriage between persons of exceedingly unequal rank. He allowed the "*donatio ante nuptias*" to be increased even during marriage.

LAW OF ADMINISTRATION

The basis of the Roman system of taxation was laid under the republic, it was altered considerably by the first emperors, and in the second century. The land tax and poll tax existed in almost the same shape as under Constantine. The word "*capitatio"* has two principal meanings, it means both the land and poll tax, when it means the land tax it corresponds with the word *"jugatio,"* or "*terrena jugatio;"* when it means the poll tax the expressions "*humana capitatio*" "*capitalis illatio" "capitatio plebeia,"* are used as synonymous with it. Cicero tells us that in his time, with the exception of Sicily, all the provinces either paid a fixed tribute (vectigal certum quod stipendiarium dicitur) or a certain proportion of their produce *(censoria locatio)* which was farmed by the censors.[471] In the beginning of the imperial period an attempt was made to impose an equal burden on all the provinces by making the land tax[472] universal. In the time of the classical jurists there was the

[471] In Verrem, lib. iii. c. 6. Schlosser, Geschichte der alten Welt, vol. viii. Savigny, Zeitschrift für Ges. Rechtsw. vol. vi. 351. Steuerverfassung and Colonat. passim.

[472] Luke, ii.: " There came forth a decree from Cæsar Augustus that all the world should be taxed." Cassiod. iii. 52. Isidor. Orig. v. 36. cit. apud Savigny.

land tax and the *tributum*[473] *capitis*. Italy was free from both. It was divided into Italy *"urbicaria"* and *"annonaria;"* the district included under the jurisdiction of the *præfectus urbis* was free from all taxes, the latter was liable to a tax in kind[474]: this was the general rule. Italy was deprived of this immunity when the empire was divided under Diocletian, for this we have direct evidence.[475] Such a privilege once taken away was never likely to be restored, especially as Italy had lost her preeminence among the nations.

In the time of Constantine the population of the villages of the empire consisted of large proprietors and their serfs, peasants, and the coloni[476], or tributarii, who were employed in the cultivation of the soil, were not allowed to depart from the land they tilled, and paid the owner of the soil a fixed portion of its produce. The coloni and citizens without land, paid a capitation tax for themselves, the proprietor paid a capitation tax for his slaves.[477] Between the accession of Diocletian and the death of Valens, the payment of taxes in kind was, generally speaking, abolished (except in Africa, Spain, and Egypt)[478], and

---

473 Dig. 1. 15. 8.§7. "Agri tribute onusti viliores hominum capita stipendio censa ignobiliora." —*Tertullian, Apol.*§13.

474 Savigny, *ubi supra,*

475 Aurelius Victor, de Cæs. 39. " Huic denique parti Italian invectum tributorum ingens malum."

476 Homines, coloni vestri. Theod. Code, xiii. 1. 3. de lustr. coil. 213. 5. 10. 1. That these unhappy men endeavoured to escape, we find from the Theod. Code in Fugit. Colon. Receptatores, lib.v. tit. ix.§2. Cod. Just. xi. 47. " Liberos colonorum esse quidem in perpetuum liberos, non autem habere licentiam relicto suo rure ad aliud migrare." Cod. Theod. viii. 2. 5., and Paulus, Receptæ Sententiæ, lib. iii. 6.§48. describes this predial servitude. " Actor vel colonus ex alio fundo in eodem constitutus, qui cum omne instrumento legatus erat, ad legatarium non pertinet nisi eum ad jus ejus fundi testator voluerit pertinere."

477 This was altered by Constantine, and finally abolished. The inhabitants of cities were freed from the poll-tax.

478 Egypt seems to have been the Roman Hindostan, and taxed in the same frightful manner as the inhabitants of Bengal are at this day, where the government takes seventy per cent of the produce, and advances to the cultivator of the richest districts in the world the pittance requisite to buy the handful of salt and rice necessary for his support, and to save him from dying of famine, which would lower the value of India stock. Ammianus Marcellinus says of the Egyptians, " erubescit apud eos si quis non inficiando tributa in corpore vibices ostendit." Compare Bishop Heber's account of the terror with which the natives looked at him because he was a European. Such is the government of placemen not responsible to the inhabitants of the soil where they rule, and which they always intend to leave

the capitation tax, a land tax, and a tax on industry was substituted for them. The land tax was levied according to an estimate which was renewed every fifteen years; cattle, slave, serfs, buildings, were comprised in it. It was easy to augment at each of these intervals the sum for which each district was responsible; at this time no steady principle appears to have prevailed, either when it was enforced or when it was forgiven. Two instances have been preserved concerning it in Gaul, from which the ingenuity of modern critics has endeavoured to extract solid statistical information; one of these is in the time of Constantine who forgave the ædui seven thousand out of the five and twenty thousand portions, for which they were liable; the other is during Julian's administration of Gaul; he lowered the tax on each portion from twenty-five pieces of gold to seven. It was the rule that every portion of ground had its tax, and, therefore, when, as often happened, districts were laid waste by invading armies or plundered by the imperial troops, or abandoned by their cultivators, the taxes due from them fell on the contiguous territories; to such an extent was this carried that, in an oration pronounced at Treves before Constantine, by Eumenius, the orator thanks the emperor for having excused the inhabitants of the cultivated land from paying the tax due from the swamps, morasses, and unfilled districts in the vicinity. But the provinces were scourged to the bone, the renewal of the estimate[479] was dreaded like some devouring pestilence, and a

---

when their fortunes are made. " The difference in favour of the first conquerors is this, the Asiatic conquerors very soon abated their ferocity, because they made the conquered country their own..... Fathers there deposited the hopes of their posterity, and children there beheld the monuments of their fathers — here their lot was finally cast." " But under the English government all this order was reversed. The natives scarcely know what it is to see the grey head of an Englishman.... Young men govern without society, without sympathy with the natives. *They have no more social habits with the people than if they still resided in England.* Every rupee of profit made by an Englishman is lost for ever to India." See Burke, East India Bill. Constantine transferred the annual tribute of Egyptian corn from Rome to Constantinople. Claudian de Bello Gildonico, v. 46.

" Ægyptia rura
" In partem cessere novam."

[479] To form an idea of the misery and depopulation of the Roman empire, it is enough to examine the laws concerning the revenue. " Ut inveniantur... quidam Romani qui malint inter Barbaros pauperem libertatem quam inter Romanes tributariam servitutem." — *Orosius,* cit. apud Lézardière, vol. i. p. 263. Constantine says (Cod.

swarm of merciless officers of the revenue spread themselves over the soil. The description given by Lactantius[480], when every allowance is made for the prejudice and exaggeration of the writer, of the condition of the people, is like Volney's picture of eastern tyranny, as he inveighs against the Heathen.

Theod. ii. tit. 27.§2.): " Provinciales egestate victús atque alimoniæ inopiâ laborantes liberos suos vendere, cognovimus." Salvian, (liv. v.) says: "Leviores his (civibus) hostes quam exactores sunt, et res ipsa hoc indicat, ad hostes fugiant ut vim exactionis evadant." Dig. 1. 15.: "Si agri portio chasmate perierit debebit percensitorem relevari, si vites mortuæ sint vel arbores aruerint iniquum eum numerum inseri censui (this shows the minute detail of fiscal regulation, and that the number of fruit trees were counted), quod si exciderit arbores vel vites nihilominus eum numerum profiteri jubetur, qui fuit census tempore, nisi causam excidendi censitori probabit." This shows that cultivation was often changed, to avoid particular taxes, from a more to a less lucrative branch of husbandry. Cod. Theod. xii. tit. 13. s. 14.: " Si qui aliarum possessionum dominus desertum prædium suum inspici forte voluerit, universa loca quæ possidet... peragrari patietur ut sareina destitutæ possessionis... possit melioribus sociari." Cod. Theod. xiii. 11, 12.: "Loca quæ præstationem suam implere non possunt præcipimus adæquari ut quid præstare possint... scribatur, id vero quod impossibile est e vasariis publicis auferatur." Cod. Just. xi. 58.1.: " Prædia deserta decurionibus loci cui subsunt assignari debent cum immunitate triennii." This shows how common the abandonment of land to escape from taxes must have been, and with what tenacity the fiscus clung to its object; but the following passage is even stronger. " Cum... Aurelianus civitatum ordines *pro desertis possessionibus* jusserit conveniri, *et pro his fundis qui invenire dominos non potuerunt*... satisfacere, servato hoc tenore præcipimus ut si constiterit ad suscipiendas possessiones ordines minus idoneos esse, eorundem agrorum onera possessionibus et territoriis dividantur accepta." Before such a law as the following could have been required, oppression must have been carried to a tremendous pitch. " Quicunque de provincialibus decurso... post hac quantolibet annorum numero cum probatio aliqua ab eo tributariæ solutionis exposcitur, si trium cohærentium sibi annorum apochas securitatesque protulerit, superiorum temporum apochas, non cogatur ostendere." Cod. Just. x. 22.§3. Constans and Constantius took away the right of appeal in fiscal causes. " Publicâ utilitate suadente in causis pensitationum debitorum que fiscalium, inhibitum est provocationis auxilium." Cod. Theod. xi. 36. 12. and ib.§19. " Abstinendum.prorsus appellatione sancimus... ut necessario in contumacem vigor judiciarius excitetur." Nov.Theod.4. says: the officers, " omnia pro arbitris extorquent," ut cum aliqua pars certa vel minima publicis comcompendiis inferatur duplam aut amplius.. avidus et prepotens executor accipiat." But when we find a decree of Arcadius and Honorius, giving to the inhabitants of Campania five hundred and twenty-eight thousand and forty-two "jugera" of land which had been abandoned, can more evidence of the deplorable condition of the empire be wanting. Cod. Theod. xi. tit. 28.§2. " Quingena viginti octo millla quadraginta duo jugera quæ Campaniæ Provincia juxta inspectorum relationum... in desertis et squallidis locis habere dignoscitur, iisdem provincialibus concessimus." And this was before the invasion of the Barbarians A. D. 395. Constantinople no doubt must have contributed much to the depopulation of Italy.

[480] DC M. P. C. 23. (6)

Zosimus accuses the Christian emperors with equal bitterness and equal truth. Salvian[481] says that the rich contrived to fling the heaviest burdens on the poor, and he accounts for the origin of the class of coloni, by a process not very dissimilar to that which induced the allodial proprietors in the dark ages to exchange their rights for a feudal tenure. He says, in consequence of this intolerable oppression, some make over their estates to the rich, and become their tenants; and even then the rent they pay is so high that they gain little by the sacrifice, "cum rem amiserint amissarum tamen rerum tributa patiuntur cum possessio ab his recesserit, capitatio non recesserit, proprietatibus carent, vectigalibus obruuntur," another class, he says, leave their patrimonial farms, "et coloni divitum fiunt.... jugo se inquilinæ abjectionis addicunt.... et rerum proprietate careant, et jus libertatis amittunt;" a third class still more miserable become slaves, "*vertuntur in servos,*"

Instead of the poll tax, from which Constantine and Licinius had exempted the inhabitants of cities, a tax was levied upon all trades[482], as pernicious and destructive to industry as the Spanish alcavala itself; we may judge of its severity from the fact that Christian sextons were released by a special law from its liabilities, and by another law which provides that it shall not be held to include the peasant who brings produce to market, or his master. The establishment of the office of *defensores* is another ominous symptom of the times; the citizens were to choose from their whole body men who were to remain in office five years to watch over the conduct of the magistrates of the city, and to protect its interests. Schlosser compares them to the schutzvogt of the middle ages. We find abundant proofs in the Theodosian code that this office was

---

[481] Salvian, de Gub. Dei, lib. v. c. 8, 9. s 4

[482] And from " Muliereulis pudicitiam prostituentibus." De Annona et Tributis, tit. i. lib. ii. Cod. Theod. ed. Ritter, vol. iv. p. 1.; tit. xvi. lib. x. Cod. Justin. Manso, Leben Constantius, p. 188. Cod. Theod. tit. i. lib. xiii. vol. v. p. 1. " De lustrali collatione." Libanius calls it, ö ἀφόρητος φορος, p. 427. Gothofred makes a desperate fight for Constantine, but the facts are all against him. Cod. Just. tit. i. lib. xi. The words of the law are (lib. xiii. tit. 1.): " Negotiatores omnes convenit aurum argentumque præbere; clericos excipi tantum qui copiatæ appellantur." (A. D. 357.) Zosimus, ii.§38., after imputing this tax, required singulis lustris, to Constantine, says it was exacted with the most unrelenting rapacity.

abused to the oppression of the people; under Arcadius and Honorius the defensores are forbidden to extort fines or to inflict torture, and an edict of Valentinian forbids all clandestine and secret trials, and requires their proceedings as judges to be carried on openly and with the usual publicity.

But no circumstance impresses the mind more forcibly with the miserable condition of the provinces than the situation of the decuriones; these were the senate, consisting of the highest municipal magistrates in their respective cities; their station was one of honour[483], dignity, and consideration; they enjoyed several exclusive and even invidious privileges. Every citizen not of this body belonged to an inferior and plebeian class, and yet so far from admission to this body being an object of honourable and legitimate ambition, it is shunned as ruin, it is dreaded as the worst and most dreadful of all calamities. It is only necessary to open the twelfth book of the Theodosian code to see the despair which the office of decurio provokes, and the ingenuity, nay, the reckless efforts by which it is avoided.[484] Rich citizens become common soldiers, they marry slaves, they fly from their residence, nay, they give themselves up to actual servitude in order to escape from functions so abhorred; yet slavery itself is no protection, the legislature meets them everywhere, and drags them back to the highest station in their native cities. The grave is the only refuge against oppression that is already intolerable, and to which every year of danger and dismay adds its own appropriate burden. Instead of being condemned to the mines and the amphitheatre, criminals were made decuriones, and though this was forbidden by special edicts, other decrees enforced it as the punishment for the scorn and refuse of mankind in all ages and countries, the profligate priest and the dastard soldier.

These decuriones were among other liabilities responsible for the collection of the imperial taxes; every magistrate was also responsible for his colleague and his

---

[483] Ausonius describes them: —
" Quos curia summos,
Municipum vidit proceres, propriumque senatum."
[484] Roth. de Re Munic. Romanorum.

successor; they were bound to undertake the management of lands that the cultivators had abandoned in despair, and above all they were immediately exposed to the violence and cruelty of the provincial governors. The rapacity and insolence of these governors were the last remaining features of the republic. If the taxes were deficient, the decuriones were bound to make them good from their private fortunes. How these laws were enforced we may judge from the edicts of Theodosius the Great, one, A. D. 381, forbidding the *rectores*[485] *provinciarum* from torturing decuriones. "Sciant neminem omnino decurionum plumbatarum[486] cruciatibus esse subdendum." Another (380), says: "Omnis ordo curialis a tormentis his quæ reis debita sunt et ab ictibus plumbarum habeantur immunes."[487] Libanius, Orat. *περὶ ἀγγαρεῖων,* says: *αἶ κατὰ τῶν βουλευόντων (de decuriones) πληγαὶ διὰ κακίαν ἄρχόντων εἶς ἔθος ἥκον.*

Citizens became decuriones from birth (as the places in the municipal senate became hereditary), from choice by the senate, to which, when the number of the senate was incomplete, every citizen was obliged to submit. When the decurio had gone through all the municipal functions, he might retire into private life, and certain high stations about the court and in the public service exonerated the holder from this situation[488] but the law on this subject was in constant fluctuation.

---

[485] Lib. xii. tit. 85.

[486] Lib. xii. tit. 80.

[487] " Venuleius Saturninus libro i. de Officio Proconsulis. Divus Hadrianus cos, qui in numero decurionum essent, capite puniri prohibuit, nisi si qui parentem occidissent, verum pœna legis Corneliæ puniendos mondatis plenissime cautum est. S."—*Dig.* xlviii. 19.§15.

"De decurionibus et principalibus civitatum, qiti capitale admiserunt, mandatis cavetur, ut, si quis id admississe videatur, propter quod relegandus extra provinciam in insulam sit, imperatori scribatur adjecta sententia a præside. Alio quoque capite mandatorum in hæc verba cavetur; si qui ex principalibus alicujus civitatis latrocinium fecerint aliudve quod facinus, ut capitalem pœnam meruisse videantur commiserint vinctos eos custodies, et mihi scribes, et adjicies, quid quisque commiserit." — *Dig.* xlviii. 19. 27.§§1,2.

[488] Cod. Theod. 12. tit. i.§5.

LAWS AFFECTING THE RELATION OF CHURCH AND STATE

With the establishment of Christianity, an element found its way into Roman jurisprudence, with which it never could altogether assimilate. The church created a legislation of its own. It was in vain that the best and wisest Christians uplifted their voices in bitter remonstrance, or pathetic expostulation. It was in vain that they deprecated, in the strongest manner, the union of what was spiritual with temporal grandeur, with the cares, and tumult, and business of the world. The address of Hilary of Poictiers to Constantine was as useless as that of Fénélon to Louis XIV.[489] It was a salutary principle of Roman jurisprudence, that no corporation should inherit unless by a special sanction from the state. Constantine abrogated this law in favour of the orthodox church A. D. 321, and permitted it to inherit without restraint.[490] But so terrible were the evils which ensued from this permission, and so enormous were the possessions absorbed by the church, that in less than half a century it was repealed by a Christian emperor.[491] "S' adoperavano con ogni via i mintstri ecclesiastici," says Paolo Sarpi, "ad acquistar beni, non avvertendo se il modo che usavano fosse legitimo, e conducente all' equità, ma purchè sortissero l' effetto, cioè che la chiesa acquistasse per qualunque

---

[489] "Qui ecclesiasticam historiam legit, quid est nisi episcoporum vitia?" said a wise, pious, and deeply learned man. Grotius, Ep. 22.

[490] Cod. Theod. xvi. tit ii.§4.

[491] Cod. Theod. xvi. 2. 20.: " Ecclesiastici, aut ex Ecclesiasticis, vel qui *Continentium* se volant nomine nuncupari, viduarum ac pupillarum domos non adeant; sed publicis exterminentur judiciis, si posthac eos ad fines earum vel propinqui putaverint de serendos. Censemus etiam, ut memorati nihil de ejus mulieris, qui se privatim sub prætextu religionis adjunxerint, liberalitate quacunque, vel extremo judicio, possint adipisci; et omne in tantum inefficax sit quod alicui horum ab his fuerit derelictum; ut nec per subjectam personam valeant aliquid, vel donatione, vel testamento, percipere. Quin etiam si forte post admonitionem legis nostræ aliquid his dem eæ feminæ, vel donatione, vel extremo judicio, putaverint relinquendum, id fiscus usurpet. Cæterum, si earum qui voluntate percipiunt, ad quarum successionem vel bona, jure civili, vel Edicti beneficiis adjuvantur, capiant ut propinqui.— Lecta in Ecclesiis Rom. iv. Kalend. Aug. Valentiniano et Valente, ill AA., coss. [370]."

via, le pareva aver fatto sacrificio a Dio."[492] It is remarkable that the account of an honest heathen of the pomp and worldliness of ecclesiastics in this age exactly corresponds with that of an honest bishop, Gregory Nazianzen, who has painted the synods of bishops of that day in the blackest colours. Any reader who will compare the account of the election of Damasus[493] to the Bishopric of Rome, in Ammianus, with the letter of Gregory[494], in which he says that he avoids all

---

[492] "Trattato delle Materie Benefic." p. 17. How much more sublime was Plato's idea of the Deity than that of these worldly churchmen! (Nόμοι, lib. x.) " There are three kinds of impiety " he says; " the first is to deny the existence of gods, the second is to deny their providence, the third is to imagine that their anger is to be turned away by sacrifices and offerings." There is also a magnificent passage in Antiphon inculcating the last sentiment. Neander, speaking of these laws, says, "the enormous wealth of the church was owing to the belief that such donations were meritorious before God as an 'opus operatum.'" — *Kirchengeschichte,* 2. b. 1. theil, p. 289. When I quote Neander, I quote a writer who unites the most fervent and simple piety, and the most amazing erudition, even in a Herman, with the most inviolable regard to truth. Also, he says, " that it was believed that these donations (Ariosto's spilt soup) were atonements for sin." A sacrilegious notion, to which half the crimes and cathedrals of the middle ages owe their origin.

[493] Ammianus Marcellinus, 27 3, 4.: " 12. Damasus et Ursinus supra humanum modum ad rapiendam episcopatus sedem ardentes, scissis studiis asperrime conflictabantur, adusque mortis vulnerumque discrimina adjumentis utriusque progressis; quæ nec corrigere sufficiens Juventius nec mollire, coactus vi magna secessit in suburbanum. 13. Et in concertatione superaverat Damasus, parte, quæ ei favebat, instante. Constatque in basilica Sicinini, ubi ritus Christiani est conventiculum, uno die centum triginta septem reperta cadavera peremptorum; efferatamque diu plebem ægre postea delenitam."

"14. Neque ego abnuo, ostentationem rerum considerans urbanarum, hujus rei cupidos ob im- petrandum, quod adpetunt, omni contentione laterum jurgari debere; cum id adepti, futuri sint ita securi, ut didentur oblationibus matronarum, procedantque vehiculis insidentes, circumspecte vestiti, epulas curantes profusas, adeo ut eorum convivia regales superent mensas. 15. Qui esse poterant beati revera, si magnitudine urbis despecta, quam vitiis opponunt, ad imitationem antistitum quorundam provincialium viverent; quos tenuitas edendi potandique parcissime, vilitas etiam indumentorum, .et supercilia humum spectantia, perpetuo numini verisque ejus cultoribus ut puros commendant et verecundos."

[494] Greg. Nazianz. Ep. 53., this is his opinion in verse: —

Ουδε τι που συνδοισιν ομοθρονος εσσμ'
εγωγε
Χηνϖν η γερανων ακριτα μαρναμε-
νων
Ενθ' ερις, ενθα μοθος τε και αισχεα
κρυπτα παροιθεν
Εις ενα δυσενεων χϖρον αγειρομενα.

But he has filled many (folio) pages with verses describing the " Episcoporum Vitia."
Mosheim, De Rebus Christ, ante Con. p. 587.§24. describes the extravagant

meetings of bishops, *πάντα σύλλογον ἐπισκόπων,* because he never knew them lead to any good, *ὅτι μηδεμίας τέλος εἶδον χρηστόν*, may form some notion of the authority due to the churchmen of that corrupt age, and of the manner in which they had degraded to a merely ritual worship the pure and spiritual morality of the Gospel. "I do not grieve," says Jerome[495] "so much for the law, but that we have deserved it;" "nec de lege conqueror, sed cur meruerimus hanc legem;" and he adds, the law is evaded by *"fideicommissa,"* as undoubtedly it was. Another injudicious law of Constantine added to the scandal given by the ambition and worldliness of the clergy, for, by exempting them, nay more, their sons and grandsons, from many temporal burdens, especially from the office of *decurio,* and the oppressive *"collatio lustralis,"* it tempted into the church a vast number of profligate, daring hypocrites.[496] Such is the way in which despotic and precipitate legislation defeats itself. To remedy this evil, A. D. 320, he issued an edict[497] commanding that no one of a decurion family, no one with sufficient fortune, no one qualified to fulfil public duties, should become an ecclesiastic, — that new ecclesiastics should be chosen in the place of those who died, and such as possessed an inconsiderable fortune, and would not be liable to the burdens of the state. Another change in legal proceedings[498] was that the sentence of the bishop, if he was taken by both parties as their judge, was without appeal. This was the basis on which such an enormous structure of imposture, chicane, and

---

pretensions of bishops, " Nova dogmata excogitabant de episc. auctoritate, quorum vim ne ipsi quidem satis assecuti fuisse videntur. Exemplo erat Cyprianus." And he quotes several instances of his absurd and blasphemous arrogance, 1. 9. He tells a poor man, who doubted the validity of his election as bishop,— " Hoc est in Deum non credere!"

[495] He says that a clergyman in the houses of rich matrons, " si pulvillum viderit, si mantile elegans, si aliquod domesticæ suppellectilis, laudat, miratur, attractat, et his se indigere conquerens non tam impetrat quam extorquet, quia singulæ metuunt veredarium urbis offendere." Cit. ap. Neander, p. 290. b. ii. th. 1.

[496] Cod. Theod. xvi. tit. 2.§2.

[497] Cod. Theod. xvi. tit. 1.§6.: " Opulentos enim sæculi subire necessitates jubet, pauperes ecclesiarum divitiis ditari."

[498] Plank. Ges. der Ch. K. Verfassung, vol. i. p. 315. th. 3.§6.

tyranny was afterwards to be reared[499]; from which were to spring the forgeries of Isidore and Gratian[500], the decretals and the canon law; the means, "weak masters though they seem," by which great monarchs were to be brought low, and whole provinces to be depopulated, till nations quailed before the seal of the fisherman, and Europe yielded to the law of him who styled himself the servant of servants, an obedience as servile as ever Asiatic slave paid to the mandate of him who was called the king of kings. But a task more humiliating now devolves on the historian of Roman law. I mean that of pointing out the intolerant and persecuting edicts which abound in the codes of the Christian emperors, and which show how completely ignorant they were of the religion which they so ostentatiously professed. In the year A. D. 319[501], Constantine issued two laws against the aruspices and sacerdotes; one says that the visits of the aruspex are to be stopped, "quamvis vetus amicitia repellatur," by a very effectual method, "concremando

---

[499] Pilati de Tassulo Loix Civiles, vol. iii. c. 12. p. 93. " Les formalités dont il est ici question sont une invention de ce même clergé pour arrêter plus long temps dans ses tribunaux et ruiner plus aisément les plaideurs séculiers (chats fourrés of Rabelais). La source de ces formalités n'est ni dans le Gouvernement Monarchique ni dansle Républicain, mais dans le pre mier et le second livre du Droit Canon..... C'est le clergé qui les a forgées après avoir établi son empire sur notre raison et nos consciences, et nous avoir accablé de son joug humiliant.... Les papes, les évêques, leurs vicaires, ont trouvé que plus ils faisoient durer un procès devant eux, plus ils y gagnoient." He adds a remark, of which there is but too frequent proof: — "Il n'y a rien de plus facile que d'éblouir les yeux du public, et de commettre mille injustices sous le voile des formalités." See Saunders's Reports and the State Trials, passim.

[500] Gratian, a native of Chiusi, in Tuscany, published his work, A. D. 1151, under the pontificate of Eugenius III.; that of Isidore (Peccator) was propagated in France in the time of Charlemagne. The latter contains the false decretals of sixty Popes, from St. Clement to St. Sylvester, and fifty canons of the apostles, and the donation of Constantine, all forgeries, but not detected till the sixteenth century. The first clause of our twentieth article, — " The church hath a power to decree rites and ceremonies, and authority in controversies of faith," was not in the articles of religion ratified by Parliament in 1571, 13th Eliz., on which act alone the legal authority of the articles depends. But this clause, printed in all the editions of the Articles since the year 1617, as if it had been so ratified, is a downright forgery. Now, if this was managed in the seventeenth century, after the discovery of printing, who can wonder at the forgeries of the dark ages? In the reign of Richard II. the clergy forged an act of Parliament for the destruction of heretics, which they said was passed at Westminster, " Quinto Regis." This was detected in the next session of Parliament.

[501] Cod. Theod. ix. 16. 1.

haruspice qui ad domum alienam accesserit," the person who invites him is punished by deportation and the loss of all his property; the informer is said to be "*dignus prœmio.*" Eusebius tells us[502], that Constantine published two other laws forbidding the worship of idols, the erection of statuse to the gods, the prediction of the future, and the slaying of victims — in other words prohibiting pagan worship. In the year A. D. 321, Constantine forbids all artificers, all the inhabitants of towns, and all judges, to pursue their callings on Sunday.[503] There is a second law, in the same year, on the same subject. In the year A. D. 341, Constantius and Constans renew the law of their father forbidding sacrifices.[504] A law, A. D. 363, forbids them on pain of death.[505] A. D. 356[506], we find a law to the same effect, "Pœnâ capitis subjugare præcipimus quos operam sacrificiis dare vel colere simulacra constiterit." A. D. 364 Valentinian renewed the laws of his predecessors[507] against those who "nocturnis temporibus aut nefarias preces aut magicos apparatus, aut sacrificia funesta celebrare conentur." Under this reign a terrible persecution was set on foot against those employed in divination, of which Ammianus has left an account[508], "everywhere," says Zosimus, "are tears and groans; the prisons cannot hold those destined to captivity." While this persecution was raging in Italy, Valens was tormenting the Eastern empire. Socrates says[509] that Valens put to death every one called Theodorus, Theodosius, Theodotus, or Theodulus. Books were destroyed by their owners; any one might ruin another by putting a treatise on magic in his library. Crowds of

---

502 Vit. Const. ii 56.
503 Cod. Just. iii. 12. 3.
504 Cod. Theod. xvi. 12. 2.
505 Cod. Theod. xvi. 10. 5.
506 Cod. Theod. xvi. 10. Strype, vii.
507 Cod. Theod. ix. 7. Bishop Jewel complained to Queen Elizabeth of the marvellous increase of witches and sorcerers, adding, "I pray God they may never practise further than on the subject." King James wrote his treatise on Demonology in great haste on account of their increase. And one of the articles of inquiry at a visitation of the diocese of London by Bishop Juxon (then, thanks to Laud, lord high treasurer), is, " Whether any minister, without licence, upon any pretence whatever, either of obsession or possession, cast out any devil, or devils? "
508 Lib. xxvi. 3.
509 Cit. ap. Cod. Theod. iv. 15.

senators were put to the torture. At length a law, A. D. 371, gave the unhappy victims respite and repose.[510] In A. D. 382, Gratian snapped the feeble thread that bound the empire to its ancient faith. He refused the pontificate; stripped the pagan worship of all its revenues; and destroyed the statue and altar of Victory. Saint Ambrose triumphed over Symmachus. It is a curious and striking proof of the confusion of men's ideas at this time on religious subjects, that Theodosius the Great actually published a law, after the pillage of the heathen temples, forbidding Christians to solicit or accept the office of Pagan High Priest.[511] Theodosius forbade divination, pagan sacrifices and worship, on pain of death. He deprived those who abjured Christianity of the right to make a will. He extended this prohibition even to catechumens.[512] He destroyed and closed the heathen temples. Other laws were enacted by his successors in the same spirit. Theodoric, the Ostrogoth, inflicts death as the punishment of heathen worship; but the occasion for such laws became less and less frequent, and probably ceased altogether after the invasion of the barbarians in Italy. In the year A. D. 561, some unhappy pagans were discovered at Constantinople — were seized — and after their hands and feet were cut off, were carried round the town on camels. Such are some of the laws in the great struggle between Polytheism and Christianity. But the laws inflicted on heretics by the orthodox church are equally severe. They are to be found in the Theodosian Code[513], deportation, exile, confiscation, beating to death with leaden poles, are among their punishments. They are forbidden to assemble, and the place where such assembly takes place is forfeited; they are excluded from all offices and dignities, with regard to which, says Gothofred[514], "elegans est Honorii dictum, ' Nullus nobis sit aliquâ ratione conjunctus qui a nobis fide ac religione discedat.'" Rewards are offered to informers

---

[510] Cod. Theod. xvi. 9. 9.
[511] Cod. Theod. xii. 112. In consequendâ Hierosynâ, &c., and Goth. note.
[512] Cod. Theod. xvi. 5. 28.
[513] Cod. Theod. xvi. tit. 5.
[514] Gothof. Parat. vi. p. 121.

against them. The definition of heretics[515] is "qui vel levi argumento a judicio Catholicæ religionis et tramite deflectunt," A. D. 395. After this comprehensive anathema, we find: "Cuncti hæretici procul dubio noverint omnia sibi loca hujus urbis adimenda esse," A. D. 396. They are deprived of life[516]: "Summo supplicio et inexpiabili pœnâ jubemus affligi... sublimitas itaque tua det inquisitores — aperiat forum — indices denuntiatoresque sine invidia delationis accipiat," A. D. 382. Such were the happy consequences[517] of conferring immense incomes on men who taught their flocks that money was the most formidable of all barriers in the path of eternal happiness; of dignifying by empty titles and pompous ornaments, men set apart to inculcate humility; in other words, of the union of church and state[518]: and such were the notions of

---

515 The laws against heretics are all condensed, Cod. Theod. lib. xvi. tit. 5. Gothof. Paratil.; and see tit. 7. De Apostatis.

516 Cod. Theod. lib. iii. tit. 7.§2. " Ne quis Christianam mulierem Judæus in matrimonium capiat, neque Judæam Christianus, nam si quis aliquid hujusmodi admiserit adulterii vicem commissi hujus crimen obtinebit; " *i. e.* it was punished by death. So St. Ambrosius exclaims: " Cave, Christiane, Judæo aut Gentili filiam tradere." Lib. i. de Abr. cap. 9.§84. Marriage with a niece, filiam fratris sororisve, was a capital offence. Ib. xii. 3. 1. After Nerva it was lawful to marry " fratris filiam non sororis." Ulpian, de Incestis, n.

517 However, when the first blood was shed by Christians, " for differing worship of the Deity," some of the most eminent complained; Sulpie, Severus, Dial. iii. c. 11. 13., and St. Ambrose, Ep. 24. St. Augustine, on the contrary, thought that pity for the death of heretics was misplaced. Ep. xlviii. ad Vincent.

518 Or, as it has been ridiculously called by those who, without Warburton's vigour of language or ingenuity uphold the absurdities it suited the purpose of that learned, violent, arbitrary, paradoxical, and not, I should think, very sincere, writer to defend — a state conscience, which makes persecution a duty. The nearest approach that has ever been made to the wretched quibbling, narrow views, and drivelling bigotry, which occupied the degraded court of Byzantium, is by modern tractarian writers; and their publications are as strong a proof of the low condition of thought, and taste, and literature among us, as the disgraceful squabbles at Constantinople were of the decrepitude of the Eastern empire. One passage from Gregory Nazianzen deserves notice. " The city of Constantinople," he says, " is full of slaves and mechanics, all of whom are profound theologians. If you ask a man for change, he teaches you how the father is different from the Son; if you ask the price of a loaf, you get for answer that the Son is inferior to the Father; and if you ask whether the bread is ready, they reply to you that the Son was made out of nothing." No wonder that the omission or insertion of the letter *(ομοουσιος* and *ομοιουσιος)* caused oceans of blood to be spilt; that while Honorius and his bishops were torturing Manichees at Ravenna, the Goths marched without resistance to Rome; and that when the Turks stormed their city the Greeks were disputing whether the light on Mount Tabor was created or uncreated.

Christianity, which under the auspices of that union[519] were promulgated from courts, and not forbidden by œcumenical councils, in the fourth century of the Christian era.[520]

CHAP. IV. JUSTINIAN[521]

JUSTINIAN was of Sclavonic origin. His father was called Sabbatius, his mother Bigleniza. His own name was Upsanda, of which Justinianus was a version: to this the name of Flavius was added. On the 1st of April, 527, he became joint emperor with his uncle Justinus, and on August of the same year, he became in consequence of the death of the latter sole master of the eastern empire.

The character of Justinian has been the subject of vehement dispute. Nor can I agree with Gibbon, that the "name of the legislator is inscribed on a fair and lasting monument." To whatever share of gratitude Justinian may be entitled as the

---

[519] Ep. 1. ad Bonifacium. I may mention that St. Chrysostom held, unequivocally, the doctrine of transubstantiation, the worship of relics, and the intercession of saints.

[520] The decisions of the councils on matters of faith were decided, as Neander says, at this time, by the Byzantine court; and the springs that set that court in motion were the same as have, in all ages, directed courts. One chief instrument, as Gregory Nazianzen tells us, Orat. xx. Theodoret, lib. iv. c. 19., was the head cook, *αρχιμαγειρος*, who was employed to prevent Basil of Cæsarea from opposing the court theology. Articles of faith were settled by lords of the bed-chamber (cubicularii), cooks, and eunuchs. Isidore of Pelusium wrote to Theodosius that, till he put a stop to the interference of his courtiers with the councils, no good could be expected for the Church. So, at the first Ephesian council, Pulcheria employed the theological controversy to deprive her enemy, Nestorius, of the see of Constantinople. In the year 476, Basiliscus changed the faith of the Church by imperial edicts; and so did Zeno and Justinian. Neander, ii. band, 1. theil, p. 287. The Church was now a political power, a political motive; it had exchanged its kingdom over the heart, for the kingdom of this world, which its founder had disclaimed; for to unite the two was and has ever been impossible; every step towards one, is a receding from the other.

[521] Gibbon. Dirksen, Civilistische Abhandlungen, vol. i. Spangenberg, Einleitung in das Römisch Just. Rechtsbuch. Zimmern, Röm. P. Walter, Gesch. Puchta, Inst. Cursus. Savigny, Geschichte, vol. i. 2. Giraud, Droit Romain. Meyer, Instit. Judiciaires. Warnkönig, Histoire externe du Droit Romain. Tigerström, Aeus. Ges. des R. R.

compiler of other men's labours, a question which shall presently be considered, it is precisely his own legislation that proves him to be one of the weakest and most bigoted, as well as *one* of the most avaricious and cruel even of Byzantine sovereigns. The ruler of a great empire who condescends to become the champion of a party in the circus, and even to share in polemical disputes; the legislator who repeatedly pronounces his own panegyric, and arms the rage of fanatics with the weapons of the law; the statesman who crushes the people whom he governs under the weight of the most oppressive taxes, while he squanders incredible sums with reckless profusion on objects of frivolous display and insulting pageantry, must be numbered among the most odious and contemptible of mankind; and deserves, as has been the lot of Justinian, that his conduct should be described in terms as bitter as the keenest satire could point, or the most implacable animosity suggest. Few of my readers probably are ignorant that Procopius[522], besides an official history of the administration of Justinian, in which, as might be expected, the most pompous eulogies were lavished on the conduct of that emperor, left a secret history which was discovered in the library of the Vatican, and published A. D. 1624, in which he represents Justinian and his Empress Theodora as two of the foulest monsters that Providence in its indignation ever raised up to be the scourges of a people. Another charge of gross and complete ignorance has been brought against him, but this which rests upon a passage in Suidas is completely overthrown. It is satisfactorily made out that Justin not Justinian is the emperor to whom the passage in question must apply. With regard to the other charges, it has been said, that Procopius must be considered altogether unworthy of belief. I confess that such is not the conclusion at which I should arrive. That he is a suspicious witness I admit, and therefore if any con-conceivable motive could be assigned for this posthumous invective, I should lend a very academic faith to the statement it contains.

---

[522] " Quamvis demersæ leges, quamvis timefacta libertas emerget aliquando." Perhaps there may be some Procopius in Russia, in spite of Siberia and the knout, at this moment *(mutatis mutandis,* of course).

But his personal interest was all the other way. That led him to praise Justinian; his secret history seems intended as a sort of expiation to truth for the falsehoods he was compelled officially[523] to propagate; and if it be said that personal malignity was a sufficient motive, let it be remembered that this objection assumes the substantial truth of the accusations. For were there no colour for charges so gross and so notorious, they would only excite ridicule among those to whom their falsehood was familiar; and to suppose that it was the sole object of Procopius to mislead remote posterity, is to ascribe to him conduct which, for inefficacy as well as virulence, is without parallel in the annals of human malignity. But, as Montesquieu[524] has observed, the miserable condition of the empire, and the laws of Justinian, corroborate the anecdotes of Procopius. Procopius cites especially the laws which made a prescription[525] of 100 years requisite against the church, as one of those which he had been bribed to enact; and, again, Procopius, not in his anecdotes, but in his work *(de Bello Persico,* 24.) attributes direct corruption to Tribonian.[526] Indeed, the reign of Justinian abounds with cruel laws capriciously applied.[527] Greater changes were made in the laws during a few years of his reign than had been made in the course of the preceding three centuries; for many of his edicts no motive can be assigned, but the desire of innovation, and as the matters to which they relate are trifling and insignificant, it is difficult to resist the conclusion that the ruler carried on a disgraceful traffic in his decisions and his laws. The bigotry of Justinian depopulated the empire, for the sects he persecuted with the sanction of his bishops were nations. Among these were the Samaritans, Montanists, the Manicheans, the Sabatians, the Arians, besides the Pagans who were scattered over the face of almost every province. Justinian imagined that

---

[523] The late Mr. Tierney, I believe, first used the happy phrase, "inveterate habits of official as- sertion."

[524] Grandeur et Décadence des Romains, c. 20.

[525] Cujacius Obs. b. v. c. 5. de Præscriptione C Annorum.

[526] "Fixit leges pretio atque refixit."

The passage in the text has been transcribed by Suidas, v. Tribonianus.

[527] The obscure and ambiguous phraseology of the 159th Novell, is generally ascribed to the corruption of Tribonian. Domat, Loix Civ. vol. ii. p. 762.

he was increasing the number of Christians, while the human race itself was diminishing under his tyranny; one instance of religious persecution deserves notice, because it certainly brought with it a tremendous retribution. Procopius tells us that, from the persecution of the Samaritans, Palestine became a desert; and, after Procopius was in his grave, the followers of Mahomet found their way through this province, which had been turned into a lair for wild beasts by religious zeal, to dismember the empire which they finally overthrew.[528]

In the year A. D. 476, when the Western empire[529] was destroyed, the following were the authenticated works on jurisprudence.

The Jurists, as they were recognised by the Law of Valentinian.

The Gregorian and Hermogenian Codes.

The Code of Theodosius II.

The Novellæ of subsequent Emperors annexed to that Code.

Even these abridgments, however, could not bring the law within the reach of the age. The Roman jurisprudence was still an object too large for its abilities to wield, or for its understanding to methodise. Ammianus Marcellinus tells us that when the name of any distinguished jurist was cited before the provincial tribunals; it was supposed to be the name of a strange vegetable, or of some foreign fish. The necessity of new reforms was still urgent, and, within thirty years after the destruction of the Western empire, four attempts were made,

---

[528] As Montesquieu says, the taxes of the emperors contributed materially to the success of the Mahometans. Thierry, " Dix Ans d'Etudes Historiques, c. sur l'Empire Romain."

[529] Cicero had already sketched an outline of a code. " Si enim aut mihi facere licuerit, quod tamdiu cogito, aut alius quispiam aut me impedito occupârit, aut mortuo effecerit, ut primum omne jus civile in genera digerat, quæ perpauca sunt; deinde corum generum quasi quædam membra dispertiat, tum propriam cujusque vim definitione declaret; perfectam artem juris civilis habebitis, magis magnam atque uberem, quam difficilem atque obscuram."—*De Orat,* 41. lib. i. But his scheme was probably unknown to Justinian.

each independently of the other, and each in a separate kingdom, to grapple with it.

The first of these was the Edict of Theodoric (A. D. 500), king of the Ostrogoths.[530]

The second was the Breviarium of the Visigoths — *Lex Romana Visigothorum* — sometimes called *Breviarium Alarici* —sometimes *Breviarium Aniani* (because no copy was to be authentic without the signature of Anianus), A. D. 506.

The third, the Lex Romana Burgundiorum, called by mistake "*Papiani Liber Responsorum,*" about 500.

And lastly the compilations of Justinian (528—534), intended for the immediate use of the eastern empire.

---

[530] Ritter, Theod. Cod. vol. ii. Prefat. That it was not intended as a perfect code, but to supply the deficiencies both of the Roman and Gothic law is proved, not only by the passage which Savigny quotes on the succession to an intestate, but by the more direct and satisfactory evidence of the edict itself; " quæ comprehendere nos edicti brevitas, vel curæ publicæ non siverunt, quoties oborta fuerint custodito legum tramite terminentur," " quibus," adds Gothofredus, " et Gothorum jus et Romanas leges innuit." The author of the Alexandrian Chronicle describes the occasion on which the edict of Theodoric was promulgated. Ind. 8. Zeno A. 11. Symmacho Consule. A lady, called Juvenalia, complained to Theodoric that her law suit had lasted three years! (How many wretched Chancery suitors would think themselves fortunate if they could only make the complaint of Juvenalia!) Theodoric sent for the judges and lawyers, gave them two days, and told them that if the question was not settled in that time he would cut their heads off *(αποκεφλιζω υμας)*. The question, as may be supposed, was determined. Theodoric, in great indignation, sent for the judges, asked why they had taken three years to do what they could do in two days, and beheaded two of the lawyers on each side. This frightened the others, and he propounded an edict: *και εγενετο φοζος, και εποιηε ιαταξιν ερι εκαστου νομου.* Without wishing for so summary a proceeding as that of Theodoric, I must say that the utter indifference of those in whose power it is to stop the delay and abuses of our law to the public good, in that respect, is monstrous, and the toleration of such a state of things is a stain on the character of the nation. " By these dilatory and expensive proceedings," said Gibbon, who certainly did not err on the side of independence, or aversion to the great and powerful, " the wealthy pleader obtains a more certain advantage than he could, hope from the accidental corruption of his judge." The system of our times is still almost as obscure and irregular as when Gibbon wrote; we have to complain of two evils seemingly opposite, but which, in fact, create and augment each other, the legislative, which is the arbitrary power of the judge, and the insane multiplication of our laws; evils which the most *practical* of nations must be content to smart under, so long as its exquisite sensibility to the convenience and gratification of the rich is only equalled by its contemptuous apathy to the mortifications and hardships of the poor.

In the year A. D. 528, one half year after the death of Justin, an attempt was made under the auspices of Justinian to compile another code, for which the three codes, the Gregorian, the Hermogenian, and the Theodosian, were to furnish the materials. In the year A. D. 529 the work was completed and promulgated under the name *Codex Justinianus.* This was called in and has completely disappeared.

About the same time Justinian with a view to guide and facilitate the labours of those employed in the still more arduous task of the Pandects, prepared fifty decisions on controverted and doubtful points of law: "cum vetus jus considerandum recepimus tarn quinquaginta decisiones fecimus, quam alias ad commodum propositi operis pertinentes, plurimas constitutiones promulgavimus."

At the end of the year A. D. 530, Tribonian received a special command to compile a book of laws out of all the works extant, which, without regard to the law of Valentinian, were authorities on subjects of jurisprudence in the Roman empire. It was to consist of fifty books and to be entitled *Pandectœ* or *Digesta.* This work Tribonian, with the assistance of sixteen colleagues, accomplished in three years. The Digests were promulgated on the 16th December, A. D. 533, and came into operation on the 30th of the same month.

Meanwhile, an elementary work had been prepared modelled on the Institutes of Gaius; this was also called "*Institutiones,*" was published on the 21st Nov. 533, and received the force of law on the same day as the Pandects.

The faults of the first, code of Justinian were rendered more glaring by these publications; and what, perhaps, in Justinian's opinion was its greatest fault, it had omitted many of his constitutions. It was, therefore, cast anew, under the auspices of Tribonian; was published under the name of *"Codex Repetitœ Prœlectionis,"* 16th Nov. 534; received the force of law on 29th Dec.534.

Justinian, on the occasion of this last publication, informed his subjects that all future edicts would be published in a collection apart, under the title "*Novellœ Constitutiones.*"

The first of these *Novella* is on the first of January, 535, the last is on Nov. 564; the number of them is 165; some of them are of very great length; some are in Latin, with a Greek transcript, but the majority are in Greek. The greatest number of these *Novellœ* is between the years A. D. 535 and A. D. 539. From A. D. 545 the activity of legislation visibly diminishes; a circumstance probably to be ascribed to the death of Tribonian, which happened in that year.

The title which Justinian gave the Pandects was "Digesta sive Pandectæ Juris enucleati ex omni vetere Jure collecti." They are divided into partes, libros, titulos, leges, paragraphos. Justinian divided the Pandects into seven parts, probably from some absurd superstition about the number seven.

The first contained the first four books, *τà πρϖτα.*

The second the next seven - - - - 5 to 11

The third the next eight - - - - 12 to 19

The fourth (*Umbilicus Pandectarum)* the next eight 20 to 27

The fifth the next nine - - - - 28 to 36

The sixth, the next eight - - - - 37 to 44

The seventh, the next sixth - - - 45 to 50

The Pandects are divided into fifty books, each of which, with the exception of the 30th, 31st, and 32nd, de Legatis primus — secundus — tertius, are subdivided into titles.

The editions vary as to the number of the titles; for instance the editions which follow the old Florentine manuscript do not reckon the title "*Pro Soluto,*" but include it under the title "de Usucapionibus et Usurpationibus," while other editions assign it a separate place. The editions which exclude the "*Pro Soluto* " as an independent head, combine the titles "de Privilegiis Creditorum" and that "de Rebus Auctoritate Judicis possidendis" and the "de Via publicâ et de Itinere publico," and the "de Via publica et Si quid." Some reckon three titles in the three books, 30, 31, 32. The number of titles, therefore, varies from 429 to 440.

Each title is divided into sections consisting of extracts from different works. These are often called "*leges,*" often "*fragmenta*;" sometimes by the Dutch "*capita,*" The number of these varies in different editions, from 9198 to 8134. Each fragment is divided into paragraphs, the first of which *(principium)* is not counted.

It was the express command of Justinian that the compilers of the Pandects should follow the order of the edict. This method was also followed in the code, notwithstanding the different subjects that were inserted in it. In the Pandects we find, after an introduction, general discussions, the doctrine of magistrates, and the constituent elements of law. Law is divided into the law of things and of persons; and the law of persons is first considered. In order to prepare the way for this inquiry the *status hominum* is investigated, and then we have an account of the chief dignitaries and officers of the empire. That this arrangement, in the main, coincided with that of the edict appears from[531] a comparison with the corresponding portion of the code, from the 14th title of the first book to the end.

The books from lib. ii. to lib. v. tit.2. relate to the civil process, and the method of proceeding in the courts of law, the title "*de Feriis et Dilationibus,*" in which the arrangement of the edict was departed from; "*de Pactis et Transactionibus*" which the order of the edict accounts for, as the code which[532] corresponds with the Digest shows; then, rules for those who represent the litigants, the doctrine of the *in integrum restitutio,* the judges, and the forum. No doubt many changes were made in this portion, as the law of process had undergone a complete revolution, and many parts of the edict were brought together as better adapted to the subject.

From the second title of the fifth to the end of the forty-sixth, Private Law is the sole subject; from lib. v. tit. 2. to the eighth book, the Law of Things is discussed in the order of the *edictum perpetuum.* The means of obtaining an inheritance as

---

[531] They correspond generally, but not altogether: between the 19th and 25th titles of the Code Tribonian has inserted matters that were not in the edict.

[532] Cod. ii.§§3. 4.

an inheritance was considered an entire thing, by legal or prætorian remedies. The *rei*[533] *vindicatio;* the "*Publiciana in rem actio,*"and the actio"*quæ*[534] *de agro vectigali proponitur*" The law of servitudes: personal, *"jus utendi fruendi," "quibus modis usus fructus vel usus amittatur,"* "*de usufructu earum rerum quæ usu consumuntur," "usufructuarius quemadmodum caveat;*" real, which fill the 8th book, the "*servitutes prædiorum urbanorum,"* and "r*usticorum."* The manner in which they may be lost.

From the ninth book of the Digest to the twenty-second, the law of obligations is laid down. These fourteen books contain three portions:

The first, *de Obligationibus ex Maleficio.*

The second, *de Obligationibus ex Contractu.*

The third, is a sort of appendix, in which the compilers have put together various matters relating to obligations and especially to contracts. Here it was that the order of the *edictum perpetuum* was most defective, and the desire of adhering to it even within very wide limits, has perplexed and bewildered the authors of the Digest. All *maleficia* are *ex dolo* or *culpa,* those which arise from *culpa* are treated of in the ninth book of the Digest where are the heads "*de pauperie," "de lege Aquilia," "de dejectis et effusis," "de noxalibus actionibus."*

---

[533] In the time of Justinian there was no difference between property " ex jure Quiritium "and that "in bonis," the "rei vindicatio," once confined to the former, applied to all property.

[534] This was called " emphyteuticarius." "Vectigales vocantur qui in perpetuum locantur, id est, hac lege, ut tamdiu pro his vectigal pendatur, quamdiu neque ipsis qui conduxerint, neque his qui in locum eorum successerunt, auferri eos liceat."—*Dig.* vii. 3. Notwithstanding Savigny, whom, on subjects connected with Roman law, I look upon as only not infallible, it appears to me that the common opinion, ascribing the dominion of these agri vectigales to the emperor or the Roman people, is unshaken. The words of Theophilus, Paraphrasis,§40. Inst. de Rerum Divisione, are insurmountable: οι τα στιπενδιαρια και τριξουταια εχοντες κατα συγχωρησιν δημου η βασιλεως ουκ ησαν δεσποται. ‘Η γαρ δεσποτεια αυτϖν η παρα τψ δημω η παρα τϖ βασιλει, αλλ’ ειχον την ε’π’ αντοις χρησιν... και εφ’ ετερων μεταφερειν και κληρονομοις παραπεμπεν; a sort of tenant right.

Then follow three mixed actions, both *in rem* and *in personam,* judicia divisoria quæ duplicia vocantur, *"finium regundorum," "familiœ erciscundœ" de communi dividundo,"* and the "*actio ad exhibendum."*[535] Then come the *interrogatories actiones.* What reason caused the insertion of these heads between the *culpa* and the *dolus* I am at a loss to conjecture; probably some association arising out of treatises which we do not possess. The next head is the *dolus malus.* The first title is *"de servo corrupto."* There is a curious title "*de*[536] *religiosis et ut funus ducere liceat,"* another *"de aleatoribus."* All these heads are founded on the Twelve Tables (the basis of the prætor's edict) which included in the same chapter civil and criminal *delicta, the furtum,* for instance, and the *si quadrupes pauperiem, &c..*

Next come the obligations *quœ ex contractu profisciscuntur,* where stands in the first place the title "*de rebus creditis,"* for which Ulpian has accounted; the first contract is the *mutui datio,* which, as one of those "*re,*" was no doubt of remote antiquity. The titles follow, *de juramentis* and the *condictiones: condictio "causþ datþ, causâ non secutâ, " "ob turpem causam," " indebiti," "sine causâ," "furtiva," "ex lege," i. e.* for any other legitimate cause. Here are placed, probably because no better place could be found for them, "*de eo quod certi loco dari oporteat,"* and "*de pecuniâ constitutâ,"* the "*actio commodati"* and "*pigneratitia."* Here the authors of the Digest omitted a great deal that the code[537] shows us was in the edict. And here, to understand the train of ideas, it is important to recollect the general rule of Roman jurisprudence, that no man could be bound except by his own act. As exceptions to this rule we have the "*exercitoria actio,"* an action given against the owner of a vessel to those who contracted with its captain or master; the *"lex Rhodia de jactu;*" the "*institoria*[538] *actio,*" of the same nature with the *exercitoria;*

---

[535] Dig. x.§4.
[536] Ulp. ad Edict. 68.
[537] Code, iv. 10. *seq.*
[538] " Seu vocat institor,
Seu navis Hispanæ magister
Dedecorum pretiosus emptor."

and the "*actio tributoria,*" by which the father was liable for so much of the contracts made by the son to whom he had given authority to act as merchant, as the *peculium profectitium* of the son would cover.

Then come the "*actio de peculio,*" the "*de in rem verso,*" then follows a sort of appendix "*de senatus consulto Velleiano*" "*de compensationibus,*" "*de deposito;*" then came the *contractus, "consensu,"* the "*mandatum," "pro socio," "de emtionibus et venditionibus,"* &'c.

Then the *actiones "infactum,"* or "*præscriptis verbis*;" to these the compilers added the "*actio pigneratitia,*" the "*ædilitium edictum et redhibitio.*" The 23d book contains the titles "*de usuris," "fructibus," "causis," "accessionibus," "morâ," "de nautico fœnore," "probationibus," "fide instrumentorum," "testibus," "juris et facti ignorantia."*

From the 23d to the 27th book, the Digest contains the law of families, "*marriage," "tutela," "curatela," "patria potestas."*

From the 28th to the 38th the greater part treats of succession by will, also of succession against the will of the deceased; then comes the "*bonorum possessio,*" and the "*sucessio legitima*"

The books from 39th to 46th contain a vast variety of miscellaneous subjects which were in the corresponding place in the Edictum. Here are the *"operis novi nunciatio," "mortis causâ donatio," "de manumissionibus," "de acquirendo rerum dominio," "de acquirendâ vel amittendâ possessione"* "*de exceptione rei judicatâ."* The interdicts, the *exceptiones,* and the "*stipulatio*" as it was arranged in the "*edictum perpetuum.*"

The books from 47 to 49 contain the criminal law. After tit. 14. lib. 49. to 50 we find the right of the *"fiscus,"* the military administration, the government of municipalities, public offices, and taxes.

The 50th book is, "*de verborum signif.," "de regulis juris.'"* Such is the actual order, if order it can be called, of topics in the Digest. The length of the extracts is quite arbitrary;

sometimes a proposition is composed of several extracts, sometimes an extract is inserted between the very words of the cited author. Generally, however, the compilers have left the extracts as they originally stood; and an external arrangement, according to which extracts from particular writings follow each other, is undoubtedly to be distinguished. It should be recollected that a classification of the more eminent waiters on Roman law was familiar to the jurists of the day. In the first year of instruction at the schools of law, the institutes of Gaius, and some commentaries on the middle of the edict were read; in the second, commentaries on the edict generally; in the third, casuistical writings of Paulus and Papinian. This we may even trace in the code of the Visigoths *(Breviarium Alaricanum)* where the Institutes of Gaius are placed first, the *Sententiæ* of Paulus second, and the *Responsa* of Papinian last. It is natural, therefore, to suppose that the commissioners of Justinian, to whom such a classification was familiar, would arrange the works they could procure in a threefold order, assigning those of less decided character to the class which might happen best to suit the convenience of the compilers.

It is certain, as has been observed in a very remarkable essay by Blume, that three classes of extracts which regularly follow each other may be remarked. Most of the titles contain extracts from all three, in which the number sometimes of the one, sometimes of the other, predominates.

The first contains extracts from the commentaries of Sabinus, from the commentators on the middle of the edict, from the Digests of Alferius, Varus, and Julianus, from the Institutiones of Gaius and of others. The second contains writings from the other commentators on the Edict from commentaries on Plautius, from the Digests of Celsus and Marcellus, and from many other writers, especially from Modestinus. The third is composed of extracts from the *Quœestiones,.Responsa,* and *Definitiones* of Papinian, especially; of the *Responsa* and *Quœstiones* of Paulus and other jurists; with an appendix of other writings, among which the Digest of Scævola is prominent. This discovery, important as regards the external order, and not without its use, even for the interpretation of the Pandects, is due as has been mentioned, to Blume, who designates the first class, as the Sabinian heap, the second, as the Edict heap, and the third as the heap of Papinianus.

Two facts may certainly be collected from the Constitutions of Justinian concerning the Pandects: one that the extracts from the writings collated were ranged according to the titles of the edict and the code.[539] The other that the extracts were compared with the corresponding titles of the code.

The following is the theory of Blume[540] upon the subject, which is certainly plausible, and to which if it run a little too much into detail and over-refinement, nobody can refuse the praise of solid learning and ingenuity.

The compilers of the Pandects divided into three classes all the works from which the selection was to be made. Each class was assigned to a separate committee. The extracts then made were compared with the code of Justinian, and arranged under a rubric, taken from the code, from the edict, or from the work actually under examination. All the matters under the same rubric were then collated, contradictions and repetitions were struck out, and such alterations made as were requisite to make the selections themselves intelligible. When each committee had completed its labours, our Pandects were composed out of the three collections. That collection was chosen for the basis of each title in which the greatest number of fragments, or fragments of most importance were contained. Then the other two collections were compared with it; on the same plan as before, repetitions were struck out, definitions and general propositions inserted. The fragments of the smaller collections, that had not been placed or struck out, were placed after the first collection; and the rule generally observed was, that the number of fragments decided which collection was to be the second, and which the third, of those comprised under the same title. Now it is obvious that when the compilers of the

---

[539] Const. Deo Auctore,§§5. 9. Const. Tauta,§14. fin. Const. δεδωκεν,§14.

[540] Blume, Ueber die Ordnung der Fragmente in den Pandecten Savigny, Zeitschrift für Ges. J. vol. iv. p. 258.

Pandects entered upon their task, each division or committee would naturally look for some comprehensive and important work, to serve as a kind of frame for the innumerable fragments of smaller works, and a standard to which the abundant but confused mass of accumulated materials might be adjusted. For this purpose they selected one work for each each committee; the works ad Edictum for one; the works ad Sabinum for another; and the Papinianæ Quæstiones for a third; the latter followed the order of the Edict. If on examining the character of these three works which were placed respectively at the head of each collection, there will be found an historical contrast between the books on Sabinus, which refer immediately to the civil law *(jus civile),* and those on the Edict, in which the prætorian law, *"jus honorarium,"* occupies the largest space. Again, in contrast with both those as dogmatical writings, we find in the third class writings almost entirely practical.

It is also remarkable, and I think it is the weak point of Blume's theory, that the commentaries on the middle of the edict, are not in the natural place, but are collated after the writings on the Ædilitian Edict.

The *Edictum perpetuum* was the model of the code, with the necessary exception of ecclesiastical law. The method of the code is the following: —

The first book to the thirteenth title, treats of ecclesiastical law.

The titles from the fourteenth title of the first book, to the twenty-seventh title of the third, contain the general introduction, and the law of civil process.

From the twenty-eighth title of the third book to the thirty-fourth they contain the law of things.

From the thirty-fifth title of the third book to the end of the fourth, they contain the law of obligations.

In the fifth book, down to the sixth title of the sixth book, they contain the law of families.

From the sixth title of the sixth book to the end of that book, the law of inheritance.

The seventh and eighth books contain various subjects. Manumission, acquisition of property, *res judicata;* appeals, concurrence of creditors, interdicts, *operis novi nunciatio;* law of pledges, *"exceptiones," "stipulatio," "patria potestas," "adoptio," "jus postlimine," "de ingratis liberis," "de infantibus expositis," "quœ sit longa consuetudo," "de donationibus."*

The ninth book contains the criminal law and process.

The tenth to the twelfth books, contain the same topics as those in the Pandects concerning public law, but in a different order.

COMPARISON OF THE PANDECTS, CODE, AND TWELVE TABLES

Introduction. General topics.

Pandects, book i.

Code, book i.

I. and II. Tables. Administration of justice.

Magistrates.

Pandects, books ii.—xii.

Code, books ii., iii.

III. Table. On contracts.

Pandects, books xii.—xxiii.

Code, book iv.

IV. Table. On parental authority and marriage.

Pandects, book xxiii., xxvi.

Code, book v. tit. 1.—xxvii.

V. Table. On the law of guardianship and inheritance.

Pandects, books xxvi.—xli.

VI. Table. Property and possession.

Pandects xli.—xlvii.

Code, book vii. tit. 25. book ix.

VII. Table. Criminal law.

Pandects, xlvii., xlviii.

Code, book ix.

Appendix.

Pandects, books xlix., 1. De Appellationibus, &c.

Code, books x.—xii.

Code, book v. tit. 27.; book viii. tit. 25.

Justinian not only deprived the original works from which his extracts were taken, and all writings save those inserted in the text of his compilations, of all authority, but in the true spirit of presumptuous despotism[541] and meddling impertinence, he forbad any commentary to be written on his codes, only short summaries *(paratitla)* and a Greek paraphrase were to be allowed.

It is of course obvious, that the very nature of Justinian's enterprise involved some great and serious evils to literature, as well as to legal science, as it was the chief object of that undertaking to abridge and to diminish the innumerable treatises, which it was impossible for any jurist in that age to comprehend, or even to peruse; it became necessary to

---

[541] The most perfect specimen of royal impertinence and presumption in modern times is, perhaps, the ludicrous mockery which the King of Prussia was pleased to call a constitution, and which his subjects have not chosen to consider one. The King of Prussia should be told what an English writer says somewhere; that if a horse knew as much as his rider, riding would be a dan-gerous amusement; where the horse knows a great deal more, and is far better educated, it must be still more perilous. It is consoling to reflect that all the hypocritical despotism of Prussia has never been able to wrest from the Rhine province the blessing of the Code Napoléon.

mutilate[542] and to deface the most precious monuments of jurisprudence. The fragments of different writers on the same subject were forced together violently, and a task to which the greatest capacity would have been unequal, and from which it would have shrunk with horror and dismay, was executed by men inflamed with all the presumption of mediocrity, and ruthless in proportion to their want of genius. "Tout abrégé d'un bon livre est un sot abrégé." The spirit of the author evaporates; all his originality and characteristics disappear, according to the admirable illustration of Cervantes, the tapestry is turned the wrong way, and if some of the limbs remain, the life that animated them has departed. Accordingly, fragments, which taken separately have no meaning, are to be met with in the Pandects, and a patchwork of particles *plane, quodsi, vero, autem, ergo,* by which sentences of different writers are inartificially combined, offends the ear, and mortifies the expectation of the reader.[543]

---

[542] Dig. vii.§3. "Et clientes" is the whole law. In Dig. xxii. 13. 25. 1. in a quotation from Paulus we stumble upon the rubbish of Tribonian, inserted as if it were part of the original: " vir simplicitate gaudens et desidiæ deditus." So Dig. iii. 5. 47.: "quia in extraordinariis judiciis, ubi conceptio formularum non observatur, hæc subtilitas supervacua est;" as if it were the text of Paulus. These insertions are called " Emblemata Triboniani."

[543] These are Gothofred's complaints of Tribonian, vol. i. p. 220. ed. Bitter: "Quod quidem non adeo improbum pro institute suo, tum et, ut cum novo jure omnia convenirent. Nisi essent ubi lucem detraxisset; nisi occurrerent, ubi propositum suum non tenuit; nisi essent, per quæ ignorantiam suam proderet; nisi denique, ubi falsi genus non unum admisit; nisi in omnibus veritati fucum fecisset. Lucem, inquam, detraxit, dum historica resecuit; dum leges discerpsit; nam cum legem viii. *Cod. Theod. de jurisdict.* in tres discerpserit, puta in 1. 8. Cod. *unde vi,* 1. *penult. de accusat. 1. un. de abigeis,* nondum tamen integram illius mentem expressit. Item, cum 1. un. *Cod. Theod. ne in sua causa,* in duas disceperet, *in l. un. C. eod. tit. et I. de testibus,* argumenti elegantiam sustulit. Propositum non tenuit; nam cum hanc legem sibi dixisset, ut quæ in præteritum respiciunt, omitteret, attamen hujusmodi nonnulla retinuit, ut constat ex collatione *l.* 18. *de operibus publ. et I.* 51. *Cod Theod. eod. tit.* ignorantiam suam prodidit, ut *in I.* 1. *de Veteranis,*. ibi perfruantur. Faisi genus non unum admisit, ut pluribus probatur in *Comment.*

"Mutilatæ constitutionis exemplum præbet L. 12. Cod. *de juris et fact. ignor.* quæ desumpta est ex L. 2. Cod. Th. *de constit. princip.* resectis quinque prioribus verbis. L. 6. Cod. *de dilationibus,* est desumpta ex L. 3. Cod. Theod. *eod. tit.* verum potissima parte truncata. L. 2. Cod. *de his, qui ven. œtat. impetr.* est ex L. 1. Cod. Theod. *eod. tit.* sed absunt elegantissimæ partes. L. 6. *de incest, nupt.* confecta est ex L. 3. Cod. Theod. *eod. tit.* sex vero locis mutilata. L. 15. Cod. *de donat, ant. nupt.* conscripta ex L. 2. Cod. Theod. *de sponsal. et ant. nupt. donat.* dimidia temen pars deest. L. 2. Cod. *de administr. tut. et curat,* hausta ex L. 4. Cod. Theod. *de*

Among other causes of error in the text of Justinian may be mentioned that of substituting "*sigla*"[544], abbreviations, for whole forms or phrases; for instance V. S. for *verborum significatio;* R. V., *rei vindicatio;* D. M. A., *dolus malus absit;* U. D. P. R. I. L. P. for *unde de plano recte ita legi possit.* Justinian, indeed, prohibited the use of these signs, but they nevertheless continued in use. Cujacius[545] enumerates several instances of the mistakes which have been thus occasioned; one in the Institutes[546], where "*senatus consultum*" has been inserted for "*sententiam constitutionis;*" another in the Digest[547], where "*fidei commissa causâ*" is put for "*fraudandorum creditorum caus â.*"

Sometimes it has happened that fragments have been inserted in the wrong place; such are called *"leges fugitivæ,"* or *"erraticæ."* So a fragment of Caius occurs[548], which ought to be found[549] where a fragment of Caius is cited which requires for its explanation the addition of the first.[550] Other laws, from their repetition, sometimes by design, sometimes by accident, are stiled *"geminatæ."*

It was the custom of the classical jurists sometimes when they referred to the work of an earlier writer, to quote not the original work itself, but another work by which they had been originally directed to it. This habit pervades the writings of the compilers of the Digest. They have constantly borrowed at second-hand their extracts from Labeo, Cassius, and Sabinus, and still more unpardonably, have inserted the quotations from

---

administr. et peric. tutor. multis etiam in locis mutilata. Ita pars prior L. 3. Cod. Theod. *de testam. et codic.* abiit in L. 17. Cod. *de testam. et quemadm. testam. ordin,* resecta sunt reliqua. L. ult. Cod. *quor. bonor,* fontem habet L. 1. Cod. Theod *eod. tit.* amputata vero sunt verba priora. L. 4. Cod. *de SCto Orphit.* collecta et interpolata ex L. 3. Cod. Theod. *de legit. hered."*

544 Sigla are singula. A. Gell. xvii. Short-hand writers were called " singularii." Cujac. xii. Obs. 40. who quotes St. Basil, διὰ τοντο σημειον χρήζουσιν, Ep., and Cassiodorus.

545 Observ. lib. iv. c. 31.

546 Inst. " qui et quibus causis," &c.

547 Dig. xl. 9. 8.

548 Dig. ii. 15. 6

549 Dig. xxix. 3.1.

550 The reader who wishes to pursue this subject should refer to Cujacius, Obs. iii. 37., where many instances are cited.

early writers in the Pandects, as if they had been taken from the authors in which they found them, without any mark to indicate the original.[551]

It may be true that Justinian was obliged to arrange his materials under the rubrics in which the imperial constitutions were distributed, and which alone were familiar to the lawyers of the age. But all internal arrangement appears to have been foreign to his thoughts, and and the complacency[552] with which he announces his provisions in favour of Papinian are quite inconsistent with any notion of a logical method in the structure of his compilation. His sole idea seems to have been (and to censure him for this would be unjust, as it would be to quarrel with an individual for the imperfection of the age), that of collecting law into a sort of cyclopædia under different heads. Wherever the genius, taste, and inventive powers of a country begin to fail, as we may observe in England at the present day, the tendency of the age shows itself in accumulating and epitomising the productions of happier ages, without regard to purity of language or elegance of form; in writing volumes of commentaries and dissertations, in heaping together masses of detail, in compiling repertories, dictionaries, and encyclopædias, and saving from ruin what it is not able to turn to its legitimate and proper use. Before the invention of printing, such a bias must have been still more irresistible, and no state of things can be imagined more adverse to scientific method and discrimination.

Ulpian's works, and especially his Commentary on the Edict were the centre of the Pandects. The writer who has suffered most is Papinian; but the neglect of the elder jurists is remarkable. Of Manerius Sabinus the Pandects contain no one original extract. The Digesta of Salvius Julianus are abundantly

---

[551] Dig. xxvii. 1.§3. compare with§2. ib.§5. compare§4.

[552] Const. Omnem Reip.§4.: "Ne autem tertii anni auditores, quos Papinianistas vocant, nomen et festivitatem ejus amittere videantur; ipse iterum in tertium annum per bellissimam machina-tionem introductus eat; librum enim hypothecariæ ex primordiis plenum ejusdem maximi Papiniani fecimus lectione, ut et nomen ex eo habeant et Papinianistæ vocentur, et (ejus reminiscentes et) lactificentur, et festum diem, quem cum primum leges ejus accipiebant celebrare solebant, peregant, et maneat viri sublimissimi præfectorii Papiniani et per hoc in æternum memoria."

quoted; but little use is made of his commentary on the Prætorian Edict.[553] Cujacius tells us on the authority of a contemporary who had seen the original work of Paulus, that almost the whole of his *Liber Singularis de Gradibus* is transcribed into the Digest[554]; the least important of Papinian's works are those to which reference is most often made. In the *de Excusationibus*[555] two thirds of the whole are taken from the *Libri Excusationum* of Modestinus, and extracts from Paulus and Ulpianus, cited by Modestinus in in the *Libri Excusationum,* are inserted in the same title of the Pandects, as if they were taken from the original works of the authors, instead of being, as they are, transcribed citations.

If the extracts from particular treatises made by the authors of the Digest are compared with extracts from the same treatises in other compilations, or even in other parts of the Pandects, for another purpose, we shall have little reason to praise the sagacity or vigilance of the compilers of the Digest. They leave out constantly, in citing an author, all the individual circumstances by which the rule or maxim under consideration was pointed; and the fragments they preserve are often far more meagre than those preserved in other compilations. This will be found to be the case if the fragments from the "*Receptæ Sententiæ*" and the *"Libri Responsorum*" of Paulus, retained in the Digest, are compared with those in the *Collatio Legum Mosaicarum et Romanarum,* and in the *Breviarium Alaricianum.* There are some passages quoted from the "*Libri Responsorum*" of Papinian, which are twice cited in the Pandects; first, as extracted immediately by the compilers from the works of Papinian; and, secondly, at second-hand from the works of another jurist, who introduces a citation from Papinian; and the fragment cited at once by the compilers of the Digest is far more scanty than that which they cite because it is embodied in another author to whom they refer. All the

[553] "Cap. xl. Graduum agnationis vetustissima descriptio.
"De gradibus librum singularem Paulus scripsit, qui totus fere continetur notissima b. *juris-consultus,* ut mihi adfirmavit vir fide dignus in cujus manus liber ille venerat integer." — *Cujacius,* vol. iii. p. 163. Obs. lib. vi. c.40.

[554] xxxviii. 10.

[555] Dig. xxvii.§1.

allusions to the ancient history of Rome and its constitution have been, almost without exception, omitted by these mechanics, the classical jurists delighted to illustrate their propositions and maxims by examples drawn from Roman history; the injury thus inflicted on science is irreparable, and is alone sufficient to call down upon its perpetrators the indignation of posterity. Cujacius has remarked more than once, in his Observations, that Tribonian[556] often filled up with his own words the chasm which he had made between two sentences of the same treatise, and that the compilers often strike out all the reasons alleged by the jurist whom they cite, and content themselves with stating the result, sometimes in their own language. When the classical jurists were called upon to apply a rule to a given state of facts, they set out the question proposed to them "*in extenso,*" and, if it was put in a foreign tongue, in the original language. The authors of the Digest have frequently contented themselves with a garbled and defective statement of the question, to which the text they insert was a solution, as may be especially remarked in the *Libri Responsorum* of Modestinus.

The later books of the Digest, as they were revised in greater haste, have suffered less by interpolation than the rest, and on this one occasion the student may applaud what he has such frequent reasons to condemn, the absurd and puerile vanity of Justinian, who was anxious, as he himself is weak enough to tell us, that the publication of the Digest and the third[557] year of his consulship, should be contemporaneous.

Savigny has insisted much on the superiority of the Justinian compilation to any other; nor, indeed, can this position, in so far as it relates to the Pandects, be disputed with any show of reason. But I must think that he has attributed an undue degree of praise to Justinian, and expresses a surprise which the circumstances do not altogether justify, at the comparative success of his commissioners. Even if it be true that Romans were employed by Theodoric and by Alaric, to

---

[556] Cujacius, Obs. xxi. c. 26. xxii. c. 21. xxiv. c. 3. See Dig. xvii. 1. 59.§4.

[557] Const. Tauta,§23.

prepare the codes which they respectively promulgated, two circumstances, to which Savigny does not allude, appear to me to go far in explaining the inferiority of their productions; the one is the condition of those for whom the legislation was intended — a consideration, surely, of vast importance, — the other, hardly, if at all, second to it, the materials at the command of Justinian, and their vast superiority to those within the reach of the contemporary legislators. The jurists employed by Justinian had the advantage of traditions unknown elsewhere; among them alone there had been a succession uninterrupted, a chain which, wretched and spurious as was the metal of its later links, had never actually been dissevered by barbarous invasion.[558] There must have been men, notwithstanding the general ignorance in the eastern empire, who knew the names of treatises, and the merit of authors, of which and of whom in Gaul and Italy all recollection had passed away. To these treatises and authors, unknown to others, if the manuscripts were, as in many instances probably they were not, within their reach, the jurists of Justinian could always turn; from them they had only to extract; there they found every thing expressed in admirable language, and arranged in systematic order; and instead of wondering that so much was done, there is reason to be surprised at the very rude and inadequate monument which the possessors of such grand materials, of such noble resources, of such unequalled treasures, have erected. Though the materials are excellent, how imperfect is the design into which they are wrought, and where the artists of the day are concerned, how imperfect its execution. There is, indeed, enough not only to excite our regret for what we have lost, but our admiration for what we have preserved; though, while we peruse the scanty fragments of Papinian, and the mutilated passages of Modestinus, we cannot help reflecting on what might have been transmitted to us, had there existed any one able to mould the whole into one immortal feature of reason and of truth; and what posterity might have inherited had the task, so important to its welfare, been undertaken in an age less degenerate, and been imposed in circumstances less

[558] There was no one school of law left in the Western Empire.

deplorable. What those circumstances were, has been already stated. The abject character of the monarch, and the incorrigible worldliness of the clergy, were fatal to all improvement. Whenever Justinian speaks his own language it is puerile, feeble, and ostentatious. It is evident that he was a slave not only to the most ludicrous vanity, but to the most insatiable avarice, and the most malignant fanaticism. His crimes increased the treasures of the church; his courtiers, of course, exasperated their master's vices; and if, as Procopius assures us, Tribonian expressed his apprehension lest Justinian, like Elijah, should be snatched up to heaven in a chariot of fire, he transgressed the wide and well-known regions of a lawyer's baseness, and encroached upon the precincts of ecclesiastical servility.

NOVELLŒ[559]

The Novells are the edicts which the emperor Justinian published to complete or modify his constitutions promulgated in the Code from the year A. D. 535. to the year A. D. 565. In the collection which has been transmitted to us there are two Novells, which emanated not from Justinian, but.from Justin the Younger, the 140th and 144th. The text of the Novells has reached us in Latin and in Greek. Some were written originally as the 17th and 66th, in both languages; a few as the 36th, the

---

[559] Biener, Geschichte der Novellen Justiniens, an excellent work. Giannone, Storia di Napoli, vol. i. p. 213. lib. iii. c. 3.§4.;, "Nelle quali veramente evvi molto che desiderare intorno all' eleganza, brevità, gravità, e dottrina; e quanto le constituzioni de' principi che da Constantino magno infino a lui (Giustiniano) fiorirono cedono alle constituzioni degli altri più antichi Imperadori da Adriano fino a Constantino tanto queste Novelle di Giustiniano cedono in brevità ed eleganza alle seconde, in guisa che s' è sempre retroceduto, ed andato di peggio in peggio, leggendosi queste ora con molta nausea, piene di loquacita, tumide, e prive affatto di quella brevità, gravità, ed eleganza delle prime: ma ciò, che piu importa, asservasi nelle medesime una certa incostanza e leggerezza inescusabile, mutandosi e variandosi ciò, che non molto prima erasi stabilito, e quel che poco anzi piacque, poco da poi si muta e si cancella. La qual cosa ha dato motivo a molti di credere, che tanta instabilità procedesse dalla leggerezza femminile di Teodora moglie di Giustiniano, che sovente s' intrigavi in sì fatte cose, e dall' avarizia di Triboniano, che per denaro sovente mutava e variava le leggi a sua posta."

37, the 111, and perhaps some others, originally in Latin, the rest in Greek. The number of the Novellœ in this collection is 168; the 140th and 144th of — Justin the Younger; the 161st, 163d and 164th of Tiberius II; the 165th to 168th from the *prœfecti prœtorio;* the remaining 159 belong to Justinian.

Other revolutions in jurisprudence followed the alterations of Justinian. The successors of this prince published a considerable number of novells, in the vain hope to adapt the Roman legislation to the wants and sympathies of their people; and the restraints imposed by Justinian were speedily set at nought. These new constitutions were written in Greek, and the disregard of the Roman language accelerated the loss of Roman legislation. In a short time after the publication of the Institutes, Theophilus published his paraphrase on the Institutes in Greek, which has descended to our times, and which, not only because it is the most ancient and authentic commentary on the Institutes that we possess, but because the author of it had access to those precious works which have since perished, has a peculiar interest, and is entitled to attentive examination. But besides this the eastern empire has transmitted to us another work on jurisprudence: this is the compilation called the Basilica. The Basilica are a Greek compilation from the Institutes, the Pandects, the Code, the Novelice, the Thirteen Edicts, and the Canons of Councils. In the space of three centuries after Justinian, the compilations of that ruler were disregarded at Constantinople; when Basil, the Macedonian, ascended the throne, he appointed a commission to prepare a Greek code; and he published meanwhile *(πρόχειρον τῶν νόμων)* in forty books; after his death, in 886, his task was continued by his son Leo, and the new code was published in the year 890, under the name of *βασιλικαὶ διατάξεις.* Fifty-five years later, this code was revised by Constantine Porphyrogenetes; it was published under the name of *τῶν βασιλίκων ανακαθαρσις (Codex repetitœ Prœlectionis).* This is the work which has reached us; it is divided into six volumes *(τεύχη),* and into sixty books, and is therefore called sometimes *ἐξάβιβλος,* sometimes *ἐξηκοντάβιβλος,* by the Greek writers who mention it. After the promulgation of the Basilica, to which the authority of law was given throughout the eastern empire, the code of Justinian was completely put aside. The Greek emigrants, after the capture of Constantinople[560], did not bring with them into Italy a single copy of the Institutes, the Pandects, or the Code of Justinian.[561]

In the year A. D. 555, when the conquest of Italy was complete, Justinian ordained that the Code, Pandects, and Noveliœ should be the law of that country. It seems, from a passage cited by Savigny, that the Goths still adhered to the edict of Theodoric. But the law of Justinian was in other respects universal. That its authority was never entirely obliterated in Italy, or France, or Spain, is proved by Savigny, in the great work which has established his reputation, by incontestable evidence,[562] The barbarians were, as Guizot has happily expressed it, entangled in the meshes of that scientific legislation, to which, in spite of their reluctance, they were for many purposes obliged to submit; and if they despised the individual Roman, they paid to the wisdom and institutions of the race from whence he sprung an involuntary tribute of admiration and obedience.[563] Savigny has cited two works as links of the chain which often hidden, but never broken through, binds the compilations of Justinian with the Glossarists, in one continued series of traditional theory or practice. The first is a work called "Petri Exceptiones Legum Romanarum," which he makes out to have been written by a Frenchman in the neighbourhood of Valence, in the eleventh

---

[560] See an admirable and very learned article in the Zeitschrift für Ges. W., vol. viii. p.157. by Professor Witte of Halle, a gentleman who combines the most various accomplishments, and besides his eminence as a jurist, has acquired great celebrity as a translator of Dante; on whom he has written some commentaries, which are remarkable for taste and erudition.

[561] In Constantinople the rulers became priests; and in France, Germany, and Italy, the priests became rulers. The first state of things produced the most contemptible, the second state of things the most oppressive, tyranny the world had seen.

[562] Savigny, Ges. des R. R. vol. ii.

[563] Guizot, Essai sur la Civ. vol. i.: " Les barbares," says this great ornament of the Republic of *Letters,* " tout en conservant leurs coutûmes, tout en demeurant les maîtres du pays, se trouvèrent pris, pour ainsi dire, dans les filets de cette législation savante, et obligés de lui soumettre en grande partie, non sans doute sous le point de vue politique, mais en matière civile, le nouvel ordre social."— p. 386. The whole passage is admirable.

century, and before the last quarter of it had begun, which contains in four books a systematic explanation of the Roman law.[564] The other called "Bra-chylogus," which is also a system of Roman law, founded on the compilations of Justinian, and especially upon the Institutes, though it contains extracts from the Code, the Digest, and the Novellœ. Savigny supposes that its author was a Lombard, who lived in the 11th and 12th centuries.

The next writers on the Roman law were the Glossators.

The Glossators divided the Pandects into three parts: —

The "Digestum Vetus," from the first book to the second title of the twenty-fourth, *de Divortiis.*

The "Infortiatum," which begins with the third title of the twenty-fourth book *(Soluto Matrimonio),* and ends with the thirty-eighth book.

The "Digestum Novum," from the first title of the thirty-ninth book, *De Operis novi Nuntiatione,* to the end.

The last part of the "Infortiatum" was made a subdivision and called by the name *"tres partes"* This portion begins in the middle of a book, in the middle of a title, in the middle of a law; nay, in the middle of a proposition; and is taken from the words *tres partes*[565], *"tres partes ferant legatarii,"* &c.

In this island, the Saxon conquest had obliterated, except in Wales, all traces of Christianity[566]; and St. Augustine found the inhabitants of England as completely Pagans, as if the

---

[564] It also contains a proof that France was divided into the Pays de droit écrit and Pays coutumier:" Omnis hæc solemnitas necessaria eat in his partibus in quibus legis jurisque prudentia viget, aliis vero partibus ubi sacratissima lex incognita est sufficit sola oblatio," &c.— *Petrus,* ii.§31.

[565]It also contains a proof that France was divided into the Pays de droit écrit and Pays coutumier: " Omnis hæc solemnitas necessaria eat in his partibus in quibus legis jurisque prudentia viget, aliis vero partibus ubi sacratissima lex incognita est sufficit sola oblatio," &c.— *Petrus,* ii.§31.

[566] Dig. xxxv. 2. 82. Savigny, Geschich. des R. R. vol. iii. p. 423.§157. whence this is taken, and Hugo, Lehrbuch der Jur. En. p. 241.

Gospel had never been preached here at all.[567] I have already quoted two passages from the laws of Canute, in which the Roman law is mentioned. Savigny has pointed out some others,[568] Vacarius[569] was the first who professed the Roman law in England. He was brought here A. D. 1136, by Theobald Archbishop of Canterbury; and composed, as we are told, in the Roman chronicle, an epitome of the Code and Digest, in nine books. King Stephen forbade the study of the Roman law[570], probably, with the view of checking the usurpations of the clergy; but that it was popularly known in some shape or other among us is proved by the extract below, from Walter de Mapes, a writer of the eleventh century, in his poem "*De Judicio extreme.*"[571] Whatever Roman law found its way into

---

[567] Nothing but the most obstinate bigotry, or the most shameless indifference to truth, can induce any one to deny that England was converted from heathenism to Christianity by Roman Catholic missionaries in the time of Gregory the Great; that is, at a time when the worst abuses of the Roman Church were prevalent, when transubstantiation, the invocation of saints, and the worship of the Virgin were fully established. To say, therefore, that the spoliation of the Roman Catholic Church was justifiable, not because it was for the public good, but St. Augustine and his missionaries taught a different religion from the Roman Catholic, or took the incomes from those who did, can only be accounted for by gross ignorance, or disgusting hypocrisy. It is an impudent perversion of historical truth; if the lands taken by Augustine for the church of Canterbury were set apart for any worship, it was that of Woden and Thor, and perhaps the sea-snake. The Saxon conquest was extermination; it obliterated all law, all usage; and changed the days of the week to those of heathen deities. These Saxons were converted by Augustine, and to Augustine they gave large estates. But putting aside these notorious facts, can any one doubt that the bulk of the property of the English church at the Reformation had been given to it after the Conquest, and by Roman Catholics, and for Roman Catholic purposes, saying masses, &c.

[568] iii. 168.

[569] Duchesne, Hist. Norm. p. 983. A.D. 1143: "Obiit Rechardus, vi. Abbas Becci, cui successit Rogerius. Magister Vacarius, gente Longobardus, vir honestus et juris peritus, cum leges Romanas anno ab incarnatione Domini MCXLIX in Anglia discipulos doceret, et multi tarn divites quam pauperes ad eum causa discendi confluerunt, suggestione pauperum de Codice et Digesta (sic) exceptos ix. libros composuit, qui sufficiunt ad omnes legum lites, quæ in scholis frequentari solent, decidendas, si quis eas perfecte noverit."

The Roman law was often quoted in the temporal courts here, till Edward II.: in Edward III.'s time it was quite exploded. Selden in Fletam, c. 7, 8, 9., has preserved some very curious instances in which it was cited. Edward I. invited the son of Accursius to Oxford to teach the civil law.

[570] " Vacario nostro indicium silentium."—*Joh. Salis. 8.* 22.

[571] " Judicabit judices judex ge-
neralis,
Ibi nihil proderit dignitas pa-

our process or institutions, came through the impure channel of ecclesiastics, and was regarded, naturally enough, with aversion and distrust.[572]

I have now concluded the task I proposed to undertake; and I own that I leave the subject with regret for less instructive occupations. To pass from the study of the French or Roman system to that of English law is to pass from a temple of Parian marble into a quarry of Portland stone. There are, no doubt, in the latter, the ordinary materials out of which a homely and convenient dwelling might be constructed, but they lie scattered about in rude disorder, and though employed by common workmen, the architect beholds them with contempt. The historian of jurisprudence in this country has a wide and almost untrodden field before him. To describe the struggle between the positive institutions of Rome and the unwritten customs of barbarians — to show by what laws Charlemagne founded his empire, and by what anarchy it was overthrown, — how the Decretals infected the institutions of Europe, and poisoned civilisation in its source, — how the Roman law was corrupted into an instrument of sacerdotal tyranny, — by what arts, what

palis.
Sive sit episcopus, sive cardinalis,
Reus condemnabitur, nec dicetur, qualis?
Ibi nihil proderit quidquam allegare,
Neque vel excipere neque replicare,
Neque ad apostolicam sedem appellare;
Reus condemnabitur, nec dicetur, quare?
Cogitate miseri, qui et quales estis!
Quid in hoc judicio dicere potestis!
Ubi nullus *Codici,* locus aut Digestis;
Idem erit dominus, judex, actor, testis."

572 "Usus (Romani) juris quâ scilicet cum Pontificio complicatur velut fere angues invicem caducei Mercurialis."—*Selden in Flet.* c. 8. p. 531. See Appendix.

perseverance, what audacity, Gregory VII. and his successors raised the monstrous edifice of ecclesiastical hypocrisy and usurpation, which the giant energy of Luther was required to shatter, and which no efforts have since been able to restore; even though in the nineteenth century, and in this Protestant country, such attempts, fortunately seconded neither by eloquence nor dexterity, have not been wanting; — these are topics which might dignify the leisure, and engross the talents, of the most distinguished writer. To such merit I have not aspired; but if what I have written shall induce any of my countrymen to disdain the grovelling superstition which it has been the object of too many crafty and interested persons among us to inculcate as Christian truth, — to exchange the mechanical drudgery of purblind routine, for those generous, though it may be less lucrative, studies which fortify the reason, and enlarge the heart, — to quit the monotonous circle of stupifying chicane for the vantage ground of history, my object will be accomplished; and I shall have contributed in some degree, and according to the measure of my abilities, to the benefit of the society in which I live.

APPENDIX

AMŒNITATES JURIS ANGLICANI. ARUNDINES SCACCARII

"Medio de fonte leporum

Surgit amari aliquid, quod in ipsis floribus angat."

APPENDIX I

IN the last number of the Exchequer Reports, there is a case called *Esdaile* v. *Trustwell.*

Without troubling the reader with details, it is enough to state that *two* reasons why the defendant was liable were stated in the declaration. It was admitted that the statement of either one of the circumstances would be sufficient — but argued that the statement of both was fatal to the claim — that two strings made the bow useless. Nobody pretended that the defendant was misled or injured in any way by the statement. Now, let us see the decision.

Parke B. — "You had better amend... I do not say you are wrong, but you had better amend." Now, the meaning of this plausible expression "better amend" is, you had better pay a fine of twenty pounds, which is probably a less sum than the amendment would cost, for the sake of inserting three or four words which tell nobody anything, or for the sake of striking out three or four more which mislead nobody, to get rid of an objection wholly beside the merits of the case. Such are the evils which people (even judges who have been the northern circuit) get out of sight by the inveterate habit of thinking through a technical medium. If, instead of saying better amend, the judge were compelled to say, "I order you, the defendant, to pay a fine of twenty pounds to the officer of the Court, just by way of smoothing matters and as the defendant seems to wish it," everybody, even an old special pleader, or a maker of new rules, would be a little startled. It is really curious to see the defendant's counsel insisting that two reasons are disclosed why his client is liable, and therefore inferring that he is not liable at all; and the plaintiff's counsel not disputing the inference, but vehemently maintaining that only one has been stated. Defendant's counsel: "The declaration would have been perfectly good if it had said that the defendant was a member at either one or other of those times." (It said he was a member at both.) Plaintiff's counsel: "The declaration shows but one distinct liability."

FEWINGS V. TINDAL, EXCHEQUER REPORTS

A servant, dismissed without warning, claimed what the law allows, a month's wages The defendant perfectly well knew what she claimed; but he says, the declaration ought to have had a special count. The Exchequer held that it ought, *overruling* a case the other way, "which broke in upon the rules of law to do justice in that particular case." *(Parke, B.)*

The servant was nonsuited. So that here you have, 1. *Ex post facto* legislation, which, probably, besides depriving the servant of her month's wages, must have cost her out of pocket, forty pounds at the lowest. 2. One case put aside to make way for a totally different principle. 3. The admission that the case so put aside, and then for the first time questioned, was against *law:* to which I will only add the question, whether a more barbarous, confused, capricious, and oppressive state of things can be imagined? Nobody here pretended that the want of a special count had been in any *way injurious* to the defendant.

If suitors were forbidden to take advantage of technical objections, without an affidavit that they had been injured by the omission or insertion which they complain of, and a distinct statement of that injury, where (except in depriving us of the display of astuteness we so often witness, and for which, elevating as it is, the ruin of so many suitors is rather too dear a price) would be the harm? If substantial justice was done *rather* more often, what injury would it do to the public? "If you *did* learn a little grammar," said Cowley to Sir Robert Howard, "what possible harm would it do you?"

MASSEY V. JOHNSON

A plea is put forward, and the question is whether that plea is supported. The Court decide that it is, and send the case back to be heard, with a hint so thoroughly characteristic of our ideas of justice that I cannot help quoting it. After saying that the plea might be proved as it was drawn, the judge, and a most excellent judge, says, in the name of the Court, "It is *unnecessary* to say whether the plea, if *proved,* is a good defence!" Why unnecessary? — to whom? — to the plaintiff or to the defendant? Can any thing be more necessary to the suitor? — unnecessary to know whether all the trouble and expense of a new trial is absolutely to be flung away! as, if the plea is bad, it must be! But such is English law, made by the rich for the rich; and for the poor literally unattainable.

The following decision would seem strange to lawyers in most countries, it is contrary to the plainest and most received maxims of jurisprudence.

MARKS V. RIDGWAY, EXCHEQUER REPORTS

"Where a defendant has been served with process, and an attorney, *without* authority, appears for him, the Court will not interfere to set aside the proceedings, if the attorney be solvent:" as if that circumstance could affect the general

principle. Why am I to be in any way whatever affected by a person who acts in my name without my sanction or authority? How such a decision could be arrived at by any one on this side Mount Atlas is really surprising!

COOK V. MOYLAN, EXCHEQUER REPORTS

A plea was held bad, because it amounted to the general issue. That is, literally, because the defendant instead of stating shortly that he was not liable to the claim, set out in a regular statement the facts on which his defence rested; which, observe, in a vast number of cases, the same law which punishes so severely his doing in this instance, would punish him for not doing with equal severity. Leave to amend was given, that is, a fine of about thirty pounds was imposed on the unhappy man whose pleader made the mistake, unless he preferred losing his right altogether. Talk of absurdity after this!

Such are the extracts from the last 300 pages of the Exchequer Reports. Let us now turn to the last 150 pages of the criminal law.

REGINA V. BENT, CROWN CASES

A statute makes it a misdemeanour *wilfully* to make a false answer to certain questions. A burgess was accused of having done this, and he was found guilty; but he was set at liberty without punishment, because the indictment imputed to him that he had committed the offence "falsely and fraudulently," without saying "wilfully," as if a man could do a thing "falsely and fraudulently" without doing it "wilfully!" Such is the drivelling folly that is called "law" in this *practical* country.

WORTLEY'S CASE

A man had stolen a poor-box in a church with the money. The fact was proved; but the discussion before the judges turned in great measure upon the question, whether the box was affixed to the freehold: if it had been, the whole character of the case would have been altered. Fortunately, the judges held that it was not. After this, who can say that Swift's account of the point taken by lawyers in a question as to the property in a cow, "whether the field I milk her in be round or square," is an exaggeration?

REGINA V. JOSEPH TOWNSEND

An assistant overseer, who had embezzled the money given him for the poor, was indicted for the embezzlement. He was found guilty: held that he must escape punishment, because he was the servant not of the *guardians,* as the *indictment* stated, but of the *overseers!*

WEST'S CASE

The prisoner was found guilty of having forged eighty scrip certificates of a railway company; he was turned loose upon the world without punishment, because, in the indictment, each instrument was called a receipt and acquittance, or a receipt, or an undertaking for the payment of money.

But the worst and most cruel case remains behind. Hitherto we have seen justice turned into a mockery by the escape of the guilty: we shall now see it turned into a scourge by the punishment of the innocent. Such a two-edged sword is the technicality of law in this country.

REGINA V. PRIVETT AND GOODHALL

Prisoners[573] took more oats than they were allowed from their *master's* granary to give their *master's horses:* held that they were felons, and that this was a larceny. Talk of the injustice done by technicality, talk of its barbarous cruelties, talk of its disregard for all philosophical analogy, after this decision which the judges, with the exception of Erie and Platt thought themselves obliged by the law as it now stands to pronounce. Lord Abinger, I know, thought otherwise. Many of the most eminent counsel to whom the outrage on all reason and humanity has been mentioned, would not believe it possible that such a law really existed. County members have undertaken to bring forward a law for its alteration. But it only affected labourers; and it remains a memorable example of the narrowness and pedantry of our law, and of the indifference of

---

[573] As an illustration of our abject ignorance of the very rudiments of jurisprudence, observe — a felony is a greater crime in our law than a misdemeanor; the man who perjures himself in a court of justice commits a misdemeanor; the labourer who gives an extra handful of his master's oats to his master's horses commits a felony: and when the law takes such pains to confound all notion of right and wrong in the minds of the people, and the church gives the money that ought to be employed in teaching them to canons and deans for doing nothing, and to bishops for voting against the Jews — we wonder at their brutality.

the legislature to the rights and interest of those who have seldom votes to give, and never power enough to make them formidable. The reasoning by which this law was supported is worthy of the law itself. It was said that as the horse ate more, he was stronger; as he was stronger, he worked more readily; as he worked more readily he gave the labourer less trouble; as he gave less trouble, what the labourer did was *lucri causâ,* therefore the labourer was a felon. In Scotus one might laugh at such a sorites as this; but when it is employed to take away the liberty, and destroy the character of a labourer, it makes the blood tingle in every vein. It takes an offence from one category, and puts it in a totally different one; and thus it appears from the same few pages that the technicalities of the English law impotent to protect society, are powerful to oppress its most helpless members; that they give impunity to the forger, to the embezzler, to the daring thief, and, if we had gone a few pages back, we might have said to the assassin, while they blight the reputation and crush the hopes of the farm labourer, who, for an offence certainly not equal to many which are hourly committed with perfect impunity by his superiors, finds himself a felon, his wife and his children degraded, and himself, it may be, ruined and broken-hearted. "Gustavi paullulum mellis, et ecce morior."

There are people who think that if about half the money now bestowed upon Masters in Chancery for their share in aggravating the miseries of Chancery suitors (which Satan himself might leave with perfect confidence to the other proceedings in equity) were given to nine or ten active and useful lawyers, for eliciting the points in dispute between parties, and stating them in a concise intelligible shape, as the French call it, "fixer l'état de la question," justice would be more attainable. But these ignorant people have never heard of Lord Hobart's justification for technicality, "these things exist that the law may be an art," not the art of the Papinians, and L'Hôpitals, but of the Cokes, and Hobarts, and Eldons. Moreover, where would be the use of all the prodigious ingenuity exemplified in the cases above cited, were so rash an innovation as the triumph of substantial justice to be introduced in our courts of law? If all people led healthy lives, and followed a temperate diet, where would be the importance of Hippocrates himself?

APPENDIX II
ORDER OF TWELVE TABLES

	GODEFROI	HAUBOLD	DIRKSEN
Table I.	De in jus vocando.	De ordine judicioorum privatorum	De in jus vocando
II.	De judiciis et furtis	De furtis.	De judiciis.
III.	De rebus crediti.	Id.	Id.
IV.	De jure patrio et jure connubii.	De manu et potestate.	De jure patrio.
V.	De hæreditatibus ettutelis.	Id.	Id.
VI.	De dominio et possessione.	De rerum mancipio, usu et possessione.	De dominio et possessione
VII.	De delictis.	De damno, injuriis aliisque delictis.	De dominio et possessione
VIII.	De juribus prædiorum.	De jure ædium et agrorum.	De delictis.
IX.	De jure publico.	De jure populi.	De jure publico.
X.	De jure sacro.	Id.	Id.
XI.	Supplem. tab. i-v.	Id.	Id.
XII.	Supplem. tab. v-x.	Id.	Id.

APPENDIX III

IN Charlemagne's Capitul. lib. i.§ 55. page 837. Lindenbrog. Cod. every priest is commanded to know the Canon Law: "Ut nulli sacerdoti ignorare liceat sanctorum canonum instituta." The best history of the efforts to introduce Roman, or rather ecclesiastical, law in this country, is to be found in Selden's Comment. ad Fletam; from which it appears that the study was introduced very shortly after the discovery at Amalfi (and here it may be remarked that we must not "mistake reverse of wrong for right," or suppose that no effect at all is to be ascribed to this circumstance in the history of the Roman Law); — that, probably from the doctrines of regal and episcopal authority incorporated with it, the study excited the hostility of the feudal lords (as of course every thing did that could contribute, however remotely, to the welfare of mankind); — that they compelled Stephen, who was very much in their power, to prohibit it[574]; — that under Henry II., one of our best and ablest princes, the study gained ground; — that Henry III. was compelled to prohibit it[575]; — that Edward I. encouraged it[576]; — that under the reign of Edward II. it fell more into disuse;—and in Edward III.'s time, *"planè neglectus rcjectusque,"*[577] was banished, nominally, from our courts of

[574] Roger Bacon who wrote in Edward I.'s time, says: " Rex quidem Stephanus allatis legibus Italiæ in Angliam publico edicto prohibuit ne ab aliquo retinerentur."

[575] Henry III.'s Mandate:— Mandatum est Majori et Vicecomitibus London, quod clamari faciant et firmiter prohiberi ne aliquis Scholas Regens de Legibus in eadum civitate de cætero ibidem leges doceat. Et si aliquis ibidem fuerit hujusmodi Scholas Regens ipsum sine dilatione cessare faciant. Teste R., apud Basing, xi. die Decembris."

[576] Writ of Edward I. to the Sheriff of Oxfordshire: — " Rex Vicecomiti. Oxoniæ salutem. Præ-cipimus tibi quod Francisco Accursii doctori legum vel ejus mandato has literæ nostras deferenti, liberes manerium (ædes tune regias ibi seu castrum) Oxoniense ad inhabitandum una cum uxore sua et familia quamdiu nobis placuerit. Nolumus, tamen, quod tu, propter hoc, impediaris quin diebus statutis in aula ipsius manerii tenere valeas comitatum. In cujus rei testimonium, &c. Teste Rege, apud Windesore, septimo die Deuembris."

[577] Selden.

justice, and was unknown to the practitioners in them from that time to the present. I say nominally, because the indirect influence exercised by the Roman Law, as it filtered through clerical judges and teachers and writers, was not quite imperceptible.

John of Salisbury (temp. Henry II.) repeatedly quotes the Roman Law, and appeals to it as binding in this country: "Nôsti siquidem" he says in a letter to some bishop, "quod et seculi leges eos acerbissime puniunt," lege *Julia repetundarum* "qui in faciendis ex officio sordidum sectantur lucrum." Again, (Epist.89.) he says, that the children of incest "nec jura civilia nec leges agnoscere."

It is remarkable that on this point he quotes "Rescriptum Divorum Fratrum de Flaviæ Tertullæ incesto," as authority; which is not extant in any collection of Roman Law that we now possess. "Monemur et temporis diuturnitate quo ignorantia juris in matrimonio avunculi tui fuisti, et quod ab aviâ tuâ collocata es, et numero liberorum. Idcircoque, cum hæc omnia in unum concurrant, confirmamus statum liberorum vestrorum in eo matrimonio quæsitorum quod ante annos xl. consitatum est, proinde atque si legitimè concepti essent."

There is a curious case (temp. Edward I.) under the statute of Marlebridge, Anno. 52. Henry III. By this statute (cap. 30.) the successors of abbots, priors, &c. might continue the actions brought by their predecessors, who were dead before judgment, against the spoilers of the church. A., prior of Wallingford, brought such an action against B. Pending the action, A. was deposed; it was continued by C. his successor. B. objected that A. was still living; the objection was overruled, erroneously, says Richard of Winchedon, a contemporary, "quia quamvis dignitate privatur morte civili non est affectus." But the reporter, a contemporary also, says, "hujusmodi privatio dignitatis vocatur prout memoriæ meæ occurrit in jure civili, media capitis diminutio." —Apud *Selden ad Flet.* c. 8.

There is a case in 5th Edward II. where the defendant had promised to marry the plaintiff, and in the meantime to support her. The question was, whether the defendant was immediately liable on his promise, "ubi Hervæus, actricis advocatus," quotes the Roman Law: "In omnibus obligationibus quibus dies non ponitur præsenti die debetur."—*De Reg. Juris,* lib. 1. *L. In Omni..* 14.

In another action by the Abbot of Abingdon, who relied on custom, for a toll on beer. The advocate of the defendant quotes the very words of Celsus: "Quia quod non ratione introductum est sed errore primo, dein consuetudine obtentum, in aliis similibus non obtinet."

If such studies had triumphed, fifteen volumes of crotchets would not have been published in the 19th century under the name of Exchequer Reports. But the instinct of hostility to improvement, peculiar to the "great vulgar and the small" in this country, combined with the barbarity of lawyers, and the selfishness of the feudal lords, put them down; and, therefore, we have kept our special demurrers, and giving colour, and fictions in ejectment.: and though we have in a fit of intemperate innovation abolished trial by battle, I do not despair, if any more reforms are made, of seeing its restoration. Whether it is or not, we have the satisfaction of knowing that our ignorance of all topics connected with jurisprudence, our incapacity to comprehend a general principle, and our tenacity of all that is most utterly indefensible in our mode of administering justice, are the jest of civilised Europe: and that the poor man had better go to law in any European nation, Russia and Naples perhaps excepted (but if the mere duty of the state, and not the character of the judge, be considered, then I say it without any exception at all), than in a country where there is no code; where juries decide on contracts, and those juries must be unanimous; where fifteen judges make the Law, when the jury does not save them the trouble; where a House of Lords, consisting of country gentlemen, soldiers, sailors, political partizans, and the personal friends of different sovereigns and different ministers, is the Supreme Court of Appeal; and a Court of Quarter Sessions is intrusted with the portion of criminal justice most affecting the interests of the humble classes; and where, — to condense in one word every notion of a suitor's misery, of a tribunal which opulence itself, in this land of opulence, trembles to address, and the name of which alone scares the poor man, however galling and outrageous be the wrong he undergoes, into submission, — that rod of scorpions, called Equity, (in other words, the accumulated fraud and folly of successive ages, the chicane of the Norman lawyer and the craft of the Roman priest,) is wielded by the unreformed, and (if I may coin a word to express an evil it is so hard to describe) the unreformable Court of Chancery.

Made in United States
Troutdale, OR
11/03/2026

56844502R00166